Second Edition

An Introduction to
COMPARATIVE LEGAL MODELS OF CRIMINAL JUSTICE

Second Edition

An Introduction to
COMPARATIVE LEGAL MODELS OF CRIMINAL JUSTICE

Cliff Roberson
Emeritus Professor of Criminal Justice
Washburn University
Topeka, Kansas, USA

Dilip K. Das
President
International Police Executive Symposium
Guilderland, New York, USA

CRC Press
Taylor & Francis Group
Boca Raton London New York

CRC Press is an imprint of the
Taylor & Francis Group, an **informa** business

CRC Press
Taylor & Francis Group
6000 Broken Sound Parkway NW, Suite 300
Boca Raton, FL 33487-2742

© 2016 by Taylor & Francis Group, LLC
CRC Press is an imprint of Taylor & Francis Group, an Informa business

No claim to original U.S. Government works

Printed on acid-free paper
Version Date: 20151120

International Standard Book Number-13: 978-1-4987-4626-7 (Hardback)

Visit the Taylor & Francis Web site at
http://www.taylorandfrancis.com

and the CRC Press Web site at
http://www.crcpress.com

Contents

Preface   xv

1   **Introduction to the Study of Comparative Legal Models**   **1**

    Chapter Objectives   1
    Key Terms   1
    Introduction   2
    Words of Art   7
       Legal Models   7
       Jurisprudence   7
       Natural Law   8
       Positive Law Approach   8
       Historical Approach   9
       Law as an Instrument of Control   9
       The Function of a Court System   10
    Rule of Law   11
       United Nations and the Rule of Law   12
       Justice Project Index   13
    Brief Examination of the Legal Models   13
       Common Law   14
       Civil Law   15
       Revival of Roman Law   18
       Commercial Law   19
       Civil Law Model Today   20
       Common Law Model   21
       Islamic Model   22
       Socialist Model   23
       Mixed-Legal Model   24
       Mexico's Reform Movement   24
    Judicial Opinion under the Common Law Model Compared
    to the Civil Law Model   26
    Law Enforcement Systems   27

Punishments   28
Comparative Violence   29
Summary   31
Questions in Review   31

2   **Common Law: The Courts**   **33**

Chapter Objectives   33
Key Terms   33
Introduction   34
    Henry II   35
    The Magna Carta   38
    Sir Edward Coke   38
    Sir William Blackstone   39
Common Law in the United States   41
U.S. Court Systems Today   42
    Federal System   42
    U.S. Court of Appeals   42
    U.S. District Courts   43
    U.S. Magistrates   44
Participants in a Criminal Case   44
    Trial Judge   45
    Defendant   46
    Prosecuting Attorney   46
    State Attorney General   48
    Defense Counsel   49
    The Right to Represent Oneself   50
    Privileged Communication   50
    Clerk of the Court   51
    Bailiff   51
    Court Reporter   52
    Court Commissioners   52
English Court System Today   52
    England, Wales, and Scotland   53
    Court of Queen's or King's Bench   53
    Supreme Court of Judicature   54
    Magistrates' Court   54
    Crown Court   55
    Royal Courts of Justice   55
Comparisons between the United States and the United Kingdom   55
Yale Kamisar on the Exclusionary Rule   57
Justice Benjamin Cardozo   57

Practice of Law   59
Canadian Legal System   62
  Court Structure   62
  Provincial and Territorial Superior Courts   63
  Provincial and Territorial Courts   64
  The Judiciary   64
  Right to Fair Trial versus Freedom of the Press   65
Scottish Legal System   65
Australian Legal System   66
  Legal System   67
  Classification of Crimes   67
Summary   69
Questions in Review   70

3 Policing and Corrections under the Common Law Model 71

Chapter Objectives   71
Key Terms   71
Policing in Common Law Countries   72
  Deviance Control or Civil Order Control   72
  Policing Models   73
  Local Policing in the United States and England   74
  Current Policing in the United States   75
  Mission of Local Police Departments   75
  Local Policing in England and Wales   77
  Hiring Requirements for U.S. and English Police Officers   78
  Salaries for English and U.S. Police Officers   79
  Training of New Officers   80
  Police Powers and Use of Discretion   80
  Community Policing under the Common Law Model   81
London Metropolitan Police Authority's Safer
Neighborhoods Policing Awareness Campaign   82
  Policing in Canada   82
Police Service in Calgary, Canada   84
  Core Values   84
  Guiding Principles   85
RCMP'S Approach to Policing in Canada   87
Corrections in Common Law Countries   88
Sentencing under Common Law Model   91
  Differences between United Kingdom and Wales   93
  Sentencing in the United Kingdom   94

Confinement   94
    Rates of Incarceration   94
    Approaches to Confinement in the United States   95
    California Penal Code, Section 1170(a)   95
    English Purposes of Confinement   95
Case Study: Confinement in Ireland   96
    Prisons Ombudsman   97
Universal Declaration of Human Rights, Article 5   97
Alternatives to Incarceration   97
Corporal Punishment   98
    Fines   98
Probation   98
    Probation in England   99
    Probation in the United States   99
Standard Probation Rules for the State of Texas (Texas Code
of Criminal Procedure, Article 42.12)   100
House Arrest   101
Death Penalty   102
Summary   104
Questions in Review   105

4 Civil Law Model: The Courts   **107**

Chapter Objectives   107
Key Terms   107
Introduction   108
Early Tribal and Feudal Laws   108
Early Legislation   109
Influence of Roman Law   109
Canon Law   111
Concordia Discordantium Canonum   111
Commercial Law   111
Development of National Legal Systems   112
Napoleonic Code   113
German Legal Science   114
Law in Action: The Inquisitorial System of Prosecution   115
Codes in Civil and Common Law Models   117
Inquisitorial Prosecution   117
German Civil Law System   118
In Germany Is It Illegal to Shoot Down a Passenger Plane That
Is Being Used by Terrorists?   120
The Death Penalty in Germany   121
    Rights of the Accused in a German Criminal Trial 123
    Principle of Territoriality   126

Law in Action: Juries in the Civil Law Model   126
Criminal Justice in France   127
Criminal Justice in Brazil   129
Summary   133
Questions in Review   134

5   Policing and Corrections under the Civil Law Model   **135**

Chapter Objectives   135
Key Terms   135
Introduction   136
Law Enforcement in France   137
  Typical Proceedings in Police Court   138
Law Enforcement in Germany   138
Law Enforcement in Brazil   141
  State Police Special Operations Battalion   142
Corrections under the Civil Law Model   142
  Pretrial Diversion   143
Plea Bargaining   145
  Confinement   148
Probation   149
Parole   150
Death Penalty   151
Fines   151
Summary   152
Questions in Review   153

6   The Islamic Law Model: The Courts   **155**

Chapter Objectives   155
Key Terms   155
Introduction   156
Muhammad   158
Origins and Evolution   159
Sources   160
Fundamental Principles   161
Structure of Penal Law   162
Murder under Islamic Law   163
Evidence of Guilt   164
  Confessions   164
  Testimony of Eyewitnesses   164
  Other Evidence   165
  Doubt as to Guilt   165

Establishing Guilt as to Adultery 166
Beheading, Not Solely an Islamic Punishment 167
Saudi Arabia 168
    Criminal Cases 169
Pakistan 170
    Article 31, Pakistan's Constitution (1973) 171
Iran 172
Summary 173
Questions in Review 175

7   **Policing and Corrections under
    the Islamic Legal Model**   **177**

Chapter Objectives 177
Key Terms 177
Introduction 177
Saudi Policing 179
    Saudi Arabia's Record on Human Rights 180
    Torture and Other Cruel, Inhuman, or Degrading
    Treatment or Punishment 181
    Arbitrary Arrest, Detention, or Exile 181
Policing in Pakistan 182
Policing in Iran 183
Corrections 184
    Amputation 186
    Blood Money 187
    Caning in Saudi Arabia 187
    Aid to Prisoners' Families 188
Corrections in Iran 188
Corrections in Pakistan 189
Summary 190
Questions in Review 190

8   **The Socialist Law Model: The Courts**   **191**

Chapter Objectives 191
Key Terms 191
Introduction 191
Legal System of Russia 192
People's Republic of China 195
    Public Trials in China 197
    Crimes 198
    Court System 199
    Confessions 201

Law of Search and Seizure   201
Rights of an Accused   201
Court Procedures   202
Legal System of Cuba   202
Court Structure   206
Trial Procedure   207
Extradition from Cuba   207
Summary   208
Questions in Review   208

9   Policing and Corrections under the Socialist Legal Model   209

Chapter Objectives   209
Key Terms   209
Introduction   210
Public Trust and Community Policing   210
Policing in Russia   211
Policing in the People's Republic of China   213
Use of Force by Police in China   214
Police Detention   215
Public Crime Statistics   215
Policing in Cuba   216
Corrections in Russia   217
Imprisonment in Russia   217
Corrections in China   218
Sentencing Rallies in China   218
Chinese Prisons   220
Early Release of Prisoners   220
Prison Conditions   220
Corrections in Cuba   221
Range of Punishments   221
Confinement in Cuba   221
Summary   222
Questions in Review   223

10   Mixed-Law Models   225

Chapter Objectives   225
Key Terms   225
Introduction   225
Bulgarian System of Law   226
Bulgarian Court System   226
Bulgarian Prosecutors   227

Crime Classification   227
Trial Procedure   228
Bulgarian Police System   229
Corrections in Bulgaria   230
Confinement in Bulgaria   230
Indian System of Law   232
Indian Legal History   232
Crime Classifications in India   233
Indian Court System   233
Policing in India   235
Criminal Process in India   236
Prosecutors   237
Corrections in India   237
Confinement in India   238
Sri Lankan System of Law   238
Criminal Justice System   239
Crime Classification   239
Sri Lanka's Court System   239
Policing in Sri Lanka   240
Trial Procedures   240
Sentencing Process   241
Confinement in Sri Lanka   242
Summary   242
Questions in Review   243

11   International Courts   245

Chapter Objectives   245
Key Terms   245
Introduction   245
ICC   247
Genocide   248
The United States and the ICC   248
Establishment of the Court   249
President of the ICC   249
Judicial Divisions   250
Prosecutor   250
Registry   250
Other Offices   250
Jurisdiction and Admissibility   250
Procedure   251

Duties of States That Are Parties 252
Selected Court Cases 252
Frequent Questions Asked of Court Personnel and Their
Answers 253
Chronology of the Development of the ICC 255
Trial Procedure of the ICC 256
International Court of Justice 257
Permanent Court of International Justice 259
Establishment of the International Court of Justice 260
Resolution of Cases 260
Practice Directions 261
Jurisdiction of the ICJ 262
Contentious Cases 262
Advisory Proceedings 263
Court of Justice of European Communities 263
Excerpts from the Establishing Treaty 265
Proceedings before the Court 266
Court of First Instance 269
Actions Relating to EU Trademarks 270
Examples of Cases Brought before the Court of
First Instance 271
Civil Service Tribune 273
Summary 274
Questions in Review 274

**12 International Criminal Justice Agencies and
Associations 275**

Chapter Objectives 275
Key Terms 275
Introduction 275
Interpol 276
Structure 276
Core Functions 278
Trafficking in Human Beings 278
Definition of Human Trafficking 279
Corruption 279
Child Sexual Exploitation 279
Interpol Databases as of December 2006 280
Public Safety and Terrorism 280
Drugs 281

Criminal Organizations   282
Financial and High-Tech Crimes   282
Fugitive Investigative Services   282
Interpol's Other Areas of Crime   283
National Central Reference Points Network   284
International Cybercrime Conference   284
Europol   285
The Europol Computer System   286
International Association of Chiefs of Police   286
International Police Association   287
United Nations Crime Prevention and Criminal Justice
Network   287
UN Commission on Crime Prevention
and Criminal Justice   288
International Center for Criminal Law Reform and
Criminal Justice Policy   288
Criminal Justice Reform Unit   289
Office for Drug Control and Crime Prevention   290
Institutes of the UN Crime Prevention and Criminal
Justice Program Network   291
Commission on Narcotic Drugs   292
UN Terrorism Prevention Branch   292
International Narcotics Control Board   293
Transnational Organized Crime   293
Trafficking in Humans   294
United Nations and Juvenile Justice   294
Differences between Trafficking and Smuggling   296
United Nations Protocol to Prevent, Suppress, and Punish
Trafficking in Persons, Especially Women and Children   296
Trafficking in Firearms   300
International Police Executive Symposium   305
International Policy Institute for Counter-Terrorism   306
Organization of American States   307
Article 3 of the Charter of the OAS   309
Child Wise   310
Summary   310
Questions in Review   310

**Appendix: Excerpts from the World Justice
Project—Rule of Law Index 2014**   **311**

References   **315**

Index   **321**

Preface

An Introduction to Comparative Legal Models of Criminal Justice, Second Edition, is an introductory text to comparative criminal justice. Both authors are professors at U.S. universities and have long been involved with criminal justice agencies in various nations. We have traveled and studied in most major nations and each have experience in the criminal justice system for more than 30 years. Our purpose is to present a text that covers the different legal models in the world that may be used in a one-semester course.

The text is presented with the theme that a country's legal model, to a great extent, determines the character of its police and corrections and its legal system. Chapter 1 contains a brief overview of the legal models. In the following chapters, each legal model is discussed and countries selected under each legal model are analyzed. In Chapters 2 through 9, we examine the legal aspects and discuss several countries that use those legal models. In Chapter 3, we present an overview of the police agencies and correctional systems used by those countries. In Chapter 10, we discuss three countries that have mixed-legal models. In Chapter 11, three international courts are examined. Chapter 12 concludes the book with a discussion on international criminal justice agencies. It was difficult to obtain information about the justice systems in some countries, and in such cases, we relied heavily on the country reports published by the U.S. State Department.

While we are listed as the sole authors of this text, there are numerous others who contributed and assisted us in this project. One person who was especially important was our editor at CRC Press/Taylor & Francis, Carolyn Spence. We also thank project coordinators Joselyn Banks and Jessica Vega. Thanks Carolyn, Joselyn, and Jessica for your professional help and backing. Corrections, comments, and recommendations for improvement may be forwarded to the authors at: cliff.roberson@washburn.edu.

New material to the second edition includes the following:

- Chapter objectives added to each chapter.
- Description of the criminal court systems for most major countries.
- Each chapter has been updated.
- The number of photographs has increased by threefold.
- Expanded discussion on the oldest known legal systems.

- Excerpts from the *Interfoto Picture Library v. Stiletto* case, where the chief judge discusses the differences between civil and common law systems.
- Extensive discussion on the "Rule of Law." The Appendix contains significant details of the World Justice Project's Rule of Law Index (2014).
- Discussion on Mexico's reform movement.
- Expanded discussion on the 800th anniversary of the Magna Carta.
- Expanded discussion on the differences between the legal models in England and Scotland.
- Discussion on the role of judges in Italian penal policies.
- Discussion on juvenile justice in Turkey.
- Discussion on women in Mexico's prisons.
- Procedures in a typical Chinese criminal trial.
- Sentencing of children in South Africa.
- United Nations actions to improve juvenile justice.
- Increased discussion on the role of the Organization of American States.

Introduction to the Study of Comparative Legal Models

1

Chapter Objectives

After studying this chapter, you should understand or be able to explain the following issues and concepts:

- The difference between the civil law and common law legal models
- The comparison between the legal models of the major legal systems
- The difference between the natural and positive law approaches
- How common law and civil law developed
- How the law functions as an instrument of control
- The meaning of the concept "rule of law"
- The primary functions of the major court systems

Key Terms

Civil law: The law of Continental Europe, based on an admixture of Roman, Germanic, ecclesiastical, feudal, commercial, and customary law. European civil law has been adopted in much of Latin America as well as in parts of Asia and Africa.

Common law: That body of law and juristic theory originated, developed, and formulated in England.

Comparative criminal justice: The study and evaluations of national criminal justice system in comparison with other nations.

Comparative jurisprudence: The study of the principles of legal science through comparison of various systems of law.

Ethnocentrism: The tendency to regard one's own group and culture as intrinsically superior to all others; regarding one's own race or ethnic group as superior.

Exegetical system of teaching: Teaching by using an explanation or commentary on the meanings of text.

International crimes: Acts that are considered to be crimes against the peace and security of humankind.

Islamic law: The expression of Allah's commands for Muslim society; in application, this constitutes a system of duties that are incumbent upon Muslims by virtue of their religious belief.

Jurisprudence: The philosophy of law or the science that treats the principles of positive law and legal relations.

Jus gentium: The law of nations; the law that natural reason has established among all individuals and that is equally observed among all nations.

Natural law: The law of nature or natural law that is said to be discoverable by the light of nature or by abstract reasoning.

Positive law: A specific law or statute that has been enacted or adopted by the proper authority of a government.

Precedent: The use of a prior court decision as authority for an identical or similar later case involving a similar question of law.

Religious law: The model of law that refers to the notion of a religious system or document being used as its legal source.

Rule of law: The rule of law implies that every citizen is subject to the law, including the lawmakers themselves, and that no person, not even the queen, is above the law.

Socialist law: The law developed in Russia after the communist seizure of power in 1917 and imposed throughout the Soviet Union in the 1920s; it is based on the concept of public ownership of the means of production and subordination of the legal system to the Soviet Communist Party.

Transnational crime: A crime that involves, directly or indirectly, more than one nation.

Introduction

There are about 192 independent nations or states in our world. So, it is impractical to study the criminal justice systems of all 192 nations. Accordingly, we will divide the systems into major types and review each major type. Independent nations or states refer to units of people who are organized into political and sovereign states. By sovereign state we are referring to a state that is an internationally recognized unit of political authority. Some nations, such as the United States, are organized into one nation with multiple "states." When we refer to states in this text, we will be referring to sovereign nations, not subordinate states.

A nation's criminal justice system is influenced by its legal system. Generally, legal systems of the world can be classified as one of five basic systems: civil law, common law, socialist law, religious law, and customary law (combinations of these). However, the legal system of each country is shaped by its unique history and so each nation incorporates individual variations.

The comparative study of criminal justice is the academic study of the criminal justice arrangements of various nations. Comparison as a study approach is relatively new when associated with other types of justice studies. Few studies of comparative justice were conducted prior to the 1980s, although there were some comparative legal studies conducted in the late nineteenth century in France, Germany, and England. There were also some comparative sociology studies during that time. It is reported that Émile Durkheim, who is credited by many with establishing sociology as a discipline, once remarked that "comparative sociology is not a particular branch of sociology; it is sociology itself" (Glendon et al., 1999, p. 2).

The Oldest Known Formal Legal System

The Code of Hammurabi is the earliest known set of codified law. The code was developed by the Mesopotamian system that emerged in the Near East about 10,000 BC and lasted until the first century BC. Mesopotamia society developed prior to the Bronze Age and encompassed the land between the Euphrates and Tigris rivers that have their headwaters in the Armenian Highlands. The area is located in what is now considered as Iraq and Kuwait.

The oldest known formal legal system is the Egyptian system that is generally believed to date back to 4000 BC. Their laws were partially codified. The pharaoh was the living god and the supreme lawmaker. There were about eight books that consisted of the ancient legal system. Documentation on prior cases were recorded and retained and often used as precedent for later cases. Judges were required to be impartial and commanded respect from the commoners.

If a comparative study of justice is so valuable, why did it take so long for researchers to examine the area? While there is no clear answer to this question, the authors believe that two factors contributed to the delay. First, most researchers find it difficult to keep up with their own system, especially with the increasing complexity of the systems, and to achieve even minimal competence in other systems takes a lot of effort. Second, many of us are convinced that we have the best system in the world and that it is self-sufficient.

There are both theoretical and practical incentives for studying the criminal justice systems of various nations. First, there is simply academic curiosity.

We want to know how different justice systems function. From a practical point of view, criminal activity does not stop at a country's border. Crime has increasingly become a global issue. And frequently crime is transnational. This is particularly true of crimes such as terrorism and cybercrime. For example, each day computer users in the United States receive e-mails from other countries involving various scams or other unlawful schemes. Another benefit of comparative study is the opportunity to learn from the experiences of others. Criminal justice systems in most nations face similar challenges (Pakes, 2004, p. 3).

The increase in transnational crime is a sufficient reason to study comparative systems. Much of the growth in transnational crime is attributed to technological advances that have resulted in the world getting smaller. Many crimes are now committed by using computers, and there are no national boundaries in this regard. These crimes can range from relatively minor consumer fraud to more serious crimes like trafficking in drugs, which involves millions of dollars.

Many legal scholars contend that people in the United States do not have the same respect for law as people in other major countries do. As will be noted later in this chapter, more individuals are killed by guns in the United States than in any other major nation. In addition, rates of confinement in penal institutions are higher in the United States. Opolot (1980) contends that it is quite common for legal scholars to opine that U.S. citizens have less respect for legal institutions. Walter Reckless (1961) stated:

> People in the United States do not have the respect for the law that people have in other countries; for example, England, Holland, Germany, Sweden, etc. The law-abiding tradition in the U.S. is not very strong. The United States has a sort of lawless tradition—at least a fairly strong subculture of lawlessness, which came with the settlement of a new country and the pushing out to new frontiers. Many persons in the United States oversubscribe to the philosophy of taking chances with the law and regulations and getting by with infractions. (pp. 2–3)

One bar to learning from other countries is the concept of ethnocentrism. And one of the goals of most studies of comparative justice is to lessen American ethnocentrism. While ethnocentrism encourages pride, confidence, and group identification in one's race, culture, or nation, it also encourages an unwillingness to appreciate and learn from others. One of our goals in examining the five major legal models that currently exist in our world today is to illustrate that each model has both positive and negative attributes when compared to other models and that there is no perfect system. The English common law has so dominated our jurisprudence that we have tended to overlook other systems; but we need to remember that our system was not created in a vacuum, nor is it the only highly developed system of law in the world (Calvi and Coleman, 2000, p. 25).

Most textbooks and other writings in comparative justice discuss only the four major legal models (common law, civil or Continental law, socialist or Marxist, and Islamic models); we have added a fifth model, which consists of a mixed system. The mixed model is one that has borrowed extensively from two or more of the other major models.

An underlying theme of this book is that a nation's criminal justice system is formed and shaped by its legal model of justice, and that the legal model of justice is formed by customs, religions, and culture. While the authors recognize that most nations do not have a true criminal justice system and that law enforcement, courts, and corrections operate independently, the term "criminal justice system" is used to refer to a nation's law enforcement, courts, and correctional system in general. Photo 1.1 is a picture of a police headquarters in Dubai. The fact that this building is used solely for law enforcement points out the degree of separation between the various branches of the criminal justice system.

This chapter begins with an overview of the five law models, followed by brief discussions of comparative policing and corrections. The chapter will conclude with a discussion of comparative violence. Subsequent chapters discuss in detail the comparative models. Included are case studies of selected countries for each legal model. After the five models are discussed,

Photo 1.1 Few police headquarters in the world are as impressive as the one pictured here, in Dubai. (Photo by Cliff Roberson.)

then we look at some world organizations that are justice related, such as the International Criminal Court and Interpol. The final chapter looks at international criminal justice organizations.

In our study of the comparative models of justice, the emphasis will be on criminal justice rather than on criminology. While it is important to look at the various causes of criminal conduct, that is beyond the scope of this book. In addition, we examine the procedural aspects or processes of justice rather than substantive criminal law. The treatment of prisoners receives more attention in the book than do victims' issues. We recognize that this approach is against the worldwide trend of emphasizing victims' issues, but we understand that an exhaustive review of all aspects of comparative justice models is not within the scope of the book and have chosen in this regard to take the traditional approach and examine only the law enforcement, prosecution, courts, and corrections aspects of justice.

Comparative justice studies in the United States have tended to focus on our justice system and on comparing it with the justice system of one particular geographic region (e.g., Asian studies). This text is a comparative study of all five major systems of justice.

When studying comparative legal models, it is important that certain "words of art" are understood. Accordingly, in the next section, some of the more important words or concepts that are used in the text are explored.

EXCERPTS FROM *INTERFOTO PICTURE LIBRARY LTD. V. STILETTO VISUAL PROGRAMMES LTD.*

1989 QUEEN'S BENCH 433

Facts of the case: Interfoto delivered 47 photographic transparencies to Stiletto in a jiffy bag. Stiletto was planning to use them for a presentation, but did not. Stiletto never opened the transparency bag or read Interfoto's standard terms and conditions, which were inside the bag. Condition 2 said there was a holding fee of £5 per transparency for each day over 14 days. After around a month, Interfoto sent a bill for £3783.50.

EXCERPTS FROM THE DECISION BY LAW JUDGE THOMAS BINGHAM, QUEEN'S BENCH

In many civil law systems, and perhaps in most legal systems outside the common law world, the law of obligations recognises and enforces an overriding principle that in making and carrying out contracts parties should act in good faith. This does not simply mean that they should not deceive each other, a principle which any legal system must recognise; its effect is perhaps most aptly conveyed by such metaphorical colloquialisms as "playing fair," "coming clean" or "putting one's cards face upward on the table." It is in essence a principle of fair and open dealing. In such a forum it might, I think, be held on the facts of this case that the plaintiffs were under a duty in all fairness to draw the defendants' attention specifically to the high price payable if the transparencies were not returned in time and, when the 14 days had expired, to point out to the defendants the high cost of continued failure to return them.

English law has, characteristically, committed itself to no such overriding principle but has developed piecemeal solutions in response to demonstrated problems of unfairness. Many examples could be given. Thus, equity has intervened to strike down unconscionable bargains. Parliament has stepped in to regulate the imposition of exemption clauses and the form of certain hire-purchase agreements. The common law also has made its contribution, by holding that certain classes of contract require the utmost good faith, by treating as irrecoverable what purport to be agreed estimates of damage but are in truth a disguised penalty for breach, and in many other ways.

Words of Art

In any discipline, certain "words of art" are used. In this section, we discuss the key words of art used in our comparative study of justice systems.

Legal Models

In the text, the phrase "legal models" refers to the different foundations of law used in various nations. "Model" refers to similar patterns and is broader than "system." For example, the U.S. legal system and Great Britain's legal system are both grouped within the common law model, but there are great differences between the two systems. We contend that the most important and influential aspect of any system of justice is its legal model—that the legal model molds or shapes a nation's criminal justice system. As used in this text, a "legal system" is an operating set of legal institutions, procedures, and rules. There are as many legal systems as there are states, nations, and organizations. A legal model is in some sense a reflection of legal tradition.

Jurisprudence

As noted in the list of key words, jurisprudence concerns the philosophy of law. The term is often wrongly applied to actual systems of law or to current views of law, or to suggestions for its amendment. "Jurisprudence" is the name of a science just as "chemistry" is the name of a science. It is the science of actual law. In the proper sense of the word, jurisprudence is the science of law.

Jurisprudence has no concern with questions of moral or political policy, since they fall under the provinces of ethics and legislation.

Natural Law

The concept of natural law originated with the philosophical jurists of Rome, and has over the centuries been extended until the phrase denotes a supposed basis common to all legal systems. If any rule of law or principle is observed by all systems, then it must be a part of the natural law, or *jus naturale*. For example, all known systems of law prohibit the unjustified killing of another human being. Accordingly, unjustified criminal homicide is a violation of natural law.

Natural law theorists contend that laws that regulate relationships among people, similar to the laws that govern the physical universe, are founded in nature. Natural law is eternal and immutable, just as God, the source of all laws, is eternal. Natural law is often referred to as a higher form of law to distinguish it from man-made laws. While discovering what "natural law is," its advocates echo the famous statement of Supreme Court Justice Potter Stewart, saying that they "know it when they see it" (Calvi and Coleman, 2000, p. 7).

Any discussion of natural law generally leads to the question of whether it is possible to legislate morality. If "legislating morality" refers to the actual changing of a person's values, then we probably cannot legislate morality. For example, whether or not it is morally permissible to obtain an abortion does not depend upon whether or not abortion is legally permissible, but on a person's moral belief about the question.

Calvi and Coleman (2000) point out that law can have an impact on morality. They note that 60 years ago, many Americans considered it perfectly acceptable to use force to keep African American children from attending certain public schools. But the years of civil rights and antidiscrimination legislation and court decisions have changed the people's views in this regard (p. 7).

Positive Law Approach

As defined in the key words, positive law is that law that has been enacted by a legislative authority. The positive law approach is that law should simply reflect the will of the majority. Under the positive law approach, morality is removed from the law, and this results in the concept of "might makes right." Under this approach, the law is in fact what the majority wants it to be. Thus, for example, the question under the positive law approach is not whether abortion is moral or immoral, but whether the majority wishes it to be legal.

Under the natural law approach, citizens who feel that a certain law is immoral may justify their steps to prevent the legalized conduct from being accomplished. For example, the natural law approach would justify the picketing of an abortion clinic by a "right to life" group. Using the positive approach, however, there is never a justification for resorting to unlawful methods to effect a change in a law.

Historical Approach

According to Berman (2005), the historical approach to the study of law was implicit in the development of the Western legal tradition beginning in the twelfth century and played a critical role in the development of the English common law in the seventeenth and eighteenth centuries, but it did not develop as a separate school of legal philosophy until the nineteenth century. Berman contends that the school emerged in the context of the debate between positivism and natural law (p. 16). The historical approach stresses the organic growth of the law. Friedrich Karl von Savigny is credited with the formalization of the historical approach. Savigny was a German jurist and legal scholar who advocated that the meaning and content of existing bodies of law be analyzed through research into their historical origins and modes of transformation. In Savigny's view, law is first developed by custom and popular faith, and next by judicial decisions—everywhere, therefore, by internal, silently operating powers, not by the arbitrary will of a law giver. He viewed law as a slow, almost imperceptible growth that is formed in much the same way as a language is. According to him, legislation and law codes merely give verbal expression to a body of existing law whose meaning and content can be discovered only by careful historical investigations.

U.S. Supreme Court Justice Oliver Wendell Holmes, Jr. (1881), also expressed the historical approach when he stated:

> The life of the law has not been logic: it has been experience. The felt necessities of the time, the prevalent moral and political theories, intuitions of public policy, avowed or unconscious, even the prejudices which judges share with their fellow-men, have had a good deal more to do than the syllogism in determining the rules by which men should be governed. The law embodies the story of a nation's development through many centuries. (p. 1)

Law as an Instrument of Control

The positivist school advocates consider law as a political instrument—a body of rules promulgated and enforced by official authorities, representing the will, the policy, of the lawmakers; in contrast, advocates of natural law treat law as essentially a moral instrument, an embodiment of principles of

Photo 1.2 The New York City Police Department, in implementing its community policing program, has established this police substation in Times Square.

reason and conscience implicit in human nature. And historicists treat law as a manifestation of the group memory, the historically developing ethos, of the society whose law it is. As stated by Harold J. Berman (2005),

> Positivists, who are today predominant among both Continental European and Anglo-American legal scholars, emphasize the source of law in the rules "posited" by legislative, administrative, and judicial authorities, and analyze those rules independently of their correspondence either to moral principles or to the historical consciousness of the given polity. (p. 13)

Many countries are using community policing as a means of helping establish law as an instrument of social control. Community policing brings law into the community as noted in Photo 1.2.

The Function of a Court System

The primary function of any court system is to help keep domestic peace. In the process of keeping peace, the courts are called upon to solve or decide controversies. For example, in a civil case there is a contract dispute that the parties cannot resolve; therefore, by submitting the dispute to the court, they call upon the judge to decide it. In a criminal case, the state accuses the defendant of a crime and demands appropriate punishment for the offense. The defendant generally denies committing the offense and certainly does not want to suffer any punishment. The judge and/or the jury decide the issues in this case. Many cases before the court are uncontested. In these cases, the judge does not act to resolve the dispute. In uncontested cases, the judge acts in an administrative capacity by formalizing the agreements of the parties.

Rule of Law

Ours is a government of liberty by, through and under the law. No man is above it, and no man is below it.

President Theodore Roosevelt (in his State of the Union Address, December 7, 1903)

Roman statesman Cicero: "We are all servants of the laws in order that we may be free."

As reported by Wormut (1949, p. 28)

The rule of law implies that every citizen is subject to the law including the king. The rule of law is an ambiguous term that has different meanings in different contexts. In the first context, the term means rule according to law. And that no individual is above the law. Accordingly, no one can be ordered by the government to pay civil damages or suffer criminal punishment except in strict accordance with well-established and clearly defined laws and procedures. In the second context, the term is used to mean rule under law. Accordingly, no branch of government is above the law, and no public official may act arbitrarily or unilaterally in violation of the law. In the third context, the term means rule according to a higher law; therefore, no written law; may be enforced by the government unless it conforms to certain universal principles of fairness, morality, and justice that transcend human legal systems.

Arguments regarding the meaning of the concept of "rule of war" can be traced back to classical Greek philosophy. The concept was familiar to the Greek philosophers such as Aristotle in their discussions regarding the best form of government as rule by the best men. In Islamic jurisprudence, it appears that the concept of the rule of law was formulated in the seventh century with the claim that no official or citizen was to be above the law.

The first known use of the phrase in English occurred about 1500 AD. The phrase "rule of law" is found in a petition to King James I of England in 1610. In 1607, English Chief Justice Sir Edward Coke stated that the King ought not to be under any man but under God and the law. In this statement, Sir Coke is referring to the concept that the king is subject to the law of the land. In 1776, Thomas Paine, in his famous pamphlet *Common Sense*, stated that in America, the law is our king. In 1780, the principle was included in the Massachusetts Constitution by the phrase "a government of laws and not of men" (Bingham, 2010).

All government officers of the United States, including the President, the Justices of the Supreme Court, state judges and legislators, and all members of Congress, pledge to uphold the Constitution. These oaths affirm that the rule of law is superior to the rule of any leader or government official.

Generally, the actual term "rule of law" is attributed to A. V. Dicey who was an English expert on constitutional law. He developed the theory for purposes of describing how the British governmental system manifested this quality. Dicey listed the basic quality of a government as a government in which citizens are equal before the law (Dicey, 1889).

Under the concept of the rule of law, we generally mean that no person, not even the queen, is above the law. One of the most exhausting studies on the rule of law was accomplished in 2014 by the World Justice Project and published in its *Rule of Law Index: 2014*. As noted in the Index, the phrase "Rule of Law" is notoriously difficult to define and measure. In order to define the phrase, the World Justice Project used a working definition based on four universal principles:

1. The government, its officials, and the public are accountable under the law.
2. The laws are clear, publicized, stable, and just.
3. The process by which the laws are enforced is fair, accessible, and efficient.
4. Justice is delivered timely by competent, ethical, and independent and neutral representatives who are in sufficient number and have adequate resources.

United Nations and the Rule of Law

According to the United Nations and the Rule of Law website (www.un.org/en/ruleoflaw), promoting the rule of law at national and international levels is at the heart of the United Nations (UN) mission. According to the UN, establishing respect for the rule of law is fundamental to achieving a durable world peace and for the effective protection of human rights. As noted by the Report of the Secretary-General on the Rule of Law and Transitional Justice in Conflict and Post-Conflict Societies (2004, p. 2):

For the United Nations, the rule of law refers to a principle of governance in which all persons, institutions and entities, public and private, including the State itself, are accountable to laws that are publicly promulgated, equally enforced and independently adjudicated, and which are consistent with international human rights norms and standards. It requires, as well, measures to ensure adherence to the principles of supremacy of law, equality before the law, accountability to the law, fairness in the application of the law, separation of powers, participation in decision-making, legal certainty, avoidance of arbitrariness and procedural and legal transparency.

According to the UN report, justice, peace, and democracy are not mutually exclusive objectives, but rather mutually reinforcing imperatives. The UN's approach to the issues involving the rule of law includes comprehensive attention to all of the nations and being sensitive to the needs of key groups and mindful of the need for complementarity between transitional justice mechanisms. The UN's main role should be not to build international substitutes for national structures, but to help build domestic justice capacities.

For the UN, "justice" is considered as an ideal of accountability and fairness in the protection and vindication of rights and the prevention and punishment of wrongs. Justice implies regard for the rights of the accused, for the interests of victims, and for the well-being of society at large. Justice is a concept rooted in all national cultures and traditions and, while its administration usually implies formal judicial mechanisms, traditional dispute resolution mechanisms are equally relevant. The international community has worked to articulate collectively the substantive and procedural requirements for the administration of justice for more than half a century.

Justice Project Index

The Justice Project after an in-depth study published rankings of the nations according to nine factors that include: constraints on government powers, absence of corruption, open government, fundamental rights, order and security, regulatory enforcement, civil justice, criminal justice, and informal justice. Then the project compiled a global ranking involving the 99 largest countries. Table 1.1 contains excerpts of the overall global rankings. The Appendix contains excerpts from the report and other selected rankings.

Brief Examination of the Legal Models

Let us start with a paradox. It is that English and Continental law irrevocably took their different courses in the very century, the twelfth, when English civilization was closer to the Continent and less insular than at any other time (Van Caenegem, 1988, p. 85).

The two major legal models in the modern Western world are the civil law and the common law models. The civil law model, also known as the

Table 1.1   The World Justice Project, *Rule of Law Index: 2014*

Rank	Countries	Score
1	Denmark	0.88
2	Norway	0.88
3	Sweden	0.85
5	Netherlands	0.83
9	Germany	0.80
11	Canada	0.78
12	Japan	0.78
13	United Kingdom	0.78
18	France	0.74
19	United States	0.71
79	Mexico	0.45

Note: The aforementioned ranking excerpts are from the Global Rule of Law Index compiled by the World Justice Project. The rule of law is calculated by taking an average of individual factors (discussed in the Appendix). The Project ranked the largest 99 countries in the world as to their performances regarding the rule of law. Only 11 selected countries are reported in this chart.

Romano-Germanic model, is the older and more influential of the two. The common law system is used in the United States and England. The civil law system is used in France, Germany, and many other European countries. It is also used in many Latin American and African countries.

The common law model prefers precedent as a basis for judgments and moves empirically from case to case. The civil law model tends to move more theoretically by deductive reasoning, basing judgments on abstract principles. Civil law is more conceptual and more scholarly than common law. Civil law also deals more with definitions and distinctions. It is often referred to as the professors' law and was molded by Roman law (Van Caenegem, 1988, p. 36).

Common Law

Common law is currently the legal model in Ireland, most of the United Kingdom (England, Wales, and northern Ireland), Australia, New Zealand, Bangladesh, India (excluding Goa), Pakistan, South Africa, Canada (excluding Quebec), Hong Kong, the United States, on a state level, and many other places. In addition to these countries, several others have adapted the common law system into a mixed system. For example, Nigeria operates largely on a common law system, but incorporates religious law.

Common law systems are those models where the decisions in cases by judges are important and often controlled. In each of those nations, there are legislatures that pass new laws and statutes but the duty of interpreting the statutes and laws belongs to the judges. The relationships between statutes and judicial decisions can be complex. In some jurisdictions, such statutes may overrule judicial decisions or codify the topic covered by several contradictory or ambiguous decisions. In some jurisdictions, judicial decisions may decide whether the jurisdiction's constitution allowed a particular statute or statutory provision to be made or what meaning is contained within the statutory provisions. Statutes were allowed to be made by the government.

Common law was developed in England, influenced by Anglo-Saxon law and to a much lesser extent by the Norman conquest of England, which introduced legal concepts from Norman law. Common law was later adopted by the Commonwealth of Nations, and in almost every former colony of the British Empire except Malta. The doctrine of stare decisis, also known as case law or precedent by courts, is the major difference between the common law systems and the codified civil law systems.

Civil Law

Generally, civil law models are subdivided into four distinct groups:

1. *French civil law*: France, Italy, Romania, Spain, and former colonies of those countries
2. *German civil law*: Germany, Austria, Switzerland, Estonia, Latvia, the former Yugoslav republics, Greece, Portugal, and their former colonies
3. *Scandinavian civil law*: Denmark, Norway, and Sweden
4. *Chinese law*: A mixture of civil law and socialist law existing today in the People's Republic of China

The civil law model is characterized by its interaction in its formative years with Roman law, Germanic law, canon law, international law merchant, and local customs. The phrase "Roman law" is commonly used to describe the entire Roman legal tradition and output from the Twelve Tables (c. 450 BC) to the Justinian compilations (c. 534 AD). The Romans were the first to consider law as a science by means of which they could look at the world, with all its people and property and their intermingling relationships, through judicial concepts that were as orderly as the laws of mathematics (Kolbert, 1979, p. 6).

Researchers of ancient Roman law generally divide it into various periods. In one of the first periods, which started about the third century BC, a class of men known as "jurisconsults," who made law their specialty, appeared and acted as consultants to lay judges who needed legal advice. While these consults acted only in an advisory capacity, they are still considered to have been the world's first professional lawyers. Whereas the orators like Cicero focused their skills on rhetoric and statesmanship, the consults developed and taught the principles of law that were later expounded in treatises.

In its early recorded history, Rome was a monarchy. By the end of the sixth century BC, the kings were expelled and a republic was established. Rome at this time was a small community on the banks of the Tiber River. The city's origin legend held that these people descended from the refugees of Troy when it was destroyed by the Greeks. The law at that time was a set of unwritten customs passed on orally from one generation to another and was regarded as part of their heritage as Romans. These unwritten rules were applied only to those who could claim to be Roman citizens. The citizen body was divided into two groups: the patricians, who were families of noble birth, and the plebeians, who were numerically greater but disadvantaged in various ways, including wealth. The individuals who determined the legal validity of particular acts were always patricians and were considered by the plebeians as not entirely unbiased. The plebeians advocated that if the customs were written into laws in advance, individuals would know what their legal positions were prior to acting in a certain situation.

In 451 BC, a commission of 10 citizens was appointed and charged with the task of writing down the customs into a set of rules. Their work became known as the Twelve Tables. The rules were approved by a popular assembly of citizens and became the law. In giving its approval to the Tables, the citizens did not feel that they were enacting new laws, only fixing more precisely what had always been the law. After being enacted in a text, they became known as *leges* (singular, *lex*, from *legere* "to read out") (Stein, 1999).

The Twelve Tables are considered the beginning of what we now know as Roman law. While the original text of the Tables has not survived, many quotations in later writings have allowed scholars substantially to reconstruct it. The Tables concentrated on points that were likely to be the center of disputes rather than on what everyone knew and accepted as the law. Procedure dominated the Tables. When disputes arose, the parties generally appeared before lay judges. The duty of the judges was to decide whether the dispute raised an issue that the law recognized, and if so, how the dispute should be resolved.

In early Rome, the law did not deal with what went on within a family. The relationships between members of a family were considered private matters, which the community had no authority to control. In cases involving homicides, a magistrate (lay judge) would take the initiative on behalf of the community as a whole to prosecute the wrongdoer in order to prevent further bloodshed between families (Stein, 1999).

During most of the duration of the Republic, the law developed through the control of legal remedies. When the concept of legal actions was first developed, there were few legal forms, and a cause of action was required to fit within one of the forms. At that time, the law was formal and rigid. It was characterized by attention to detail, and often a cause of action was lost because of a small mistake by one of the parties.

Beginning around 367 BC, a special magistrate, called a *praetor,* was elected to deal exclusively with the administration of justice. Even though the praetor had no legal training, he was expected to supervise the formal stage of every legal action. At that time, each formal legal action had two stages. In the first stage, the legal issue was categorized into one of the existing legal forms. The second stage, which was relatively informal, consisted of an actual trial of the issues. Since the second stage was more time consuming, citizens without any legal training were appointed as lay judges to decide the issues in that stage.

During this time the citizens realized that many disputes arose not because of a disagreement about the law, but through a disagreement as to what actually happened (the facts of the case). Therefore, during the second half of the Republic, magistrates began to allow parties to express their claims and defenses rather than adhering to the fixed forms. After the magistrate discovered what the issue was, he would set out in hypothetical terms in a written document known as a *formula* (literally, a "small form"). The formula declared what law was involved in the dispute and what a party had to establish in order to obtain recovery. The praetor could grant a formula in a case in which there was no precedent. While unofficially the praetor was making new law, he was considered just to be implementing existing law.

As Roman conquests expanded and Roman rule was extended over the western Mediterranean in the third century BC, the number of noncitizens involved in the legal system increased. At first, the system acted under the fiction that the foreigners were citizens. In 242 BC, a second praetorship was instituted; this praetor especially dealt with cases in which one or both parties were not citizens. The two praetors were distinguished as "urban" and "peregrine." The Romans considered that the civil law was their proud possession and should not be extended indiscriminately to "peregrines" ("travelers," or noncitizens). In addition, during this period Romans, being citizens, were expected to observe higher standards of conduct than were foreigners. Accordingly, Roman law at that time consisted of two kinds of institutions. The first one was the institute for Roman citizens and the second one the "law of nations" or *ius gentium.* The *ius gentium* was available to both citizens and noncitizens. Some referred to the *ius gentium* as natural law; it was accepted that the law of nations and natural law were similar because they were based not on traditional practice but on common sense, or natural reason.

The first and second centuries AD are considered the high mark in the development of Roman law. This era, referred to as the "Classical period," marked the most sophisticated and refined developments in Roman law—a paradox, because during these centuries the Roman Empire sometimes had brutal, lawless emperors such as Nero, Caligula, and Domitian. At its apex, Roman law was considered "a body of practical wisdom of a kind the world had not seen before" (Glendon et al., 1999, p. 18). This period of Roman law likely ended with the civil war that commenced around 235 AD.

Most of the ancient sources of Roman law were lost. In the sixth century AD under the direction of Emperor Justinian, Byzantine jurists codified Roman law into the Corpus Juris Civilis of Justinian. Corpus Juris was divided into four parts: the Institutes, the Digests, the Code, and the Novels. The Byzantine Roman lawyers did more than copy the law of earlier periods. They added and modified laws and continued the movement away from formalism, which they accomplished by reducing the emphasis on the technical aspects of legal procedure. The Corpus Juris was the product of selecting some parts of the prior law and rejecting other parts. The Code and the Digest were designed to be the complete and authoritative restatement of Roman law.

The most important part of the Corpus Juris was the Digest. It was a summary of what the writers believed were the most valuable parts of prior writings on Roman law and dealt with the subjects of torts, unjust enrichment, contracts, and remedies. Since almost all prior writings on Roman law have been destroyed, it has become our principal source of knowledge about early Roman law. The Institutes contained an introductory text for students of Roman law. The Code was a systematic collection of prior legislation. The Novels contained the legislation that was enacted after the Code and the Digest were completed.

After the fall of the Roman Empire, the Germanic invaders used Roman law to govern their Roman subjects and applied their own law to their own people. After the fall of the Empire and until the revival of Roman law in the eleventh century, the Roman Catholic Church assumed the functions of government and imposed its canon law. Canon law, however, was developed by applying Christian notions to Roman law.

Revival of Roman Law

About 1050, Europe entered a period of political, economic, and cultural transformation. The return of political order and relative economic stability led to a search to establish predictability and efficient methods of dispute resolution. This search led to the revival of Roman law. The revival started in northern Italy around the end of the eleventh century.

Students from all over Europe assembled at the University of Bologna to hear lectures on Roman law. The university became the leading center for legal learning. It also had the first women law professionals, most of whom were nuns. At first, the lecturers proclaimed the superiority of the Justinian Digests. These lecturers became known as "glossators" because they tried to reconstruct accurately and explain the Digests; in English, "gloss" is another word for "marginal commentary" or "definition." Later lecturers, in about the thirteenth century, saw their work as adapting the laws discussed in the Digests to contemporary issues. The later lecturers became known as "commentators" because they were also influenced by the spirit of rational inquiry and speculative dialectic. Included in the commentators was Thomas Aquinas. But the most famous was Bartolus (Bartolo de Saxoferrato, 1314–1357) of the University of Perugia.

Bartolus, the most famous master of the dialectical school of jurists, was born in 1314, at Sassoferrato, is also styled Bartolo de Saxoferrato. His reputation dates from his appointment in 1343 to a chair of civil law in the University of Perugia, where he lectured for many years, raising the character of the law school of Perugia to equal that of Bologna. He died in 1357 at Perugia. Bartolus is considered to have been the professor who introduced the dialectical method of teaching law. His reputation probably owed more to the fact that he revived the exegetical system of teaching law in a spirit that gave it new life. He imparted to his teaching a practical interest, from the judicial experience he had acquired while acting as an assessor to the courts at Todi and at Pisa before he assumed a professorial chair. His treatises *On Procedure* and *On Evidence* are among his most valuable works, and his *Commentary on the Code of Justinian* has in some countries been regarded as of equal authority with the Code itself (Ullmann, 1962).

The Roman civil law as reconstructed and supplemented by the glossators and commentators was considered the law of Europe. John Henry Merryman (1985) describes the era: "There was a common body of law and of writing about law, a common legal language and a common method of teaching and scholarship."

Commercial Law

As discussed earlier, Europe in the Middle Ages was regulated by Roman law and canon law handed down by the church. In addition, a body of law developed to deal with the emerging commerce between countries and with maritime trade. Commercial law developed because Roman law and canon law were not flexible enough to handle the issues involved in commercial transactions. Merchants' courts were established, and these courts in turn established their own procedures to govern the cases. Their rules were informal and designed to expedite the issues before the courts. Eventually, the "law merchant," as their rules were called, became an international body of accepted commercial rules. For a period of time, however, the law merchant was ignored by the civil courts in Europe. Eventually, the civil courts reluctantly accepted the law merchant as a valid body of law.

Civil Law Model Today

> The judgments of the courts have no binding force except in the causes in which they are rendered. Judges are forbidden in matters of their jurisprudence to make any ruling of general application or regulation.
>
> **Civil Code of Colombia (1887, Article 17)**

The civil law model is also known as the "inquisitorial model." While civil law is commonly tied to Roman law, it cannot be traced to a single source. There are many nations that use the civil law model, and each of them has its own originality. The Justinian Code is the cornerstone of today's civil law model (Calvi and Coleman, 2000, p. 34).

The civil law countries include France, Germany, the Netherlands, Sweden, Austria, Switzerland, Italy, Spain, Sweden, Denmark, Norway, Finland, Belgium, and Portugal. While the historical development of the civil law system in these countries is quite complicated, much of the credit is given to Napoleon Bonaparte, who encouraged comprehensive modernization of the Continental legal system and, as part of his plan for a united Europe, provided for the drafting of the Napoleonic Code Civil, which contained a restatement of the ancient principles in modern terms (Opolot, 1980, p. 10). Spain and Portugal had for many years used the Roman law for most purposes. Opolot claims that Spain's inhabitants had become thoroughly romanized on the basis of cultural influence (p. 11).

The civil law, as practiced in Spain and Portugal, was transported to Latin America by the *conquistadores* and other settlers and became part of the culture, just as the Spanish and Portuguese languages did. The pattern of transporting the civil law model to Africa was very similar. The French carried civil law into Algeria, Niger, Togo, Mali, Chad, and the Comoro Islands (the present legal model in the Comoro Islands is considered a mixed system, since both French and Islamic law formed the basis of a new consolidated code). Belgians transported their legal system into parts of Central and East Africa. Portuguese settlers took their legal system into Angola, Guinea Bissau, the Cape Verde Islands, and Mozambique. The Spanish imposed their legal system in the Spanish Sahara and Equatorial Guinea. The Italians imposed theirs in Libya and Somaliland (Opolot, 1980).

Opolot (1980) lists the tenets of civil law as follows: it is an inquisitorial system; there is limited use of the jury; it emphasizes a written code; and precedent is not used.

Common Law Model

> Common law is that body of law and juristic rules which was originated, developed, formulated, and administered in England... common law comprises the body of principles and rules of action... which are derived from usages and customs of immemorial antiquity.

> *Black's Law Dictionary*

The common law model is regarded as an "adversarial" model. Today, countries that use common law include the United States, Canada, the United Kingdom, and most of the former British colonies including Australia, New Zealand, India, and parts of Africa and the Caribbean. Most historians trace the origin of the common law in England to the reign of William the Conqueror. At the time of his conquest of England (1066), there was no uniform criminal law there.

The first known English code had been written in the seventh century by King Aethelbert. His proclamations of the code were called "dooms" and were influenced by the social class structure of the time. Punishments under the dooms were often determined by the status of the victim. For example, stealing from a holy man was punished by a fine three times the value of the property stolen, whereas stealing from the king was punished by a fine nine times the value of the property—or by death.

When William and his Norman lords seized the throne, England was divided into tribal areas known as "shires." Justice was administered by "shire-reeves" who presided over the shire courts. The shire-reeves later became known as "sheriffs." Prior to the conquest, the law was based on ancient custom and varied with each tribal area. Each county was controlled by a shire-reeve who also controlled the courts in that county. Since the shire-reeve determined the law in the county, there was no uniform English system.

William took over the county courts and made them royal courts. He sent representatives to the courts to record their decisions and then distributed selected court decisions. As the routine of these courts became firmly established, it became possible to predict their decisions by reference to similar cases that had been decided and published. From this beginning, the doctrine of *stare decisis* developed in the eighteenth century. William compiled the law of crimes that most areas of the kingdom observed in common. These became the common law crimes of England.

Lux v. Haggin, 69 Cal. 255, 10 P. 674 (1886)

In ascertaining the common law of England, we may and should examine and weigh the reasoning of the decisions, not only of the English courts but also of the courts of the United States and of the several states, down to the present time. We are not limited to the consideration of the English decisions rendered prior to July 4, 1776. The common law of England may be said to consist of a collection of principles found in the opinions of sages, or deduced from universal and immemorial usage, and receiving progressively the sanction of the courts. It was imported by our colonial ancestors, so far as it was applicable, and was sanctioned by royal charters. The best evidence of the common law is found in the decisions of the courts, contained in numerous volumes of reports, and in the treatises and digests of scholars that have been multiplying from the earliest periods of English history down to the present time.

Opolot (1980, p. 38) lists the following tenets of common law: it is largely unwritten; it contains the principle of *stare decisis*; it is an adversary system; it uses judicial review; it utilizes trial by jury.

Islamic Model

The sacred law of Islam is an all-embracing body of religious duties, the totality of Allah's commands that regulate the life of every Muslim in all its aspects.

Schacht (1964, p. 1)

In this section, we will discuss traditional Islamic law, and later in the text, the trends and modernization of Islamic law in countries such as Egypt, Afghanistan, and Pakistan will also be discussed.

Islamic law is the epitome of Islamic thought. Total and unqualified submission to the will of Allah (God) is a fundamental tenet of Islamic law. Islamic law is simply an expression of Allah's commands for Muslim society. Islamic law has been described as a system of duties that are incumbent upon Muslims by virtue of their religious beliefs. Known as *shari'ah*, Islamic law constitutes a divinely ordained path of conduct that guides Muslims toward a practical expression of their religious conviction in this world and the goal of divine favor in the world to come.

Muslims believe that Muhammad brought to the world not only the word of God in the form of the Qur'an, but also a divine law specific to Islam, a law whose roots are contained completely in the Qur'an but whose crystallization was not possible without the words and deeds of the Prophet. The schools of Islamic law (*shari'ah*), both Sunni and Shi'ite, consider that the Sunnah (deeds and actions) and *hadith* (anecdotes) of the Prophet serve as the primary source of Islamic law after the Qur'an. In Islam even a prophet is not by himself a legislator; instead, God is ultimately the only legislator (*al-Shari'*). Muslims believe, however, that, as God's prophet, Muhammad knew the divine will as it was meant to be codified in Islamic law. His actions and juridical decisions therefore played an indispensable role in the later codification of the *shari'ah* by various legal schools (Berman, 2005).

The Islamic criminal process consists of two parts: the trial and the administration of penalties if warranted. The purpose of the trial is to identify the wrongdoer. The state acts as a third party to ensure that justice is done. The administration of penalties segment is similar to the common law punishment hearing.

The primary objective of Islamic law is to prevent evil. The law has two main tenets, equality and good faith. According to Opolot (1980, p. 82), Islamic law is the most victim-centered system in criminal justice history. Its criminal justice system focuses on both the victim and the offender, not only during the trial but also after conviction.

Socialist Model

The socialist model of law was first developed in Russia after the communist seizure of power in 1917 and imposed throughout the Soviet Union in the 1920s. After World War II, the Soviet legal model was also imposed on Soviet-dominated regimes in eastern and central Europe. Later, ruling communist parties in China, North Korea, and Vietnam adopted variations of Soviet law. Soviet law, which has changed radically since it was first introduced in the Soviet Union, revived certain features of earlier tsarist law, shared key elements with the law of other dictatorships, and introduced public ownership of the means of production and subordination of the legal system to the Soviet Communist Party. Presently, the People's Republic of China is considered a socialist legal model, but it has many features of a mixed-legal model.

Most of the basic features of Soviet law came into effect very soon after the 1917 Russian Revolution. The new government immediately placed itself above the law and gave the head of the Communist Party powers similar to those enjoyed by the tsars. The government decreed that enemies of the Revolution should be eliminated without the need for trials; it expropriated land, banks, insurance companies, and large factories; and it promulgated its ideology and suppressed opposing speech. The communist ideology was hostile to law, proclaiming, on the authority of Karl Marx, that the state and all its institutions (including legal ones) would eventually "wither away" after the socialist revolution.

The classic socialist model has three purposes: (1) to provide for national security; (2) to regulate economics by using socialist principles; and (3) to educate the general population as well as lawbreakers about the law (Vago, 1997, p. 12). The People's Republic of China represents the typical socialist model. Its constitution establishes the nation as a "socialist country under the people's democratic dictatorship and led by the proletariat on the basis of a worker-peasant alliance. Socialism is the political system of the country where all power belongs to the people" (Du and Zhang, 1990, p. 214).

The constitution also provides that the state's economic system is based on the concept of socialist public ownership.

Criminal procedure was designed to favor the state. Although the criminal justice system generally followed the Continental European model, which uses extensive preliminary investigations, the investigator in cases of serious crimes was an official of the Party and not a judicial official, as in western Europe. The investigator, who was also the prosecutor, could hold a suspect without contact with legal counsel for months.

Mixed-Legal Model

Algeria is an example of a nation with a mixed-legal model. Its legal system was derived from French and Arabic legal traditions and influenced by socialism. Although Algeria's constitution mandates an independent judiciary, the executive branch exercises some influence over its operations. Ordinary courts have initial jurisdiction over civil proceedings. Each of the 48 provinces has a court of appeal that reviews initial court decisions. The Supreme Court has the highest jurisdiction. Administrative courts have jurisdiction over minor disputes. The State Council, which was established in 1998, regulates the administrative courts.

The three main sources of Algerian law are treaties or conventions ratified by the president, the legal code, and Islamic law. French jurisprudence has not been observed since 1975. According to the constitution, defendants are entitled to a public trial, during which they are presumed innocent, they may confront witnesses, and they may present evidence. They also have the right to appeal the verdict.

As noted earlier, the People's Republic of China while presently considered as a socialist legal model is moving into a mixed-law system with many aspects of civil law system. Cuba is another nation whose legal system was considered as socialist law but has now embraced many aspects of Spanish civil law.

In addition, there is the Scandinavian civil law that is used in Denmark, Norway, Finland, and Iceland. The latter system uses many civil law concepts from France and Germany. Scandinavian law is generally considered pliable and less dogmatic than the European legal systems. Under this system, great attention is paid to the rules and principles that have evolved in practice, especially in the courts. The extensive participation by nonlegally trained individuals has contributed to the pragmatic and flexible character of their system.

Mexico's Reform Movement

Mexico is moving toward an adversarial system used in the common law legal models and from the civil law system. At this time, however, it is unclear as to the status and future of this movement. In 2008, there was

Photo 1.3 Traffic control is one of the more routine duties required of law enforcement officers. This photograph shows a Mexican policeman directing traffic in a small Mexico city. (Photo by Cliff Roberson.)

judicial reform legislation that provided an apparent avenue for reform. In addition, the courts have become more of an adversarial system and away from the Spanish civil law system. As of the date of the revision of this text, Mexico's progress has not been encouraging. A shift from the civil law to the adversarial system involves retraining judges, lawyers, and prosecutors. In addition, textbooks need to be rewritten and court-rooms remodeled. Antonio Garza, a former U.S. Ambassador to Mexico, estimates that the cost of the change will exceed $4 billion (Garza, 2015). A 2007 Gallup Poll indicated that less than 40% of the Mexican citizens had confidence in their judicial system. Photo 1.3 shows a Mexican police officer directing traffic. It was noted that many motorists ignored his directions.

Mexico's 2008 judicial reforms have four main elements:

1. Changes to criminal procedure through the introduction of new oral, adversarial procedures, alternative sentencing, and alternative dispute resolution mechanisms
2. A greater emphasis on the due process rights of the accused (i.e., the presumption of innocence and an adequate legal defense)
3. Modifications to police agencies and their role in criminal investigations
4. Tougher measures for combating organized crime (Shirk, 2010)

Judicial Opinion under the Common Law
Model Compared to the Civil Law Model

To illustrate the difference between the common law and the civil law models, we will use an actual case that occurred in the County of Maui, State of Hawaii.

Facts of the case: Police officers of the Maui Police Department received a phone call from an anonymous person and proceeded to the Puu Olai beach at Makena to look for nude sunbathers. On reaching their destination, the police surveyed the beach from a ridge using both their naked eyes and binoculars and saw the defendants lying on the beach completely nude, one on his stomach and the other on his back. The officers then approached the defendants and arrested them for indecent exposure. It was admitted by the police officers that defendants were not at any time engaged in any activity other than sunbathing. At the time of the arrest, there were several other people on the beach who were nude. The first issue the court was asked to decide on appeal was whether defendants created a common nuisance by sunbathing in the nude on a public beach.

The Hawaii statute (HRS § 727-1) reads as follows:

> The offense of common nuisance is the endangering of the public personal safety or health, or doing, causing or promoting, maintaining or continuing what is offensive, or annoying and vexatious, or plainly hurtful to the public; or is a public outrage against common decency or common morality; or tends plainly and directly to the corruption of the morals, honesty, and good habits of the people; the same being without authority or justification by law:... as for example:... Open lewdness or lascivious behavior, or indecent exposure.

The opinion by the Hawaii Appellate Court (using common law principles):

> Sunbathing in the nude is not per se illegal. It must be coupled with the intent to indecently expose oneself. As authority for this statement, the court cited the case of *The King v. Grieve*, 6 Haw. 740 (1883). The court, citing *Messina v. State*, 212 Md. 602, 606, 130 A.2d 578, 580 (1957) held that the intent necessary is a general intent, not a specific intent; i.e., it is not necessary that the exposure be made with the intent that some particular person see it, but only that the exposure was made where it was likely to be observed by others. Thus, the intent may be inferred from the conduct of the accused and the circumstances and environment of the occurrence. The court then looked at the "public place" requirement and stated: "The place is a public one if the exposure is such that it is likely to be seen by a number of casual observers. *Van Houten v. State*, 46 N.J.L. 16, 17 (1884)."

Decision of the Appellate Court: The conviction was *affirmed* (*approved*).

(*State v. Rocker*, 52 Haw. 336, 475 P.2d 684, 1970 Haw. LEXIS 135 [Haw. 1970])

Comment: Note how the justices used prior court decisions (precedent) to justify their decisions. How would a civil law judge look at the same issues? Note that the civil law judge does not look at prior court decisions and must make his or her decision based on the statute and logical reasoning.

Note: The common law judges are generally expected to follow earlier decisions, because one of the goals of a legal system is to render law that is uniform and predictable justice. In the civil law countries, the doctrine of judicial precedent does not apply. The judge should apply the law as created by the legislature. In the civil law system, the judge's decision is not binding in future cases.

Law Enforcement Systems

It is important to distinguish between "police" and "policing." *Policing* describes the set of processes that are used in an attempt to maintain security through surveillance and the threat of sanction. It is a relatively broad concept and encompasses a wide range of activities. For example, a basketball referee conducts policing when he or she works a basketball game; in contrast, the word *police* refers to the body of people who carry out much of the policing function. *Police* also refers to the institution or the agency involved in law enforcement (Pakes, 2004, p. 26). For our purposes, we will use "police agencies" and "law enforcement agencies" interchangeably.

In a review of various nations' law enforcement systems, we tend to see two basic types of systems: one where the national police dominate law enforcement, and one where it is dominated by local law enforcement agencies with limited national involvement.

An example of the national police type is Angola. There, the National Police is a militarized force whose duties include the defense of democratic legality, the preservation of public order and calm, respect for the regular exercise of the fundamental rights and liberties of citizens, defense and protection of state, collective and private property, and prevention of delinquency and reduction of criminal activity (*World Police Encyclopedia*, 2006, vol. 1, p. 25).

An example of a nation where primary law enforcement is dominated by local law enforcement agencies is Canada. While each of Canada's 10 provinces makes laws that prescribe standards for such matters as the governance, recruitment, and training of police officers, municipalities are responsible for urban policing. There are approximately 300 police organizations in Canada. In addition, Canada has several national police organizations, including the Royal Canadian Mounted Police (RCMP).

The RCMP provides policing services under contract to 8 of the 10 provinces and support for the local police departments. In addition, the RCMP is responsible for enforcement of federal statutes (Das and Palmiotto, 2006, vol. 1, p. 158).

Punishments

The earliest forms of state-imposed sanctions generally included social control by means of ordering financial compensation. For example, in the Middle Ages, offenders were ordered to pay a certain amount of money to the victim or his or her family. The motivation for the use of financial compensation was to reduce the likelihood of blood feuds between families. Often the amount of money paid depended more on the status of the victim rather than on the harm done to him or her.

Imprisonment or physical restraint as a form of punishment did not appear until relatively late in history. Despite its late appearance, confinement is now very popular worldwide. In 2002, there were approximately 8.5 million people in confinement.

According to Pakes (2004), differences in sentencing practices among countries tell us something about various jurisdictions' visions of social inclusion and social control. He contends that punishment is an area almost made for comparative research. As discussed in the next section, the United States has the highest rate of firearms ownership and the highest rate of firearms killings per 100,000 people. The United States also has the highest rate of confinement. For example, in 2002, there were more than 8.5 million people in prison worldwide. The highest incarceration rates existed in the United States (about 700 per 100,000 individuals) and in Russia (about 665 per 100,000), while Germany had only about 95 per 100,000 and the United Kingdom had 125 per 100,000. While the data listed in this section and the next could support an argument that the United States is the most violent country in the world, the issue is far more complex.

There are four generally accepted goals used to justify confinement of individuals convicted of crimes: retribution, deterrence, rehabilitation, and incapacitation. "Retribution" refers to the practice of punishing an individual because he or she committed a crime and therefore should suffer. "Deterrence" can be subdivided into *general deterrence* and *specific deterrence*.

"General deterrence" refers to punishing an individual in order to prevent others from committing similar acts. "Specific deterrence" refers to punishing an individual in order to prevent that individual from committing crimes in the future. "Rehabilitation" involves the concept that the offender needs and should receive treatment or correction. "Incapacitation" refers to the notion that while an individual is confined, he or she cannot commit other crimes against the general public. The problem in researching which theories are being used by the various countries is that most of the time we are unaware of what theory the sentencing judge uses when he or she sentences a person to imprisonment. Another complicating factor is that some of the sentencing goals are mutually exclusive.

As we examine the various countries, we will discuss their particular sentencing goals. For the reasons stated earlier, the sentencing goals used in specific countries will be discussed in general terms. For example, it appears that the most popular sentencing goal in the United States in the 2000s is incapacitation.

Comparative Violence

In April 2007, a student at the Virginia Institute of Technology gunned down 32 people and then killed himself. Within 24 hours of the murders, Australian Prime Minister John Howell criticized the gun control laws in the United States and stated that the "gun culture is such a negative in the United States" (Begley, 2007, p. 43). While other nations have experienced mass murders, it appears that the United States has had more than its proportionate share. A popular theory about why the United States has a high number of violent crimes blames its lack of gun control. Begley noted in her study that the percentage of individuals owning guns in the United States is the highest of any industrialized country. She stated that there are 90 firearms per 100,000 population in the United States, compared to only 32 per 100,000 in France. She also noted that there were 10.08 annual deaths by firearms in the United States per 100,000 individuals, compared to 4.93 in France. Her study indicated that the annual gun death rate per 100,000 in England, with its strict licensing requirements, is only 0.31. Begley also concluded that rates of violence are highest in mobile societies where it is hard to put down roots and form enduring connections. Table 1.2 provides an overview of selected countries' legal models.

Table 1.2   List of Selected Countries and a Brief Description of Their Legal Models as of June 2015

Country	Legal System Based on or Influenced By
Argentina	West European civil law
Australia	English common law
Belgian	French civil law
Brazil	Civil law
Bulgaria	Civil law
Canada	English common law except Quebec where law is based on French civil code
Chile	West European civil law
China	Civil law influenced by Soviet legal model
Columbia	Mix of French and Spanish legal models
Costa Rica	Spanish civil law
Cuba	Mix of Soviet and Spanish civil law
Denmark	Civil law
Dominican Republic	French civil law–criminal procedure modified in 2004 to include accusatory system.
Egypt	Islamic law
Finland	Swedish civil law
France	Civil law
Germany	Civil law
Greece	Civil law based on Roman law
Hungry	French civil law
Iceland	Danish civil law
Italy	Civil law
Japan	German civil law with Anglo-American influence
Mexico	In process of changing from Spanish civil law to common law
Netherlands	French civil law
Norway	Mixed system of civil, common, and customary law
Pakistan	Mixed system of common and Islamic law
Peru	Civil law
Portugal	Civil law
Puerto Rico	Mixed Spanish civil law and U.S. federal system
Russia	Mixed civil and Soviet law systems
South Africa	Mixed Roman, Dutch, common law, and customary law
Sweden	Roman-Germanic and customary law systems
United Kingdom	Common law
United States	Common law

Summary

- There is an increased need to study the criminal justice systems of other countries because of the increase in transnational crime.
- Ethnocentrism is a bar to learning about other countries' criminal justice systems.
- A country's criminal justice system is formed and shaped by its legal model of justice.
- The historical approach to the study of law was implicit in the development of the Western legal tradition.
- The two major legal models of the modern Western world are the civil law and the common law models.
- The Romans were the first to consider law as a science by means of which they could look at the world, with all its people and property and their intermingling relationships.
- Europe in the Middle Ages was regulated by Roman law and church canon law. During this period, commercial law developed because Roman law and canon law were not flexible enough to handle the demands of trade.
- Under civil law, judgments of courts are not binding except in the causes in which they are rendered. The civil law model is based on an inquisitorial model. While it is commonly tied to Roman law, it cannot be traced to a single source.
- The common law model developed in England and comprises the body of principles and rules of action derived from traditional usages and customs.
- The common law model is an adversarial model.
- Under the Islamic model, the sacred law of Islam is an all-embracing body of religious duties. It is the epitome of Islamic thought. The primary objective of Islamic law is to prevent evil.
- The classic socialist model has three purposes: to provide for national security, to regulate economics by socialist principles, and to educate the general population as well as lawbreakers about the law.
- Law enforcement systems tend to be either dominated by the national police or dominated by local agencies.

Questions in Review

1. Why do the authors consider that the comparative study of criminal justice is an academic study of criminal justice arrangements of various nations?
2. Explain the meaning of the word "jurisprudence."

3. Explain how the positive law approach differs from the natural law approach.
4. Why did Supreme Court Justice Oliver Wendell Holmes, Jr., state that the life of law has not been logic, but experience?
5. What is the primary function of a nation's court system?
6. What are the chief differences between the civil law and common law models?
7. How do the socialist model and the Islamic model of law differ?
8. Explain the meaning of the phrase "rule of law."

Common Law
The Courts

2

Chapter Objectives

After studying this chapter, you should understand or be able to explain the following issues and concepts:

- The basic concepts used by common law courts
- The dual systems of courts in the United States
- The role of counsel in common law courts
- The role of the trial judge in common law courts
- The codification of laws

Key Terms

Appointed counsel: Counsel appointed by the trial judge to represent an indigent defendant.

Arraignment: The initial court hearing in federal and state courts where a defendant is advised of the charges and his or her rights.

Bailiff: An officer of the court who is assigned the duty of peacekeeping, prisoner custody, and other activities by the trial judge.

Codification: The process of collecting and arranging the legislative enactments of a nation into one unified code of laws.

Court clerk: An officer of the court who is responsible for maintaining the written records of the court.

Defendant: The person against whom a criminal or civil action is brought.

Dual federalism: In reference to U.S. court systems, the institution of both state court systems and a federal court system, with each system having final authority in selected areas; also used to describe the concept of two coexisting complete court systems.

Indictment: Formal document issued by a grand jury charging a person with a crime.

Information: A legal document that constitutes a formal accusation of criminal misconduct against an individual; generally used in inferior courts instead of an indictment.

Misdemeanor: A minor crime.

Prosecuting attorney: The attorney who represents the state or federal government in a criminal trial.

Retained counsel: Private counsel who has been hired by a defendant.

Substantive criminal law: That portion of the law that creates, defines, and declares what acts constitute crimes and establishes punishments for those crimes.

Introduction

The law embodies the story of a nation's development through many centuries, and it cannot be dealt with as if it contained only the axioms and corollaries of a book of mathematics. In order to know what it is, we must alternately consult history and existing theories of legislation. But the most difficult labor will be to understand the combination of the two into new products at every stage.

**U.S. Supreme Court Justice Oliver Wendell Holmes, *The Common Law*
(1881, p. 6)**

The first legal model that we examine is the common law model. This model is not the oldest, but it is the one with which most readers of this text will be familiar. In Chapters 2 and 3, we will explore the common law model as currently existing in the United States and the United Kingdom. As noted in Chapter 1, the phrase "legal model" has a broader meaning than "legal system." For example, both the United States and Great Britain use the common law model, but their legal systems are vastly different. In Chapter 2, we will examine the legal model in general and then discuss the differences between the U.S. and British court systems. In Chapter 3, we will explore the differences between police systems and corrections in the two countries and conclude with a discussion of other common law countries. In later chapters, the common law model will be compared with the other four legal models.

For centuries, the common law of England consisted of a system of legal remedies. Each remedy had its own procedure. Common law prefers precedent as the basis for judgments. Thus, it is built empirically, or established from a case-to-case approach. The modernization of common law came relatively early in England when compared with the modernization of civil law on the Continent. As R. C. Van Caenegem (1988, pp. 36–37) noted, the activity of the justices and the various actions with which they dealt formed a coherent whole and were grasped and described as such. Van Caenegem describes the new law (in the eleventh century) as national and loyal to the king. The king and his central justices were considered to be the bearers of the whole system, and its application was nationwide.

Following the Norman Conquest of 1066, England was essentially two "nations" within one. And the two nations were separated by a wide gulf. The two nations were the Franci (French) and the Anglici (native English persons). The French were individuals of Continental origin, spoke French, and ruled the country and largely controlled the church. They also controlled the wealth and held land in both their native Normandy and England. The Franci had little respect for the traditional values of the English people. English individuals were mainly peasants who were barred from high office and generally relegated to a humble life of farming.

The common law developed as essentially feudal land law. In its formative years, common law was shaped and defined by the French invaders. The formal language of common law was French until the seventeenth century. Common law had little concern for the peasants until the thirteenth century. During that century, the two nations fused into one nation. Van Caenegem (1988) states that it was during the thirteenth century that the common law that bound together freemen of any descent became truly English and distinct from Continental law. He contends that common law helped to create a sense of nationhood and greatness in late medieval England and made people aware of their distinctness, as compared with the nations on the Continent.

Selected court decisions were published in Year Books, and those decisions were considered to be directives for judges in future cases. Individuals training to be lawyers received their training in the Inns of Court. At the Inns, they learned their craft as other medieval craftsmen did, in contact with senior lawyers and judges. English law during that era worked within the framework of feudalism.

Henry II

Henry Curtmantle (1133–1189), the Duke of Normandy and later the King of England (r. 1154–1189), expanded the Anglo-French domains and strengthened the royal administration, including the courts in England. Henry developed new judicial forms and solidified common law. As noted by Van Caenegem (1988, p. 38), no essential elements of common law were developed during Henry's reign, but he decided which elements were to be included as part of the common law and how the elements were to fit together. In general, he made the system work.

During Henry's reign, the people of England and Normandy were intel-
lectually alive and enterprising. Although few had formal legal education,
probably many had a passing acquaintance with the common law. The justices,
clerics, and laymen attained a high degree of professionalism in the law.
Henry was probably the wealthiest ruler of that time, and his administration was the most efficient. According to Van Caenegem (p. 39), the judicial
machinery he set up was on a scale never seen before. Henry's system of
justice yielded profits for the king. It was during this period that England
became an island in a sea of Roman law. England's semi-feudal, semi-modern
common law is considered an anomaly in the history of Western civilization
(Van Caenegem, 1988, pp. 40–41). Photos 2.1 and 2.2 indicate the popularity
of the Magna Carta.

Photo 2.1 The most cherished existing copy of the Magna Carta was deposited
in the U.S. Congressional Library in Washington, D.C. on November 28, 1939,
for the duration of World War II by British Ambassador Lord Lothian. Librarian
Archibald MacLeish (left) is shown thanking Lord Lothian after accepting the
document which can be seen in the background. The Magna Carta was on
display for the public in a spot opposite the Declaration of Independence and the
U.S. Constitution. (Courtesy of the Library of Congress.)

Photo 2.2 Shortly after the historical Magna Carta was placed in the U.S. Congressional Library for safekeeping by British Ambassador Lord Lothian, the public was allowed to view it under the watchful eyes of library guards. (Courtesy of the Library of Congress.)

The Great Writ Is over 800 Years Old

On June 15, 2015, the Magna Carta, the forerunner of the concept of due process, celebrated its 800th anniversary. The Carta is one of the world's most recognized symbols of liberty under law. The overriding principle of the document is that no person is above the law.

In his inaugural address in 1941, President Franklin Delano Roosevelt stated: "The democratic aspiration is no mere recent phase in human history...it was written in the Magna Carta."

Two important principles of Liberty noted in the Magna Carta:

- No freeman shall be taken, imprisoned, disseized, outlawed, banished, or in any way destroyed, nor will
- We proceed against or prosecute him, except by the lawful judgment of his peers or by the law of the land.

"To no one will We sell, to no one will We deny or delay a right to justice."

The Magna Carta

King John of England (r. 1199–1215) quarreled with the Roman Catholic Church, and the barons united against him and forced him to sign the Magna Carta in 1215. John's problems had started with the loss of Normandy. He then formed a coalition of rulers in Germany and the Low Countries to assist him against the French king. John's efforts to defeat the French king were very costly, and the taxes he raised to pay for the campaign were very unpopular. John also levied inheritance duties on some barons, adding to his troubles. By the spring of 1215, the barons joined in protest against John's abuse and disregard of law and custom.

On June 15, 1215, the rebellious barons met John at Runnymede on the Thames. The king was presented with a document known as the Articles of the Barons, on the basis of which the Magna Carta was drawn up. The Magna Carta is an undramatic document. It is filled with problems of feudal law and custom that are largely alien to modern English people. However, it is remarkable in many ways. For instance, it was not written purely in the baronial interest but aimed to provide protection for all freemen. It was an attempt to provide guarantees against the sort of arbitrary disregard of feudal rights that three previous kings had made familiar.

Some clauses derived from concessions already offered by the king in efforts to divide the opposition. For example, Clause 39, which promises judgment by peers or by the law of the land to all freemen, had its origin in a letter sent by Pope Innocent III to the king. The barons, however, were not attempting to dismantle royal government; in fact, many of the legal reforms of Henry II's day were reinforced. Nor did they seek to legitimate rebellion; rather, they tried to ensure that the king was beneath rather than above the law. In immediate terms, the Magna Carta was a failure, for it was no more than a stage in ineffective negotiations to prevent civil war. John was released by the pope from his obligations under it. The document was, however, reissued with some changes under John's son, with papal approval, and so it became, in its 1225 version, a part of the permanent law. For the next five centuries, England developed its system of limited monarchy, with government power shifting from the crown to Parliament.

Sir Edward Coke

Sir Edward Coke (1552–1634) was one of the most eminent jurists in the history of common law (his name is pronounced like "cook"). Coke was elected to Parliament in 1589 and rose to become first solicitor general and then speaker of the House of Commons. In 1606, he became the chief justice of the King's Bench. He was dismissed as chief justice in 1616 (Bowen, 1956).

Coke was inclined to be overbearing and impatient both at the bar and on the bench, and he was not always logical. His knowledge of law, however, was unequaled. He was an expert on the Year Books. Coke has been accused of manipulating precedents and using them to support his view of the common law. Between 1600 and 1615, Coke issued 11 volumes of his Reports, a series of detailed commentaries on common law, in which he systematized the principles of English law by relating and commenting on decisions. Two additional volumes of the Reports were published posthumously.

In 1626, Charles I called on Parliament to levy taxes. He was involved in a war and was desperate for money, and by that time, parliamentary action was required to levy taxes. Parliament refused to do so, and Charles imposed a forced loan on certain knights. Those who refused to pay the loan were imprisoned. Several of the knights were tried in 1627 in a famous case known as "Case of the Five Knights." The knights lost their case and remained in jail. In 1628, Charles released them and called for Parliament to convene. When Parliament met, feelings were strong against Charles. Coke, then aged 76 years old, had been reelected to Parliament. He made an impassioned plea, saying that the rights of Englishmen had suffered numerous attacks in the past few years. The Parliament drafted the Petition of Right, which sought recognition of four principles: no taxes without consent of Parliament, no imprisonment without cause, no quartering of soldiers on subjects, and no martial law in peacetime. Charles reluctantly accepted the petition.

Sir William Blackstone

In the seventeenth century, a frequent grievance against the common law was its uncertainty. The common law, having grown by the accumulation of cases, was buried in hundreds of volumes of court reports. Abridgments or summaries of the law were unofficial and often unreliable. No official organization had the responsibility to compile abridgments or summaries. In addition, the acts of Parliament were disorganized and not codified. Between 1765 and 1769, Sir William Blackstone (1723–1780) published his *Commentaries on the Laws of England*. They were accepted as correct statements on the status of common law at that time.

William Blackstone was the fourth and posthumous son of Charles Blackstone, a silk merchant of moderate means. His mother died when William was only 12 years old, and he was educated by his uncle Thomas Biggs, a London surgeon. He was only 18 when he graduated from Oxford University and entered the Middle Temple, one of the Inns of Court, to study law. In 1746, he had become a barrister. In 1770, Blackstone refused the office of solicitor general but accepted that of judge of the Court of Common Pleas. In the 10 years of his judgeship, he administered the law satisfactorily but attained no special distinction. Toward the end of the 1770s his health failed; he died in February 1780.

To assess the impact that Blackstone has had on today's common law, the authors conducted a computerized search of court decisions of federal and state appellate courts in the United States over 5 years (2003–2007). In almost 600 cases in U.S. and state courts, Blackstone's commentaries were cited in court decisions. For example, the U.S. Supreme Court in 2006, in the case of *Dixon v. United States*, 126 S. Ct. 2437, stated:

> Duress was an established defense at common law. See 4 W. Blackstone, Commentaries on the Laws of England 30 (1769). When Congress began to enact federal criminal statutes, it presumptively intended for those offenses to be subject to this defense. Moreover, Congress presumptively intended for the burdens of production and persuasion to be placed, as they were at common law, on the defendant. Although Congress is certainly free to alter this pattern and place one or both burdens on the prosecution, either for all or selected federal crimes, Congress has not done so but instead has continued to revise the federal criminal laws and to create new federal crimes without addressing the issue of duress. Under these circumstances, I believe that the burdens remain where they were when Congress began enacting federal criminal statutes.

The Maryland State Supreme Court in 2007, in *Wisneski v. State*, 2007 Md. LEXIS 188 (Md. 2007), stated:

> In order to examine properly the public element of common law indecent exposure, therefore, we then must explore English common law extant in 1776 in which the offense of indecent exposure constituted a misdemeanor. Sir William Blackstone commented generally: [M]isdemeanors are a breach and violation of the public rights and duties, owing to the whole community, considered as a community, in its social aggregate capacity... All crimes ought therefore to be estimated merely according to the mischiefs which they produce in civil society: and, of consequence, private vices, or the breach of mere absolute duties, which man is bound to perform considered only as an individual, are not, cannot be, the object of any municipal law; any farther than as by their evil example, or other pernicious effects, they may prejudice the community, and thereby become a species of public crimes. Thus the vice of drunkenness, if committed privately and alone, is beyond the knowledge and of course beyond the reach of human tribunals: but if committed publicly, in the face of the world, its evil example makes it liable to temporal censures... The only difference is, that both public and private vices are subject to the vengeance of eternal justice; and public vices are liable to the temporal punishments of human tribunals.

A U.S. District Court in the Western District of Texas, in *Martinez Aguero v. Gonzalez*, 2005 U.S. Dist. LEXIS 2412 (W.D. Tex. 2005), stated:

> In his Commentaries, Blackstone describes the concepts of allegiance expected from and governmental protections due citizens and aliens.
>
> Allegiance, both express and implied, is however distinguished by the law into two sorts or species, the one natural, the other local; the former being

also perpetual, the latter temporary. Natural allegiance is such as is due from all men born within the king's dominions immediately upon their birth... Natural allegiance is therefore a debt of gratitude; which cannot be forfeited, cancelled, or altered, by any change of time, place, or circumstance, nor by anything but the united concurrence of the legislature.

Local allegiance is such as is due from an alien, or stranger born, for so long time as he continues within the King's dominion and protection: and it ceases the instant such stranger transfers himself from this Kingdom to another. Natural allegiance is therefore perpetual, and local temporary only: and that for this reason, evidently founded upon the nature of government; that allegiance is a debt due from the subject, upon an implied contract with the prince, that so long as the one affords protection, so long the other will demean himself faithfully.... As therefore the prince is always under a constant tie to protect his natural-born subjects, at all times and in all countries, for this reason their allegiance due to him is equally universal and permanent. But, on the other hand, as the prince affords his protection to an alien, only during his residence in this realm, the allegiance of an alien is confined (in point of time) to the duration of such his residence, and (in point of locality) to the dominions of the British empire.

William Blackstone, Commentaries on the Laws of England (1769, pp. 357–359, available at http: //www.yale.edu/lawweb/avalon/ blackstone/bk1ch10.htm, accessed May 21, 2015)

Thus, the influence of Blackstone still exists in common law courts, more than 300 years after his death. He was probably the most influential jurist in the history of common law.

Common Law in the United States

When English settlers came to America in the seventeenth century, they brought the English common law with them. Except for few modifications, English common law became the common law of the colonies. During the American Revolution, there was a great deal of hostility toward the English in America. This hostility extended to the common law system. Accordingly, most of the new states enacted new statutes defining criminal acts and establishing criminal procedures. The statutes, however, basically enacted into statutory law what was formerly English common law.

Today, the criminal law of the individual states is a written set of regulations that is largely the result of legislative action. These regulations are recorded in some official record within the states and are often referred to as the "penal code." Criminal laws vary somewhat among the states. In some states, there is no reliance upon the common law to determine what is right and wrong. The statutes spell out specifically each act that is made a crime and the punishment that may be inflicted for the commission of such an act. For example, the code may state that manslaughter is the unlawful killing of a human being without malice. This definition will be followed by a statement that one convicted of manslaughter may be imprisoned for a period not to exceed 4 years. The statutes of other states may provide that "manslaughter" is punishable by imprisonment not to exceed some other prescribed number of years, but may not define what acts constitute manslaughter. The courts must then look to the common law to determine the interpretation of manslaughter.

U.S. Court Systems Today

There are two court systems in the United States—federal and state. The term "dual federalism" is used to describe the concept of two complete court systems. The majority of criminal cases are tried in state courts. There are some counties whose state courts prosecute more criminal cases each year than are prosecuted annually in the entire federal system, including Los Angeles County, California; Harris County, Texas; and Cook County, Illinois.

Federal System

> The judicial power of the United States shall be invested in one Supreme Court....
>
> **U.S. Constitution (Art. III, Sec. 1)**

The U.S. Supreme Court is the highest court in the federal system. The court is composed of one chief justice and eight associate justices. Justices are appointed by the president with the "advice and consent" of the U.S. Senate and may be removed only by impeachment. The court always decides cases as one body. Except in unusual situations, the court acts as an appellate court and decides cases based on trial briefs, records of trial from the trial courts, and arguments of counsel. The Supreme Court also acts as a supervising authority over other federal courts.

U.S. Court of Appeals

The federal court system is divided geographically into 12 judicial circuits (including the District of Columbia, which has its own circuit and is the only one not numerically designated). A U.S. Court of Appeals is located in each judicial circuit. Like Supreme Court justices, Court of Appeals justices

Photo 2.3 The Byron White Federal Courthouse in Denver, Colorado. The courthouse was named after Justice Byron White, the only U.S. Supreme Court Justice to have played football in the National Football League. In the United States, the pace of trials in federal courts is more relaxed than in the very busy state courts. (Photo by Cliff Roberson.)

are appointed by the president with the "advice and consent" of the Senate. The Courts of Appeals differ in the number of justices appointed to each. A Court of Appeals normally hears cases in a panel of three or five judges. In rare cases, a Court of Appeals will decide a case en banc, that is, as a whole court with all justices present. Photo 2.3 is of one of the U.S. Federal Courthouses.

U.S. District Courts

The basic trial court in the federal system is the U.S. District Court (USDC). There is at least one district court in each state, and most states have more than one. In those cases, the state is divided geographically into federal judicial districts. For example, Iowa is divided into two federal districts, northern and southern. In Texas, there are four federal judicial districts: U.S. District Court for the Southern District of Texas, U.S. District Court for the Eastern District of Texas, U.S. District Court for the Western District of Texas, and U.S. District Court for the Northern District of Texas.

Federal district court judges are appointed by the president with "advice and consent" of the Senate. District judges are appointed for life. In most judicial districts, more than one judge sits as the district court. For example, the U.S. District Court for the Southern District of New York (New York City) has more than 100 judges, each sitting as the U.S. District Court for the Southern District of New York.

In special cases (and rarely), the USDC can sit and decide a case as a "three-judge" district court. The vast majority of cases are, however, presided over by a single judge. In all criminal cases heard in the USDC, the accused has a right to a jury trial.

U.S. Magistrates

U.S. magistrates are part of the federal judicial system but are not considered as separate courts. The federal magistrates are required to be attorneys and are appointed by the presiding judge of the judicial district for a specific term. Magistrates try minor offenses and perform pretrial matters and similar duties. They are considered to be judicial officers and therefore can issue search and arrest warrants.

Participants in a Criminal Case

The major participants in a U.S. criminal case are the judge, prosecuting attorney, defense counsel, clerk of the court, bailiff, and court reporter. All are considered officers of the court. The criminal trial procedure varies little, whether the charge is a felony or misdemeanor, or whether the trial is a court trial or jury trial. The defendant is entitled to a fair trial before an impartial judge and an honest jury, in an atmosphere of judicial calm.

The justice system is an adversary system, meaning that it has two sides. In a criminal trial, these are the prosecution and the defense. Each is permitted to present evidence on its own behalf. Theoretically, both sides come into the trial on an equal basis. But as Justice Byron White of the U.S. Supreme Court, in *United States v. Wade*, 388 U.S. 218 (1957), pointed out, this system is not a true adversary system with both sides entering the trial on an equal footing. He stated:

> Law enforcement officers (and prosecuting attorneys) have the obligation to convict the guilty and to make sure they do not convict the innocent. They must be dedicated to making the criminal trial a procedure for the ascertainment of the true facts surrounding the commission of the crime. To this extent, our so-called adversary system is not adversary at all: nor should it be. But defense counsel has no comparable obligation to ascertain or present the truth. Our system assigns him a different mission. He must be and is interested in not convicting the innocent, but absent a voluntary plea of guilty, we also insist that he defend his client whether he is innocent or guilty. The State has the obligation to present the evidence. Defense counsel need present nothing, even if he knows what the truth is. He need furnish no witnesses to

the police, reveal any confidences of his client, nor furnish any other information to help the prosecution's case. If he can confuse a witness, even a truthful one, or make him appear at a disadvantage, unsure or indecisive, that will be his normal course. Our interest in not convicting the innocent permits counsel to put the State to its proof, to put the State's case in the worst possible light, regardless of what he thinks or knows to be the truth. Undoubtedly there are some limits which defense counsel must observe but more often than not, defense counsel will cross-examine a prosecution witness, and impeach him if he can, even if he thinks the witness is telling the truth, just as he will attempt to destroy a witness who he thinks is lying. In this respect, as part of our modified adversary system and as part of the duty imposed on the most honorable defense counsel, we countenance or require conduct which in many instances has little, if any, relation to the search for truth.

Trial Judge

Although the terms "judge" and "the court" are used interchangeably, they should be distinguished. The judge presides over the trial proceedings and exercises those duties and power imposed by law. The court is a judicial proceeding presided over by a judge. The judge plays a very important role both before and during the trial. There is a great deal of power and authority, and many decisions are solely at the judge's discretion. Since unscrupulous acts could seriously affect the administration of justice, the judge's actions are subject to review by appellate courts. This avoids any abuse of power or authority by the judge. Fortunately, most are honest individuals who endeavor to do a conscientious job.

In most states, the judges of the superior or district court, or its equivalent, are elected by the people of the judicial district where they serve. The superior or district courts are the major trial courts in the various states. As in the case of state superior or district court judges, lower court judges are elected in most states. They are elected by the people of the judicial district where they serve, but this district may be only a portion of a county. The qualifications for this position vary greatly among states. In many outlying rural areas there is not enough court business to justify a full-time judge, so the judge may be a local practicing attorney elected to act as the judge when court business is required.

The trial judge has many duties prior to the trial. For example, the judge is required to hold arraignments and preliminary hearings. At these hearings, the defendant will be advised of the charges, his or her plea will be entered, and motions may be presented. In felony cases or cases in which the defendant could be confined, an indigent defendant will have counsel appointed. In addition, the judge must make rulings (decisions) on motions presented by either the prosecution or defense. Typical motions include motions to suppress evidence, for continuances, and to dismiss for failure to receive a speedy trial.

During the trial, the judge has the primary responsibility for seeing that justice is carried out. The judge has a duty not only to protect the interests of the defendant but also to protect the interests of the public, ensuring that the guilty are convicted. The judge controls all proceedings during the trial and limits the introduction of evidence and arguments of counsel to relevant and material matters with a view to the expeditious and effective ascertainment of the truth. The judge must control the conduct of the defendant and the spectators; determine the competency of witnesses and the admissibility of evidence; rule on objections made to questions asked by the attorneys; protect witnesses from harassment during cross-examination; interpret for the jury the laws involved in the particular case; and in some jurisdictions, comment on the weight of the evidence presented and the credibility of witnesses. In many jurisdictions, the judge sentences the defendant after conviction. If the trial is a court trial, the judge renders a verdict of guilt or innocence. Additional duties during the trial will be enumerated as the discussion of the trial progresses (Roberson et al., 2015).

Defendant

The perpetrator of a crime is guaranteed certain rights. Many aspects of criminal procedure are controlled by the U.S. Constitution, specifically in the Bill of Rights (the original 10 Amendments to the Constitution). These federal constitutional protections concerning individual rights are, for the most part, binding on state courts.

These rights attach to the perpetrator early in the criminal procedure process, and violation of them may result in the case being dismissed. For example, if the perpetrator confesses to the crime of murder, and that confession is obtained in violation of his or her constitutional rights, it may be suppressed. If the confession is the only link connecting the defendant to the crime, the case may have to be dismissed. When these types of incidents occur, it is very difficult for the victim to understand why the defendant goes free when there has been a confession.

Prosecuting Attorney

The primary duty of a prosecutor in the U.S. system is not to convict, but to promote justice. (Roberson, 2003)

The prosecuting attorney is known by a variety of names. In some places he or she is known as the district attorney, abbreviated "D.A." and in other areas as the county attorney. In the federal system, the title is U.S. Attorney. The "public official" role of the prosecuting attorney is comparatively recent. For many years, it was the responsibility of victims or their relatives to prosecute when a crime was committed. Attorneys were employed by these persons to assist in the prosecution. As time passed, it was deemed advisable to have a full-time public prosecutor because the offense was actually committed against society, and the office of the prosecuting attorney was established.

In most states, the prosecuting attorney is an elected official of the county. In large urban areas it is a sought-after position, as it holds prestige and pays well, and the prosecuting attorney has a number of deputies for assistance. In many places, there may be no staff, and in sparsely settled counties, the position may be only a part-time job. When not engaged in handling official duties, the prosecuting attorney in such counties may have a private law practice. A few states have permitted several counties to form a "judicial district" and employ a single prosecuting attorney to handle the duties.

Prosecuting attorneys have a great deal of power, irrespective of personal capabilities or jurisdiction of service. They are charged with grave responsibilities to the public, demanding integrity, zeal, and conscientious effort in the administration of justice. As stated by the U.S. Supreme Court in the *Gideon* decision, prosecuting attorneys "are everywhere deemed essential to protect the public's interest in an orderly society." The public prosecutor institutes proceedings before magistrates for the arrest of persons charged with or reasonably suspected of committing a public offense. In addition to acting as prosecutor, in most instances he represents the county on all civil matters.

The prosecuting attorney enters the justice procedural picture early in the prosecutive process. A great number of arrests are made by law enforcement officers on their own determination that there is reasonable cause to believe a crime has been committed. Unless the alleged offender is released by the arresting agency without further action being taken, the prosecuting attorney must be consulted to determine whether prosecutive action will be taken against the arrested person.

The prosecuting attorney evaluates the weight of evidence against the accused and the nature of the charge in making the decision whether to prosecute. If the prosecuting attorney decides against prosecution, the accused will be released. If it is decided that prosecutive action should be taken, a complaint will be prepared by the prosecuting attorney and filed with the appropriate court. The accused is then taken before a committing magistrate for the initial appearance, or arraignment, as it is referred to in some jurisdictions. Often law enforcement agencies conduct an investigation of alleged violations before making an arrest. In these instances, the prosecuting attorney is usually consulted to determine whether there is sufficient evidence against the accused to justify prosecutive action, if a complaint should be filed, and a warrant of arrest obtained. The prosecuting attorney may prefer to present the charge to the grand jury to determine whether prosecutive action should be taken, or whether a secret indictment should be sought. This procedure is followed in felony charges in most states. If the crime for which the arrest was made is a less serious misdemeanor, the prosecutive decision may be left to the discretion of the law enforcement agency involved. Even the preparation of the complaint and the prosecution during the trial may be handled by the officer, and the prosecuting attorney may not even appear on the scene unless some special problem arises. In the more serious misdemeanor cases and on felony charges, the prosecuting attorney will be involved from the time of arrest through the appeal.

If the charge is a serious one and the prosecuting attorney decides to prosecute, there are many decisions and duties to perform. The first decision is to determine what charge, or charges, the evidence will support so that the appropriate accusatory pleading may be filed. The prosecuting attorney must decide whether the charges, when more than one, are to be separated into different trials or consolidated into one. In some jurisdictions, if the charge is a felony, it must be decided whether the facts are to be presented in a preliminary hearing or to a grand jury. The information or the indictment must be prepared depending on the type of hearing conducted. Where appropriate, the granting of motions requested by the defense must be disputed. At the time of the trial, another responsibility is to present enough evidence to prove the defendant guilty beyond a reasonable doubt. The prosecuting attorney must also assist in the selection of the jury, decide what witnesses to call, and determine what physical evidence should be introduced. It is not necessary that every person who has some knowledge of the facts in the case be called, nor is it necessary that all physical evidence collected by the law enforcement officers during an investigation be presented during a trial. The prosecuting attorney must present enough witnesses and physical evidence to ensure the defendant a fair trial, and may not withhold any evidence that would be advantageous to the defendant. If the defense presents witnesses in its behalf, the prosecuting attorney must cross-examine them. The responsibilities of making recommendations to the judge on the severity of the sentence and assisting the state attorney general with appeals also fall to the prosecuting attorney.

State Attorney General

In most states, the attorney general has broad authority to coordinate local prosecutions. This authority includes the right to prosecute on his own and to supervise, assist, and consult local prosecuting attorneys. If a local prosecuting attorney needs assistance or fails to perform his or her duties, the attorney general is free to act. Unless called on by the local prosecutor, or unless the local prosecutor fails to prosecute when the facts warrant it, the state attorney general does not ordinarily intervene. There are a few states where the attorney general has no authority over local prosecutions. If there should be malfeasance in office by a local prosecuting attorney in those states, the governor could be called to appoint a special prosecutor to perform the duties of the local prosecutor. When a case is appealed, in most jurisdictions it is the responsibility of the state attorney general to present the case to the appellate court. The attorney general will be assisted by the prosecuting attorney of the county in which the trial took place.

Defense Counsel

The defense attorney represents the rights and interests of the defendant. Unlike the prosecutor, who is concerned with justice and fairness, the defense attorney's obligation as established by the American Bar Association's General Standards of Conduct is to use all of his or her courage, devotion, and skills to protect the rights of the accused. Many defense attorneys interpret this obligation as requiring that they do everything possible to obtain an acquittal even if they know that the defendant in fact committed the offense.

The Sixth Amendment to the U.S. Constitution states that those who are accused of crimes have a right to be represented by an attorney. The Supreme Court in the landmark case of *Gideon v. Wainwright* established the principle that all defendants have a right to counsel in all felony cases, even if they cannot afford to hire their own attorneys. The court extended this concept to misdemeanor cases in *Argersinger v. Hamilin,* holding that, absent a waiver, no person may be imprisoned for any offense, either misdemeanor or felony, unless he or she has been represented by an attorney.

There are basically four types of defense attorneys: public defenders, contract defense services, assigned defense counsel, and private defense counsel. Public defenders are hired and paid by the government and are appointed to represent those persons charged with crimes who cannot afford to hire attorneys to represent them. Many counties have public defender's offices that are staffed by very able, aggressive attorneys.

However, there are instances where, for a variety of reasons, the public defender's office has a conflict of interest in a case. For example, this might occur if there were two defendants in one case. In this situation, the court might appoint an attorney from the contract defense services to represent one of the two defendants. Contract defense services are normally comprised of a group of attorneys who have entered into an agreement with the county to represent indigent defendants for a specified fee.

Assigned defense counsel exists in the majority of counties in the United States. Many of these counties are small and cannot afford the cost of maintaining a public defender's office. Under the assigned defense counsel format, the court maintains a list of attorneys who are willing to be appointed to represent indigent criminal defendants. When a defendant appears in court, the judge appoints the next attorney on the list to represent the accused.

The last form of defense attorney is the private defense counsel. These attorneys usually represent defendants who are capable of paying for their services (Roberson et al., 2015).

The Right to Represent Oneself

The U.S. Supreme Court has held that the Sixth Amendment right to counsel allows a defendant to proceed *pro se*, or to represent himself or herself without counsel. The rationale is that the right to counsel guaranteed by the Sixth Amendment is a personal right of the accused, not a right bestowed upon an attorney representing the accused. The defendant who desires to proceed *pro se* must make a knowing and intelligent waiver of his right to an appointed counsel. The right to represent oneself does not mean that the defendant can engage in disrespectful or disruptive conduct in court. Additionally, the courts have stated that when a defendant knowingly waives the right to counsel, he or she cannot later raise the issue of ineffective representation, because in essence the accused has waived any appeal on this issue (Roberson et al., 2015).

Privileged Communication

Defense counsel are often placed in a most awkward position because of the age-old relationship of "privileged communication" between attorney and client. This relationship provides that information furnished to an attorney in confidence by a client may not be revealed without the permission of the client. Law enforcement agencies may be unaware of crimes discussed by a client. In one instance, a client told his attorney about two murders he had committed and where the bodies were buried. The problem created by receiving this information is whether the attorney should furnish it to the appropriate law enforcement agency or keep it in strictest confidence. The answer to this question has been debated by many legal scholars with no concrete answer forthcoming. It would appear that the better view would be to furnish the information to the appropriate law enforcement agency in order that the bodies be recovered and relatives notified. Society, as well as the criminal, is entitled to some consideration and justice. In most instances, prosecutive action could not be taken because the exclusionary rule would prohibit the use of the information as evidence.

If the facts of a case are such that an attorney absolutely cannot accept the responsibility of effectively defending a client, the case should be refused. Once the case is accepted, it is the attorney's duty to remain until it has been brought to a logical conclusion. The defense attorney has many functions to perform, both before and during the trial. A conference with the accused should be held as soon as practically possible. This conference should be private and unobserved, even if the accused is in jail at the time. If there are codefendants, the defense counsel must decide whether all can be effectively represented without a conflict of interest. If either counsel or one of the defendants feels that being represented by just one counsel would result in prejudice, each defendant is entitled to and must be provided with individual counsel.

The defense counsel will advise the defendant on the plea that should be entered at the arraignment, and counsel will be present for the purpose of cross-examining witnesses at the preliminary hearing. Counsel also has a right to be present during an identification of "lineup" procedure if the defendant has been formally charged; however, the attorney has no right to interfere with the lineup or to prohibit the defendant from participating. The counsel will file those motions that are in the best interest of the defendant. The defendant is entitled to sit with counsel at the counsel table during the trial so that they may confer on the defense. This assistance is another reason why a defendant is entitled to be present during a trial. Defense counsel will cross-examine prosecution witnesses when appropriate and will present such evidence on behalf of the defendant deemed necessary under the circumstances. Further duties of the defense counsel will be pointed out in the discussion of trial procedures (Roberson et al., 2015).

Clerk of the Court

With the judge, the prosecuting attorney, and the defense counsel all playing dramatic roles during a criminal trial, one could easily overlook the clerk of the court, or county clerk, as the position is also known. This official also has an important function in the justice system, not only during the trial but before and after as well. The main function of the court clerk is to maintain all records of a particular case. These records include items such as copies of all the accusatory pleadings and motions that have been filed. The clerk also issues subpoenas, and, in many jurisdictions, prepares the jury panel. He or she attends trials to swear in witnesses, mark exhibits, and maintain the evidence that is introduced. The clerk also keeps copies of the court transcripts, judgments rendered, and motions for appeals.

Bailiff

The court bailiff may be a permanent member of the justice system or an individual appointed to assist in a particular trial. In some jurisdictions, the bailiff is a member of the county government and carries the title of marshal. The bailiff assists the judge in maintaining order in the court and calls the witnesses to testify. If the defendant has not been released from custody, it is the duty of the bailiff to guard the defendant in the courtroom. When the jury is sequestered, it is the responsibility of the bailiff to make certain that the jurors are free from all contact with the public; the bailiff will return the jury to the courtroom after they have reached a verdict. In many jurisdictions, the bailiff serves court orders and other court papers.

Court Reporter

The responsibility of recording everything said during the trial proceeding belongs to the court reporter. This includes the testimony of all the witnesses, objections made to the attorney's questions, rulings made by the judge, and conferences between the attorneys and the judge. If the case is taken up on appeal, the recorded notes must be transcribed. The court reporter must be highly skilled to record transactions as they take place, often at a rapid pace. The court reporter may record the proceedings in shorthand or with a stenotype machine. When first used in the courtroom, tape recorders were not very reliable. However, today many jurisdictions are using audio tapes to record the trial proceedings. These tape recorders have improved in both their reliability and the quality of recording.

Court Commissioners

In many judicial districts, court commissioners are appointed to assist trial judges. In most instances, they must possess the same qualifications as a judge, and a commissioner may substitute for a judge in an emergency situation. Otherwise, the commissioners hold hearings on motions filed, set and accept bail, and perform other duties as may be imposed on them by law.

English Court System Today

A significant difference between the U.S. system and the English court system is that the United Kingdom has a unitary judicial system in which all courts fit into a single national hierarchy. As noted earlier, each U.S. state has its own court system, and there is a federal system as well, so that there are numerous court systems in the United States.

The highest court in the English system is the House of Lords, which hears some of the most important cases on appeal and a few special classes of cases as a court of original jurisdiction. The judicial functions of the House of Lords are conducted by a small, select group of judges who are appointed to the House to act in this capacity.

England, Wales, and Scotland

The legal model of England and Wales is identical. Scotland, on the other hand, has a completely different system. The Scottish criminal justice system is considered by many to be more welfare-oriented and less adversarial and punitive. A curious issue is that in Scotland's criminal courts, the defendant may be found guilty, not guilty, or not proven. When a verdict of not proven is returned it generally means that the jury probably thinks that the defendant is guilty but that the prosecutor has failed to establish his or her guilt beyond a reasonable doubt. It appears that the not proven verdict is returned more frequently than a not guilty verdict. A not guilty verdict is considered generally as a statement by the jury that they do not believe that the defendant committed the crime charged.

In England and Wales the jury size is 12. In Scotland it is 15. Scotland also limits the challenging of jurors without cause. Generally to remove a prospective juror without cause both parties must agree. A jury's guilty verdict in Scotland is reached when a bare majority of jurors, 8, agree on a guilty verdict. For example, if 8 jurors vote guilty, 4 vote not guilty, and 3 vote not proven; the defendant is found guilty. If on the other hand, 7 jurors vote guilty, 3 vote not guilty, and 5 vote not proven; the defendant is acquitted. In England and Wales, a unanimous verdict is preferred, but in most cases a verdict agreed to by 10 of the 12 jurors will be accepted.

In Scotland, most criminal trials take place in sheriff's courts or district courts. Most cases are prosecuted by local prosecutors generally known as "Procurators Fiscal." The label "Fiscal" is historically tied to the fact that originally the prosecutors were primarily used for the collection of tax revenue. The Procurators Fiscal are independent and are thus protected from outside influence. It is very difficult to challenge a decision made by a member of the Procurators Fiscal.

Court of Queen's or King's Bench

The Court of the Queen's or King's Bench was originally held *coram rege* ("before the monarch") and traveled wherever the king or queen went. The court heard cases that concerned the sovereign or cases affecting great persons privileged to be tried only before him. The Bench could also correct the errors and defaults of all other courts. Only gradually did it lose its close connections with the king and become a separate court of common law.

The Court of King's Bench exercised jurisdiction over criminal and civil cases and over the other superior common law courts until 1830, at which time the Court of Exchequer Chamber became the court of appeal from the three superior common law courts. King's Bench heard appeals from the Court of King's Bench in Ireland until the end of the eighteenth century and exercised important jurisdiction over officials and others by means of prerogative writs (habeas corpus, certiorari, prohibition, and mandamus). The Judicature Act of 1873 merged the court in the Queen's Bench Division of the High Court of Justice. The Queen's Bench Division now consists of a chief justice—who is the lord chief justice of England—and 24 judges assigned to the division. Appeals from inferior courts come before a divisional court, composed of two or three judges of the division.

Supreme Court of Judicature

The Judicature Act of 1873 also abolished many of the historical English courts that had overlapping judicial powers. The Act established a Supreme Court of Judicature consisting of the Court of Appeal and the High Court of Justice, the latter having five divisions: the Chancery; Queen's (or King's) Bench; Common Pleas; Exchequer; and Probate, Divorce, and Admiralty.

In 1881, the system was again modified and the Queen's Bench Division absorbed the courts of Common Pleas and Exchequer. In 1971, the court system of England and Wales was further modified by the abolishment of certain specialized courts and the replacement of those courts by the Crown Court. The Supreme Court of Judicature sits as a comprehensive body, below the House of Lords, which is the final court of appeal.

The Court of Appeal is divided into a Civil Division and a Criminal Division. The High Court of Justice is made up of three divisions, which have both original and appellate jurisdiction: the Chancery Division, presided over by the lord chancellor, or vice chancellor, and dealing with land sales, estates, and so on; the Queen's Bench Division, presided over by the lord chief justice and dealing mainly with contract and tort (the Admiralty Court and the Commercial Court being both part of the Queen's Bench Division); and the Family Division, headed by a president, which deals with adoption, matrimonial proceedings, and other familial matters.

Magistrates' Court

The magistrates' courts in England and Wales are inferior courts that are concerned primarily with criminal jurisdiction over a wide range of offenses, from minor traffic violations to more serious crimes like petty theft or assault. There are several hundred such courts in England and Wales, presided over by a bench or panel of two or more lay (not legally trained), unpaid magistrates. The magistrates study the facts of a case and are advised on points of law by the clerk. The clerk is responsible for the administrative functions of the court. Magistrates' court proceedings are held in open court, except when the magistrates sit as "examining justices." When sitting as examining justices, they carry out inquiries prior to trial in serious matters that are required before the accused is committed to a higher court for trial. All criminal charges are initially brought before magistrates' courts. More serious charges are subsequently committed for trial at the Crown Court.

The magistrates' courts have limited authority to imprison or fine a defendant. Appeals from a magistrates' court go to the High Court or the Crown Court. The magistrates' court also hears juvenile cases involving care of children under the age of 14 years and cases involving children aged 14–15 years, except for homicide cases.

Crown Court

The Crown Court is an intermediary court that is above the magistrates' courts but below the High Court of Justice and the Court of Appeal. The Crown Court is concerned mostly with criminal cases. It hears trials on indictment, as well as sentencing and appeals from the magistrates' courts. There are six court circuits: Southeastern (with London as the administrative center); Wales and Chester (with Cardiff as the center); Western (Bristol); Midland and Oxford (Birmingham); Northeastern (Leeds); and Northern (Manchester). The Crown Court is governed under the directives of the lord chief justice, with the agreement of the Lord Chancellor.

Royal Courts of Justice

The Royal Courts of Justice, also called the Law Courts, is housed in a Victorian Gothic structure designed by George Edmund Street, who died during its construction. Located in London, it includes several towers, more than a thousand rooms, and ornate decorations and furnishings. The building is a complex of courtrooms, halls, and offices concerned primarily with civil (noncriminal) litigation. Statues of Christ, King Solomon, King Alfred, and Moses are placed above its main doors. Its main hall is about 240 feet long and 80 feet wide. Extensions were added to the building in 1911 and 1968. It lies in the Greater London borough of Westminster on the boundary with the City of London. Within the complex are held sessions of the Court of Appeal, the High Court of Justice, and the Crown Court.

Comparisons between the United States and the United Kingdom

The United Kingdom and the United States have been described as "two countries separated by a common law" because there are so many differences between them in terms of the legal framework. One of the major differences is that the United Kingdom has no written constitution and no judicial review, whereas every court in the United States possesses the power to pass judgment on the constitutionality of legislation and on other official actions. Another major difference is that the United States has a very complex federal court system and its relationship to state court systems is difficult to understand, whereas the United Kingdom has one unitary system.

Both nations appear to placing an increasing reliance on statute law and codification as instruments of legal development. When the United Kingdom entered the European Economic Community, it was thought that there might be pressures to make English law more accessible by codifying it along the lines of the Continental model. Harmonization of the laws of the member states, however, has not thus far required this.

In the United States, the legal sovereignty of the states impedes such a radical change, but uniform state laws are becoming more common. In U.S. federal courts and in most state courts, jury verdicts must be unanimous; if the jury is unable to agree, a new trial before another jury can be held. In England, verdicts by margins of 10 to 2 or 9 to one are acceptable after the jury has deliberated for at least 2 hours.

McKenzie (1994) contends that the U.S. system relies on a due process model that emphasizes the rights of the defendant, while the United Kingdom's crime control stresses the role of the criminal justice system to punish the guilty (Deflem and Swygart, 2001, p. 58).

In the area of substantive criminal law on the issue of what conduct is a crime, the two nations are very similar. There are, however, important differences in the rules of criminal procedure. Criminal procedure in the United States has become a constitutional matter, with a kind of federal common law of criminal procedure overriding state law in many instances. The "due process of law" under the Fourteenth Amendment has been used by the U.S. Supreme Court to require state criminal courts to provide state criminal defendants most of those due process rights listed in the federal Constitution.

A major difference between English and U.S. safeguards is that English protections rest on statute or case law and may be changed by ordinary statute, whereas U.S. safeguards are constitutional and cannot be relaxed unless the Supreme Court later reverses its interpretation or the U.S. Constitution is amended.

If the evidence was obtained in violation of a defendant's federal constitutional rights, the exclusionary rule does not allow that evidence to be admitted to establish the defendant's guilt. The exclusionary rule was forced upon the state criminal courts by the U.S. Supreme Court in 1961 in the case of *Mapp v. Ohio*. The rule had been used in federal courts since 1914. The English courts do not have the exclusionary rule. Even today, more than 50 years after the rule was forced upon the state courts, it remains a controversial issue.

Yale Kamisar on the Exclusionary Rule

A court which admits [evidence illegally obtained] manifests a willingness to tolerate the unconstitutional conduct which produced it.... A court which admits the evidence in a case involving a "run-of-mill" Fourth Amendment violation demonstrates an insufficient commitment of the guarantee against unreasonable search and seizure. (62 Judicature, pp. 66–84, August 1978.)

Justice Benjamin Cardozo

(Excerpts from *People v. Defore*, 242 N.Y. 13 [1926])

The criminal is to go free because the constable has blundered...The pettiest peace officer would have it in his power, through overzeal or indiscretion, to offer immunity upon an offender for crimes most flagitious. A room is searched against the law, and a body of a murdered man is found. If the place of discovery may not be proven, the other circumstances may be insufficient to connect the defendant with the crime. The privacy of the home has been infringed, and murderer goes free...

Photo 2.4 is a photo of Justice Cardozo.

Both nations recognize the double jeopardy rule whereby a defendant cannot be tried twice for the same offense except under certain conditions. In England, unlike the United States, a retrial may be ordered if "new and compelling evidence" comes to light after an acquittal for a serious crime. In addition, in England, if it is established by reasonable doubt that an acquittal was obtained by violence or threats of violence to a witness or juror the defendant can be retried.

The U.S. Supreme Court, in *Miranda v. Arizona*, 384 U.S. 436 (1966), held that before interrogating a suspect who is in custody, law enforcement officers must inform the suspect of certain rights under the Fifth Amendment privilege against self-incrimination. Suspects must be informed in clear and unequivocal terms that they have the right to remain silent and that anything said can and will be used against them in court. If the defendants remain silent, a report of their silence is not admissible in evidence.

The Criminal Procedure and Investigations Act 1996 (CPIA) replaced the English prosecutor's common law duty to disclose information to the defense. The CPIA established a two-stage reciprocal discovery scheme. In the primary disclosure, the prosecutor must disclose any prosecution material not previously disclosed which in the prosecutor's opinion might undermine the case for the prosecution. The defendant is then required to disclose his defense to the charge. Defense disclosure is compulsory in cases tried on

Photo 2.4 Justice Benjamin N. Cardozo (1870–1938) was a noted American Jurist who served on the New York Court of Appeals and was later appointed to the U.S. Supreme Court by President Hoover to fill the seat of the legendary Oliver Wendell Holmes. Justice Cardozo wrote extensively on the exclusionary rule. (Courtesy of the Library of Congress.)

indictment, and optional in cases tried summarily; in both situations, the right to secondary disclosure is conditioned upon prior defense disclosure. After the defendant has made disclosure, the prosecutor must make secondary disclosure to the defense of material that might be reasonably expected to assist the accused's defense as disclosed by the defense statement.

The CPIA restricts defense access to the unused material possessed by the prosecution. The defendant's initial access depends entirely upon prosecutorial screening of police files under a subjective test. Secondary access depends upon prosecutorial screening, this time under an objective test that is subject, on application by the defense, to judicial review. Such secondary access, however, is conditioned upon the defendant's disclosure of his defense. The English system, with its formal mechanisms for revealing the results of police investigations, both inculpatory and exculpatory, to the prosecutor, is distinctly different from the informal disclosure practices currently used in most U.S. jurisdictions.

The English Police and Criminal Evidence Act, 1984, provides that the Home Secretary shall issue codes of practice in connection with the detention, treatment, questioning, and identification of persons by police officers. Based on that authority, the Home Secretary has issued Code of Practice C, which requires that a suspect must be cautioned before any questions about the suspected criminal activity are put to him. The "caution" must be as follows: "You do not have to say anything. But it may harm your defence if you do not mention when questioned something which you later rely on in court. Anything you do say may be given in evidence." The actual warnings, or caution, about the right to remain silent are fairly similar in the United States and England. The major difference between the two nations is that in England, the fact that the defendant remained silent may be admissible in evidence against the defendant. In most cases, the mere mention of the fact that the accused invoked his or her Miranda rights is grounds for a mistrial or reversal of a conviction. Also since England does not have the exclusionary rule, a statement taken in violation of regulations promulgated in Code of Practice C is still admissible in court, whereas the violation of the Miranda rule for the most part makes the defendant's statement inadmissible.

Once a defendant is convicted and a sentence is pronounced, he or she has a right to appeal in both nations. In U.S. federal courts and in most state courts, a defendant cannot appeal his or her sentence if the sentence is within statutory limits for the offense. In England, the defendant can appeal his or her sentence.

Practice of Law

In the United States, admission to practice law is generally reserved to the individual states. After an individual has been admitted to practice law in a state and has practiced for a period of time, he or she can file a petition to be admitted to practice in federal court. An exception to this general rule is the District of Columbia, where the practice of law is regulated by the District of Columbia Bar Association in a manner similar to the practices in the individual states.

The District of Columbia Bar is a unified bar association. Its core functions, supported by member dues, are the registration of lawyers, operation of a lawyer disciplinary system, maintenance of a Clients' Security Fund, and certain other administrative operations. The bar is governed by a Board of Governors composed of 20 lawyers selected by the active membership and three members of the public appointed by the bar itself as nonvoting members.

In the individual states, there are two types of bar associations: the unified bar association, which requires membership in the bar association before an individual may practice law within that jurisdiction; and the voluntary bar association, where the right to practice law is not controlled by the bar association. In those states where membership in the bar association is voluntary, admission to the bar and regulation of attorneys are generally accomplished by the State Supreme Court.

Generally, an attorney is required to be admitted to practice in each state in which he or she wishes to practice. For example, author Cliff Roberson is admitted to practice law in the states of California and Texas and before the U.S. Supreme Court. Should he wish to practice law in New York, for example, he would either need to obtain special permission of the New York court or be admitted to practice law in New York.

Prior to being admitted to practice law in a state, an individual is required to pass a state bar examination. An exception to the bar examination requirement is permitted in 45 states. In those states, an attorney with at least 5 years' experience as an attorney in another state may, with the sponsorship of local attorneys, petition for admission to the local bar. Prior to taking the bar exam, generally an applicant must have completed both an undergraduate education and 3 years' study in an accredited law school. For the most part, once an attorney is admitted to practice law in a state, the attorney may practice in all types of cases.

In England, legal training is by study at an Inn of Court. The Inns of Court are voluntary societies, unchartered and unincorporated. Their early history is obscure. Since the Middle Ages, the Inns have been devoted to the technical study of English law. At an Inn, students listened to arguments in court and discussed law among themselves.

Unlike the practice of law in the United States, there are two types of practicing lawyers in England, barristers and solicitors. Barristers engage in advocacy (trial work), and solicitors in office work. There is, however, considerable overlap in their functions. For example, a solicitor may appear as an advocate in the lower courts, while barristers are often called upon to give advice or to draft documents.

Appearance as advocates before the English High Court is limited to barristers. Barristers are known collectively as "the bar." It is from the bar that the most important judicial appointments are made. A barrister must be a member of one of the four Inns of Court. A prospective barrister must pass a series of examinations established for the Inns by the Council of Legal Education and must satisfy certain traditional requirements, such as eating a certain number of dinners at the respective Inn. In addition, the Inns still stress the pupillage system, whereby students read with practicing barristers for specified periods of time. The General Council of the Bar sets standards for the bar and acts in matters of general concern to the profession.

Barristers are generally required to accept any case for a proper professional fee, whereas U.S. attorneys have more latitude in refusing to accept certain cases. U.S. attorneys must decline cases when they have doubts that their ability or professional training are adequate to perform the duties of an attorney successfully in the particular case.

If a U.S. attorney does not get paid by a client, the attorney may bring legal action against the client. However, if a barrister does not receive payment for work, the barrister may not take action in court to obtain it. A significant number of U.S. attorneys are members of a law partnership. Barristers cannot form partnerships with other barristers or with solicitors, nor can they carry on any other profession or business.

In the United States, disciplinary matters are handled by either the bar association or the state supreme courts. In England, disciplinary matters concerning barristers are handled by the governing body of each Inn, known as the "benchers" (judges of the High Court or barristers). For the most part, disciplinary power has been delegated to the Senate of the four Inns of Court, established in 1966.

Solicitors confer with clients, give advice, draft documents, conduct negotiations, prepare cases for trial, and retain barristers for advice on special matters or for advocacy before the higher courts. They may appear in all courts as the agents for litigation or representatives of their clients, and they are deemed officers of the court, but they may appear as advocates only in the lower courts. Since their activities make up the greater part of the work of lawyers, there are many more solicitors than barristers.

Solicitors are required to complete a law school course. In addition, unlike attorneys in the United States, solicitors are required to serve an apprenticeship for about 3–5 years. Solicitors are required to be British Commonwealth citizens, but barristers are not.

The official organization of solicitors is the Law Society, a voluntary group, incorporated by Parliament. The Law Society has extensive authority in setting and enforcing standards for solicitors. A solicitor, unlike a barrister, may sue for his fees. In England, the Inns of Court (the governing body of barristers) and the Law Society (the governing body of solicitors) have the power to disbar or remove the attorneys within their respective organizations from the rolls.

Canadian Legal System

Canada is a federalist country and a member of the British Commonwealth. It is divided into 10 provinces and 3 territories. It has a parliamentary democratic government in which the executive and legislative power is split between the central and provincial units. Responsibility for the various parts of the criminal justice system is shared and divided among the federal, provincial, and municipal levels of government.

Canada's legal system was modified by the Constitution Act, 1867. Under the provisions of that act, the authority for the judicial system in Canada is divided between the federal government and the 10 provincial governments. The provincial governments are given jurisdiction over the administration of justice in the provinces and include the constitution, organization, and maintenance of the courts, civil and criminal, in the province, as well as civil procedure in those courts. Canada has a Dominion Criminal Code, which covers major crimes. It also has a Canadian Bill of Rights and provincial laws such as the Ontario Human Rights Code.

The authority to appoint the judges of the superior courts in the provinces—which includes the provincial courts of appeal as well as the trial courts of general jurisdiction—is given to the federal government. In addition, the federal government has the obligation to provide for the remuneration of those judges and the authority to remove them.

The federal government also has jurisdiction over criminal law and exclusive authority over the procedure used in criminal courts. The present court system gives the provincial governments jurisdiction over the constitution, organization, and maintenance of, and the appointment of judges to, the lowest level of courts, while the federal government has authority over the constitution, organization, and maintenance of, and the appointment of judges to, the Supreme Court of Canada, the Federal Court of Appeal, the Federal Court, and the Tax Court of Canada. Authority over the superior courts in each province is divided. Accordingly, for these courts to function properly, the federal and provincial governments must cooperate in the exercise of their respective authorities.

Court Structure

The courts in Canada are organized in a four-tiered structure with the Supreme Court of Canada at the top. The Supreme Court of Canada functions as a general court of appeal for Canada and hears appeals from both the federal court system, headed by the Federal Court of Appeal, and the provincial court systems, headed in each province by that province's Court of Appeal. Unlike the U.S. Supreme Court, the Supreme Court of Canada functions as a national, and not merely federal, court of last resort.

The next highest level of court consists of the Federal Court of Appeal and the various provincial courts of appeal. Two of these latter courts also function as the courts of appeal for the three federal territories in northern Canada—the Yukon Territory, the Northwest Territories, and Nunavut Territory.

The third level of courts consists of the Federal Court, the Tax Court of Canada, and the provincial and territorial superior courts of general jurisdiction. The territorial superior courts are the only court in the system with inherent jurisdiction in addition to jurisdiction granted by federal and provincial statutes.

At the lowest level are the courts typically described as "provincial courts." These courts are generally organized within each province into various divisions defined by the subject matter of their respective jurisdictions; hence, one usually finds a Traffic Division, a Small Claims Division, a Family Division, and a Criminal Division.

The Supreme Court of Canada sits only in Ottawa. The other three federally established courts—the Federal Court of Appeal, the Federal Court, and the Tax Court of Canada—sit at 17 permanent locations. The provincial and territorial courts sit at more than 700 locations. These include 15 permanent provincial and territorial appellate court sitting locations, one in each province and territory except for Quebec and Alberta, which have two each.

Judicial System of Canada

- Highest court(s): Supreme Court of Canada (consists of the chief justice and 8 judges); note—in 1949, Canada finally abolished all appeals beyond its Supreme Court to the Judicial Committee of the Privy Council (in London).
- Judge selection and term of office: Chief justice and judges appointed by the prime minister in council; all judges appointed for life with mandatory retirement at age of 75.
- Subordinate courts: federal level: Federal Court of Appeal; Federal Court; Tax Court; federal administrative tribunals; courts martial; provincial/territorial: provincial superior, appeals, first instance, and specialized courts; in 1999, the Nunavut Court—a circuit court with the power of a superior court and the territorial courts—was established to serve isolated settlements.

Source: CIA World Fact Book, available at: https://www.cia.gov/library/publications/resources/the-world-factbook, accessed May 14, 2015.

Provincial and Territorial Superior Courts

The superior courts of each province and territory include both a court of general trial jurisdiction and a provincial court of appeal. A photograph of a

Photo 2.5 The Court of Appeals & Supreme Court for British Columbia, Canada, are located in downtown Vancouver. (Photo by Cliff Roberson.)

Canadian appellate court can be seen in Photo 2.5. Their jurisdiction is not limited to matters over which the provincial governments have legislative jurisdiction. Unlike state courts in the United States, the superior courts have jurisdiction over disputes arising in many of the areas over which the federal government has legislative jurisdiction—for example, criminal law. If federal legislation calls for the exercise at some point of judicial authority, but says nothing about which body is to exercise that authority, it is assumed that the authority will reside with the provincial and territorial superior courts. These courts are considered the primary courts in the Canadian legal system.

Provincial and Territorial Courts

The provincial and territorial courts handle the overwhelming majority of cases that come into the Canadian court system. They deal with a broad range of criminal matters, family law, and all civil litigation in which the amount at issue is relatively small. Like the U.S. inferior state courts, these are the courts that an average citizen is more likely to have contact with.

The Judiciary

Members of the judiciary in Canada, regardless of the court, are drawn from the legal profession. Judges appointed by the federal government, which includes the judges of all of the courts except the judges in the provincial and territorial courts, are required to have been members of a provincial or territorial bar for at least 10 years. Judges in Canada are subject to mandatory retirement at either the age of 75 or 70, depending on the court.

Right to Fair Trial versus Freedom of the Press

One area where the Canadian system is different from the U.S. system involves the issue of freedom of the press. Vidmar (1996) states that the Canadian legal system, unlike the U.S. system, stresses the right to a fair trial over the rights of free press, and that a Canadian judge has the right to ban the public and the press from the courtroom if this is deemed to be in the best interest of public morality or necessary to maintain order.

Scottish Legal System

At the union of the parliaments of England and Scotland in 1707, the legal systems of the two countries were very dissimilar. Scotland had adopted much of the Roman law that had been developed by the jurists of Holland and France as the foundation of its system when there was a gap in its own common law. There is considerable infusion of civil law, especially in legal nomenclature and in the emphasis on principle rather than following precedent.

The Scottish legal system is different from that of the English and is closer to the Continental pattern. The supreme Scottish court is the Court of Session. The court has two principal functions. It has original jurisdiction in a very wide range of cases, which is exclusive in a few matters; in its appellate capacity it hears appeals from the nine Court of Session courts of first instance (the Outer House), each presided over by a lord ordinary, and also from the sheriff courts. The appellate court (Inner House) sits in two divisions, the first and second, presided over by the lord president of the Court of Session and the lord justice clerk. While all judges are referred to by the courtesy title of "lord," they are not all peers.

The lower civil court is the sheriff court, which is an ancient court dating back to the twelfth century. Scotland is divided into several sheriffdoms, each staffed by a sheriff-principal and a number of full-time sheriffs. Courts are held in the major towns. These courts have both civil and criminal jurisdiction. In civil cases, the sheriff normally makes decisions alone, although sometimes he is assisted by a jury of 7. In criminal cases, the accused is tried summarily or with a jury of 15. In a civil jurisdiction, the appeal lies to the sheriff-principal and then to the Court of Session, or directly to the Court of Session; in a criminal jurisdiction, it lies to the High Court of Justiciary.

Australian Legal System

For thousands of years, Australia was inhabited by indigenous peoples, now known as the Aborigines. In 1788, a British penal colony was established in the southeastern part of the Continent. Other settlements of European people were subsequently established elsewhere, leading to the creation of six independent British colonies: New South Wales, Victoria, Queensland, Western Australia, South Australia, and Tasmania. These colonies became a federation in 1901, and eventually formed the states of the Commonwealth of Australia, although since then, the Northern Territory and the Australian Capital Territory have been granted self-government.

The Commonwealth of Australia has nine separate parliaments or legislatures, most of which have lower and upper houses. There are also several hundred local government authorities, known as councils or shires. The state or territory governments have primary responsibility for criminal justice.

The Commonwealth of Australia is a federalist government composed of a national government, six state governments, and two territory governments. The government of the Commonwealth is responsible for the enforcement of its own laws. The most frequently prosecuted Commonwealth offenses are those related to the importation of drugs and the violation of social security laws. Offenses against a person or against property occurring in Commonwealth facilities are also regarded as offenses against the Commonwealth.

The states are primarily responsible for the development of criminal law. Queensland, Western Australia, and Tasmania are described as "code" states because they have enacted criminal codes that define the limits of the criminal law. The remaining three states—New South Wales, Victoria, and South Australia—are regarded as "common law" states because they have not attempted codification. In practice, however, there is little difference in the elements of the criminal law between the "code" and "common law" states.

Local governments can pass legislation, known as bylaws. These generally include social nuisance offenses as well as traffic and parking rules. Local government officials or the state and territory police generally enforce the local government bylaws. The maximum penalty that can be imposed for conviction of a bylaw offense is a monetary fine. However, nonpayment of fines can result in imprisonment.

Judicial System of Australia

- Highest court: High Court of Australia (consists of seven justices, including the chief justice); note—each of the six states, two territories, and Norfolk Island has a Supreme Court; the High Court is the final appellate court beyond the state and territory supreme courts.

- Judge selection and term of office: Justices appointed by the governor-general in council for life with mandatory retirement at age 70.
- Subordinate courts: Subordinate courts at the federal level: Federal Court; Federal Magistrates' Courts of Australia; Family Court; subordinate courts at the state and territory level: Local Court—New South Wales; Magistrates' Courts—Victoria, Queensland, South Australia, Western Australia, Tasmania, Northern Territory, Australian Capital Territory; District Courts—New South Wales, Queensland, South Australia, Western Australia; County Court—Victoria; Family Court—Western Australia; Court of Petty Sessions—Norfolk Island.

Source: CIA World Fact Book, available at: https://www.cia.gov/library/publications/resources/the-world-factbook, accessed May 14, 2015.

Legal System

Australia was originally settled as a prison colony for the English. Photo 2.6 shows one of the oldest prisons in Australia. The structure of the Australian legal system is derived from, and still closely follows, that of the United Kingdom. In addition to parliament-made law, there is the "common law" inherited from the English courts, which has since been developed and refined by Australian courts. It should be noted, however, that since 1963 Australian courts have ceased to regard English decisions as superior or even equal in authority to those made by Australian courts. The legal system is adversarial in nature and places a high value on the presumption of innocence. Because of the federalist system of government, there are nine separate legal systems in operation. Although there are some significant differences among these systems, they are essentially similar in structure and operation.

Classification of Crimes

Crimes can be classified as felony, misdemeanor, or minor offenses, but more commonly they are classified as indictable or nonindictable offenses. Indictable offenses are those that are heard by the superior courts and may require a jury, whereas nonindictable offenses, which comprise the vast majority of court cases, are heard in magistrate's courts, where no juries are employed.

While there are some classification differences among the various jurisdictions, in all jurisdictions indictable offenses generally include homicide, robbery, serious sexual and nonsexual assault, fraud, burglary and serious theft. In some jurisdictions, such as South Australia, there is a group of

Photo 2.6 Port Arthur Prison, Tasmania, Australia. The Port Arthur Prison was established in 1830 as a timber camp that used prisoners as convict labor. Only 3 years later it became a punishment station for repeat offenders. From 1833 until 1853, it was the destination for the hardest of convicted British criminals, those who were secondary offenders having reoffended after their arrival in Australia. Rebellious personalities from other convict stations were also sent there, a quite undesirable punishment. In addition, Port Arthur had some of the strictest security measures of the British penal system. (Photo by Cliff Roberson.)

"minor indictable" offenses that can be heard in either the superior or lower courts, according to the wish of the accused.

Judicial System of the United Kingdom

- Highest court(s): Supreme Court (consists of 12 justices including the court president and deputy president); note—the Supreme Court was established by the Constitutional Reform Act 2005 and implemented in October 2009, replacing the Appellate Committee of the House of Lords as the highest court in the United Kingdom.
- Judge selection and term of office: Judge candidates selected by an independent committee of several judicial commissions, followed by their recommendations to the prime minister, and appointed by Her Majesty The Queen; justices appointed during period of good behavior.

- Subordinate courts: England and Wales—Court of Appeal (civil and criminal divisions); High Court; Crown Court; County Courts; Magistrates' Courts; Scotland—Court of Sessions; Sherrif Courts; High Court of Justiciary; tribunals; Northern Ireland—Court of Appeal in Northern Ireland; High Court; county courts; magistrates' courts; specialized tribunals.

Source: CIA World Fact Book, available at: https://www.cia.gov/library/publications/resources/the-world-factbook, accessed May 14, 2015.

Summary

- The common law system was established from a case-to-case approach.
- At first, English common law developed as essentially feudal land law, and later in its formative years was shaped and defined by the French invaders.
- The Magna Carta, signed by King John in 1215, was the forerunner of many of the protections involving individual rights.
- Coke, one of the most eminent jurists in the history of common law, issued volumes of reports on common law principles.
- For centuries, Blackstone's *Commentaries* have been considered a source of the laws of England.
- When English settlers came to America in the 1600s, they brought English common law with them.
- There are two court systems in the United States, federal and state. The term "dual federalism" is used to describe the concept of the federal and state systems.
- The justice system in the United States and England is considered an adversary system in that there are two sides and the judge acts as the umpire or referee.
- In the United States, many aspects of criminal procedure are controlled by the U.S. Constitution and the judicial interpretation of the Constitution.
- The U.S. Constitution provides that a defendant has the right to the assistance of counsel.
- Communications between a U.S. defense attorney and his or her client are generally considered privileged communications.
- The English court system has a unitary judicial system in which all the courts fit into a single national hierarchy.

- The English Supreme Court of Judicature consists of the Court of Appeal and the High Court of Justice.
- In the United States, the systems rely on a due process model that emphasizes the rights of defendants, while the English system stresses crime control. English courts do not have the exclusionary rule.
- In Canada, the responsibility for various parts of the criminal justice system is shared and divided among the federal, provincial, and municipal levels of government.

Questions in Review

1. Explain why the U.S. system of government is called a federalist system.
2. How important was Henry II in the development of English common law?
3. What is the role of federal courts in the prosecution of state criminal cases in the United States?
4. In the United States, what is the primary duty of a prosecutor?
5. Why does a guilty defendant have the right to counsel in a state criminal case?
6. What are the functions of a U.S. magistrate?
7. What are the duties of a bailiff in a U.S. court?
8. How is the Canadian system of courts organized?

Policing and Corrections under the Common Law Model

3

Chapter Objectives

After studying this chapter, you should understand or be able to explain the following issues and concepts:

- The principles in which community policing is based
- How punishment is determined under the common law model
- Punishment philosophy under the common law model
- The functions of police under the common law model
- The various policing models
- The differences in policing in Great Britain and the United States
- The requirements to be a police officer in Great Britain and the United States
- The Royal Canadian Mounted Police's approach to policing

Key Terms

Community policing: A concept of policing that advocates that the government and community should work closely together and that the police and the community are coproducers of safety.

Corporal punishment: Physical punishment such as whipping, branding, dunking, and maiming.

Deterrence: A punishment philosophy that focuses on future outcomes rather than past misconduct and is based on the theory that creating a fear of future punishments will deter crime.

Federal government: A government of states in which sovereignty is divided between a central authority and component state authorities.

Incapacitation: Punishment philosophy that advocates incarcerating offenders for a period of time to protect society from a particular threat. At least while prisoners are in confinement, they are unlikely to commit crimes on innocent persons outside of prison.

Rehabilitation: An approach that believes that punishment should be directed toward correcting the offender; also called the "treatment" approach.

Retribution: A punishment philosophy based on the ideology that the criminal is an enemy of society and deserves severe punishment for willfully breaking its rules.

Policing in Common Law Countries

The term "police" was derived from the Greek word *polis*. The police are that function of the government charged with the preservation of public order and tranquility, the promotion of public health, safety and morals, and the prevention, detection, and punishment of crimes (*State ex rel. Walsh v. Hine*, 59 Conn. 50, 21 A. 1024, [1890]).

"Police" was defined by Jeremy Bentham as follows:

- Police is in general a system of precaution, either for the prevention of crime or of calamities.
- Its business may be distributed into eight distinct branches:

  1. Police for the prevention of offenses.
  2. Police for the prevention of calamities.
  3. Police for the prevention of epidemic diseases.
  4. Police of charity.
  5. Police of interior communications.
  6. Police of public amusements.
  7. Police for recent intelligence.
  8. Police for registration. [As reported in *Board of Canal & Lock Comm'rs v. Willamette Transp. & Locks Co.*, 6 Ore. 219 [Oregon (1877)]

Deviance Control or Civil Order Control

Dammer and Fairchild (2006, p. 105) classify police duties into two major tasks: deviance control and civil order control. To them, deviance control refers to the police mission to reinforce community values and laws. In this task, the police protect citizens against lawbreakers. The deviance control function is conservative in nature and consists of protecting the community against nonconformists and trying to keep violators of community norms under control. Civil order control differs from deviance control in that in civil order control there is often a strong political component to the activities being controlled. Actions that disturb the civil order may be threatening to a government. For example, when the police act to control a mass strike or political rally, they are performing civil order control. Frequently, the police in this latter type situation have confrontations with citizens.

Canada, England, and U.S. civil police are basically organized to carry out the deviance control task. However, all have at times carried out civil control tasks in situations involving labor troubles, student protests, and riots of various kinds. For example, in the 1980 riots in Liverpool, Birmingham, and London, the English police used tear gas for the first time in dealing with the unruly crowds (Reiner, 1985). The English police now use pepper spray for crowd control (Tyler and King, 2000). Local police in the United States have also been used to carry out civil order control. For example, the Los Angeles City Police have been used on occasion to combat rioting and for crowd control, especially during the Watts riots in the 1960s and those following the Rodney King incident in the 1990s.

Policing Models

Wright (2002) uses four models to distinguish between public policing depending upon the type of relationship existing among the police, the state, and the military. His four models are as follows:

The civil police model: The police and the military are completely separate in terms of organization and objectives. The police deal with crime and the military deal with national security issues. The police tend to be decentralized with wide discretion. England, Canada, and the United States utilize this model of policing.

The state police model: The influence of the state is strong; while the police and the military are separate, the military is allowed to get involved in public order operations. The police also use military-type deployments and may use special military equipment. As we will discuss when we examine the civil law model countries in Chapter 5, Germany and France use the state police model.

The quasi-military model: The state has a great deal of control over the police, and the police serve the interests of the state. The police and the military are to a considerable extent interchangeable.

The martial law model: Actually a stronger version of the quasi-military model. There is no separation of police and military forces. Both are under the same command and control of the state.

The United States and England typify countries that have developed the civil police model with its decentralized police organizations. There is a tendency for countries with the common law legal model to have highly decentralized police organizations, whereas countries whose criminal justice system is based on the civil law model tend to have centralized national police forces. According to Banton (2007), the classification of police as centralized or decentralized organizations is a relative concept. The English police, for example, are generally considered to be a decentralized force; however, when they are compared to police forces in the United States, they appear quite centralized.

The two key differences between U.S. and English local police are the extent to which police officers should be armed, and whether the emphasis should be on crime control or peacekeeping. The traditional U.S. emphasis has been on crime control, in contrast to the traditional English emphasis on keeping the peace (Pakes, 2004, p. 29).

Local Policing in the United States and England

The structure of U.S. law enforcement has its roots in the English system. The structure of policing in the United States can be divided into three levels: local, state, and federal. The United States considers itself a federal type of government, with the national government having only those powers granted to it by the U.S. Constitution or necessarily implied by the Constitution. In addition, the central or federal government does not have unlimited authority in the area of criminal justice. As noted in Chapter 2, the majority of the criminal prosecutions in the United States are in state, not federal courts. For example, in the majority of cases the crime of murder is a state offense. It is a federal crime only if there is a special circumstance attached to it to give the federal authorities jurisdiction, such as murder on federal property, murder on the high seas, or murder of federal officers. While murder is generally a state crime, it is normally investigated and prosecuted by local police departments. Photo 3.1 shows a pretrial holding facility where prisoners are kept while awaiting trial.

Photo 3.1 A pretrial holding facility in Denver, Colorado, used by the Denver Police to hold individuals awaiting trial. (Photo by Cliff Roberson.)

Consider this scenario. A murder is investigated by the local police department, the suspect is convicted in a state district or superior court for the murder, and then the defendant submits a writ to a federal court alleging that his rights, which are guaranteed under the U.S. Constitution, were violated by the local police when he was arrested. In this case, all three levels of government, local, state, and federal, were involved in the prosecution. This is not an unusual situation. Therefore, it is essential that the three levels of government actively coordinate with one another and establish an ongoing need to work together.

Current Policing in the United States

Local U.S. police departments in 2006 had about 581,000 full-time employees, including about 452,000 sworn personnel. There were about 11,000 more sworn and 4000 more nonsworn employees than in 2000. Racial and ethnic minorities comprised 23.6% of full-time sworn personnel in 2006, up from 22.6% in 2000, and 14.6% in 1987. Women comprised 11.3% of officers in 2006, up from 10.6% in 2000, and 7.6% in 1987. From 2000 to 2006, the number of African American local police officers increased by 1500 or 3%; Hispanic or Latino officers by 4700 or 13%; officers from other minority groups by 850 or 7%; and female officers by 4400 or 9% (Bureau of Justice Statistics, 2006).

Although 74% of all local police departments served fewer than 10,000 residents, these agencies employed just 14% of all officers. About half of all officers served a jurisdiction with 100,000 or more residents. While departments serving the largest cities had thousands of officers on average, those serving fewer than 2500 residents had an average of just four full-time employees, including three sworn officers (Bureau of Justice Statistics, 2006). There are approximately 362 local police officers in the United States per 100,000 citizens, compared to about 345 for England.

Mission of Local Police Departments

As noted earlier, traditionally local police departments in the United States focus on crime control, whereas English police departments focus on keeping the peace (Pakes, 2004, p. 28). For example, the mission and value statements of the New York City Police Department are as follows:

> *Mission*: The Mission of the New York City Police Department is to enhance the quality of life in our City by working in partnership with the community and in accordance with constitutional rights to enforce the laws, preserve the peace, reduce fear, and provide for a safe environment.
> *Values*: In partnership with the community, we pledge to:
> • Protect the lives and property of our fellow citizens and impartially enforce the law.

- Fight crime both by preventing it and by aggressively pursuing violators of the law.
- Maintain a higher standard of integrity than is generally expected of others because so much is expected of us.
- Value human life, respect the dignity of each individual, and render our services with courtesy and civility (New York City Police Department, 2007).

The London Metropolitan Police Authority's (MPA) mission statement is "Making London safe for all the people we serve." And the MPA vision statement is "To make London the safest major city in the world."

Both the mission and value statements of the NYPD indicate an emphasis on crime control. Those statements were compared with the following statement of the MPA, which was posted on its website: "The Metropolitan Police works together with the people of London to make our capital city safe" (London Metropolitan Police Authority, 2007). The MPA focus as evidenced by their mission and vision statements is on peacekeeping. Similar comparisons of police units in the United States and England reflect this difference in focus of the two police systems.

Most U.S. police departments have adopted the concept of community policing where the police are involved in the community. Photo 3.2 shows a typical community policing station. The development of community policing is discussed later in this chapter.

Photo 3.2 A Houston Police Department Community Policing Substation located in a shopping center in the "Chinatown" section of the City of Houston, Texas. (Photo by Cliff Roberson.)

Local Policing in England and Wales

Like the police organizations in the United States, policing in England and Wales is fragmented. Both the United States and England have a historical distrust of a strong state police organization. There are 43 police forces in England and Wales, each one is responsible for a certain area of the country. There are also special police forces, such as the British Transport Police, the Ministry of Defence Police, and the Port of London Authority Police, responsible for the policing of particular installations. Generally, the police agencies are maintained and provided resources by central and local government agencies, with immediate oversight by local county committee councils and magistrates (police authorities).

The Metropolitan Police Force polices London and is directly answerable to the UK Government Minister. The UK Government Minister is responsible for both crime control and other interior affairs. In 2005–2006, the Metropolitan Police Service employed 30,871 officers, 13,769 police staff, 400 traffic wardens, 2,308 Police Community Support Officers (PCSOs), and 1,070 Specials (London Metropolitan Police Department, 2007). Photo 3.3 shows a picture of an early police strike in London.

For the most part, the chief or commander of each police force, also known as the chief constable, is not answerable to anyone on operational matters, but is accountable to a committee on matters of efficiency. He or she must prepare an annual report on the work of the force concerned. Local police authorities select a force's most senior officers, subject to the

Photo 3.3 Police strike in London, England about 1910. (Courtesy of the Library of Congress Prints and Photographs Division.)

approval of the Home Secretary. The chief constable can also appoint other officers. With the exception of the Metropolitan Police, all police forces are required to undergo statutory inspection by Her Majesty's Inspectorate of Constabulary.

Some common services to police forces are provided centrally. The most important of these is the compilation of criminal records information. Liaison with the International Criminal Police Organization (Interpol) is provided by the Metropolitan Police. Other central bodies are the National Drugs Intelligence Unit and a National Criminal Intelligence Service (NCIS). The Police National Computer records, among other things, registration and relevant history of all motor vehicles.

There are about 135,000 sworn police officers and 55,000 civilians employed by the 43 police forces. Approximately 15% of these officers are female, and fewer than 5% of officers serving in England and Wales are of an ethnic minority. Recruitment campaigns for such officers periodically appear in the press.

Hiring Requirements for U.S. and English Police Officers

The hiring requirements for NYPD officers are as follows:

- Candidates must be at least 21 years of age on or before the day of hire.
- Candidates must be a U.S. citizen on or before the day of hire. On or before the day of hire, candidates must have successfully completed either 60 college credits with a 2.0 GPA from an accredited college or university or 2 years of full-time, active military service in the U.S. Armed Forces with an honorable discharge and have a high school diploma or its equivalent.
- Candidates must reside either within one of the five boroughs of New York City or one of the surrounding counties of New York City, Suffolk, Westchester, Orange, Rockland, Nassau, or Putnam Counties, on the day of hire.
- Candidates must possess a valid, unrestricted New York State Drivers License on the day of hire.
- Candidates must pass a drug/alcohol screening.
- Candidates must pass a character and background investigation.

In contrast, the MPA has no formal education requirement as long as the individual is proficient in English. Other MPA requirements for hiring include being at least 18.5 years old at the time of attending training school, being of good moral character, being able to cope with the physical and mental demands of the job, and having been a resident of the United Kingdom for at least 3 years. An individual of any nationality may apply, provided he or she has permanent right to remain without restriction in the United Kingdom if from a non-EEA country.

Salaries for English and U.S. Police Officers

The annual starting pay for the English recruit officer was £21,009 and on completion of initial training (end of 31 weeks) it rose to £23,454. There is also a cost-of-living allowance for the Metropolitan Police Service (MPS) London of £4,338 and a living allowance of £2,055. Therefore, during training pay is £27,402 and thereafter £29,847.

The starting pay for a police sergeant was £32,985; a police inspector, £44,118; and a chief inspector, £48,645. Officers must complete their 2-year probation period before they can apply for promotion (London Metropolitan Police Authority, 2015).

According to the City of Los Angeles Personnel Department, the starting pay and benefits for police was $57,420 per annum. Upon completion of probation and advancement to rank and pay grade of Officer II, the annual salary increased to $60,552. In addition to these base salaries, there is overtime earning, holiday pay, night differential, and uniform allowance.

The number of motor vehicles used by police officers in England and Wales is approximately 25,000, amounting to about 20 vehicles per 100 officers. In U.S. local police departments, there was one vehicle for every two sworn officers. Most English and U.S. local police agencies have a computerized crime recording system and control and dispatch system.

One of the two major differences between the U.S. and English police is that the English police do not routinely carry firearms. A Police Federation survey with responses from more than 42,000 members in 1995 indicated that about 80% of English officers did not wish to be routinely armed while on duty. However, the survey indicated that over 60% of English officers believed that police officers should be trained to use firearms and allowed to carry them under special circumstances (Das and Palmiotto, 2006, p. 885). Approximately 7000 of the officers are certified firearms officers, but even these officers do not routinely carry weapons. In the survey, about 80% of officers felt that more officers should be firearms certified, and about half favored the mandatory wearing of body armor for all operational duties.

The standard weapon carried by English police officers is a wooden staff or truncheon. A weapon capable of inflicting more harm, a side-handled baton, promises to replace the truncheon in the future.

Training of New Officers

Local police academy training in the United States is not uniform in either content or the number of hours required for certifying a police officer. The number of weeks required for a local police recruit training can range from as little as 8 or 10 weeks to as much as a year. For example, the state of Georgia requires 8 weeks of recruit training for police recruits; the Wichita, Kansas, Police Department requires 22 weeks or 840 hours; and the Los Angeles, California, Sheriff's Department requires 1 year of training. A Bureau of Justice Statistics survey of more than 12,000 law enforcement agencies found that on average, departments required 640 training hours of new police recruits. Higher-level training for police officers is generally accomplished at state academies and the FBI Academy in Quantico, Virginia (Birzer and Roberson, 2006, p. 206).

English police recruits remain on probation for the first 2 years of their service. Much of their training is carried out in the workplace under the supervision of a veteran officer. Their initial training generally consists of a week with whatever constabulary is involved, followed by a longer period of training at "training school" held at a central training center. Once the recruit has completed training school, he or she returns to the constabulary and works under the supervision of a tutor constable. All recruits enter as "constables" (Das and Palmiotto, 2006, p. 883). Higher-level training is generally carried out by the Police Staff College at Bramshill in Hampshire, also known as Centrex.

Police Powers and Use of Discretion

In the area of police powers and the use of discretion by police officers, the United States and England have very similar rules and regulations. The key difference is that the authority of U.S. police officers is restricted by the U.S. Supreme Court's interpretations of the U.S. Constitution. The English police are generally restricted by national statutes and police regulations. As noted in Chapter 2, the English courts do not use the exclusionary rule to exclude illegally seized evidence.

The Police and Criminal Evidence Act of 1984 allows an English police officer to stop, detain, and search persons and vehicles for stolen goods, weapons, or other tools of crime, and they may set up roadblocks in certain circumstances. The officer must state and record the grounds for taking this action and record what was found.

The English police have powers to enter and search premises and to seize and retain property. The police may seize anything which on reasonable grounds is believed to be evidence of the offense under investigation, or of any other, or which had been obtained following an offense. U.S. police officers are restricted by the Fourth Amendment to the U.S. Constitution as to

Photo 3.4 A California Highway Patrol car on display in Copenhagen, Denmark. (Photo by Cliff Roberson.)

their authority to enter and search premises. The general rule in the United States is that prior to entering a home the police must get a warrant, unless circumstances do not allow for the delay necessary in obtaining a warrant.

An arrest may occur without a warrant where a person is reasonably suspected of having committed an arrestable offense, or a magistrate may issue a warrant. The Police and Criminal Evidence Act 1994 allows a police constable to use reasonable force if necessary to detain or search a person or vehicle. What is reasonable force will depend on the circumstances and the extent to which the citizen resists. The arrest authority of the English and U.S. police is very similar in this regard. Photo 3.4 is a picture of a patrol car used in California.

Community Policing under the Common Law Model

According to Dammer and Fairchild (2006, p. 126), the modern origins of community policing started with the work of Sir Robert Peel and his locally based and accountable police forces. The Police and Magistrates' Court Act of 1994 and the Criminal Justice and Public Order Act of 1994 are the basis for current community policing efforts in England. These efforts include London's recent Safer Neighborhoods Policing Awareness Campaign.

Community policing in the United States grew from a few small foot patrol projects in the 1950s and 1960s to the preeminent reform agenda of modern U.S. policing. Birzer and Roberson (2006, p. 78) state that community-oriented policing in the United States is not a program but a philosophy or a strategy—a way for all police officers to view their jobs and duties. Community-oriented policing is based on the concept that the police and citizens working together in creative ways can solve contemporary community problems related to crime, fear of crime, social and physical disorder, and general neighborhood conditions. Both nations appear to adopt the philosophy of community-oriented policing.

London Metropolitan Police Authority's Safer Neighborhoods Policing Awareness Campaign

In 2007, the London Metropolitan Police Authority (MPA) started a Safer Neighborhood program. Safer Neighborhood is about local policing, police and partners working with you, to identify and tackle issues of concern in your neighborhood. Safer Neighborhood teams will be deployed in each neighborhood. Each team is normally made up of six police and Police Community Support Officers (PCSOs). Their aim is to listen and talk to you and find out what affects your daily life and feelings of security. These might be issues such as antisocial behavior, graffiti, noisy neighborhoods, yobs (hoodlums), or vandalism. Then they work in partnership with citizens and other social agencies to find a lasting solution (London Metropolitan Police Authority, 2007).

Policing in Canada

Under Section 91 of the 1867 Constitution Act, the Canadian Parliament was given exclusive jurisdiction to pass criminal laws and establish rules for criminal procedures. Under Section 92, the provincial governments have jurisdiction over the administration of justice in each province. This jurisdiction includes the interpretation of the constitution, the maintenance and organization of provincial courts in both civil and criminal jurisdictions, and civil procedure as applied in provincial courts. Police forces are generally divided into provincial, municipal, and federal units. Photo 3.5 shows a police headquarters in Canada.

The Canadian Narcotic Control Act (1970) was designed to control the flow of narcotics by making a federal crime of narcotic offenses. Violations of this act are prosecuted by federally appointed counsel. Besides listing the drugs that are illegal under this federal statute, it guides the prosecution and enforcement process (e.g., requirements for police officer entry, search, and seizure), sentencing, and the appeal process in Canada.

The provinces establish the standards for their own police. There are about 300 police organizations in Canada. About 16.5% of Canada's police officers are female. The total number of racial and cultural representation

Photo 3.5 Central Police Department Headquarters, Vancouver, Canada. (Photo courtesy of Dwayne Roberson.)

is unknown because these data are not reported. There are approximately 60,000 police officers in Canada, of whom about 27% (about 15,600) are sworn Royal Canadian Mounted Police (RCMP) and are generally under the control of the national government.

The RCMP is a federal police agency accountable to the Minister of Public Safety. It is responsible for enforcement of federal statutes, national security investigations, security of federal institutions, important persons and foreign missions, and relations with foreign police services. The RCMP is involved in investigating crimes involving drugs, narcotics, organized crime, and cybercrime. In addition to being the federal police agency for all of Canada, in three provinces the RCMP also acts as the provincial police. In 8 of the 10 provinces, the RCMP provides different degrees of policing under paid contract with the provinces. Only in Ontario and Quebec does the RCMP not provide some degree of local policing. The RCMP is the only policing agency serving the Yukon and Northwest Territories, which account for more than one-third of Canada's geographical area.

Since 1886, all basic training of RCMP recruits is conducted at the Depot Division in Regina. The course is 6 months in length and includes a variety of subjects from basic criminal law to driving and shooting. Since 1974, women have been recruited into the force and undergo the same training as male constables. Female members of the force are assigned to the remote northern communities, highway patrols, or desk jobs on the same basis as their male counterparts. Photo 3.6 is a photograph of an early mounted policeman.

Photo 3.6 A Royal Canadian Northwest Mounted Policeman on horseback, Dawson, Yukon Territory, Canada in 1917. (Photo courtesy of the Library of Congress Prints and Photographs Division.)

Police Service in Calgary, Canada

The Calgary Police Service, located in Calgary, Alberta, Canada, is made up of more than 1570 police officers and 803 civilian members. In concert with other agencies and the citizens of Calgary, the Calgary Police Service strives to preserve the quality of life in the community by maintaining Calgary as a safe place to live, work, and visit.

Core Values

All members of the Calgary Police Service are expected to adhere to the core values of the Service, conducting themselves at all times with honesty, integrity, ethics, respect, fairness and compassion, courage and commitment.

Honesty: Tell the truth with candor in a way that is clear and to the point.
Integrity: Display actions and express oneself in a manner consistent with the values of the Service.
Ethics: Consistently align behaviour with the Service's values and goals.

Respect: Treat all people with value and decency. Listen to the views of others and maintain open communication.

Fairness and compassion: Deal with people fairly and in a manner that displays empathy and understanding.

Courage: Take a stand on issues of value and importance to oneself and the Service. Make decisions and take action regardless of the possible consequences, to maintain public safety.

Commitment: Build strong working relationships with members of the Service and the community through open and timely communications. Consistently do what is right, delivering on commitments and recognizing others' talents so as to develop mutual trust.

Mission: "To optimize public safety in the city of Calgary"

The Calgary Police Service, in concert with other agencies and the citizens of Calgary, is instrumental in preserving the quality of life in our community by maintaining Calgary as a secure place in which to live. In so doing, we are dedicated philosophically and operationally to the concept of community-based policing.

The primary focus is on crime prevention, crime detection and apprehension, and traffic safety. The most effective tools are positive community relations, education, problem solving, and the use of current technology to analyze conditions, project trends, and deploy resources.

Guiding Principles

To promote an understanding that the true measure of police effectiveness is the absence of crime and disorder, not the visible evidence of police action in dealing with them.

To secure the cooperation of the public in voluntary observance of laws by encouraging understanding and communication between the citizens of Calgary and their Police Service.

To maximize individual and collective skills within the Service in terms of crime prevention, crime detection, and traffic safety.

To promote a professional police image by demonstrating impartial service to the law and by offering service and friendship to all members of the public without regard to gender, race, religious beliefs, color, ancestry, or place of origin.

To use only the minimum force required on any particular occasion, and only when persuasion, advice, and warning are found to be insufficient to obtain public observance of the law.

To recruit qualified candidates who reflect the diversity of the community.

To provide training, education, and developmental capability within
   the Service that maximizes the potential of all members.
To achieve the foregoing within an acceptable cost framework (Calgary
   Police, 2007).

   Municipal police forces have jurisdiction over the most heavily populated areas (e.g., Metropolitan Toronto), utilize the largest amount of police
resources, and are comprised of city, village, county, and township police
forces. Most forces are organized along lines similar to the Ottawa municipal
police force (highest to lowest): attorney general, chief of police, and three
deputy chiefs—of field operations (traffic and patrol), of staff operations
(investigations), and of administration and staff services. The provinces,
by law, must financially support municipal police forces. Municipal police
force enforce all laws relating to their area of jurisdiction, which includes the
Criminal Code, provincial statutes, the bylaws of the municipality and (in
recent years) certain federal statutes, such as the Narcotic Control Act and
the Food and Drugs Act (Kurian, 1989).
   Police services can be contracted out on the municipal level as well. For
instance, various cities and towns may contract with the provincial police or
the RCMP, which acts as provincial police in eight provinces, in lieu of establishing their own municipal police. In cases where the RCMP is contracted
out to a municipality, the unit is accountable to the municipal chief executive
(Kurian, 1989).
   Provincial policing is largely decentralized. Ontario and Quebec are currently the only provinces that operate their own provincial police. Generally,
their duties cover those geographic areas not already covered by the municipal police, although there are continuous exchanges of information between
the two agencies.
   The Ontario Provincial Police is headed by the Ontario Provincial Police
Commissioner, who is supervised by the Solicitor General. The commissioner oversees three separate department heads: the provincial commander
of field operations, the provincial commander of services, and the provincial
commander of investigations.
   Other types of policing agencies include: the RCMP Marine Services, the
Air Section of the RCMP, the Canadian Pacific Railway Police, the Canadian
National Railway Police, and the National Harbors Board Police. Although
the Department of National Revenue, the Department of Justice, the Post
Office Department, and the Immigration Service primarily have only investigative powers, they may collaborate with the RCMP in law enforcement
efforts.
   Policing in the First People's (Canadian Native) Reserves is determined
by their governing bodies, and they may contract with other agencies for
policing services or establish their own. The Canadian national government

contributes about 58% of the cost of providing police services to the reserves and the local reserve pays the remaining portion.

Except for the RCMP, most Canadian police officers are members of a labor union. The Canadian police unions tend to be politically conservative and support tougher laws, sentencing, and punishment.

The Canadian police have arrest and search and seizure powers very similar to those possessed by English and U.S. police officers. The Charter of Rights and Freedoms prescribes the circumstances under which the powers may be exercised.

RCMP's Approach to Policing in Canada

The Royal Canadian Mounted Police is the Canadian national police service and an agency of the Ministry of Public Safety Canada.

The RCMP is unique in the world since it is a national, federal, provincial, and municipal policing body. They provide a total federal policing service to all Canadians and policing services under contract to the three territories, eight provinces (except Ontario and Quebec), more than 200 municipalities, 165 Aboriginal communities, three international airports and numerous smaller airports. RCMP's approach to policing:

- Police services based on the community policing philosophy.
- Communities help police recognize, develop, and determine community policing needs.
- They are also active partners in many of the principal police tasks, such as crime prevention services, operational support, and enforcement. (Royal Canadian Mounted Police, 2007)

The purpose of the RCMP's Cadet Training Program (CTP) is to provide cadets with a clear understanding of their roles and responsibilities in Canadian society and to enable them to realize and further the objectives of community policing. The CTP is based on principles of adult learning and community policing. It revolves around a system that teaches cadets to focus on the client's perspective in any given situation.

Cadets are responsible to a large extent for their own learning and development. They are required to seek out appropriate information, resolve problems in consultation with partners, and ensure continuous assessment and improvement of work practices. Assignments and training activities are completed individually and in groups.

Training is delivered using a variety of methods, such as scenario training (problem-solving exercises), role play, lectures, panel discussions, research, presentations, and community interaction. The emphasis is on lifelike scenarios. In 1996, a model detachment was constructed at Depot to simulate a realistic work environment and to enable cadets to develop skills in an operational context.

Since 2002, the average age of RCMP recruits has been at least 27. The Depot will train approximately 1020 cadets per year. The Depot is a designated postsecondary institution, so cadets can qualify for an education credit on their income tax (RCMP website: http://www.rcmp-grc.gc.ca/ccaps/ contract_e.htm, accessed May 31, 2007).

Corrections in Common Law Countries

Garland (2001) contends that sentencing differences between countries tell us something about the position and perception of offenders in the various countries. According to him, differences in sentencing practices are likely to reveal information regarding countries' visions of social inclusion and social control. If Garland is correct, what does this reveal to us regarding the differences in visions of social inclusion and social control between the United States and England, or Canada, one of the closest neighbors of the United States? As will be discussed later in this chapter, there are significant differences in rates of incarceration between the United States and the other two common law countries, England and Canada.

The ultimate purpose of criminal sanctions is generally considered to be the maintenance of social order. Herbert Packer (1968) contends that the two major goals of criminal sanctions are to inflict suffering upon the wrongdoers and to prevent crime. Robert Dawson (1969) writes that the major purpose of the criminal justice system is to identify, in a legally acceptable manner, those persons who should be subjected to control and treatment in the correctional process. According to Dawson, if the corrections system does not properly perform its task, the entire criminal justice system suffers. An inefficient or unfair correctional process can nullify the courts, prosecutors, and police alike. Conversely, the manner in which the other agencies involved perform their tasks has an important impact on the success of the process: a person who has been unfairly dealt with prior to conviction is a poor subject for rehabilitation.

The four common goals of criminal sanctions are retribution, deterrence, incapacitation, and rehabilitation. Retribution generally means "getting even." Retribution is based on the belief that the criminal is an enemy of society and deserves severe punishment for willfully breaking its rules. Retribution is often mistaken for revenge. There are, however, important differences between the two. Both retribution and revenge are primarily concerned with punishing the offender, and neither is overly concerned with the impact of the punishment on the offender's future behavior or the behavior of others. Unlike revenge, however, retribution attempts to match the severity of the punishment to the seriousness of the crime. Revenge acts on passion, whereas retribution follows specific rules regarding the types and amounts of punishment that may be inflicted.

Retribution is also referred to as "just deserts." The just deserts movement reflects the retribution viewpoint and provides a justifiable rationale for support of the death penalty (discussed later in this chapter). This viewpoint has its roots in a societal need for retribution. It can be traced back to the individual need for retaliation and vengeance. The transfer of the vengeance motive from the individual to the state has been justified based on theories involving theological, aesthetic, and expiatory views. According to the theological view, retaliation fulfills the religious mandate to punish the sinner. Under the aesthetic view, punishment helps reestablish a sense of harmony through requital and thus resolves the social discord created by the crime. The expiatory view is that guilt must be washed away, or cleansed, through suffering. There is even a utilitarian view that punishment is the means of achieving beneficial and social consequences through the application of a specific form and degree of punishment deemed most appropriate to the particular offender after careful, individualized study of the offender.

Deterrence is a punishment viewpoint that focuses on future outcomes rather than past misconduct. It is also based on the theory that creating a fear of future punishment will deter crime. There is substantial debate over the validity of this concept. Specific deterrence works only on the offender, whereas general deterrence works on others who might consider similar acts. According to this viewpoint, the fear of future suffering motivates individuals to avoid involvement in criminal misconduct. This concept assumes that the criminal is a rational being who will weigh the consequences of his or her criminal actions before deciding to commit them.

One of the problems with deterrence is determining the appropriate magnitude and nature of punishment to be imposed in order to deter future criminal misconduct. For example, an individual who commits assault and then feels bad about the act may need only slight punishment to achieve deterrent effects, whereas a professional shoplifter may need severe, fear-producing punishments to prevent future shoplifting.

Incapacitation is the idea that we incarcerate offenders for a period of time to protect society from a particular threat. At least while the prisoner is in confinement, he is unlikely to commit crimes on innocent persons outside of prison. To this extent, confinement clearly helps reduce criminal behavior outside of prison. Under this incapacitation viewpoint, there is no hope for the individual's rehabilitation; therefore, the only solution is to incapacitate the offender.

There are two variations of the incapacitation viewpoint. Collective incapacitation refers to sanctions imposed on those who commit a certain offense without regard to their personal characteristics. Selective incapacitation refers to the incapacitation of certain groups of individuals who have been identified as high-risk offenders, such as robbers with a history of drug use. Under selective incapacitation, offenders with certain characteristics or history would receive longer prison terms than others convicted of the same crime. The purpose of incapacitation is to prevent future crimes, and the moral concerns associated with retribution are not as important as the reduction of future victimization. An early English prison is shown in Photo 3.7.

The rehabilitation approach pronounces that punishment should be directed toward correcting the offender. This approach is also called the "treatment" approach. This approach considers that criminal misconduct is a manifestation of a pathology that can be ameliorated by some form of therapeutic activity. While this viewpoint may consider the offender "sick," it is not the same as a medical approach. Under the rehabilitation viewpoint, we need to teach offenders to recognize the undesirability of their criminal behavior and make significant efforts to rid themselves of that behavior. The main difference between the rehabilitation approach and the retribution approach is that under the rehabilitation approach offenders are assigned to programs designed to prepare them for readjustment or reintegration into the community, whereas the latter approach is more concerned with the punishment aspects of the sentence.

Photo 3.7 A photograph of a British prison in Portland, England in 1900. (Photo courtesy of the Library of Congress Prints and Photographs Division.)

Sentencing under Common Law Model

In no other area of the U.S. justice system is there greater variation among states than in the sentencing phase of justice proceedings. If a defendant is tried for more than one offense, or if he is presently serving a sentence for another crime, it is important to question if the sentences for each offense will be served consecutively or concurrently. In a consecutive sentence, one sentence must be served before the other begins. Concurrent sentences are served at the same time—concurrently.

On conviction of a misdemeanor, the statutes of most states provide that the penalty imposed shall not exceed 1 year imprisonment in a jail and/or a fine. Generally, for a felony, the defendant may be imprisoned for more than a year. In the majority of states, it is the prerogative of the judge to impose sentence. In some states, like Texas, the defendant may elect to be sentenced by a jury.

To assist judges in attempting to arrive at an equitable sentence and to more nearly make the sentence fit the crime and offender, most states provide for a presentence investigation (PSI) in felony cases. The PSI is usually conducted by a staff member of the probation department. The investigation generally includes such matters as the offender's family status, educational background, work experience, and prior criminal record. Often the PSI will report the defendant's attitude toward the crime, and whether the offender is remorseful over having committed the crime or is only unhappy about being caught.

In 2012, 68% of all U.S. convicted felons were sentenced to a period of confinement—42% in state prisons and 28% in local jails. Jail sentences are for short-term confinement (usually for a year or less) in a county or city facility, while prison sentences are for long-term confinement (usually for over a year) in a state facility. An estimated 31% of all convicted felons were sentenced to probation with no jail or prison time to serve. Over 90% of all convictions for murder and nonnegligent manslaughter resulted in a prison sentence, as did a majority of felony convictions for sexual assault (59%) and robbery (71%).

An offender convicted of multiple offenses receives a sentence for each offense. If multiple prison sentences are imposed, the court then decides whether the convicted felon will serve the sentences concurrently (at the same time) or consecutively (one after another). For persons with consecutive sentences, the total time is the sum of the sentence lengths, and for persons with concurrent sentences, the total time is the same as the longest sentence. For persons convicted of a single offense, the total time refers simply to the sentence for that offense.

Whenever an offender receives a prison sentence range, such as 5–10 years, the total time refers to the maximum amount of time. For the

United States in 2015, the mean felony sentence incarceration (prison or jail) was 3 years; the median was 1 year and 7 months. The mean length of sentences to state prison was 4 years and 5 months; the median term was 3 years.

The mean prison sentence for murder and nonnegligent manslaughter was 18 years and 9 months; the median was 20 years. Life sentences are rare among convicted felons, whether measured as a percentage of all sentences (0.5%) or as a percentage of prison sentences (1.1%). However, among the 8990 persons convicted of murder or nonnegligent manslaughter, 24.1% were sentenced to life in prison. Not all 8990 persons convicted of murder or nonnegligent manslaughter were subjected to the death penalty. Thirteen U.S. states did not authorize the death penalty in 2015. In the 37 states that did, only certain types of murder were capital offenses.

The amount of time felons actually serve in prison in the United States is typically some fraction of the total sentence received. Two primary reasons explain the difference between sentences received and time served. In states that impose indeterminate sentences, a judge specifies the minimum and/or maximum sentence length, but a parole board decides when the prisoner will actually be released. In 2015, about a quarter of prison releases were determined by a parole board decision.

In most but not all states, prisoners gain early release through time credits that they receive automatically or that are granted to them for good behavior or special achievements—provisions that are intended to help correctional officials manage institutional populations. For both types of sentence reduction, released offenders usually serve the remaining portion of their sentences under supervision in the community.

The median time from arrest to state court sentencing in 2005 was about 6 months. In 2002, 7% of all convicted felons in state courts were sentenced within the first 30 days following their arrest, and 49% of felons were sentenced within 6 months. An estimated 78% of convicted felons were sentenced within 1 year of arrest.

On average, murder cases took the most time to process in 2005. Fewer than half (42%) of all felons convicted of murder in state courts were sentenced within 1 year of their arrest. Guilty pleas accounted for 95% of all felony convictions, and trials accounted for the remaining 5% (U.S. Department of Justice, Bureau of Justice Statistics Bulletin, Felony sentences in state courts, January 2012).

U.S. Prison Population

In 2015, the United States had roughly 5% of the world's population but was home to approximately 25% of the world's inmates. In 2015, there were roughly 2.4 million inmates in state and federal prisons in the United States. The annual cost to confine these prisoners exceeds

$80 billion per year. About 40% of the inmate population are African American. Only about 17% of the U.S. inmate population are incarcerated for drug offenses. Even if all of them were released, the United States would still have the highest rate of incarceration per 100,000 population.

Source: "Briefing: Opening the prison doors," *The Week Magazine*, April 24, 2015, p. 11.

Differences between United Kingdom and Wales

Sentencing in the United Kingdom is more uniform and is regulated by the Ministry of Justice, which was established in May 2007 as part of the English government's drive to reform courts, prisons, and the probation service. The Ministry of Justice (MoJ) is responsible for criminal law and sentencing, for reducing reoffending, and for prisons and probation. The MoJ also encompasses the responsibilities of the former Department for Constitutional Affairs (DCA), overseeing the Magistrates' Courts, the Crown Court, the Appeals Courts, and the Legal Services Commission.

When an English offender is convicted following a trial or guilty plea, the court has a range of sentencing options available. These depend on the type, the seriousness, and the circumstances of the crime and the maximum penalty available by law. The judge or magistrate giving the sentence must consider punishing the offender, reducing crime, rehabilitating the offender, protecting the public, and having the offender make reparation. The sentence will be a combination of these aims. All offenses have a maximum penalty set out in law, and a limited number of crimes have a minimum sentence, as follows:

- A mandatory life sentence for murder.
- An automatic life sentence for a second serious sexual or violent offense (there is a list of qualifying offenses, all of which have a maximum penalty of life). For offenses committed after April 4, 2005, this penalty has been replaced with new public protection sentences.
- A minimum 7-year prison sentence for third-time trafficking in Class A drugs. This provision applies to importation, production, supplying and possession with intent to supply Class A drugs. The maximum penalty for these offenses is life imprisonment.
- A minimum 3-year prison sentence for third-time domestic burglary. The maximum penalty for burglary is 14 years' imprisonment.
- A minimum 5-year prison sentence for possession or distribution of prohibited weapons or ammunition. The maximum penalty is 10 years imprisonment.

Magistrates' and Crown Courts have different sentencing powers. The serious cases are sentenced in the Crown Court and less serious offenses are sentenced in the Magistrates' Court. When deciding upon the appropriate sentence, courts have guidelines to assist them. The Sentencing Guidelines Council, created in 2004, has responsibility for producing guidelines for use in all criminal courts. Any guidelines that are issued by the Council must be followed or reasons must be given by the judges or magistrates if they depart from them.

Sentencing in the United Kingdom

For the most serious offenses, a court may impose a prison, or custodial sentence. The length of sentence imposed by the court will be limited by the maximum penalty for that crime. The sentence imposed by the court represents the maximum amount of time that the offender will remain in custody.

Under English law, a custodial sentence can only be imposed if (1) the offense is so serious that neither a fine alone nor a community sentence can be justified for the offense; or if the offender refuses to comply with the requirements of a community order; or if the offender is convicted of a specified sexual or violent offense under the Dangerous Offender provisions under Criminal Justice Act 2003 and the court finds that the offender poses a risk of harm to the public.

The United Kingdom modified its release regulations in April 2005, and now prisoners serving standard determinate custodial sentences of 12 months or more will serve half of the sentence in custody and the second half on license (i.e., parole) in the community. During the period of license, offenders may be recalled into custody if they commit a further offense or break the conditions of their license. For those offenders assessed as "dangerous" and serving indeterminate or extended sentences for public protection, the regulations provide that these offenders are not released from prison until and unless their level of risk to the public is assessed by the Parole Board as manageable in the community. If the risk is not reduced to a safe level, they may never be released.

Confinement

Rates of Incarceration

With the exception of the United States, the majority of countries using the common law legal model have relatively low rates of confinement. The rate of incarceration in prison and jail in the United States on December 31, 2004 was 724 inmates per 100,000 residents, up from 601 in 1995. At year's end in 2004, one in every 138 U.S. residents was incarcerated in a state or federal prison or a local jail (U.S. Department of Justice, Office of Justice

Programs, Bureau of Justice Statistics Bulletin "Prisoners in 2004," October 2005, NCJ 210677). Of the major industrialized countries, the United States has the highest rates of incarceration. In 2004, the United Kingdom had an incarceration rate of about 141 inmates per 100,000 residents, compared to Ireland's rate of 76. Canada's rate in 2004 was about 108 inmates per 100,000 (International Centre for Prison Studies, 2007).

Approaches to Confinement in the United States

The United States has used various approaches to justify the confinement of criminals. The idea of rehabilitation started with the reformatory era in the 1870s. At first, rehabilitation was not viewed in explicit medical terms. Later, in early 1900s, prisons began to incorporate medical advances into corrections, and by the 1960s correctional programs began to take a genuine medical approach to corrections. When the Federal Bureau of Prisons was created in the 1930s, the classification of prisoners became more refined and the medical model provided a state-of-the-art clinical orientation by developing diagnostic and treatment methods.

By the 1960s, treatment or rehabilitation was clearly the dominant approach. This changed in the late 1970s. Since then, the United States in general has used a punishment approach or one of incapacitation. If there is a dominant philosophy today in the United States, it is one of incapacitation. One of the problems in the United States in determining the approach to punishment is the fact that under the federalist form of government, each state, subject to the restrictions set forth in the U.S. Constitution and federal court cases interpreting the Constitution, sets its own goals and approaches.

California Penal Code, Section 1170(a)

The Legislature finds and declares that the purpose of imprisonment for crime is punishment. This purpose is best served by terms proportionate to the seriousness of the offense with provisions for uniformity in the sentences of offenders committing the same offense under similar circumstances.

English Purposes of Confinement

The United States is not the only country that has had problems determining the proper purposes of punishment. It appears that most other countries have the same problem. An examination of the English Statement of Purposes (EPS), quoted in the following, indicates that the English have similar problems. The EPS declares that it "serves the public by keeping in custody those committed by the courts," and that its duty is to "look after them with humanity and help them lead law-abiding and useful lives in custody and after release." The purposes are divided into a series of goals:

- To keep prisoners in custody
- To maintain order, control, discipline, and a safe environment
- To provide decent conditions for prisoners and meet their needs, including health care
- To provide positive regimes to help prisoners address their offending behavior
- To allow prisoners as full and responsible a life as possible
- To help prisoners prepare for their return to the community (Morris and Rothman, 1995, p. xi)

Case Study: Confinement in Ireland

O'Sullivan and O'Donnell (2007) conducted a study of coercive confinement in Ireland. The authors concluded that between 1951 and 2002, the rate of coercive confinement in Ireland was radically reduced. "Coercive confinement" is defined not only as formal sites of incarceration associated with the criminal justice system, but also psychiatric hospitals, homes for unmarried mothers, and the various residential institutions for children placed by the courts.

Four main observations were noteworthy regarding confinement rates in 1951 versus 2002: (1) the massive downsizing of the confined population from more than 31,000 to fewer than 5,000; (2) the narrowing in the range of institutional sites; (3) the changing gender balance of those held in coercive confinement from primarily female to primarily male; and (4) the increasingly dominant role of the state. The decline in the use of coercive confinement stands in sharp contrast to what has occurred in other nations and cannot be attributed either to a fiscal crisis or to a shift in regulatory tactics. The authors argue that the most likely reason for the decline in the coercively confined population in Ireland is the diminishing supply of potential deviants. A shift occurred between 1951 and 2002 in the extent to which institutional confinement was seen as an acceptable response to poverty or sexually transmitted diseases. The authors refer to this shift as a waning in the culture of control. In analyzing the shift away from punitive policies in Ireland, the authors specifically compared the state of coercive confinement in 1951 to that of 2002 for three main reasons: (1) these dates mark high and low points in the use of imprisonment; (2) they were census years, so reliable demographic information about the population was available; and (3) it was possible to obtain population counts for all of the sites of institutional confinement for these 2 years.

Prisons Ombudsman

The English prison system has an ombudsman who is appointed by the Home Secretary and is an independent point of appeal for prisoners and those supervised by the Probation Service. For the purpose of investigations, the ombudsman has full access to Prison Service information, documents, establishments, and individuals, including classified material and information provided to the Prison Service by other organizations, such as the police. For medical records, the prisoner's consent is required for disclosure. England also has a chief inspector of prisons. This officer is independent of the Prison Service and reports directly to the Home Secretary on the treatment of prisoners, the conditions of prisons in England and Wales, and such other matters as the Home Secretary may require.

In the United States, because of the federalist form of government, state prisons are regulated by the state governments. Accordingly, there is no central ombudsman. The federal courts, especially the U.S. Supreme Court, have been active in overseeing the status of prisoners in state institutions based on the concept that the treatment and care of state prisoners are protected by the U.S. Constitution's Eighth and Fourteenth Amendments.

Universal Declaration of Human Rights, Article 5

No one shall be subjected to torture or to cruel, inhuman or degrading treatment or punishment. (United Nations Department of Public Information)

The Universal Declaration of Human Rights is not a treaty; but it has an effect similar to a treaty. It is a declaration adopted by the General Assembly of the United Nations "as a common standard of achievement for all peoples and all nations." (See the Universal Declaration of Human Rights; Restatement [Third] of Foreign Relations Law § 701, Reporter's Note 6 ["The Declaration has become the accepted general articulation of recognized rights"], and *Beharry v. Reno*, 183 F. Supp. 2d 584 [E.D.N.Y. 2002].)

Alternatives to Incarceration

Probably the search for alternatives to confinement started with the first wholesale use of confinement. As will be noted in later chapters, the search for alternatives was intense in Europe in the later part of the nineteenth century. As noted by Franz von Liszt, a prominent German criminologist in the 1880s: "The short prison sentence in its present form is worthless, indeed, it does not improve, it contaminates" (quoted in Kalmthout and Tak, 1988, p. 3). Both the Council of Europe and the United Nations have promulgated resolutions promoting the use of alternatives to incarceration (Dammer and Fairchild, 2006, p. 240). Popular alternatives to confinement include fines, forfeitures, restitution, community service, probation, and house arrest.

Corporal Punishment

The use of corporal punishment in the common law countries has basically disappeared. This does not mean that prisoners no longer are mistreated or abused. It means that as a court-ordered punishment, none of the common law countries presently authorize it. In 1994, the American public was outraged because a young American traveler was sentenced to caning in Singapore. He received four lashes for defacing automobiles and other acts of vandalism.

Fines

A fine is a monetary penalty imposed generally on the conviction of minor offense. Fines as the sole punishment are more popular in Japan and Western Europe than in the United States. One problem with the use of fines in the United States is the constitutional prohibition against confining a person for the failure to pay a debt. The U.S. Supreme Court held in *Williams v. Illinois*, 399 U.S. 235 (1970), that imprisoning a defendant who was indigent and unable to pay a fine was a violation of the Equal Protection Clause of the U.S. Constitution. Fines are used in 95% of the criminal cases in Japan and in about 85% of the cases in Western Europe.

Probation

Probation can be traced to the common law practice of "judicial reprieve." Under judicial reprieve, a judge would suspend punishment so that convicted persons could demonstrate that they had reformed their behavior. The practice of "recognizance" was also used to enable offenders to remain free if they agreed to pay the state a sum of money in lieu of punishment. Often the debt was structured so that the defendant was required to pay it only if he or she was determined to be engaged in subsequent criminal conduct. In some cases, before the judge would accept the defendant's recognizance contract, sureties were required. The sureties (persons other than the defendant) were responsible for the behavior of the defendant after release.

Probation generally involves replacing a part of a defendant's sentence of confinement with a conditional release. Probation is essentially a contract between the defendant and the court. If the probationer complies with certain orders of the court (conditions of probation), the court will not require the defendant to serve a certain sentence (normally a sentence to confinement). If the defendant later violates the terms of the contract, the court is no longer restricted by the contract and may sentence the defendant to serve a stated punishment.

Probation in England

For many years, probation was supervised by 54 autonomous local services. The National Probation Service (NPS) was created in 2001 to supervise probation in the United Kingdom. Under the Criminal and Court Services Act (2000), NPS also has a statutory duty to offer contact, consult, and notify victims about important aspects of release arrangements of offenders convicted of a sexual or violent offense leading to a sentence of 12 months or more in custody.

Each year the probation service supervises some 175,000 new offenders. The caseload on any given day is in excess of 200,000. Approximately 90% are male and 10% are female. Just over one-quarter of offenders serving community sentences are aged 16–20 years, and just less than three-quarters are aged 21 years and over. Approximately 70% of offenders supervised will be on community sentences, and 30% imprisoned with a period of statutory license supervision in the community as an integral part of the sentence.

The NPS combines continuous assessment and management of risk and dangerousness with the provision of expert supervision programmers designed to reduce reoffending. Enforcement of the order/license conditions is a priority. Each year the NPS assists magistrates and judges in their sentencing decisions through the provision of about 246,000 presentence reports and 20,000 bail information reports. The probation service staff finds and supervises some 8 million hours of unpaid work by offenders in local communities, to ensure that they meet the requirements of their community punishment orders.

Probation in the United States

The probation system in the United States also varies by state. In some states, defendants at the time they are placed on probation are informed as to the terms of the sentence being probated. For example, a defendant may be sentenced to prison for a term of 3 years, with the actual serving of the time probated for 5 years. If the defendant stays out of trouble for 5 years, then the sentence is never served. If the defendant's probation is revoked, then the defendant serves 3 years from the time the probation was revoked. In other states, the defendant is placed on probation for a certain period of time.

If the probation is revoked, then the defendant receives a sentence the length of which is determined at a sentencing hearing after the probation is revoked.

Probation is the most popular sentence given in felony cases in the United States. In some states, the juries may recommend probation. However, even in those states where the juries may decide the punishment (e.g., Texas), only the judge may grant probation. Most states have restrictions on the granting of probation for certain serious crimes. In addition, it appears that the death penalty may not be probated. This is based on the fact that the death penalty is limited to those cases where the defendant is beyond rehabilitation. The length of the probation period may vary. A 5-year period appears to be a common one for felony cases. In fact, the Federal Criminal Code recommends that federal probation periods last for 5 years.

In some cases, the judge grants probation only if the defendant agrees to serve a period of local time (in a jail). For example, one judge as a matter of policy will not grant probation in felony cases unless the accused does at least 30 days' time in the local jail. This practice is known as "split sentencing."

"Shock probation" is frequently used in the case of first-time offenders. In these cases, the judge grants probation only after the accused has sampled prison life. Shock probation is designed to give defendants a "taste of the bars" before placing them on probation. Evaluations of shock probation have indicated that its rate of effectiveness may be as high as 78%. Critics of shock probation claim that even a brief period of incarceration can reduce the effectiveness of probation, which is designed to provide the offender with nonstigmatized, community-based treatment.

There are approximately 1900 probation agencies in the United States. About half are associated with a state-level agency and the remainder with county or city governments. Approximately 30 states have combined probation and parole agencies. While prison populations have been increasing at a rapid rate in the past 20 years, it appears that the number of persons on probation has been increasing at an even faster rate. On any given day, there are approximately 1.8 million individuals in the United States on probation. One of the reasons for the popularity of probation is its low cost.

Standard Probation Rules for the State of Texas (Texas Code of Criminal Procedure, Article 42.12)

1. Commit no offense against the laws of the state of Texas or of any other state or of the United States.
2. Avoid injurious or vicious habits.
3. Avoid persons or places of disreputable or harmful character.

4. Report to the probation officer as directed.
5. Permit the probation officer to visit him at his home or elsewhere.
6. Work faithfully at suitable employment as far as possible.
7. Remain within the county unless travel outside the county is approved by probation officer.
8. Pay any fines imposed and make restitution or reparation in any sum that the Court deems proper.
9. Support your dependents.
10. Participate in any community-based program as directed by the court or probation officer.
11. Reimburse the county for any compensation paid to appointed defense counsel.
12. Compensate the victim for any property damage or medical expense sustained by the victim as a direct result of the commission of the offense.

In the United States, as a general rule, there is a probation office for each felony court. In large urban areas, the probation offices of several courts may be merged into one office. The individual in charge of a probation office is normally called the chief probation officer (CPO). The duties of the CPO are to carry out policy and to supervise the probation officers. Probation officers (POs) are generally charged with four primary tasks: investigations, intake, diagnosis, and treatment supervision.

The investigation functions are usually related to the presentence investigation that the court uses in deciding on the appropriate sentence. The intake task refers to the process by which probation officers interview individuals regarding cases that have been scheduled in court for the initial appearance. Intake is normally used only in minor cases and is directed toward the possibility that the case may be settled without further court action.

House Arrest

Electronic surveillance technology was first developed in the mid-1960s. It was not used with offenders in the United States until the 1980s. Since then, however, it has developed into one of the most popular intermediate sanctions in that country. It is estimated that more than 1 million persons in the United States will ultimately be placed on some form of electronic monitoring.

Not only is the number of offenders placed on electronic monitoring house arrest increasing, but the types of offenders are becoming more diverse. At first, it was used for offenders awaiting trial or sentencing and offenders released from institutional correctional facilities. In addition, it was often used first for property offenders. The growing popularity of electronic monitoring has been due in large measure to the increasing demand to effectively supervise offenders and protect the communities. Public support in the United States for the use of monitoring as an alternative to imprisonment is probably based on public knowledge of the high cost of incarceration.

Death Penalty

The United States is the only major Western country where the death penalty is widely used. Both the United Kingdom and Canada's laws do not provide for the death penalty. In the United States, it varies considerably by states. Nineteen states have abolished it. Most of these are located in the northern part of the United States. The most recent include Nebraska (2015), Maryland (2013), Connecticut (2012), Illinois (2011), New Mexico (2009), New Jersey (2009), and New York (2007). The strongest support for the death penalty in the United States is found in Texas, Oklahoma, and the Southeast. The federal government also has a death penalty statute. As noted later, in the exercise of the death penalty the states are restrained by the U.S. Supreme Court's interpretation of the U.S. Constitution.

The death penalty is a controversial one. Heated arguments have taken place over the years concerning its merits. Many contend that there is no place in a civilized society for the death penalty. They also argue that it does not act as a deterrent. Some opponents state that it is in violation of the Eighth Amendment because it is cruel and unusual. Proponents contend that it is a deterrent and as such it should be retained. One major problem with the death penalty is the long delay between the imposition of the penalty and the execution.

The Supreme Court in *Furman v. Georgia* (408 U.S. 238 [1972]) stated that the death penalty as such was not cruel and unusual punishment, but the discriminatory manner in which it was applied made it cruel and unusual and thus in violation of the Eighth Amendment. Later, the opinion in *Woodson v. North Carolina* (428 U.S. 280 [1976]) held that a statute that made the death penalty mandatory on conviction for certain offenses was unconstitutional because it did not allow any consideration to be given to the character and record of the offender. The Supreme Court stated: "Consideration of both the offender and the offense in order to arrive at a just and appropriate sentence has been viewed as progressive and humanizing development."

In *Gregg v. Georgia* (428 U.S. 153 [1976]), a Georgia statute that allowed the judge or jury to take into consideration aggravating and mitigating circumstances in imposing the alternative sentences of life imprisonment or death was considered constitutional. As required by *Woodson,* alternative sentencing procedure must be used in death penalty cases. Now in a few states that have the death penalty, a trial is first held to determine the guilt or innocence of the accused. If the accused is found guilty, a second trial is held to determine whether the death penalty should be imposed or whether the defendant should be given life imprisonment. In other states with the death penalty, only one trial is held. The jury first deliberates on the guilt or innocence of the defendant. If the defendant is found guilty, then the same jury deliberates on the penalty to be imposed. Under each method during the sentencing phase, the jury or judge must consider both the aggravating and mitigating circumstances of the case.

The *Gregg* case upheld the death penalty for first-degree murder with aggravating circumstances. The Supreme Court in *Coker v. Georgia* (433 U.S. 584 [1977]) held that the death penalty for the rape of an adult woman was excessive and disproportionate to the crime. In *Godfrey v. Georgia* (446 U.S. 420 [1980]), the Supreme Court held that the death penalty amounted to cruel and unusual punishment when pronounced on the defendant. The Georgia statute in question provided that the death penalty could be imposed where the offense of murder was "outrageously or wantonly vile, horrible, or inhuman." The Court held that while the evidence established that the defendant shot both victims in the head with a shotgun and that they died instantly, there was no evidence of serious suffering by the victims or that the crime was outrageously or wantonly vile, horrible, or inhuman. In *Enmund v. Florida* (458 U.S. 782 [1982]), Enmund and two other defendants entered into a conspiracy to rob a victim of money. The three went to the home of the victim. Enmund remained in the car while the other two went into the house to rob the victim. The victim's wife pulled a weapon and shot one of the defendants. The other defendant killed the victim and his wife. All three defendants were convicted of first-degree murder and were sentenced to death. Enmund appealed the death sentence on the grounds that, under the circumstances, the sentence of death was cruel and unusual. He alleged that he did not participate in the actual killing and had no intent to kill during the robbery. The Supreme Court agreed and set aside the death penalty in his case. Accordingly, it appears that the U.S. Supreme Court will approve the death penalty only in those cases involving first-degree murder with aggravating circumstances.

In the United States, there are many state and federal prisons.

Summary

- "Police" refers to that function of the government that is charged with the preservation of public order and tranquility, the promotion of public health, safety and morals, and the prevention, detection, and punishment of crimes.
- Dammer and Fairchild classify police duties into two major tasks, deviance control and civil order control.
- There are four models of policing: the civil police model, state police model, quasi-military model, and martial law model.
- The structure of U.S. policing has its roots in the English system. Its structure can be divided into three levels: local, state, and federal.
- Traditionally local police departments in the United States focus on crime control, whereas English police focus on keeping the peace.
- Local policing in England and Wales is fragmented, with a distrust of a strong state police system.
- The training of local police in the United States is not uniform in either content or the number of hours required for certifying a police officer. The rules regarding police discretion are very similar in the United States and England.
- Both the United States and England have adopted community policing concepts.
- In Canada, the provinces have jurisdiction over the administration of justice in each province.
- About 27% of Canadian police are in the Royal Canadian Mounted Police. In Canada, municipal police forces have jurisdiction over the most heavily populated areas of Canada.
- The differences in sentencing practices of nations tell us a lot about the nations.
- In the United States, in no other area of the justice system is there greater variation among the states than in the sentencing phase of justice proceedings. Sentencing in the United Kingdom is more uniform and is regulated by the Ministry of Justice.
- Confinement rates in the United States are among the highest in the world. The use of corporal punishment has basically disappeared in common law countries.
- Common law countries rely heavily on the use of probation as an alternative to confinement.
- The only major common law country that retains the death penalty is the United States, and there it is not used in many states.

Questions in Review

1. What are the key differences when the police in New York City are compared to London?
2. How are the Canadian police organized?
3. Why could it be said that sentencing is more uniform in England than in the United States?
4. Should the United States retain the death penalty?
5. How is probation administered in the United States?

Civil Law Model
The Courts

4

Chapter Objectives

After studying this chapter, you should understand or be able to explain the following issues and concepts:

- The principles involved in the civil law model
- The role of canon law in the development of the civil law model
- The importance of the historical school of jurisprudence
- The role of the principle of territoriality in civil law
- The influence of Roman law
- The sources of civil law
- The development of the Napoleonic Code
- German legal science
- How civil law uses the inquisitorial system

Key Terms

Canon law: The body of law and procedure developed by the Roman Catholic Church.

Codification: The grouping of laws on a particular subject into a systematic order or arrangement.

Commercial law: The body of law and procedure developed by merchants for the regulation of trade.

Decretal letter: A reply in writing by the pope to a particular question of church discipline that has been referred to him.

Historical school of jurisprudence: A school of jurisprudence that advocated the analyzing of laws based on their historical origins and modes of transformation.

Principle of territoriality: The concept that before a nation has jurisdiction over an individual for his or her conduct, there must be some territorial connection with the nation.

Introduction

In this chapter, the civil law model is examined with an emphasis on the courts. In Chapter 5, policing and corrections under the civil law model will be examined. The civil law model of justice is the oldest and most widely distributed form of justice. Unlike the common law model, the sources of civil law cannot be traced to a single source. The three principal sources of civil law are Roman civil law, canon law, and commercial law. In most civil law jurisdictions, the law is modeled into five basic codes: the civil code, commercial code, code of civil procedure, penal code, and code of criminal procedure.

There are many legal systems that fit under the civil law model, and each has its own originality. It should also be noted that in many systems, the civil law model has suffered encroachment by common law traditions (Opolot, 1980, p. 14). According to Merryman (1985, p. 3), many scholars consider the civil law model to be culturally superior to the common law model and that attitude itself has become part of the civil law tradition.

Two major nations utilizing the civil law model, France and Germany, developed their legal systems under vastly different circumstances. As will be discussed later in this chapter, the French code was based heavily on the ideology that was present during the French Revolution. The French style of codification had little, if any, impact on the development of German law. The German system was based on German legal science that was never adopted in France. The national civil law systems in today's world, while utilizing the civil law model, include a number of national legal systems in Europe, Latin America, Asia, Africa, and the Middle East. It is probably more accurate to state that those national legal systems, while vastly different, have all adopted the prevailing attitude of the civil law model of justice.

Early Tribal and Feudal Laws

Prior to the development of feudal law, tribal law had existed for many generations. There were provincial codes in Sweden as early as the thirteenth century. The codes reflected a relatively uniform body of private law and a static rural community made up of free landowners who lived in villages and were organized into "hundreds." The two basic groups of the community were the "village" and the "kin." When a crime was committed, the family or kinship group, and not the state, was regarded as the injured party. The family had the duty to stone the offender or carry out blood feud. Early German justice was based on tribal rules, also known as folk peace. Other tribes had legal systems that were similar to those of the Swedish and German tribes.

With the development of feudalism in Europe, the concept of protection by kinship groups was replaced by the duty of the lords and bishops to protect the residents of their lands. With grants of land to lords came the responsibility to administer justice and to hold court for the residents.

Early Legislation

The courts with their rights of forfeiture were profitable for the lords (Opolot, 1980, pp. 16–17). As monarchies became more public and looked for more financial support, the courts were inviting targets. In about 1350, Sweden adopted uniform legal codes with separate codes for the boroughs and the countryside. By the sixteenth century, the consent of parliament was required before the king could enact major legislation. A new legal code was enacted in Sweden in 1734 that covered private, criminal, and procedural laws. The new code was more practical in nature, but relied heavily on the medieval traditions. The new pattern of legislation spread throughout Europe until France adopted the Napoleonic Code. The introduction of the Napoleonic Code ended the movement from tribalism to feudalism to monarchy, in which feudal law replaced tribal law and state law replaced feudal law.

Influence of Roman Law

While no single source can be traced to its beginning, scholars commonly use 450 BC as the date of origin for Roman law. That is the supposed date of the publication of the Twelve Tables (see Chapter 1). The civil law model is a composite of several distinct legal traditions, including Roman civil law, canon law, commercial law, and legal science. In AD 528, Emperor Justinian collected the laws of the empire and published them as the Code of Justinian or *Corpus Juris Civilis*.

After the *Corpus Juris Civilis* was published, Justinian forbade any references to the works of jurisconsults. He had included in his code those works that he had approved. He had also forbidden the preparation of any commentaries on the law except those that included in the code. His goal was to abolish all prior law except that included in the *Corpus Juris Civilis*. He also ordered the burning of other documents that discussed the status of law that were based on any book other than his code. His command that there be no commentaries on the law other than his work, however, was not very effective and was widely disregarded during his lifetime (Merryman, 1985, p. 9).

With the fall of the Roman Empire, the *Corpus Juris Civilis* fell into disuse and was replaced by less sophisticated versions of Roman law mixed with the Germanic tribal legal customs of the invaders. This produced what is referred to as "vulgarized" or "barbarized" Roman law and today is of interest primarily to legal historians.

The revival of Roman law is generally thought to have started in Bologna, Italy, late in the eleventh century. There was, however, an earlier revival in the ninth century with the publication, in Greek, of a compilation of law called *Basilica*. While the *Basilica* had less influence than the later Italian revival, it acted as an important source of law in Greece until the adoption of the first Greek civil code after World War II.

As noted in Chapter 1, it was in Bologna that the first modern European university with law as its major study was established. Several other universities with law as their major field of study soon opened in other northern Italian cities. The law studied at the universities was the Corpus *Juris Civilis* of Justinian, not the law as modified by the Germanic invaders. Merryman (1985) contends that there were two major reasons why the universities studied the unmodified works of Justinian. First, the conception of a Holy Roman Empire was very strong. Justinian was thought of as an emperor sanctioned by God; his works were considered imperial legislation, and they had the authority of the pope behind them. Second, the founders of the school saw the original works, which they called "written reason," as far superior to the barbarized compilations that had been used by the Germanic invaders.

Within a short period of time, Bologna and the other northern Italian universities became the legal center for the Western world. Groups of scholars, known as glossators and commentators, produced an immense volume of literature on the law. The works of the glossators and commentators along with the Justinian Code became the basis of a common law of Europe, which was later referred to as *jus commune* by legal historians.

Roman law may be the greatest contribution that Rome made to Western civilization, and the Roman way of thinking has influenced both common and civil law lawyers (Merryman, 1985, pp. 2–4). Even though Roman civil law had an influence on common law, its influence on civil law was more direct and more pervasive.

Alan Watson

According to Alan Watson, an expert on civil law models, what civil law got transferred from Rome to Modern Europe was not a detail body of rules as such but a systems structure. He claims that modern legal systems, including common law and civil law, are inconceivable without the input of a systematic structure.

Source: Samuel, G., *An Introduction to Comparative Law and Theory and Method*, London, UK, Hart Publishing, 2014.

Canon Law

The canon law of the Roman Catholic Church is widely considered to be the second oldest component of the civil law tradition, behind Roman civil law. The church developed a body of law and procedure for its own governance and to regulate the rights and obligations of its members. While Roman civil law was the universal law of the temporal empire, canon law was the universal law of the spiritual domain. Much of canon law reflected legal concepts contained in the Justinian Code (Calvi and Coleman, 2000, p. 23). The primary source of canon law, however, was the various decretal letters, authoritative papal statements concerning controversial points in doctrine or ecclesiastical matters (Reichel, 2005, p. 120).

Concordia Discordantium Canonum

Around 1140, John Gratian, a monk, compiled the *Concordia discordantium canonum* ("Harmony of Contradictory Laws"), later called the *Decretum Gratiani* ("Gratian's Decree"). It was a collection of canon law and also a systematic application of the Scholastic method to all legal material. The *Decretum* dealt with the sources of the law, ordinations, elections, simony, law of procedure, ecclesiastical property, monks, heretics, schismatics, marriage, penance, and sacraments and sacramentals. Although primitive, it provided a foundation for systematic compilation of the legal material by the canonists and for the expansion of canon law. It was the basis for the education in canon law that started in the schools of Bologna, Paris, Orleans, Canterbury, Oxford, and Padua.

The church claimed jurisdiction over the entire life of Christians, and therefore, conflict resulted between the church and the empire's jurisdiction. The conflict reached its apex during the era of Pope Leo I (r. 440–461), and by Pope Gregory's time (590–604) canon law had secured a strong foothold in the legal system of the empire. One reason for the ascendancy of canon law was its flexibility. During that time, canon law operated as a living law and provided a written contemporary system (Reichel, 2005, p. 120). Canon law was also absorbed by the Germanic tribes.

Commercial Law

A third source of civil law, after Roman law and canon law, was commercial law. Some form of commercial law has existed since the start of commerce. The commercial law of Western Europe was developed in Italy about the time of the Crusades. It was during the Crusades that European commerce regained dominance in the Mediterranean countries. Italian merchants formed guilds, and the guilds established rules for the conduct of commercial affairs, the law of merchants. The Italian cities of Amalfi, Genoa, Pisa, and Venice became commercial centers and were influential in the development of commercial law. Unlike Roman and canon law, which was considered bookish and dominated by scholars, commercial law was created by merchants for merchants and was very practical. Disputes in commercial matters were decided by merchant courts, and these courts were presided over by merchants. Commercial law eventually penetrated the commercial world even into Northern Europe and England.

By the ninth century, both canon law and Roman law had experienced their heyday. As Germanic and other invaders conquered the empire, they provided modifications to both canon and Roman law. By the eleventh century, however, both canon law and Roman law were reestablished as superior systems. Scholars from various European countries studied the *Corpus Juris Civilis*, and it provided the basis for a common law of Europe, *jus commune*, which prevailed until the fifteenth century. In the fifteenth century, the concept of national sovereignty prompted the rise of national laws (Reichel, 2005, pp. 121–124).

Development of National Legal Systems

The concept of sovereignty is generally traced to the work of a group of European scholars, most notably Hugo Grotius (see drawing in Photo 4.1). Grotius is also referred to as the father of international law. The scholars considered sovereignty to be a fundamental concept for the ordering of international affairs between nations.

During the emergence of the nation-state concept, national legal systems were also developed. These developments destroyed the legal unity previously provided by the common acceptance of Roman-canonic *jus commune* in feudal Europe.

Events including the decay of feudalism, the Reformation, and the weakening authority of the Holy Roman Empire resulted in the emergence of monarchies as the power of the nation-states. The new centralized states stood in opposition to the medieval autonomy of classes and land commonly associated with those classes. The nation-states then became the unique source of law. National law systems replaced the *jus commune* as the law of the nation, with the maxim that "the prince's pleasure is the law." The content of the law, however, continued to be drawn largely from the *jus commune*, but the authority for it now rested with the nation-state.

The notion of a national civil law system emerged in France in the sixteenth century. It was also during the sixteenth century that Parisian French was made the national language, even though it was spoken by only a minority

Photo 4.1 Hugo Grotius, who is considered to be the father of international law. The drawing was created in about 1700. (Courtesy of the Library of Congress Prints and Photographs Division.)

of the population of France at the time. Louis XIV's royal *ordonnances* in the seventeenth century also fostered the notion of a national law system (Glenn, 2000, p. 124).

Napoleonic Code

Prior to the French Revolution, the judiciary was one of the surviving institutions of feudalism in France. Judicial offices were considered property that one could buy, sell, or leave to one's heirs. The judges were an aristocratic group that sided with the wealthy and powerful in France. Judges frequently made more law than they interpreted (Merryman, 1985, p. 15). In the decades before the Revolution, there was an intellectual revolution led by a number of writers, including Montesquieu and Rousseau, who advocated the doctrine of separation of powers within a government. A drawing of Montesquieu is shown in Photo 4.2. After the French Revolution, the Napoleonic Code was developed. Two of the key points involved in drafting the code were reduction of the power of judges and separation of governmental powers.

In 1804, under the leadership of Napoleon, the code became the world's first systemic, rational codification of a national system of law. The code

Photo 4.2 Charles Secondat, Baron de Montesquieu, who advocated for the doctrine of separation of powers within the French government. (Courtesy of the Library of Congress Prints and Photographs Division.)

expressly repealed all prior laws in the areas it covered. Any prior principle of law that was included in the code was considered to have derived its authority not from tradition, but from the Code itself. For years after the enactment of the Napoleonic Code (French Civil Code of 1804), the fiction was maintained that history was irrelevant to the interpretation and application of the code. A frequently quoted statement by lawyers at the time was: "I know nothing of the civil law; I know only the Code Napoleon" (Merryman, 1985, p. 29).

Under the Napoleonic Code, judges were not permitted to interpret the law. The legislature alone could make laws, and the sole function of the judges was to apply the law as written by the legislature. The French codifiers sought to establish an entirely new legal order. As Merryman noted (1985, p. 26), the ideology of the French codification, though more temperate than that of the immediate post-revolutionary period, accurately reflected the ideology of the French Revolution.

German Legal Science

German *Allgemeines Landrecht* ("general state law"), the law of the Prussian states, began during the reign of Frederick the Great (1740–1786) but was not promulgated until 1794 under his successor, Frederick William II. It was to be enforced wherever it did not conflict with local customs. The code was adopted by other German states in the nineteenth century and remained in force until it was replaced by the civil code of the German Empire effected in 1900.

Throughout the nineteenth century, German legal scholars argued about the type of national code that should be written and, indeed, whether one should be written at all. German legal science was primarily the creation of nineteenth-century German legal scholars and evolved from the ideas of Friedrich Karl von Savigny (1779–1861), a German jurist and legal scholar who is considered one of the founders of the influential "historical school" of jurisprudence. He advocated that the meaning and content of existing bodies of law be analyzed through research into their historical origins and modes of transformation. Savigny advocated against following the French codification and the secular concept of natural law. According to him, a necessary first step to codification was a thorough review of the legal order in order to identify and correctly state the principles in a uniform system of law.

Only with the formation of the German Reich in 1871 was a program of national codification undertaken. Commissions were established, and, when the first draft of the code was presented for critical appraisal in 1888, it was rejected as being too Roman. A second draft was promulgated in 1896 and went into effect in 1900. As the French sought to establish a new legal code with no historical basis, the German scholars sought to codify the existing principles of law into a uniform code.

The German scholars compiled their studies in the *Digests* (German, *Pandekten*). The *Digests* were highly systematic treaties based on principles taken from Roman law. Their work culminated in the German Civil Code of 1896. Their methods and concepts were applied to other fields of law and dominated legal scholarship of Germany. The concept of German legal science is based on the assumption that laws (statutes, regulations, and ordinances) are naturally occurring phenomena or data from which the scientist can ascertain inherent principles and relationships, just as mathematicians discover the laws of mathematics (Merryman, 1985, p. 62). The German Civil Code has had an important influence on the law of other countries, particularly Japan, Switzerland, and Greece. It has influenced the law of Austria and, in conjunction with the Swiss Civil Code, that of Russia and the Scandinavian countries, among others.

Law in Action: The Inquisitorial System of Prosecution

A common comparison between the civil law model and the common law model is that civil law uses the inquisitorial system whereas common law uses the accusatorial system. Merryman (1985) contends that this may

Table 4.1   A Brief Comparison between Accusatorial and Inquisitorial Systems

Function	Accusatorial System	Inquisitorial System
Role of accusor	Prosecutor	Investigating judge
How truth is determined	The trial is a competition between prosecution and defense	From a continuing investigation with emphasis on screening
Role of judge	As a referee	As an investigator and fact finder
Role of defendant	Defendant is not required to cooperate	Defendant is expected to but not required to cooperate

be correct from a historical perspective, but is inaccurate and misleading when applied to present-day systems. He notes that civil law has evolved away from the true inquisitorial system and common law has moved away from the abuses and excesses of the accusatorial system. The result is that the two systems are converging from different directions toward roughly equivalent mixed systems of criminal justice. Table 4.1 is a comparison of the two systems.

The historical characteristics of the inquisitorial system of prosecution include the following:

- An affirmative obligation by the state to carry out policies of criminal procedure
- An emphasis on publication of written materials compiled through the trial process by an investigating attorney
- A procedure that is under the control of a judicial officer who is not neutral but takes the initiative in investigation
- A concern with enforcing the law by treating the accused as one of the primary sources of evidence (Opolot, 1980, p. 21)

What Role Do Judges Play in Italian Penality?

According to Professor Zelia Gallo, since the 1970s, Italian judges have had a variable effect on Italian penality; they have produced pressures in favor of punitiveness and of moderation. They have contributed to the fluctuation between repression and leniency in the assessing of criminal punishment. Gallo focused on the relationship between the judiciary and the political class and the penal repercussions that have followed from their changing interaction.

He contends that the variations in penality can be best understood in terms of evolving judicial legitimacy. And whose highs and lows can be linked to the expansion and contraction of judicial powers. During the periods when there was high legitimacy manifest in increasing political reliance on judicial action, the punishments tended to be harsher.

During the periods of low legitimacy, manifested in conflict between the judges and politicians, the punishments awarded were more moderated.

Source: Gallo, Z., Legitimacy and punitiveness: The role of judicial actors in Italian penality in *Punishment and Incarceration: A Global Perspective*, edited by Deflem, M., Bigley, UK, Emerald Books, 2015, pp. 1–30.

Codes in Civil and Common Law Models

Often civil law is described as "code law," implying that "codes of law" are present only in civil law models. This is inaccurate. Attorneys who practice law in states like California, Florida, New York, and Texas will quickly point out that most U.S. states have adopted extensive codes of law, such as penal codes, civil codes, tax codes, vehicle codes, and health and safety codes. In addition, there is the Uniform Commercial Code, which most states have adopted, and the federal codes adopted by the U.S. government. The State of California has more codes of law than any other civil law system.

The conception of what is a code, however, is different in civil law countries than in common law countries. Subject to some exceptions, when codes are adopted in a common law system, the code is considered a restatement of existing principles of law. If there is a problem with the interpretation of a code provision, common law and other laws are examined for an answer. In the civil law systems, codes are generally considered the development of a new subsystem of law; for clarification of problems, the judges should look to legislative intent. Another important difference is that in civil law countries, a code is considered a complete statement of the law in an area, whereas in common law countries a code is not generally considered a complete body of law in an area.

Inquisitorial Prosecution

A basic difference between the common law and the civil law models is the civil law principle that prosecutors must prosecute all crimes that they believe have been committed. This means that "deals" or "plea bargains" are not officially sanctioned and are rare. Judges play an active role in shaping the proceedings; they are responsible for investigating the facts and deciding whether the defendant is guilty or not. The lawyers play a secondary role, simply highlighting pieces of evidence that favor their interpretation of the case. Because there is no inexperienced jury that could be misled, there are many fewer technical rules for determining what sort of evidence the judge (and, in more serious cases, two lay jurors) hear. Thus, many advocates for the civil law model claim the proceeding is much more "truth oriented"; there is less fighting about what can be considered by the judges, and more focus on what "actually happened."

German Civil Law System

To understand the present criminal procedure used in Germany, we need to look to the former German Democratic Republic (GDR) and how on Reunification Day, October 3, 1990, the two Germanys became one again.

The basis for Germany's modern-day statutory criminal law is the German Penal Code, which was codified in 1871. Prior to this code, each German state had its own penal code. When it was adopted, retribution was the dominant philosophy and heavy emphasis was placed upon prevention through punishment. Satisfaction with the penal code was short-lived, and as early as 1882 scholars called for reform of criminal sanctions toward an emphasis on prevention through special deterrence, which emphasizes deterring the offender, not the offense.

The Penal Code of 1871 was substantially modified in 1920 with the required provisions to register served sentences, in 1923 by the creation of a special juvenile criminal law, and in 1924 with the introduction of fines to replace short-term prison sentences. The Nazi era (1933–1944) introduced sweeping and harsh reforms with an emphasis upon general deterrence through extreme severity. These reforms left the basic penal code intact but introduced punishment on order of the Führer.

After World War II and while Germany was divided into two sectors, the new Federal Republic of Germany, created in 1949, made a serious attempt to reform the law with the appointment of the "Grand Criminal Law Commission," whose membership consisted of legal scholars, practitioners, and politicians. The Commission created a reform called the "Draft of a Penal Code." In 1962, the draft code was not adopted by the Federal Assembly because of its alleged weakness in formulating a criminal policy with regard to punishments. The draft was criticized because of its emphasis on punishment and retribution and its conservative view and rigidity on sexual mores.

After the failure of the first draft, a second reform group was established. The Special Committee on Criminal Law Reform was comprised of German and Swiss legal scholars and criminologists. This committee developed the "Alternative Draft of a Penal Code." This draft recommended restricting the application of criminal law to socially harmful conduct and emphasized restructuring the sanction system to fit the philosophy of rehabilitation.

Criminal law reform introduced reform in partial steps, the main elements contained in five Criminal Law Reform Acts beginning in 1969.

The Criminal Law Reform Acts emphasized restructuring sentencing to make sentences more conducive to the rationale of rehabilitation. Many acts were decriminalized and others redefined with a more practical working definition. A second major reform consisted of a permanent restriction on short-term prison sentences and the substitution of fines. Additionally, changes were introduced in the general law as well as in the alternative sanctions that could be applied. The German government also passed legislation that regulated the environment and established new economic, hostage-taking, and aircraft hijacking crimes.

The Unification Treaty Act of August 31, 1990 (*Einigungsvertragsgesetz*), replaced, in large part, the laws of the former German Democratic Republic (East Germany) with those of the Federal Republic of Germany. Limited exceptions, however, allowed laws from the former East German Penal Code to exist in the former eastern states.

Presently, the Federal Republic of Germany is a federal state created by the German Federal Constitution. Germany consists of 16 states, each with its own constitution. The federal government and the states have concurrent jurisdiction (police powers, cultural issues, local government matters, and the application of civil and criminal laws). Federal laws establish a framework for the individual states. If any conflict arises between a federal law and that of a state, the federal law prevails.

Laws are created by the *Bundestag*, or lower house of the German parliament. The upper house (*Bundesrat*) is a representative body of the states based on their population. The legal system is guided by federal laws that apply nationwide. Those specifically applicable to the criminal justice system are the Penal Code and the Code of Criminal Procedure. Other laws that concern the criminal justice system are the *Betaübungsmittelgesetz* (drug statutes), the *Betübungsmittel-Verschreibungsverordnung* (drug prescription regulation), *Strassenverkehrsgesetz* (traffic laws), and the *Gesetz der Ordnungswidrigkeiten* (laws governing administrative or regulatory offenses). The following are the levels of courts in Germany that deal with criminal matters:

- Local courts (*Amtsgerichte*): Local courts have jurisdiction in criminal matters where a punishment of not more than 3 years of imprisonment can be imposed.
- Regional courts (*Landgerichte*): Both *Amtsgerichte* and *Landgerichte* are courts of first instance. In addition, the regional courts serve as a court of general appeal (*Berufung*), along with the higher regional courts.
- Higher regional courts (*Oberlandesgerichte*): Courts of appeal for both *Amtsgerichte* and *Landgerichte*; they may also hear cases at first instance.

- Federal High Court (*Bundesgerichtshof*): Hears appeals on questions of law; it is divided into various panels.
- Federal Constitutional Court (*Bundesverfassungsgericht*): The highest court in the land; it considers only cases involving violations of constitutional law. The court does not serve as a regular court of appeals from lower courts or the Federal Supreme Courts as a sort of "super appellate court" on any violation of federal laws. Its jurisdiction is focused only on constitutional issues.

There is a separate court for juveniles that has jurisdiction for those persons between 14 and 18 years of age. Young adults between the ages of 18 and 21 years may be dealt with in juvenile court and may also be institutionalized in juvenile facilities up to the age of 25. Juvenile courts use the same penal codes but employ different sanctions and procedures from those used for adults.

In Germany Is It Illegal to Shoot Down a Passenger Plane That Is Being Used by Terrorists?

In a 2006 decision, the German Federal Constitutional Court struck down an antiterrorism provision that empowered the Ministry of Defense to order that a passenger airplane be shot down, if it could be assumed that the aircraft would be used against the life of others and if the downing of the plane would be the only means of preventing the present danger. Under the Court's reasoning, shooting down a plane violates the fundamental right to life and the right to dignity enshrined in the German Constitution. The treatment of the passengers as objects without proper legal protection is in the Court's view unconstitutional. The Court's decision is interpreted by some scholars as asserting that the power granted to officials under the law to shoot down planes is unconstitutional. Under this view, the dignity of the (innocent) passengers on such an airplane is violated by the (legal) powers granted to officials under the law. What makes the law therefore unconstitutional is the content of the law that is incompatible with the dignity provision (Lepsius, 2006).

The German court system differs from that of other federal-type governments, such as the United States, in that all the trial and appellate courts are state courts while the courts of last resort are federal. All courts may hear cases based on law enacted on the federal level, though there are some areas of law over which the states have exclusive control.

A case may be heard for the first time in any of the first three courts, depending upon the type of offense. It may be taken to one or two more on appeal or revision on a legal point. Even though all German courts have the jurisdiction to review the constitutionality of governmental action within their jurisdiction, only the Federal Constitutional Court may declare national statutes unconstitutional. The Federal Constitutional Court was provided for in the German constitution adopted after World War II. The High Court was designed to prevent another Nazi-like administration in which the power of the federal government was unchecked. While there is limited precedent for judicial review in German constitutional history, the far-reaching jurisdiction of the Federal Constitutional Court was influenced primarily by the model of the U.S. Supreme Court and the Austrian Constitutional Court. The court is headquartered in Karlsruhe, Baden-Württemberg. It was established in 1951.

Judicial System of Germany

- Highest court(s): Federal Court of Justice (the court consists of 127 judges including the court president, vice presidents, presiding judges, and other judges; and is organized into 25 Senates subdivided into 12 civil panels, 5 criminal panels, and 8 special panels; Federal Constitutional Court or *Bundesverfassungsgericht* (consists of 2 Senates each subdivided into 3 chambers, each with a chairman and 8 members).
- Judge selection and term of office: Federal Court of Justice judges are selected by the Judges Election Committee, which consists of the Secretaries of Justice from each of the 16 federated States and 16 members appointed by the Federal Parliament; judges are appointed by the president of Germany; judges serve until mandatory retirement at age 65; Federal Constitutional Court judges—one-half are elected by the House of Representatives and one-half by the Senate; judges are appointed for 12-year terms with mandatory retirement at age 68.
- Subordinate courts: Federal Administrative Court; Federal Finance Court; Federal Labor Court; Federal Social Court; each of the 16 German states or Land has its own constitutional court and a hierarchy of ordinary (civil, criminal, family) and specialized (administrative, finance, labor, social) courts.

Source: CIA World Fact Book, available at: https://www.cia.gov/library/publications/resources/the-world-factbook, accessed May 14, 2015.

The Death Penalty in Germany

Many scholars contend that Article 102 of the Grundgesetz (Basic Law), which abolished the death penalty in Germany, was motivated by disgust at the excessive use of the death penalty in Germany by the National Socialist regime. During the 12 years of Nazi dictatorship, more than 30,000 death sentences were handed down—in addition to the mass extermination directed at "undesirable" populations. German scholars have voiced this opinion concerning the Parliamentary Council's 1949 decision to call for the abolition of the death penalty in the Basic Law.

The Federal Constitutional Court has two separate panels (called senates) of eight judges each, and each senate has jurisdiction over distinct areas of constitutional law. Judges serve a single, nonrenewable 12-year term. Half the judges are elected by the *Bundesrat* (the upper house of the German legislature), the other half by a special committee of the *Bundestag* (the lower house). To be elected, a judge must secure a two-thirds majority of votes cast.

The U.S. Supreme Court accepts fewer than 200 cases a year from thousands of requests for review and hears all of its cases en banc (with all justices involved). The German Federal Constitutional Court's workload is about 5000 cases annually. The Federal Constitutional Court also hears cases by panels (senates) divided according to subject matter jurisdiction. The Federal Constitutional Court is not considered an appeals court, but rather a trial court with first and final competence. Its decisions are binding on state and federal legislatures and on all other courts.

Anyone claiming an infringement of his or her basic rights may bring a constitutional complaint. If there is doubt in any trial or appellate court proceedings as in the constitutionality of a law, the court must stay the proceedings and forward the question to the Federal Constitutional Court.

The Federal Constitutional Court, unlike the U.S. Supreme Court, may exercise abstract judicial review. For the U.S. Supreme Court to take a case, there must be an actual case pending, whereas under abstract judicial review the federal or a state government or one-third of the members of the Bundestag may petition the court on the constitutionality of a statute, even before the statute has taken effect. Most of the cases heard by the court are constitutional complaints by individuals, a form of action that is free of court costs and does not require counsel. See Figure 4.1 for a diagram of the present German court structure.

The classification of crimes in Germany is very similar to that of the United States. In Germany, criminal offenses are classified as *Verbrechen* (felony) and *Vergehen* (misdemeanor). Less serious offenses have, through a lengthy reform process, either been decriminalized, upgraded into misdemeanors, or reclassified as *Ordnungswidrigkeiten* (regulatory or administrative offense). *Verbrechen* denotes an act punishable by a minimum prison sentence of 1 year. *Vergehen* is punishable by a sentence of less than 1 year or a fine. *Verbrechen* comprises serious crimes involving severe injury or extensive property damage or loss (for instance, homicide, rape, robbery, arson), while *Vergehen* applies to offenses such as simple assault, theft, or vandalism. *Ordnungswidrigkeiten* includes disturbing the peace, illegal practice of prostitution, illegal assembly, and possession of materials to make and distribute forged documents or money.

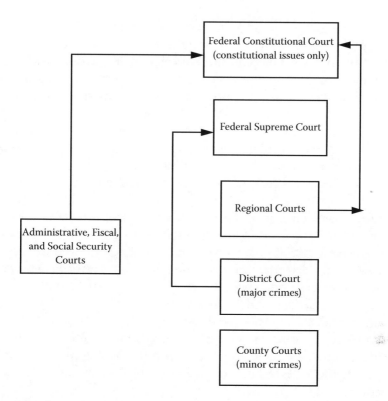

Figure 4.1 The German court structure.

The age of criminal responsibility in Germany is also very similar to that in the United States. Persons who commit an offense while under the age of 14 are not held criminally liable for their offense. Criminal liability attaches at the age of 14.

Rights of the Accused in a German Criminal Trial

Prior to and during the trial, the accused has the following rights:

- The suspect has the right to be heard and can request that evidence be taken before a writ of indictment is issued.
- If the suspect is interrogated by police, the suspect must be told of the charges against him or her.
- Once the Public Prosecutor's Office has completed its inquiry, the writ of indictment is communicated to the accused before the court decides to open the main proceedings.
- The counsel for the accused has an absolute right to inspect all evidence against the accused.

- A defendant may plead guilty to a lesser offense. A guilty plea, however, does not automatically end the trial, and more often than not the
  court will review the evidence presented by the prosecutor to determine if it supports the guilty plea. A guilty plea can be changed at any
  time, in which case the court would weigh the evidence presented to
  determine if a change in plea can be supported. At the district court
  level, where the defendant can receive up to a maximum sentence of
  3 years of incarceration, the defendant can be tried either by a single
  judge or by a judicial panel consisting of one professional judge and
  two lay judges. There is no jury system in German courts.

The accused must be provided with legal representation under the following circumstances: where the defendant is facing a trial in the regional
court or higher regional court, where the defendant is charged with a serious
crime, where the defendant may be prohibited from practicing a profession,
or where the defendant has been incarcerated for at least 3 months and is not
expected to be released until 2 weeks prior to the trial.

The defendant may choose up to three attorneys. Legal representation
under these circumstances is compulsory; it is provided by the state if the
defendant cannot afford an attorney. Attorneys are obliged to provide legal
services for the accused and are paid a fixed salary by the state for their
services.

The procedures for bringing an accused to trial are usually initiated by
either the police or the Public Prosecutor's Office, or both. When sufficient
evidence exists to indicate a criminal offense has occurred, the prosecutor
will initiate an inquiry. If the inquiry suggests that an indictment should be
issued, the prosecutor's office will issue the indictment. The power to indict
is vested in the Public Prosecutor's Office. If the prosecutor refuses to indict,
an injured party can turn to the courts to appeal the decision.

The indictment will then be reviewed by the relevant court. If sufficient
grounds to proceed exist, the court moves the case on to the main proceedings. If insufficient evidence exists, the court issues an order refusing to open
the main proceedings.

The Public Prosecutor's Office is legally obligated to investigate any criminal offense, providing sufficient evidence exists to support the allegation
that a crime has occurred (that is, a police investigation, citizen's complaint,
or press report). Although in most cases offenses are prosecuted by the Public
Prosecutor's Office in the court of appropriate jurisdiction, there are limited
exceptions to this rule. For instance, tax authorities may apply directly to
the court to impose fines, bypassing the prosecutor's office, in criminal tax
offenses.

In some cases, such as libel, slander, trespass, and simple assault and
battery, the injured party may seek an indictment without having to rely

on the prosecutor's office. The injured party takes the role of the Public Prosecutor's Office. If in such cases the prosecutor's office files an indictment, the injured party may join the public proceedings as an accessory to the prosecution. This role grants the injured party specific rights in reviewing defense material, calling witnesses, rejecting a judge, and being heard in court.

There are various alternatives to trial that exist for certain cases of minor offenses, such as when the prosecutor asks for a punishment order to be granted by the court. This out-of-court settlement occurs when the judge allows the defendant to make payments or forfeit a driver's license rather than face trial. The accused then has the option of refusing the order and requesting a hearing, at which time the main hearing will resume. The prosecutor can also exercise discretion and drop the charges against the accused under the following conditions: (1) the suspect's role is limited and prosecution serves no public function or interest; (2) the defendant is being tried for another more serious crime; or (3) in the case of a minor offense, the prosecutor moves for a conditional waiver and the judge and the accused agree to the conditions and orders that are sufficient to accommodate the public interest in a prosecution.

At the district court level, a single professional judge will preside. It is also possible for a professional judge and two lay judges to preside. The votes of lay judges carry the same weight as those of professional judges. They determine guilt or innocence as well as the sentence. While a unanimous decision is not required, a two-thirds majority of judges, both lay and professional, is necessary for a decision against the accused. Lay judges are chosen by the lay judge election committee and serve for a period of 4 years.

In the regional courts, a chamber consisting of three professional judges and two lay judges hands down decisions concerning serious crimes at first instance or may rule on appeals against judgments of the judicial panel at the District Court (*Bezirksgericht*). The Small Criminal Chamber (*Kleine Strafkammer*), consisting of one professional judge and two lay judges, makes the determination in cases involving hearing an appeal of a decision made by the professional judge. In their appellate function, the Criminal Panels of the Higher Regional Courts sit as panels of three professional judges. If sitting as a court of first instance, the panel sits as a panel of five professional judges. The Criminal Panels of the Federal Supreme Court are composed of five professional judges.

Cases may be filtered out of the system with an informal punishment order whereby the judge allows the defendant to make payments rather than face trial. All other cases, even those in which the defendant has made a confession and entered a guilty plea, will be moved to the main hearing for trial. Plea bargaining, entering a guilty plea in exchange for a lighter sentence, exists on a very limited basis in Germany.

Principle of Territoriality

The basic principle for determining jurisdiction in criminal matters is that the authorities and courts of the state or province in which the offense was committed are competent to investigate and adjudicate it. One interesting aspect of German law deals with the jurisdiction of German criminal courts. In most nations, for the criminal courts to have jurisdiction, the offense must have some connection with the nation: this is the "principle of territoriality." The German constitution prohibits the extradition of Germans to foreign countries. The purpose of this prohibition is not to make Germans immune from criminal trials for offenses committed abroad but to ensure them a trial before a German court. In order to achieve this, the jurisdiction of German courts is extended beyond the basic principle of territoriality to include all offenses committed by Germans, even those committed abroad.

Law in Action: Juries in the Civil Law Model

Civil law countries use juries on a more limited basis and in a different manner than juries are used in common law countries. One problem with using juries in the civil law system is that there is no concept of a trial as used in the common law countries. The typical proceeding in a civil law country is actually a series of isolated meetings and written communications between counsel and the judge (Merryman, 1986, p. 112). Most civil law and socialist law countries use a "mixed bench" in which the lay judges (functional equivalent to jurors) and professional judges are combined into a single body (Reichel, 2005, p. 257).

The appointment of assessors was started in the late nineteenth and early twentieth centuries throughout much of Continental Europe as an attempt to limit the influence of the jury system, which had been introduced in the wave of egalitarian reforms that followed the French Revolution. The freedom of the nonprofessional jury to determine the guilt of an accused was so contrary to the civil law tradition of the professional judge, so the legislatures appointed assessors who would sit and decide cases alongside professional judges.

In France the jury of nine, which sits only in the assize courts, where only the most serious crimes are tried, is in reality a group of assessors who must decide in conjunction with three professional judges. Juries may circumvent the judges, as a majority of 8 votes are needed for conviction, but in practice the judges generally are able to influence the jury and gain a majority.

In Germany, there are *Schöffen* (lay jurists) who sit with professional judges to decide the guilt or innocence of the accused. Italy uses a similar system (Opolot, 1980, p. 23).

Judicial System of Spain

- Highest court(s): Supreme Court or *Tribunal Supremo* (consists of the court president and is organized into the Civil Room with a president and 9 magistrates; the Penal Room with a president and 14 magistrates; the Administrative Room with a president and 32 magistrates; the Social Room with a president and 12 magistrates; and the Military Room with a president and 7 magistrates); and the Constitutional Court or *Tribunal Constitucional de Espana* (consists of 12 judges).
- Judge selection and term of office: Supreme Court judges appointed by the monarch from candidates proposed by the General Council of the Judicial Power, a 20-member governing board chaired by the monarch and includes presidential appointees, and lawyers and jurists confirmed by the National Assembly; judge tenure NA; Constitutional Court judges nominated by the General Assembly, executive branch, and the General Council of the Judiciary, and appointed by the monarch for 9-year terms.
- Subordinate courts: National Court; High Courts of Justice (in each of the autonomous communities); provincial courts; courts of first instance.

Source: CIA World Fact Book, available at: https://www.cia.gov/library/publications/resources/the-world-factbook, accessed May 14, 2015.

Criminal Justice in France

The French legal system is based on the principal of a unity of the civil and criminal justice systems, which means that the same court can hear both criminal and civil cases. The 1992 Penal Code retained the tripartite distinction of crimes, misdemeanors, and violations, which was first established by the Penal Code of 1810.

The three basic trial courts in the French criminal justice system are the police courts, correctional courts, and assize courts. The police courts have jurisdiction over minor violations of law. Correctional courts have jurisdiction over offenses that can incur a maximum of 10 years of imprisonment. The assize court has jurisdiction over serious crimes that have possible life imprisonment sentences. The assize court sits on an ad hoc basis (not as a permanent court). Its decisions are permanent and cannot be brought for appeal.

The Chamber of Correctional Appeals hears appeals of decisions brought to it by the police and correctional courts. The Criminal Chamber of the Supreme Court of Appeal oversees the application of law in all courts. It verifies judicial decisions to ensure that the application of the law and the resulting sentences are sound, but does not actually hear any cases. Its judges determine the appropriate application of the law in a case, but do not draw any conclusions as to the facts of the case.

The Court for Children hears cases involving minors charged with offenses that would be brought to the police and correctional courts if they were adults (misdemeanors and violations). The Assize Court for Minors handles cases involving minors charged with more serious offenses.

The accused in a French criminal court has the right to a self-obtained lawyer or to a lawyer chosen by the state. The accused also has the right to appeal the judge's decision. At appeal, the accused is brought in for temporary custody under the Chamber of Accusation. The accused has the right to ask the president of the Chamber of Accusation to suspend any sentence until a decision is made on the appeal. The accused has the right to the assistance of an attorney.

Generally, the procedure by which a case is brought to court becomes more elaborate as the seriousness of the crime increases. There are two procedural stages preceding trial. In the police stage, the police conduct a preliminary investigation under the direction of the public prosecutor. This process involves a search for the suspect, a hearing of the suspect, and an observation of the suspect, once arrested. During this investigation, the suspect is kept under observation for 24 hours, which can be lengthened under authorization of the public prosecutor. Another type of investigation takes place when the suspect is caught while committing the crime. Police officers can make observations at the scene of the crime and relate their information to the public prosecutor.

The judiciary stage can be initiated by either the public minister or the victim, although the public minister studies the legalities involved in the charges and prosecutes the suspect. The public minister decides whether the case should be brought before a judge or disposed of alternatively. The victim can also initiate prosecution by bringing a civil suit against the suspect, forcing the public prosecutor to take action.

Under the Chamber of Accusation, preparatory instructions for the case are given to an examining magistrate who has the power to proceed with the examination of the suspect. (In 1993, the term "accuse" was replaced by the term "put under examination.") The magistrates can interrogate, confront, and bring warrants against the suspect. They can also arrest the suspect and bring him or her before judicial authority. Another set of instructions is given for the bringing of appeals.

The examining magistrate reads the charge and the statement of the defense. Judges of the correctional court must explain the reasoning for their decisions. The public minister can also prosecute a suspect. Suspects are not allowed to plead guilty.

Judicial System of France

- Highest court(s): Court of Cassation or *Cour de Cassation* (consists of the court president, 6 divisional presiding judges, 120 trial judges, and 70 deputy judges organized into 6 divisions—3 civil, 1 commercial, 1 labor, and 1 criminal); Constitutional Council (consists of 9 members).
- Judge selection and term of office: Court of Cassation judges appointed by the president of the republic from nominations from the High Council of the Judiciary, presided by the Court of Cassation and 15 appointed members; judge term of appointment NA; Constitutional Council members appointed—3 by the president of the republic and 3 each by the National Assembly and Senate presidents; members serve 9-year, nonrenewable terms with one-third of the membership renewed every 3 years.
- Subordinate courts: Appellate courts or *Cour d'Appel*; regional courts or *Tribunal de Grande Instance*; first instance courts or *Tribunal' d'instance*.

Source: CIA World Fact Book, available at: https://www.cia.gov/library/publications/resources/the-world-factbook, accessed May 14, 2015.

Criminal Justice in Brazil

Brazil is a republic with a federal district (Brasília) and 27 states. Brazilian law is divided into civil, commercial, civil procedure, penal, and penal procedure codes and is preceded by a *Parte Geral*, which is an overview of concepts and principles derived primarily from legal scholarship. The emphasis of Brazilian codes is on inclusive definitions, neat conceptual distinctions, and broad general rules. Lawyers are trained to make the facts fit into conceptual structures, to preserve rules from exception, and to smooth out the rough spots (Merryman, 1985, p. 78).

Brazilian crimes are classified, very similar to the United States, as felonies and misdemeanors. Felony offenses include the serious crimes and misdemeanors, the less serious. The Penal Code applies to persons aged 18 years or older. Juvenile offenders between the ages of 12 and 17 are subject to juvenile law, the Statute of Children and Adolescents (1990). Juveniles cannot be sentenced to imprisonment, but they may be detained in appropriate institutions under secure training orders.

In Brazil, as in other civil law countries, every crime and penalty must be embodied in a statute enacted by the legislature. Criminal procedure is inquisitorial, written rather than oral, and the role of accuser is appropriated by a public official. Trials are not averted by a plea of guilt. While a confession can be admitted as evidence, only the court can determine guilt. There is no formal plea bargaining, but as discussed later there is an informal process. The accused does not have a right to a public trial as does one in the United States. Generally, the procedure is restricted to defense counsel, prosecutor, and magistrate. Cases are normally prepared by a prosecutor (member of the *Ministério Público*), but inquests are generally conducted by a police district officer (*delegado de polícia*), who is a law school graduate and a full-time public employee.

In matters involving organized crime, judges are free to seek evidence themselves and to control the nature and objectives of investigative and examining phases as well. In other criminal cases, the dossier compiled is open to inspection by the defense counsel.

Frequently, criminal cases are initiated by reports of alleged offenses made by victims or their representatives to the authorities (police, prosecutors' office, or a criminal court). Procedure can also be initiated by persons other than victims and their representatives. After the initiation of a case, further action is always determined by the *delegado de polícia*, a judicial police district officer. The officer is responsible for ordering investigations, screening cases subsequent to arrest in order to determine which should be prosecuted or dropped, notifying defendants of the charges, and setting bail.

Next, the case is forwarded to a prosecutor, who decides whether to declare a case pending or, if he or she cannot form an *opinio delicti*, request more evidence, by returning the file to the *delegado*. During the phase of investigation and adjudication (*instrução criminal*), the accused normally remains free, except in a case of organized crime or where the individual is "caught in the act." "Caught in the act" refers to those situations where the person was committing the crime, had just perpetrated it, was being pursued by the police, offended the victim or any citizen, or was found close to the crime scene with incriminating evidence (weapons, stolen property, records, documents, concrete objects, or circumstances).

Within 24 hours after an arrest, the accused is notified of the reason for the arrest and the names of the witnesses to the crime. Notification is then sent to the judge, who may grant pretrial release (*liberdade provisória*). If the judge agrees that the accused was indeed detained for being "in the act," the judge will order a trial within 10 to 30 days.

Authorization for police inquests is granted for a period of 10 to 30 days. In exceptional cases, prosecutors can order searches and evidence gathering without authorization from the court. They must notify the judge and request confirmation of the procedure within a few hours. Any evidence obtained illegally may be excluded from the proceedings.

An accused has the following legal rights:

- To be informed specifically and clearly of the charges
- To be assisted by family, attorney, or legal aid to advise of arrest
- To be assisted, during the preliminary investigation, by a defense attorney or public defender
- Not to give self-incriminatory evidence
- To request investigation of the facts or circumstances that might establish innocence
- To declare directly to a judge
- To be informed of the content of the investigation
- To adhere to the constitutional precept of silence, or to declare while not under oath
- Not to be tortured, or treated in a cruel, inhumane, or degrading manner; not to be tried in absentia, except in cases of involvement with organized crime (still controversial and not universally accepted by judges). Jury decision is by secret ballot

In large jurisdictions that have a large number of criminal cases, there is informal pretrial diversion through bargaining that is unacknowledged by judges, and worked out between prosecutors and defense attorneys who plead guilty on behalf of their clients in exchange for a shorter sentence.

The trial process begins when the judge accepts a complaint and fixes a date for questioning the defendant and ordering his or her notification by a prosecutor. The trial procedure includes the following.

Immediately after questioning, or within 3 days, the defendant may submit written allegation and enlist his or her witnesses.

There is direct examination of witnesses, starting by the state's witnesses. The prosecutor or plaintiff may request any sort of inquest they consider necessary.

Both parties may present evidence at any phase of the criminal process.

If, in view of the evidence presented, the judge is convinced that the defendant is guilty as charged (of an inexcusable crime against life, including inducing/helping another person to commit suicide or abortion), defense counsel or prosecutor may request the second phase of the case to be handled by a jury court (*tribunal do júri*), composed of a judge and 21 jurors, chosen from a yearly revised list of eligible names (300–500 in larger jurisdictions).

On the prescribed date for the trial, the state's witnesses are taken away to places where they cannot hear the debates, and seven people selected from the 21 prospective jurors are present, so that a jury or *conselho de sentença* can be formed. Once the jury is formed, jurors cannot communicate to anyone or express their opinions on the case.

Jurors receive copies of relevant documents; hear state's witnesses, judge, defense counsel, plaintiff, and prosecutor; and may, if they so wish, question defense's witnesses. A verdict is reached after jury deliberation by secret vote of the majority of jurors.

The role and prestige of prosecutors (*promotores de justiça*) as control agents have increased enormously since the promulgation of the federal constitution in 1988. They are salaried, full-time federal or state government employees, organized in a permanent institution professionally structured, whose essential function is to defend the legal order and the democratic regime, as well as social and individual interests. In Brazil, compared to other systems of criminal justice, prosecutors' functions are reduced. This is because the screening of cases immediately after arrest and decisions on which cases should be prosecuted, fixing bail, and notifying defendants remain the legal prerogatives of the *delegados de polícia*.

Defendants cannot be tried or sentenced without legal representation; very infrequently (that is, unless they are trained lawyers) defendants are allowed to represent themselves, provided the magistrate believes their defense will be adequate. If the defendant cannot afford an attorney, the court will appoint a public defender, a full-time government employee who specializes in representing criminal suspects in need. Public defenders are members of the *Defensoria Pública*, a professionally structured agency, whose functions in criminal matters are to sponsor private defense and guarantee the individual rights of people in detention. Defendants may also be represented by a private defense attorney.

Brazilian judges are full-time public servants who earn a fixed salary and benefits. They are members of an institution whose hallmark is uniformity, differing, thus, from the judiciary mosaic in America, where no two state court systems are identical, and court names tend to vary regardless of functions.

Judicial System of Brazil

- Highest court(s): Supreme Federal Court (consists of 11 justices).
- Judge selection and term of office: Justices are appointed by the president and approved by the Federal Senate; justices are appointed to serve until mandatory retirement at age 70.
- Subordinate courts: Federal Appeals Court; Superior Court of Justice; Superior Electoral Court; regional federal courts; and state court system.

Source: CIA World Fact Book, available at: https://www.cia.gov/library/publications/resources/the-world-factbook, accessed May 14, 2015.

Summary

- There are many legal systems that are classified as civil law systems.
- Two major civil law nations, France and Germany, developed their legal systems under vastly different circumstances. The German system is based on German legal science and the French system is based heavily upon the ideology that was present during the French Revolution.
- One of the first legal codes was the Swedish Code, which was developed in about 1350.
- The introduction of the Napoleonic Code in France is seen as the end of the movement from tribalism to feudalism to monarchy.
- Roman law cannot be traced to a single source. Scholars commonly use 450 BC as the date of its origin.
- The civil law model is a composite of several distinct legal traditions, including Roman law, canon law, commercial law, and legal science.
- The revival of Roman law is generally thought to have started in Bologna, Italy, late in the eleventh century. There was an earlier revival in the ninth century with the publication of the *Basilica*.
- Roman law is considered by many as the greatest contribution that Rome made to Western civilization. The Roman way of thinking has influenced both common and civil law lawyers.
- Canon law was developed by the Roman Catholic Church and is considered the second oldest component of the civil law model.
- After the French Revolution, the Napoleonic Code was developed. Two features of it were the reduction in power for judges and the separation of governmental powers.
- German legal science was an attempt to analyze existing bodies of law through research into their historical origins and modes of transformation.
- While both common law and civil law systems have codes of law, there are vast differences between the two types of codes.
- The basis for present-day criminal procedure in Germany is the 1871 German Penal Code.
- Civil law juries are used on a more limited basis and in a different manner than juries in common law countries.
- The three basic trial courts in the French criminal justice system are the police courts, corrections courts, and assize courts.

Questions in Review

1. How are juries used differently in civil law systems from common law systems?
2. Explain the differences between the inquisitorial and accusatory models of trial procedure.
3. Explain the functions of a French police court.
4. Describe the impact of the French Revolution on present-day criminal justice procedures in France.
5. What role did German legal science play in the development of the present criminal procedure in Germany?

Policing and Corrections under the Civil Law Model

5

Chapter Objectives

After studying this chapter, you should understand or be able to explain the following issues and concepts:

- Policing under the civil law mode
- The four common models of policing under the civil law model
- The typical proceedings in police courts
- Pretrial diversion under the civil law models
- Plea bargaining under the civil law models
- Punishment concepts under the civil law models
- Probation and parole under the civil law models

Key Terms

Bundegrenzschutz (**BGS**): Germany's primary federal police force.

Bundeskriminalamt (**BKA**): German Federal Crime Investigation Bureau.

Conditional discharge: One form of pretrial diversion used in Germany that is based on the concept of conditional discharge by which prosecutors may dismiss a defendant from the criminal proceedings.

Gendarmerie Nationale: French police in rural areas and small towns.

Parole: Conditional release of a prisoner from prison after he or she has served a portion of his or her sentence.

Plea bargaining: The process by which a defendant and a prosecutor bargains for a mutually satisfactory disposition of the case.

Probation: A sentence imposed by the court under which the defendant is not imprisoned as long as he or she maintains a certain standard of behavior.

Rikspolis: The national police force in Sweden.

Introduction

From a historical point of view, the major nations using the civil law model (e.g., Germany, Spain, and France) have tended to have strong national governments when the civil law model was adopted or assumed, whereas the nations using the common law model have historically been more responsive to the demands of their citizens and have generally had national governments whose powers were not absolute. Technically, all nations who have multiple-force law enforcement agencies have at least one national-level agency with overlapping authority that transcends the concerns of subordinate governments, such as the Federal Bureau of Investigation in the United States and the Royal Canadian Mounted Police in Canada (Reichel, 2005).

Countries that have adopted the common law model tend to favor decentralized control of police forces, whereas countries that follow the civil law model tend to favor a centralized model of policing. However, there is considerable variation among the centralized police organizations of the civil law countries. Most civil law nations fall under one of four categories regarding their police models: (1) complete centralization in one police force; (2) high centralization, with a small number of national police forces; (3) regional centralization under federal authority; and (4) decentralized local policing, with a strong national agency.

Sweden would be an example of a country with a completely centralized police force. The Rikspolis, the one national police force, is made up of a number of police authorities, each of which is responsible for policing one of the counties of the country. The counties are further subdivided into police districts.

France, Italy, and Spain fit into the model of high centralization of police control with a small number of national police forces. There are two national police agencies in France: the National Police (*Police Nationale*) and the Gendarmerie Nationale. The National Police operates in cities, whereas the Gendarmerie Nationale polices rural areas and small towns. A third force, the State Security Police (*Compagnies Républicaines de Sécurité*), is a part of the National Police but is organized like a military unit.

Germany's policing would be considered regional centralization under a federal authority, with the basic policing structure resting on the state or province police forces. The Belgian police system could be described as decentralized local policing, with a strong national agency. The Belgian system has a federal police force, which brings together the former Gendarmerie and the national criminal investigation unit, and numerous local police forces, each of which is responsible to a mayor. Belgium's system of policing is closer to the ones used in the common law nations than the other civil law centralized systems.

Law Enforcement in France

The responsibility for France's internal security is assigned to two major forces: the National Police and the National Gendarmerie. Generally, there is one police officer for every 229 inhabitants (Das and Palmiotto, 2006). The advantages of having two major police forces, according to Horton (1995), are that a nation can use a "divide and conquer" strategy when the quality of police services or the loyalty of one of the forces is questioned. With two forces policing each other, there is a better chance of ensuring the civil liberties of the citizens. Horton also notes the ability to transfer cases from one force to the other when there are complaints against one force. Bayley (1992) notes that in general there have not been any serious problems encountered between the two police groups in France, and those encountered pale in comparison to those in Italy with its five national police forces.

The French national police forces are under the authority of France's Minister of the Interior. The highest police authority in France is the general director of the National Police. There are four major divisions of the National Police. The Central Division of General Information oversees informational services concerning political, economic, and social issues. The Central Division of the City Police supervises law enforcement in cities. The Central Branch of the Judiciary Police coordinates the search for the most dangerous delinquents and the investigation of the most serious offenses. The Division of Territory Surveillance is responsible for state security (Borricand, 2002).

In France, the administrative police generally are responsible for maintaining peace and order, such as the regulation of traffic. A special squad of administrative police, the Intervention Group of the State National Police (*Groupe d'Intervention de la Gendarmerie Nationale*), was created for anti-terrorist operations. In addition, municipal police contribute to law enforcement in the municipalities.

The state police force is under the authority of the defense minister. It fulfills the role of the administrative and judicial police in rural areas. There are also special customs police who work to control illegal entry of persons into the country to attack the public order.

The French police have broader investigative powers than U.S. police; however, France's Code of Criminal Procedure limits the exercise of these broad powers to a select group of police: the officers of the Judicial Police(s). OJPs are designated by ministerial decree from a list of persons declared eligible by statute. The Attorney General may suspend or revoke the designation, if an OJP abuses his or her powers, and certain judges also have disciplinary powers over OJPs and other members of the police (Frase, 1990).

Policing in France is more closely integrated with the prosecution function than it is in the United States. The prosecutor is to be notified without delay when the police learn of an offense, and immediately if it is a "flagrant" offense. If a prosecutor arrives on the scene, his or her authority supersedes that of the police officer previously in command. Individual prosecutors have all the powers of an OJP previously in command and may also order the police to conduct investigations, whether or not the offense is flagrant. While the prosecutors rarely take direct charge of an investigation and infrequently order investigation of facts that the police would not themselves investigate, the mere possibility of such intervention may serve a valuable function in checking the power of the police. Since the French prosecutor must be kept informed, at an early stage, of the existence and progress of the investigation, the prosecutor has more input into the direction and methods of investigation (Frase, 1990).

Typical Proceedings in Police Court

The *tribunal de police* (police court) is presided over by a single judge, but the court is constituted with the addition of a prosecutor and a recording officer (*greffier*). The judge is a member of the judicial hierarchy (the *tribunal de grande instance*) who has been designated to sit in a lower court (the *tribunal d'instance*). The prosecutor is a *procureur de la Republique* or a deputy *procureur* (*substitut*), or a *commissaire de police*. The greffier notes by hand what transpires at the hearing and subsequently types it up so that it can be placed in the record (*dossier*).

The judge, the procureur or the commissaire de police, and the greffier sit together on the bench during a hearing. The judge manages the hearing, interrogates the defendant (*prevenu*) (if present) and any civil party (*partie civile*) or witness. The dossier recording the investigation is available on the bench and is consulted by the judge during the hearing.

Law Enforcement in Germany

The Federal Republic of Germany (FRG) is a federation consisting of 16 individual states. Germany has a limited federal police force. Basically, all police functions are the responsibility of the state police agencies. Their jurisdictions are strictly divided and autonomous, and almost all police activity takes place at the local level, or in cases of rural settlements, by the state police. The administration of the police falls under the control of the state Ministry of the Interior. The states have jurisdiction for organization and personnel matters pertaining to the state police forces.

In the study of police structure in Germany, the impact of the Allied forces who occupied Germany after World War II must be considered. The Potsdam Agreement of 1945 tasked the Allied forces with the duty of decentralizing, democratizing, and demilitarizing areas of public life in Germany, including the police. The Allied forces agreed on the need to decentralize the police, but had different ideas about what constituted decentralization, and so this was approached differently by the British, French, and Americans (Reichel, 2005). In addition, the Soviet Union assumed control over portions of Germany until the reunification. The British organized the police in a manner similar to that of the British system, and the police function in their occupation zone was limited to the maintenance of law and order and the detection of crime. The traditional administrative functions of the police in the British zone were transferred to other governmental units. The French, however, had no problems allowing a centralized control of the police in their zone. In the American zone, the police retained central police control as an organizational principle for the communities with populations of fewer than 5000. In the larger cities, the Americans established police organizations very similar to those in major U.S. cities, and the mayors were responsible for supervision of the police forces (Reichel, 2005).

After the German officials complained that the communal police forces in small towns were impractical and that the mixture of police structures was ineffective, in 1950 the Allied High Command allowed state governments to centralize their police at the state level. The centralization was not completed until 1975, when the city of Munich eliminated its communal police force. Today in Germany, policing is essentially a state matter.

The *Bundegrenzschutz* (BGS) is the primary federal police force. It performs special police duties in the security of the FRG and is under the control of the Federal Ministry of the Interior. The BGS operates nationwide and has approximately 30,000 sworn officers. The duties of the BGS include providing protection of the borders of the FRG; railway policing; security of air traffic; protection of federal institutions and federal ministries; and police duties in periods of emergency.

There is, within the federal police, the Federal Crime Investigation Bureau (*Bundeskriminalamt* or BKA). The primary duties of the BKA are to act as a central clearinghouse for information and communications of all federal police forces and to combat crime through such means as collection and analysis of police intelligence, compilation of statistics, research, identification, and forensic science laboratory services. The BKA also conducts limited investigations in specific areas (e.g., counterfeiting, drugs, arms, and explosives, and if there are international aspects to the case, terrorism and political crimes). They may be ordered or requested to conduct investigations to aid local authorities.

The state ministers of the interior have adopted a joint security program that provides for a relatively uniform state police organization throughout the states. The chief executive is the minister of the interior of the state. There is a crime investigating office in each state, which serves the same function at the state level that the Federal Crime Investigating Office serves at the federal level. Each state has the following police components: uniformed police, including special emergency units such as those for crowd or riot control, as well as marine police units responsible for policing rivers, harbors and coastal areas; a detective branch or criminal police, which carries out criminal investigations, except for special investigations, at the local level; and a police academy.

The police academy, river police office, central crime investigation office, telecommunications center, payments office, and mobile police fall within the state police administrative structure, but outside the immediate chain of command. The police directorate is at the lower level and consists of uniformed officers and the detective branch. This is directed by the common chief officer, who maintains a central command and control function. At the higher level is the district police department, which is responsible for several police directorates as well as for specialized functions such as special operational units, motorway police stations, and the forensic laboratory.

Juvenile Justice in Turkey

It appears that when individuals discuss juvenile delinquency issues in Turkey they refer to it as juveniles pushed into crime instead of delinquents. The general opinion of the Turkish experts is that juvenile crime is caused solely by external influences. Accordingly, those juveniles who break the law are treated as victims and passive actors.

Turkey did not develop a separate juvenile justice system until the late 1980s. Prior to that juveniles were prosecuted in the adult criminal justice system. While a separate system for juveniles was created by legislative action in 1979, it was not implemented until 1987.

Under the present Turkish system, there are three classes of juveniles who are involved in criminal misconduct: (1) those who are 12 years of age or younger, (2) those between 13 and 15 years of age, and (3) those between 16 and 18 years of age. Those under the age of 13 are not considered as criminal responsible for crimes they may commit. For those in the middle range of 13–15 years of age, the question of whether or not they may be held criminally responsible for their act must be determined by psychologists. Those in the older age range, 16–18, are presumed to be criminally responsible for their criminal misconduct, but when punished receive lesser sentences than adults.

There are separate jail facilities for arrested juveniles. Adjudicated juveniles may be placed in a reformatory or juvenile training home.

There are also juvenile prisons for those awaiting trial for serious offenses or having been adjudicated as having committed a serious offense. The youths can be held in juvenile prisons until they reach the age of 21.

Source: Serkan Tasgin. (2015). Juvenile justice and incarceration in Turkey. In Mathieu Deflem (Ed.), *Punishment and Incarceration: A Global Perspective.* Bigley, UK: Emerald Books, pp. 31–52.

Law Enforcement in Brazil

Brazil is a republic composed of a federal district (Brasília, capital of the union) and 27 states. Brazilian police forces are organized at federal, state, and municipal levels. Most of Brazil's law enforcement officers are members of the military police, whose units are commanded at the state level. While the Brazilian police force has historically been linked to the armed forces and to the ideological tendencies of the administration in power, the military police have operated independently of the armed forces since 1988.

During the period from 1964 to about 1985, the police were used mainly as an instrument of political repression. Since 1985, the police have been used primarily to combat crime. Under the Federal Constitution of 1988, law enforcement on the streets is assigned to the military police. There are also state troopers, who are part of the military police and are responsible for patrolling state highways (Das and Palmiotto, 2006).

Violence and corruption among police are serious concerns in Brazil, exacerbated by low wages and educational attainment. Each year police in São Paulo and Rio de Janeiro are implicated in hundreds of extrajudicial killings as well as in drug trafficking, kidnapping, theft, and other crimes. Attempts at reform have been frustrated by the sheer number of such incidents and by frequent conflicts between police agencies (Brazil, 2007).

The federal police, within the federal jurisdiction, report to the Ministry of Justice, and their jurisdiction is nationwide. A primary mission of the federal police is to detect criminal offenses against the political and social order and against the goods, services, and interests of the federal government, its autonomous bodies, and public enterprises, as well as other offenses with interstate or international repercussions. They are also responsible for prevention and control of illicit trafficking in narcotics and other illegal drugs, contraband, and of attempts to evade the maritime, air, and border police and federal police enforcement.

The state police are divided into civil police and military police. The military police perform typical civil police duties. The military police are not an internal force of the national military. They have retained the military police name, which was given to them when the force was created in 1977 by a military-led national government.

The military police are responsible for actual policing and preservation of public order. Their primary mission is daily patrols and the pursuit of criminals. Both the civil and military state police report to the governors of the states, the Federal District, and the territories. In each state, the chief of police is the secretary of public security, who directly assists the governor and is responsible for any acts of law enforcement and crime prevention in the course of duty.

The civil police function as state judicial police and investigate criminal offenses, with the exception of military offenses and those offenses under the jurisdiction of the federal police.

State Police Special Operations Battalion

In October 2007, a new movie opened in Rio de Janeiro: *Tropa de Elite* ("Elite Squad"). The movie is about the Brazilian State Police Special Operations Battalion, known as BOPE, during a crime sweep in Rio in 2005. This is one of the most popular movies that has played in Brazil. The BOPE attempted unsuccessfully to keep it out of the theaters.

The BOPE has approximately 400 members. Its members wear a badge that has a skull and crossed pistols. At one time it had a reputation as an honest haven for honest cops in Rio. According to the *New York Times*, that reputation for being incorruptible is fading.

According to the *Times*, the film traces the true story of Operation Holiness, in which BOPE was tasked with making the area safe for a brief visit by Pope John Paul II in 1997, and continues covering their activities until 2005. It was alleged that during the 4-month period prior to the pope's visit, the BOPE killed about 30 people in an effort to exterminate a drug gang working in a favela (slum) near the home of Rio's archbishop. A spokesman for the movie stated, "The police have forgotten their main mission and are fighting a private war against drug traffickers" (Barrionuevo, 2007, p. 3).

Corrections under the Civil Law Model

It is often stated that we can assess the quality of justice in a country by looking at the treatment reserved for offenders. Differences in sentencing practices reveal meaningful information about a nation's visions of social inclusion and social control (Garland, 2001). Punishment is an excellent area for comparative research because it provides us with a look at what the nation aims to achieve by the imposition of it (Pakes, 2004). Criminal justice systems react differently to similar crimes. One factor influencing this difference is based on how each nation perceived the seriousness of offenses and the perceived severity of the various types of punishment. According to Labardini (2005), countries with a common law legal tradition seem to allow for nominally harsher penalties than do civil law countries.

According to Nestler (2003), sentencing in Germany indicates that the German approach to sentencing is far less punitive than in the United States, although both countries belong to the so-called Western world and have rather similar political and economic structures. Nestler indicates that the motives by which sentencing is driven in Germany are primarily retribution, deterrence, a little bit of rehabilitation, and a lot of pragmatism.

In Germany, sentences are handed down either by the single professional judge or by the judicial panel. There must be at least a two-thirds majority vote to determine the sentence. During a punishment hearing, information is collected by the presiding judge about the defendant's personal life, problems, and financial means. If deemed necessary by the court, a psychological or psychiatric evaluation may be conducted to aid the court in the determination of guilt or innocence as well as the sentence and placement of the accused. An aide to the court, the *Gerichtshilfe*, will conduct an examination of the individual's personality, home environment, and school or work performance to make recommendations to the court on the appropriate adjudication and disposition. Criminal responsibility can be mitigated as a result of the mental state of the offender. This may include acts committed under the influence of alcohol or drugs. The introduction of legal reform has provided other types of penalties, such as the suspended sentence, *Weisungen* (instructions), *Auflagen* (orders), declaration of guilt without imposition of sentence, community service, and probation. Photo 5.1 is a picture of a typical Spanish prison.

In France, the sentence is determined by the judge. The judge who sets the punishment also decides how the punishment will be carried out. The accused, the victim, and the public minister can express their opinions during the sentencing process. Expert witnesses, such as psychiatrists, have great influence. The French courts will generally abide by the conclusions of expert witnesses.

In Brazil, the judge may discharge a defendant and hold the execution of his or her penalty in abeyance upon good behavior (*suspensão condicional da pena*).

Pretrial Diversion

One form of pretrial diversion used in Germany is based on the concept of conditional discharge, by which prosecutors may dismiss a defendant from the criminal proceedings. Although unconditional discharge has a long tradition in Germany, the first provisions having been enacted in 1924,

Photo 5.1 A prison near Madrid, Spain. (Photo by Cliff Roberson.)

conditional discharge is an offspring of the reform movement of the 1970s. At that time courts needed relief from their high caseload. The solution was a procedural decriminalization through a transfer of parts of the courts' sentencing power to the public prosecutor (Meier, 2004).

Conditional discharge is provided for in para. 153a, section one of the German Criminal Procedure Statute (StPO), which provides that the public prosecutor has the power to stop the proceedings and dismiss the defendant if the defendant fulfills the orders and instructions imposed upon him within a given time period, usually 6 months. The option depends upon the defendant's and the trial judge's consent. The public prosecutor may choose this option if the defendant is charged with a misdemeanor, which means an offense with a minimum sentence of less than 1 year of imprisonment, and if the severity of the offender's guilt does not require a formal charge. While the ranges of the orders and instructions that may be imposed upon the offender are unlimited, the law states that the offender can be obliged to do the following: make restitution for the damage caused by the offense; make a payment to a charitable organization or to the state; do community service; pay maintenance claims; engage in victim–offender mediation; or participate in seminars for offenders.

In Germany, other diversion programs exist for cases of minor offenses, such as when the prosecutor asks for a punishment order to be granted by the court. This out-of-court settlement occurs when the judge allows the defendant to make payments or forfeit a driver's license rather than face trial.

In the case of a minor offense, the prosecutor moves for a conditional waiver, and the judge and the accused must agree to the conditions and orders that are sufficient to accommodate the public interest in a prosecution.

In Brazil, pretrial diversion is available. It is obtained by a meeting of the opposing parties in a case with a judicial officer for the purpose of stipulating matters of agreement. It is not required to file a motion for diversion. During the period of diversion, the trial dossiers compiled on a case remain permanently open to inspection by counsel and prosecution alike. In jurisdictions with a large criminal caseload, there is an undetermined amount of pretrial diversion through bargaining that is not acknowledged by judges and worked out between prosecutors and defense attorneys who plead their clients guilty in exchange for a shorter sentence. In recent years, there has been an increasing amount of diversion (i.e., formal halting or suspending of traditional criminal proceedings), involving counseling, tutoring, crisis intervention, job assistance, and guidance with school and family problems.

Plea Bargaining

Civil law systems are ideologically opposed to plea bargaining because it is seen as inconsistent with a judge's duty to determine guilt and to apply the law uniformly to all offenders (Pizzi, 1993, p. 1361). At one time plea bargaining was considered impossible to contemplate in a civil law country because it undercuts a judge's obligation to determine the truth about the charges (whether or not the defendant confesses to the crime) and also because plea bargaining has the potential to introduce varying sentences between defendants charged with the same crime. The civil law tradition also emphasizes the need for uniformity and verdicts that are fully explicable under applicable law.

In the 1980s, many scholars reported admiringly that the German system had successfully avoided any form or analog of plea bargaining in its procedures for cases of serious crimes. Another group stated that in France plea bargaining was virtually nonexistent. To these French and German scholars, the very idea of commercialized justice was abhorrent to civil law legal tradition (Pizzi, 1993). But, according to Pizzi (1993), informal forms of plea bargaining, usually between the judge and defense counsel, have emerged in both Germany and France. Pizzi states that such plea bargaining has become a problem that is defended by practitioners and condemned by scholars.

According to Langer (2004), in Germany and France, the influence of U.S. plea bargaining is undeniable. Each jurisdiction has adopted a form of plea bargaining that contains substantial differences from the U.S. model, either because of decisions by the legal reformers in each jurisdiction or because of structural differences between U.S. criminal procedure and the criminal procedures of the civil law tradition. Not only has each adopted a version of plea bargaining different from the U.S. model, but also, each one of these jurisdictions has adopted forms of plea bargaining different from one another. The German and French plea bargains differ substantially from each other because of decisions by legal reformers in each country, the differing ways in which the practice has been introduced, and the resistance it has generated (Langer, 2004).

According to Canivet (2003), the French Department of Justice has one form of plea bargaining with a project called "appearance in court on a previous recognition of guilt" (*comparution sur reconnaissance préalable de culpabilité*). That procedure will apply to any person who admits to having committed a crime punishable by 5 years of imprisonment at the most and will result in a deal on sentencing that will be approved by the judge and that will lead to a sentence of no more than 6 months of imprisonment without parole. According to Canivet, the French simply transplanted plea bargaining into their legal culture only for its virtue of efficiency, without any effort to adapt its underlying philosophy to their cultural background. He indicates that under the economic theory of law, plea bargaining is a win–win contract and a rational allocation of resources between the parties. The rationale is that since each criminal trial is uncertain in its result, the rational accused is induced to avoid a trial where he could be sentenced to a harsher penalty than the one he deserves, and the prosecutor is induced to avoid a long and costly trial that could result in too light a sentence or in an acquittal. After the defense lawyer and the prosecutor agree, the parties follow a more or less informal procedure sealed by a written agreement approved by a judge in open court, on a lesser sentence than the maximal penalty provided for by the law, in exchange for relinquishment by the accused of his right to trial and to due process of law.

Canivet describes the dominant penal philosophy in France as very distrustful of the economic and utilitarian model of sentencing in the common law. In France's legal culture, individual rights normally are not legal titles that can be disposed of freely by their holders. The right to a fair trial and the right of due process are absolute and inalienable; they cannot be negotiated or traded off, whatever the anticipated benefit for their holder or for third parties. Canivet argues that the French ignored this philosophy when they transplanted plea bargaining into their system.

According to Turner (2006), as late as 1979, Germany could still be considered as a "land without plea bargaining." Since then, however, plea bargaining has grown rapidly in Germany, largely unnoticed at first and has been much more open since the 1990s. In 1986, a study found that plea bargaining occurred almost exclusively in white collar and drug cases; by 2007, it also happened frequently in sexual violence, organized crime, and corruption cases, and less often in homicide cases.

The practice of plea bargaining in Germany developed organically, without direction from any written rule change or centrally established policy. Judges and prosecutors were looking to save time and resources as their caseloads grew and became more complex, and defendants were looking for more certainty and a sentence reduction for their cooperation. In the absence of legislative guidance, trial judges were relatively free to define their own role in the process. The higher courts stepped in occasionally, but even when they did so, they established only very broad limits on plea negotiations.

Germany's model of plea bargaining entrusts the judge with the duty to ensure the fairness and accuracy of plea bargaining. The judges act as both a party to and a supervisor of plea negotiations. This proactive approach is in large part a function of Germany's inquisitorial tradition, which entrusts judges with the primary responsibility to discover and verify the substantive truth of the case. Active involvement in the plea negotiations allows judges to fulfill that responsibility in the context of plea bargaining and helps ensure that the plea bargains are fair and consistent with the true facts of the case.

Judges in Germany also have substantial control over the charges filed, which makes them an indispensable part of the plea bargaining process. When the charges do not adequately reflect the underlying events, judges can, after giving notice, convict the defendant on different charges. The judge can, pursuant to a plea bargain, also change the charges. Similarly, judges decide whether charges should be dismissed once the formal accusation has been filed, and their approval is often needed for a prosecutor to decline to file charges. In deciding whether to adjust or dismiss charges, judges can probe into the relevant facts on their own initiative, going beyond the investigative file compiled by the police and presented by the prosecution.

German judges also have broad discretion over the defendant's sentence. Sentencing and trial form part of a unitary proceeding in Germany. The court deliberates on punishment and sentence at the same time, and in the mixed court, which hears more serious criminal cases, lay and professional judges deliberate together. At the end of trial, the judgment must describe in detail "how the court evaluates the evidence and which facts it finds to be true." It must also provide reasons for the punishment imposed, but the law imposes relatively few limits on the court's sentencing discretion.

For the most part, informal plea bargaining is based on the amount of discretion that the judge or the prosecutor has. With the civil law tradition of compulsory prosecution that stems from the concern that broad prosecutorial discretion would lead inevitably to local differences in the enforcement of the criminal law, civil law prosecutors have traditionally had only limited discretion. In the common law systems, in contrast, prosecutorial discretion is seen as part of a political tradition that is built on a preference for local control over political power and on an aversion to strong centralized governmental authority and power (Pizzi, 1993).

In Brazil, there is no explicit plea or sentencing bargaining. There is, however, a functional equivalent. Brazilian courts use it to manage their caseload without giving every defendant a full-blown investigation and adjudication of his or her case. It is like pretrial diversion, except that charges are not dropped (as occurs in pretrial diversion programs in the United States), and like probation, except that there are no probation officers involved.

Confinement

In France, there are five types of penal institutions:

1. *Central houses* receive offenders who have been sentenced to more than 1 year in prison.
2. *Detention centers* can also receive offenders with long sentences, but are oriented toward the resocialization of offenders.
3. *Stop houses* receive offenders with less than a 1-year sentence.
4. *Penitentiary centers* are a hybrid of stop houses and central houses and receive offenders with both long and short sentences.
5. *Semiliberty centers* house offenders who can be released for short periods of time to go to work, school, or professional training or undergo medical treatment.

In France, the prison administration is under the minister of justice and consists of the central administration service and exterior services. The prison central administration service is headquartered in Paris. Prison exterior services operate at both regional and local levels, along four areas of interest: the application of judicial decisions, reintegration, human resources, and general administration. Inmates in the French prisons are not obligated to work, although in principle, prisons are obligated to provide work for inmates to do. About 40% of the prisoners are provided with paid work.

In Germany, prisons are administered only at the state level. There are neither federal prisons nor private prisons. The German institutions are classified as either open or closed institutions. Open institutions are characterized by minimal restrictions and lack of high-security walls, fences, or armed guards at the perimeter. Open institutions house nonviolent offenders with relatively short sentences. Closed institutions are characterized by high security at the perimeter as well as within the institutions. However, in closed institutions it is not uncommon to find low-security tracts, particularly in women's prisons, where young mothers are often allowed to keep their children with them in the prison until the child reaches a designated age. There are about 25 open institutions and 200 closed institutions (Aronowitz, 2002).

In Brazil, the maximum period of incarceration is 30 years. The penalties vary considerably, pending on the seriousness and circumstances of the offense, and the personality and behavior of the offender. Most offenses are punishable with prison sentences.

Probation

The Boston shoemaker John Augustus is credited by many with being the founder of the concept of probation as a substitute for imprisonment. The first legislation in Massachusetts that formally established probation was in 1878. Probation developed in England in a similar manner to that in the United States. In fact, many credit Matthew Hill, an English court reporter, with the development of the concept of probation. In 1841, Hill would identify juvenile offenders whom he considered not wholly corrupt and hand them over to English citizens willing to act as guardians (Reichel, 2005). Whether Hill or Augustus should be credited with the development of probation, it is clear that the concept developed in a common law country. The civil law countries lagged behind in utilizing probation by at least 40 years.

France was the first civil law country in Europe to utilize probation. While a law was enacted in France in 1891 that contained aspects of probation, not until 1958 did the French allow for a formal sentence of supervised probation (Reichel, 2005). By 1891, Switzerland was using a form of probation.

Probation in Germany started as a form of conditional pardon. One method used in Germany to reduce the number of prisoners is the suspension of prison sentences. Suspended sentences were first introduced to German law in 1953. After the first experiences were quite encouraging, their scope was considerably enlarged in the reform period of 1969–1974 and once again in 1986. Today, suspension is possible with sentences of up to 2 years. The requirements that must be met if a prison sentence is to be suspended vary depending on the duration of the reference prison sentence (Nestler, 2003).

In the Brazilian penal system of justice, probation is a component in the administration of justice embodied by an agency or organization in charge of running the process, including the preparation of reports for the courts, or supervision of probationers by probation officers. Probation in Brazil is known as *suspensão condicional da pena*, a suspension of the penalty based on testing of the conduct of the accused, a benefit subject to the defendant's admitting the charges. The penalty must not exceed 2 years of imprisonment and it can be suspended for a maximum of 2–4 years, provided the convict is not guilty of a serious crime.

Parole

In France, first-time offenders usually are paroled after serving one-half of their sentences; recidivists are eligible for parole after a longer period of imprisonment. In 2002, a formal system for dealing with the early release of prisoners on grounds of ill health was introduced in France (Steiner, 2003). In the 5 years following its enactment, the legislation had been applied successfully in cases of seriously ill and elderly prisoners.

In France, prisoners may also apply for a remission of a sentence. French inmates can apply for early release to the Penalty Application Commission. The reduction cannot exceed 3 months per year of incarceration and 7 days per month for incarceration over 1 year. Time reduction is also permitted if the French inmate passes an academic exam or completes university or professional studies. However, this form of reduction cannot exceed 2 months per year of incarceration. French prisoners with life sentences can also obtain parole. The total reduction of sentence cannot exceed 20 days or a month per year of incarceration.

Germany has a formal program for parole. In cases where a determinate sentence has been imposed, conditional release for good behavior may be granted to a German inmate who has served two-thirds of the sentence. In special cases in Germany, an individual may be released after half the sentence is served. In Germany, punishment of life without the possibility of parole is not permitted. When an individual has received a life sentence, the court may consider conditional release after the individual has served at least 15 years. Supervisory assistance in the form of a parole officer is available to inmates released early from prison.

Prisoners in Brazil who have served at least one-third of their maximum sentence or made restitution for the loss or damage caused may be granted parole. Parolees, until a final discharge is granted, must sustain good behavior and remain under the supervision of an institution or agency approved by the court. As with probation, the power to grant parole is held by the courts.

Women in Mexico's Prisons

The social anthropologist Elena Azaola conducted an extensive research project on women confined in Mexico's federal prisons in 2013–2014. She noted that while male population increased by 40% from 1999 to 2010 than that of female prison population, more than doubled during that period. The majority of female prisoners in Mexico's federal prisons were incarcerated for drug-related offenses. Over 90% of the female prisoners had never been convicted of a felony prior to present conviction.

In general, Dr. Azaola contends that women prisoners face more adverse life conditions than male prisoners, the level of vulnerability and violence they suffer in their family was higher, and the employments they had access to were almost always informal and poorly reattributed.

Source: Personal interview with Dr. Azaola on April 16, 2015.

Death Penalty

The death penalty has been increasingly banished throughout the world. According to Amnesty International, a total of 118 countries have abolished the death penalty in law or practice, and only 78 countries and territories retain and use the death penalty; however, the number of countries actually executing prisoners in any 1 year is much smaller. In fact, in the decade 1995–2005, three countries a year on average abolished the death penalty for all crimes (Labardini, 2005).

The Western country where the death penalty is most widely accepted and used is the United States. Even there, however, the death penalty has had a checkered career. The death penalty was outlawed in Germany on May 23, 1949, by Article 102 of the *Grundgesetz* (Constitution) of the FRG. In France, the death penalty was repealed by the law on October 9, 1981. In Brazil, the death penalty has been abolished for ordinary crimes and is permitted only in case of war declared by Congress and as a response to aggression by a foreign nation.

Fines

According to Meier (2004), in Germany, fines have proved to be very efficient in reducing the number of imprisoned offenders, and a provision in the Penal Code establishes the priority of fines over short-term prison sentences. This provision is the result of the reform movement of the late 1960s and early 1970s and is grounded in the widespread belief that short-term prison sentences have more disadvantages than advantages because they take the offender from his social setting and commit him to an institution where he has contacts with other offenders; moreover, the time they spend in prison is too short to stabilize them socially and offer them help they may need. Fines are also used in France and appear to be the most popular punishment there.

Summary

- The major nations using the civil law model (e.g., Germany, Spain, and France) have tended to have strong national governments when the civil law model was adapted or assumed, whereas the nations using the common law model have historically been more responsive to the demands of their citizens and have generally had national governments whose powers were not absolute.
- Countries that have adopted the common law model tend to favor decentralized control of police forces.
- Those countries that follow the civil law model tend to favor a centralized model of policing. However, there is considerable variation among the centralized police organizations of the civil law countries.
- Most civil law nations fall under one of four categories regarding their police models: (1) complete centralization in one police force; (2) high centralization, with a small number of national police forces; (3) regional centralization under federal authority; and (4) decentralized local policing, with a strong national agency.
- The responsibility for France's internal security is assigned to two major forces: the National Police (Police Nationale) and the National Gendarmerie.
- The French National Police forces are under the authority of France's Minister of the Interior. Highest police authority in France is the general director of the National Police.
- French policing is more closely integrated with the prosecution function than in the United States.
- Germany's policing is considered regional centralization under federal authority, with the basic policing structure resting on the state or province police forces.
- Germany has a limited federal police force. Basically, all police functions are the responsibility of the state police agencies.
- Brazilian police forces are organized at federal, state, and municipal levels. Most of Brazil's law enforcement officers are members of the military police, whose units are commanded at the state level.
- Sentencing in Germany indicates that the German approach to sentencing is far less punitive than in the United States.
- In Germany, sentences are handed down either by the single professional judge or by a judicial panel.
- In France, the sentence is determined by the judge. The judge who sets the punishment also decides how the punishment will be carried out. The accused, the victim, and the public minister can express their opinions during the sentencing process.

- At one time plea bargaining was considered impossible to contemplate in a civil law country because it undercuts a judge's obligation to determine the truth about the charges (whether or not the defendant confesses to the crime) and also because plea bargaining has the potential to introduce varying sentences between defendants charged with the same crime.
- The civil law countries lagged behind in utilizing probation by at least 40 years.
- France was the first civil law country in Europe to utilize probation. Probation in Germany started as a form of conditional pardon. One method used in Germany to reduce the number of prisoners is the suspension of prison sentences.

Questions in Review

1. Why are punishments in civil law courts generally considered less punitive than sentences handed down in U.S. courts for similar offenses?
2. What are the key differences between police departments in civil law countries and those in common law countries?
3. Should all countries eliminate the death penalty?
4. In many U.S. states, life imprisonment without the possibility of parole is a permissible punishment. In many civil law countries, it is not a permissible punishment. Which side do you support? Why?
5. German and French courts appear to rely more on the recommendations of medical experts in formulating an appropriate sentence than do the court in the United States. Which do you think is the better practice? Why?

The Islamic Law Model
The Courts

6

Chapter Objectives

After studying this chapter, you should understand or be able to explain the following issues and concepts:

- The concept of *hudud* crimes
- The concept of *qisas* crimes
- Criminal proceedings under the Islamic law model
- The influence of the Prophet Muhammad on Islamic law
- The key concepts of Islamic law
- The structure of Islamic penal laws
- Evidence principles under Islamic law

Key Terms

Hudud **crimes:** Crimes against God. They include defamation, denunciation of Islam, theft, banditry, defamation, drinking alcohol, apostasy (turning away from Islam), and sexual offenses such as sodomy and adultery.

Qadi: A judge.

Qisas **crimes:** Crimes against private persons. These crimes are more serious than *ta'zir* crimes, but not as serious as *hudud* crimes.

Qur'an: The holy text of Islam and literally means "reading." The highest source of Islamic jurisprudence.

Secular law: Law that does not pertain to religion or to any religious body.

Shari'ah: A body of rules of conduct that was revealed by God to the Prophet Muhammad and recorded in the Qur'an, whereby people are directed to lead their lives.

Ta'zir **crimes:** The least serious crimes in Islamic penal law.

Unzil: Refers to that which descended from Heaven.

Introduction

In studying Islamic law, our problem is that there is a multiplicity of schools of thought, and not one national legal system. No school can be regarded as the "parent" of Islamic law, and no school can be given precedence on that basis. As far as possible when studying Islamic law as a model, we must remember that each model is focused on its geographical location. Accordingly, when studying Islamic law was applied in Morocco, for instance, we would need to focus on the diacritics Mālikī school of thought (Harasani, 2014).

The different Islamic nations have adopted different schools of thought. For example, Saudi Arabia follows the Hanbali school of thought, while Morocco adheres to the diacritics Mālikī school of thought. However, the legal systems of the two countries are not exclusively Hanbali or diacritics Mālikī. In addition, many of the laws in the Islamic legal systems are secular and not based on Islamic legal doctrine (Harasani, 2014). This makes a national legal system of an Islamic country difficult to justify as a model for Islamic law when undertaking comparative legal research. Accordingly, we have used the general elements of such legal systems to exemplify the manifestations of Islamic law.

In general, the legal tradition of Islamic law rests on the teachings of the Prophet Muhammad. The most difficult feature of Islamic law for most Westerners to grasp is that no separation exists between church and state. The religion of Islam and the government are one (Wiechman et al., 1996).

The first two models of law that we have studied, common law and civil law, are considered secular in nature. Neither of them claims to have any force of religion behind it. Sacred law legal tradition is the law that is based on some sacred text or body of religious doctrine. Islamic law clearly falls in that category.

When the Islamic legal model is discussed, we tend to think of countries in the Middle East and North Africa as the major Islamic law countries. The American naval historian A. T. Maham is credited with first using the term "Middle East" in 1902. At the time he was referring to the region around the Persian Gulf. The term was later used in the British House of Lords in 1911 by Lord Curzon during a discussion of the state of affairs in Persia and Turkey.

Today, the nations that embrace the Islamic legal model are fragments that have formed from the universal Muslim community that was first formed about 1400 years ago (Opolot, 1980).

The countries that have majority Muslim populations have adopted diverse legal systems. Those that were once English colonies (Bangladesh, Jordan, and some of the Persian Gulf states) generally accepted common law systems. Those that were once under French colonial influence (countries of the Maghreb and other parts of North Africa, including Egypt, as well as

Syria and Iraq) generally adopted civil law systems. A third group of countries retained or later adopted Islamic law—called the *shari'ah*—with few or no reforms (Saudi Arabia and Iran). While the last shah had reformed a large amount of the law in Iran, building on previous colonial laws, common law concepts were almost totally replaced following the Islamic revolution in that country in 1979.

Although Islamic law is used, at least in part, in 53 Muslim countries and a number of non-Muslim countries, such as India, only a few countries apply traditional Islamic criminal law. And most of those, for instance, Iran and Sudan, have systems that are blended with the civil or common law model. Saudi Arabia has applied Islamic criminal law in its traditional form since it was founded in 1927 (Esmaeili and Gans, 2000).

The Muslim system of criminal justice evolved from the justice initiated by the Prophet Mohammed. In the United States, the separation of church and state is a constitutional requirement. In those countries using the Islamic law model, the administration of criminal justice is so interwoven with religion and Muslim society that it cannot be studied without some understanding of the religion and the way of life it entails.

Muslims believe that Muhammad was the most perfect of God's creatures. While he was not divine, he was not just a man among men but "like a ruby among ordinary stones." The ethical teachings of Islam are rooted in the Qur'an and the model of perfect ethical character, Muhammad. The virtues that characterize him are humility and poverty, magnanimity and nobility, and sincerity and truthfulness. Muhammad loved spiritual poverty and was also close to the economically poor, living very simply even after he had become "the ruler of a whole world." He was always severe with himself and emphasized that if exertion in the path of God (*al-jihad*, commonly translated as "holy war") can sometimes mean fighting to preserve one's life and religion, the greater jihad is to fight against the dispersing tendencies of the concupiscent soul.

Islam has used these virtues as models and sources of inspiration for all Muslims, and they have been applied on many levels from the most outward to the most inward. The great classical texts of Islamic ethics, such as those of al-Qushayri and al-Ghazali, which are still widely read, are expositions of ethical and spiritual virtues that all Muslims believe the prophet possessed on the highest level. The key points to studying Islam legal models include the concept that Islam's law comprises a comprehensive outlook on life. As one looks from a satellite at this planet, the shar'iah see the earth as a single "city" with diverse inhabitants—in modern parlance, a "global village." Islam looks to the benefit of the society as a whole from a general perspective and presents a theoretical model that if followed provides safety and protection for society (Kamali, 1999).

Muhammad

The Prophet Muhammad (also spelled Mohammed) was born in 570 AD in Mecca, in present-day Saudi Arabia, and died on June 8, 632. His full name is Abu al-Qasim Muhammad ibn 'Abd Allah ibn 'Abd al-Muttalib ibn Hashim. He is considered the founder of the religion of Islam. His name is invoked in reverence several billion times every day. Yet, Muhammad has been one of the most reviled figures in the history of the world since the seventh century. He is the only founder of a major world religion who lived in the full light of history and about whom there are numerous records in historical texts, although like other premodern historical figures, not every detail of his life is known.

Although the Qur'an is considered by Muslims to be the word of God and not that of Muhammad, it nevertheless reveals the most essential aspects associated with the prophet. There are also the sayings of Muhammad himself (the *hadith*) and accounts by his followers of his actions (the *sunnah*).

Muhammad is considered the ultimate prophet of Islam and a messenger from God. His father died before he was born and his mother died when he was 5 years old. He was raised by his uncle. Muhammad was known for his handsome features, uprightness, intelligence, charity, and knowledge of the environment surrounding him.

As a young boy he traveled with his uncle in a merchants' caravan to Syria, and some years afterward he made the same journey in the service of a wealthy widow named Khadijah. She was pleased with the way he transacted her business, and the report of his behavior, which she received from her servant who had accompanied him. Soon afterward they married, though she was 15 years older than he was. Their marriage lasted until her death 26 years later. After her death, he took other wives, but he always mentioned her with the greatest love and reverence. The marriage gave him wealth and rank among the notables of Mecca, while his conduct earned him the surname al-Amin, "the trustworthy."

It was his practice to retire often to a cave in the desert for meditation. His usual month for retreat was Ramadan (the month of heat). It was there, one night toward the end of his quiet month, that he claimed the first revelation came to him when he was 40 years old.

He claimed that he heard a voice say: "Read!" He said: "I cannot read." The voice again said: "Read!" He said: "I cannot read." A third time the voice, more terrible, commanded: "Read!" He said: "What can I read?" The voice said:

"Read: In the name of thy Lord Who createth."
"Createth man from a clot."
"Read: And it is thy Lord the Most Bountiful"
"Who teacheth by the pen,"
"Teacheth man that which he knew not."

Haykal (1976), Bahgat (1993), and Souryal (2004)

Origins and Evolution

In its purest and simplest form, the message of Islam is relatively brief: instill-
ing monotheism and social justice. Without the former, the latter is irrelevant,
and without the latter, the former is illogical.

Souryal (2004, p. 19)

The word "Islam" is a noun that stems from the same Semitic root as
Arabic "salam" and Hebrew "shalom." The word "Islam" can have two meanings: "peace," as in "peace be with you," and "submission," referring to whole-
hearted submission to God. The same room gives us the word for believers in
Islam, "Muslim," which Europeans have also spelled "Moslem" or "Muslin."
(Arabic words are pronounced differently in various parts of the Islamic
world.) The word "Muhammadan" has also been applied by Westerners to
Muslims, but it is considered objectionable by Muslims because the Qur'an
explicitly forbids worshiping the Prophet Muhammad. Souryal (2004) states
that using the word "Muhammadan" would be the same as referring to
Christians as "Jesusites" or Jews as "Mosesites."

Souryal (2004) contrasts Islam with Christianity and Judaism on the basis
of three fundamental theological doctrines: Christians believe that Jesus is
the son of God; Jews believe that they are God's chosen people; and Muslims
believe that the Qur'an is God's literal word that physically descended (*unzil*)
upon Muhammad.

Hallaq (2005) traces the origins of Islamic law to Mecca, the city in
which Muhammad was born. Muhammad began to preach in the early
seventh century, and his teachings eventually reflected significant cultural, religious, political, and legal influences from many corners of the
world. During the early development of Islamic law, first under the direction of Muhammad and later that of his political and religious descendents,
Muslims drew on these influences and combined them with the indigenous
ideas and norms present in the Qur'an and developed a different approach
to legal thinking.

Hallaq contends that the next stage of the legal development began with
the rise of professional *qadis* (judges). The judges, who were appointed by the
political authorities, quickly achieved a measure of independence from the
state. The judges began as arbitrators, administrators, and even storytellers,
but they quickly began to create specific legal administrative structures. Later,
according to Hallaq, the judges developed into a fully independent cultural
and religious institution that was dependent on political authorities for financial support, but was not controlled by them.

Hallaq explains that as the judgeships became increasingly regular-
ized, a parallel class of legal specialists developed who became member
of, or worked to advise, the judiciary. In the decades following the death

of Muhammad in 632, these specialists formed small discussion groups in order to develop reputations for embodying religious knowledge and thereby developing epistemic authority with the sole power to interpret the religious texts. By the ninth century, two dominant trends had developed: one that emphasized traditionalism (antirational), and another that sought to promote human reason as the primary tool for interpreting Allah's revelations. Following the failed inquisition (*mihna*) (833–850) of traditionalist scholars of the Abbasid Caliphate, which was encouraged by the rationalists, a middle path between reason and traditionalism developed. The scholars who had promoted the middle path also promoted the formation of doctrinal schools (*madhhab*). According to Hallaq, with the establishment of these doctrinal schools, Islamic law reached its full maturity and remained as one a unique experiment in mediating the relationship between religion and state.

Sources

Nader (1990) summarizes the key concepts of Islamic law as follows:

- The law is not made, but was been revealed by God.
- The teachings of leading Muslim jurists have only amplified the law. Islamic law is valid regardless of whether or not it is recognized by the state. The law originates only in divine revelation and not from customs and traditions.
- Islamic law is comprehensive and all-embracing and covers every aspect of the legal system.
- It is not the nature of what the law should be, but what the law actually is.

The two schools of Islamic law (*shari'ah*) associated, respectively, with the Sunni and Shi'i sects both agree that the *sunnah* and *hadith* of the prophet serve as the most important source of Islamic law after the Qur'an. In Islam even a prophet is not a legislator; instead, God is the only legislator (*al-Shari'*). Muslims believe that as God's prophet, Muhammad knew the divine will as it was meant to be codified in Islamic law. His actions and juridical decisions therefore played an indispensable role in the later codification of the *shari'ah* by various legal schools. Muslims believe that Muhammad brought not only the word of God in the form of the Qur'an to the world but also a divine law specific to Islam, a law whose roots are contained completely in the Qur'an but whose crystallization was not possible without the words and deeds of the prophet.

For the few serious crimes mentioned in the Qur'an, judges must specify punishments. The judges have much greater freedom in punishment for less serious crimes. "*Shari'ah*" means the "path" to follow God's law. Shari'ah law is holistic or eclectic in its approach to guiding the individual in most daily matters. It controls, rules, and regulates all public and private behavior. The three major crime categories are *hudud* crimes, the most serious; *ta'zir* crimes, the least serious; and *qisas* crimes, those for which the victim has a right to seek retribution and retaliation.

Non-Muslims are not bound by the same standard as are Muslims. However, both Muslims and non-Muslims must abide by laws such as tax laws, traffic laws, and laws pertaining to white collar crimes and theft. The *mazalim* courts try these and many other crimes similar to common law crimes, as well as civil, family, and other cases. Islamic law has separate courts for Muslims for religious crimes, and contemporary nonreligious courts for other criminal and civil matters.

Saudi Arabia adopted Islamic law when it was founded in 1927. Other countries employing more or less traditional Islamic law include Iran, Syria, Egypt, Iraq, Lebanon, and Kuwait.

In Iran during the reign of Reza Shah, the modern Iranian criminal, judicial, and penitentiary systems were founded. France's Napoleonic Code was used as the model for penal codification. In 1979, with the overthrow of the shah and the establishment of the Islamic Republic, all laws and regulations were newly reformulated based on Islamic rules. The procedures of Iran's present justice system are considered by international observers to be inconsistent with and inattentive to the rights of defendants.

Fundamental Principles

Souryal (2004) states that the Islamic theory of responsibility is governed by four fundamental principles that must be observed in all cases, regardless of whether the crime is *hudud*, *qisas*, or *ta'zir*. The four principles are as follows:

1. The principle of individual responsibility
2. A presumption of innocence
3. Nullification of penalty by doubt
4. Guarantees for an accused

The principle of individual responsibility rejects a more traditional theory under which parents or other family members could be held responsible for crimes committed by a son, daughter, or other relative. Souryal notes that the Qur'an is replete with religious provisions that establish the concept that nobody can be held criminally responsible unless he or she is involved in the commission of a prohibited act as either a principal or an accomplice. This Islamic principle preceded the same theory that currently exists in civil and common law countries. Apparently, the first reference to a Western theory of individual responsibility was in France shortly after the French Revolution (Sanad, 1991).

The concept of presumption of innocence was also recognized by Islamic law prior to any acknowledgment in Western legal thought. According to Sanad (1991, p. 72), the Prophet Muhammad stated in a *hadith:* "Avoid condemning the Muslim to *hudud* crimes whenever you can, and if you can find a way out for the Muslim, then release him; for if the Imam errs it is better that he errs in favor of innocence than in favor of guilt." In conjunction with the presumption of innocence is the principle of nullification of penalty by doubt. According to Souryal, quoting Abu-Zunra, this rule rests on the *hadith:* "Prevent punishment in case of doubt. Release the accused if possible, for it is better that the ruler be wrong in forgiving than wrong in punishing" (Souryal, 2004, p. 121).

Souryal describes a criminal proceeding in Islamic law as a contest between a defendant and the government acting on behalf of the society. This is very similar to a description of a common law trial. Since each side seeks to win and since the government is more powerful than the defendant, the defendant is guaranteed certain basic rights, such as freedom from warrantless searches and seizures, freedom from illegal arrest and investigative detention, and guarantees against certain types of interrogation. Other basic rights in an Islamic trial that are similar to those in civil law or common law countries include the right to present a defense and the right to an impartial trial. One right that is present in Islamic law and not present in all civil law or common law countries is the right to damages for wrongful conviction.

Structure of Penal Law

Under the common and civil laws, substantive, evidential, and sentencing codes are largely independent. Under Islamic criminal law, the definition of crimes, the means of establishing proof, and appropriate punishments are intimately related. Under Islamic law, the types of punishment under consideration determine which legal rules govern a criminal trial (Esmaeili and Gans, 2000).

There are three categories of punishment set out in the *shari'ah*. The first, applicable to *hudud*, are punishments that are fixed by the Qur'an and Sunnah and cannot be altered by any judicial authority. Such punishments include lashing, life imprisonment, hand amputation, and stoning to death. These punishments are attached to only a few crimes, which are regarded as crimes against God.

The second category for punishment is *qisas* (retaliation), which includes such crimes as murder and assault. Like *hudud*, *qisas* is provided for in the *shari'ah* and the courts have no initial sentencing role. The third category is *ta'zirat* (discretionary punishments). This category, which applies to the remaining crimes, is Islamic criminal law's closest analogy to common law sentencing. *Ta'zirat* punishments are dispensed by the secular authority (traditionally, a king). In practice, a list of *ta'zirat* crimes and their associated punishments, which can include lashing, prison, banishment, or capital punishment, is specified in written form. *Shari'ah* judges can also, at their discretion, punish any person considered to have committed a sin under Islamic law (Esmaeili and Gans, 2000).

The same crime may be subject to several categories of punishment. This is so because the definition of crimes attracting certain *hudud* and *qisas* punishments and the rules governing their proof are more stringent than those attracting *ta'zir* punishments. Thus, a criminal who is deemed not liable to receive a *hudud* or *qisas* punishment may still be found guilty of a *ta'zir* crime and sentenced to a discretionary punishment. For example, a person may be found not guilty of the *hudud* crime of theft, because of the stringent conditions that Islamic law attaches to the fixed penalty of hand amputation, but may nonetheless be found guilty of sinful conduct and receive the *ta'zir* penalty of lashing. In the case of murder, the defendant may be subject to the *qisas* punishment of retaliation, if strict definitions and rules of proof are satisfied, or a *ta'zir* penalty, such as imprisonment, if less strict conditions are met (Esmaeili and Gans, 2000).

Islamic law restricts the free proof of facts in criminal trials to a much greater extent than does the common law. Whereas evidence law in common law jurisdictions consists of a set of limited exclusionary rules and, otherwise, permits all evidence that satisfies the low threshold of relevance, Islamic law exhaustively defines all categories of evidence that can be used to sustain a criminal conviction (Esmaeili and Gans, 2000).

Murder under Islamic Law

Similar to civil and common law, under Islamic law there are three degrees of murder (*qatl*): *qatl al-amd* (intentional murder), *qatl al-shabih al-amd* (nonintentional murder), and *qatl al-khata* (accidental murder). Only the first of these categories attracts the possibility of the *qisas* retaliatory measure of capital punishment, although the other categories may still result in the lesser *qisas* remedy of *diyya* (monetary compensation).

Intentional murder (*qatl al-amd*) occurs when the killer intends to kill and uses *mimma taqtulu ghaliban* (some means likely to lead to killing). The requirement that the killer use a means likely to kill is a safeguard to ensure that the killing was intentional. The courts are occasionally faced with the problem of defining which weapons are "deadly," even when they are otherwise certain that a killing was intentional. The use of a firearm, a knife, a hammer, or suffocation satisfies the criteria for intentional murder.

Evidence of Guilt

The Islamic rules of proof in criminal trials are complicated by the intersection between Islamic sentencing and trial law. The boundaries of each category of permissible evidence will vary according to the punishment being contemplated in court. For some crimes, the restrictions are almost an insurmountable barrier to any conviction. Since intentional murder can result in beheading, there are many restrictions on the evidence that can be used to prove a murder charge. A further complication is that there is disagreement both between and within the various Islamic juristic schools, about the content of the restrictions (Sanad, 1991).

Confessions

Perhaps the most practical and effective method of proof allowed under Islamic law is confessional evidence. Islamic law provides two significant barriers to the use of confession as evidence in criminal trials. First, like common law courts, it requires a voluntary confession. Accordingly, a confession that resulted from torture, beating, threats, deception, or any inhumane treatment will not be accepted, even if the court has reason to believe that the confession is true. A second limitation is the general principle of Islamic criminal law that an accused person can withdraw a confession, even a voluntary one, at any time. Juristic writings on this point concern mainly crimes that attract *hudud* punishments. The prevailing view is that a confession to a *hudud* crime can be withdrawn until the moment of punishment. Thus, for example, a defendant's retraction of a confession to theft, instants before her or his hand is amputated, will prevent the completion of the punishment unless other permissible evidence was available to prove the crime. In some cases, the defendant's escape from legal custody can be regarded as an implicit withdrawal of a confession. The ability to withdraw confessions in cases involving less serious punishments, as opposed to *hudud* crimes, is uncertain. One view is that the same rules should apply in both cases. Arguably, withdrawn confessions should not be available to justify the application of the death penalty, which generally attracts the strictest rules of proof. On the other hand, some of the aspects of the Islamic law of withdrawn confessions, for example, the recommendation that *shari'ah* judges positively encourage defendants not to confess or to withdraw their confessions in relation to some crimes, seems to sit more comfortably with *hudud* crimes, seen as crimes against God or society, than with *qisas*, or personal crimes (Sanad, 1991).

Testimony of Eyewitnesses

The classic method for proof of criminal charges under Islamic law is the oral testimony of two pious Muslim males. The required content of the testimony varies according to the punishment sought. To justify a conviction for capital murder, considerable detail is required. Each witness must describe the precise nature of the murder, including such facts as the portion of the victim's body that was struck by the murder weapon. If the witnesses contradict each other on these details, then their testimony is not acceptable. If the witnesses can only specify a lesser degree of detail, then a lesser degree of murder may be proven, but capital punishment will be unavailable.

The requirement of *adala* (piety) on the part of each witness provides a further obstacle for use of this eyewitness evidence. The Hanbali school of jurisprudence requires the court to make a positive inquiry into the good character of every witness. Witnesses must have obeyed the demands and prohibitions of the religion of Islam and have a sense of honor (Sanad, 1991).

Other Evidence

The use of evidence other than eyewitness testimony and confession is controversial in Islamic law. A number of jurists take the view that to permit other methods of testimony would be to allow a judge to become a witness in a trial where he is supposed to reach a verdict. In particular, the judge's personal observation cannot be evidence of serious crimes, including murder. This prohibition extends to the judge's use of inferences from *al-qrain* (circumstantial evidence) where they are unfavorable to the accused. The law does permit the use of such evidence in a murder trial to reach a verdict that would result in a noncapital punishment, such as the payment of blood money.

Some jurists argue that it is wrong to restrict evidence in criminal trials to testimony and confession. Other jurists argue that the ban on the use of the judge's personal observation should be limited to *hudud*, the most serious crimes in the Islamic calendar, and should be permitted to prove *qisas* crimes such as murder. In Iran, one of the main modern jurisdictions that practice Islamic criminal law, the judge's personal observation can support any criminal charge (Sanad, 1991).

Doubt as to Guilt

All Muslim jurists agree that *shubha* (semblance of doubt) will result in *dar'a* (nullification) of *hudud* punishments. In one *hadith*, the prophet said: "Nullify the *hudud* if there is doubt and lift the death penalty as much as you can." In another, the prophet said: "If the judge makes a mistake in amnesty it is better than a mistake in punishment." The jurists do not specify a particular degree of doubt that will result in nullification, such as the common law standard of reasonable doubt. Rather, the texts speak in terms of examples, such as a man accused of adultery who thought his sexual partner was his wife or did not realize that adultery was a crime (Sanad, 1991). Photo 6.1 shows a modern crime laboratory is an Islamic country.

Photo 6.1 The Crime Laboratory of the Dubai Police Department. (Photo by Cliff Roberson.)

Establishing Guilt as to Adultery

To prove the crime of adultery, the Qur'an requires either four confessions in open court or the testimony of four Muslim males who must testify that they had a full view of the precise act of sexual penetration. If one of the witnesses fails to testify satisfactorily, then the remaining witnesses will be found to have committed the Hadd crime of slander. The Qur'an provides that those who launch a charge against chaste women and do not produce four witnesses to support their allegations should be punished by flogging them with 80 strips (Sanad, 1991).

If *shari'ah* judges are faced with doubts in the evidence, weak evidence can be supplemented by a procedure called *qasama* (oath). *Qasama* has no parallel in the West. The procedure requires that the judge have a high, albeit not itself sufficient, degree of certainty that an accused person is guilty. In this circumstance, termed *lawth*, the judge may ask 50 members of the family of the victim to swear that the defendant murdered their relative. Where 50 relatives are unavailable, the oath of just one, made 50 times, will suffice. This procedure can apply even when the evidence falls short of the strict requirements of proof set out earlier, for example, because a confession has been withdrawn and there is only one eyewitness (Sanad, 1991).

Beheading, Not Solely an Islamic Punishment

Beheading was practiced in common law, civil law, and Islamic legal systems. For example, Charles I, the King of England, was beheaded on January 30, 1649, in London. As noted in Photo 6.2, there is a statute in London of Charles I. He had been charged with high treason and "other high crimes against the realm of England." The ancient Greeks and Romans regarded it as a most honorable form of death. Before execution the criminal was tied to a stake and whipped with rods. In early times an axe was used, but later a sword, which was considered a more honorable instrument of death, was used for Roman citizens. Japan used a form of ritual decapitation from the fifteenth through the nineteenth century. A symbolic consequence of the French Revolution was the extension of the privilege of beheading to criminals of ordinary birth by means of the guillotine. Beheading was last used

Photo 6.2 An 1890 drawing of the Statute of Charles I, located in London, England. Charles I was beheaded on January 30, 1649. (Courtesy of the Library of Congress Prints and Photographs Division.)

in France in 1939. During World War II, the Japanese beheaded prisoners of war, not a tribute to their nobility but to show contempt toward them.

In today's world, Saudi Arabia still favors public beheading, and Iran has used it in special cases. It is now terrorists who use it to the greatest effect, for instance, widely distributing a video of the beheading of the *Wall Street Journal* reporter Daniel Pearl and using it as recruiting propaganda. There is a verse in the Qur'an that may support beheading, but the translations of the verse vary so much that it is impossible to be sure what it really means. Some indicate that the verse only means that the neck of the enemy may be struck, and others contend that it means that enemies should be beheaded (Dalrymple, 2005; *Encyclopaedia Britannica*, 2007).

Saudi Arabia

Saudi Arabia has an area of 2,240,000 square kilometers (864,869 square miles) and a population in 2005 of 25.6 million (UN estimate). Its population density is about 11.4 persons per square kilometer. It is situated on the Arabian Peninsula. Saudi Arabia has the world's largest oil reserves (about 20% of proven deposits) and is also currently the world's largest producer. Oil and natural gas products now account for 35% of Saudi gross domestic product, 75% of government revenue, and 85% of export income.

The southern region of the peninsula was occupied by Abyssinians (ancestors of today's Ethiopians) until they were driven out in the sixth century by the Persians, who made it a province of their empire. In 622, considered the beginning of the Muslim era, the Prophet Muhammad fled from his home town of Mecca to nearby Medina. In Medina, he organized his followers and launched a successful campaign to recapture Mecca. After Muhammad's death in 632, the Muslims continued their expansion across the Arabian Peninsula and into Syria, Mesopotamia (present-day Iraq), Persia, and westward into Egypt and the rest of North Africa.

Arabia was absorbed into the Turkish Ottoman Empire during the sixteenth century, but the local rulers were allowed a great deal of autonomy. In 1914, the British government made an agreement with the sherif (local ruler) of Mecca under which the area would acquire independence if the sherif supported Britain's military campaign against the Turks. After the Turkish defeat, the Kingdom of Hijaz (a region on the peninsula) was recognized as independent under the 1920 Treaty of Sèvres. On the other side of the peninsula, the leading potentate was Abdul Aziz Ibn Abdar-Rahman, better known as Ibn Saud, ruler of the province of Najd. In 1915, the government of India, then under British rule, recognized Najd and some other territories along the Persian Gulf as possessions of Ibn Saud. Throughout the 1920s, military clashes between Ibn Saud's troops and forces loyal to the Hashemite king of Hijaz, Hussein, grew more frequent as the decisive struggle for control of the peninsula took place.

The British and other Western powers switched their support between the two sides as it suited them. Eventually, Ibn Saud pushed out the Hashemites, and in 1926 was recognized as ruler of the Kingdom of Hijaz and Najd. In 1932, this became the United Kingdom of Saudi Arabia. Saudi Arabia now occupies four-fifths of the Arabian Peninsula, with coastlines on the Red Sea and the Persian Gulf.

Saudi Arabia is an absolute monarchy with no political parties. The king appoints a council of ministers to run day-to-day affairs. A consultative council (*majlis as-shura*), numbering about 60, has been established to advise the monarch; it has no formal powers.

Criminal Cases

The Saudi Nizam Al-Assasy (Basic Law of Government), Article I, declares that Saudi Arabia is an Arab Islamic state with the Qur'an, the holiest text of Islam, and the Sunnah (the sayings and practice of the prophet) as its constitution. The traditional subjects of law, including criminal law, are exclusively defined by the *shari'ah* (traditional Islamic law). All legal matters are regulated by royal decrees. The Islamic legal model differs from both common law and civil law models in that it is based on divine revelation and was not developed through a hierarchy of judicial decisions or by written codes (Esmaeili and Gans, 2000).

As in most Islamic nations, ordinary criminal courts are often supplemented by police courts, which tend to deal with lesser criminal offenses, and military courts, which hear questions affecting security and military matters.

The main sources of the law are the Qur'an, the Sunnah (sayings and practice of the prophet), *ijma* (consensus of Muslim jurists), and *qiyas* (juristic analogy). Although the Qur'an is considered the most important source of law, fewer than 100 of its 6300 verses deal with legal issues, including criminal law. The bulk of its prescriptions concern Islamic rules for prayer and fasting, and subjects such as theology, morality, and history (Esmaeili and Gans, 2000).

The Saudi criminal courts were established in 1927 by royal decree and are administered by the Saudi Ministry of Justice. The general courts have jurisdiction over all criminal matters except for minor crimes. In cases involving the death penalty, stoning, or amputation, the court consists of a three-judge panel.

The appeals courts were established by the same royal decree in 1927. The highest court is the Supreme Judicial Council, which reviews all penalties involving death or amputation. If the council confirms the general court's

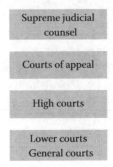

Figure 6.1 Saudi Arabia's court structure.

verdict, then the case is submitted to the king for his decision, since the king is the supreme judicial authority. In capital murder trials, the appeals courts only review the determination of guilt or innocence. Neither appeals court nor the king has the authority to commute a death sentence in a murder trial (Esmaeili and Gans, 2000).

Traditional Islamic law provides for a very simple criminal procedure. There is no jury system. There is no prosecutor. Judges conduct the investigation and the examination and issue the verdict.

Legal representation for defendants is neither required nor prohibited under the *shar'iah*. However, *shari'ah* generally entitles individuals and legal entities to a *wakil* (representative), who may be a lawyer. Islamic law provides for open trials and, ordinarily, Saudi criminal trials are public. However, the court may close the proceedings to protect public morals and individual privacy.

Islamic law provides for the following procedural safeguards: the presumption of innocence, a high standard of proof in criminal matters, a right to cross-examination, and a right to appeal. Additionally, under Saudi law, compelled confessions are forbidden and accused persons have a right to confront those who testify against them. The simplicity of Saudi trial procedure and the lack of a formal role for lawyers in both the trial and appeal courts often leaves the protection of accused persons entirely in the hands of *shar'iah* judges and the Saudi king (Esmaeili and Gans, 2000). Figure 6.1 describes the court structure of Saudi Arabia.

Pakistan

Pakistan came into being as an independent, Muslim-majority nation in 1947, following years of disenchantment with English colonial rule and the development of irresolvable differences between Pakistan's future leadership and the Hindu leadership of what would become the independent, secular republic of India. Of Pakistan's three constitutions, only the 1973 constitution is recognized as a democratic document, both in its substance and in the procedure that led to its adoption. The 1973 constitution was adopted in the aftermath of the 1971 civil war in Pakistan, which led to the creation of independent Bangladesh (formerly East Pakistan).

Article 31, Pakistan's Constitution (1973)

Islamic way of life:

(1) Steps shall be taken to enable the Muslims of Pakistan, individually and collectively, to order their lives in accordance with the fundamental principles and basic concepts of Islam and to provide facilities whereby they may be enabled to understand the meaning of life according to the Holy Quran and Sunnah.

(2) The State shall endeavour, as respects the Muslims of Pakistan
   (a) to make the teaching of the Holy Quran and Islamiat compulsory, to encourage and facilitate the learning of Arabic language and to secure correct and exact printing and publishing of the Holy Quran;
   (b) to promote unity and observance of the Islamic moral standards; and
   (c) to secure the proper organisation of zakat, ushr, auqaf and mosques.

In addition to Article 31, another important principle of policy is expressed in Article 33, which states that "the State shall discourage parochial, racial, tribal, sectarian and provincial prejudices among the citizens."

Pakistan has an extensive penal code of some 511 articles, based on the Indian Penal Code of 1860, extensively amended during both the pre-independence and postindependence eras, and an equally extensive Code of Criminal Procedure. Numerous other laws relating to criminal behavior have also been enacted. Much of Pakistan's code deals with crimes against persons and property—including the crime of "dacoity" (robbery by armed gangs) and the misappropriation of property.

According to Usmani (2006), Pakistan was involved in a raging debate on the issue of *hudud* laws since they were introduced in 1979. *Hudud* are considered penalties that the Qur'an and Sunnah of the prophet have prescribed for certain crimes. Usmani claims that the *hudud* laws are but a small part of Islamic teaching.

Judicial System of Saudi Arabia

- Highest court(s): High Court (consists of the court chief and organized into circuits with three-judge panels except the criminal circuit which has a five-judge panel for cases involving major punishments).
- Judge selection and term of office: The High Court chief and chiefs of the High Court Circuits appointed by royal decree following the recommendation of the Supreme Judiciary Council, a 10-member body of high-level judges and other judicial heads; new judges and assistant judges serve 1- and 2-year probations, respectively, before permanent assignment.
- Subordinate courts: Court of Appeals; first-degree courts composed of general, criminal, personal status, and commercial courts, and the Labor Court; hierarchy of administrative courts.

Note: In 2005, King Abdullah issued decrees approving an overhaul of the judicial system and which were incorporated in the Judiciary Law of 2007; changes include the establishment of a High Court and special commercial, labor, and administrative courts.

Source: CIA World Fact Book, available at: https://www.cia.gov/library/publications/resources/the-world-factbook, accessed May 14, 2015.

Iran

The 1979 Islamic Revolution in Iran changed Iranian law fundamentally, especially Iranian criminal law. The 1979 constitution provides that all legislation must be consistent with Islamic criteria. After the Islamic Revolution, the legislature was required to ratify or rectify the codes in coordination with rules of Islam. Under Islamic law, some norms differ according to religion, gender, and other criteria. Islamic scholars believe that the differences between people on the basis of religion and gender are not indicative of discrimination, and that such differences are justifiable under Islamic law. For example, the Iranian Penal Code, enacted in 1991, holds that the murderer of a Muslim man shall be executed. The Code refers only to a Muslim man's blood money. The provisions appear to imply that if a Muslim man kills a non-Muslim, intentionally or unintentionally, he is not to be executed. If a Muslim man is killed by another man, whether by a Muslim or non-Muslim, the murderer is executed. But if a Muslim man kills a non-Muslim, intentionally or unintentionally, the murderer will only pay the *diye* (blood money) (Rahmdel, 2006).

The Iranian judiciary consists of a Supreme Court, a Supreme Judicial Council, and lower courts. The chief justice and the prosecutor general are specialists in Shi'ite canon law who have attained the status of *mujtahid*. Under the 1979 Constitution, all judges must base their decisions on the *shari'ah*. In 1982, the Supreme Court struck down any portion of the law codes of the deposed monarchy that did not conform with the *shari'ah*. In 1983 and 1991, the penal code was revised to ensure that the penal code embraced the form and content of Islamic law. The present penal code implements a series of traditional punishments, including retribution (Arabic *qisas*) for murder and other violent crimes—wherein the nearest relative of a murdered party may, if the court approves, take the life of the killer. Violent corporal punishments, including execution, are now the required form of chastisement for a wide number of crimes, ranging from adultery to alcohol consumption. In view of the high number of clergy within the judiciary, the state in 1987 implemented a special court outside the regular judiciary to try members of the clergy accused of crimes (Iran, 2007).

Judicial System of Iran

- Highest court(s): Supreme Court (consists of a president and NA judges).
- Judge selection and term of office: Supreme Court president appointed by the head of the Supreme Judicial Council in consultation with judges of the Supreme Court; president appointed for a 5-year term.
- Subordinate courts: Penal Courts I and II; Islamic Revolutionary Courts; Courts of Peace; Special Clerical Court (functions outside the judicial system and handles cases involving clerics); military courts.

Source: CIA World Fact Book, available at: https://www.cia.gov/library/publications/resources/the-world-factbook, accessed May 14, 2015.

Summary

- Sacred law legal tradition is the law that is based on some sacred text or body of religious doctrine. Islamic law clearly falls in the category of a sacred law legal tradition.
- Islamic law is used, at least in part, in 53 Muslim countries and a number of non-Muslim countries, such as India; only a few countries apply traditional Islamic criminal law.

- Muslim criminal justice evolved from the Islamic justice initiated by the Prophet Mohammed.
- The word "Islam" is a noun that stems from the same Semitic root as Arabic *salam* and Hebrew *shalom*. The word "Islam" can have two meanings: "peace" and "submission."
- Key concepts of Islamic law are as follows: The law is not made, but has been revealed by God; the teachings of leading Muslim jurists have only amplified the law; Islamic law is valid regardless of whether or not it is recognized by the state; the law originates only in divine revelation and not from customs and traditions.
- Islamic law is comprehensive and all-embracing and covers every aspect of the legal system.
- The *sunnah* and *hadith* of the prophet serve as the most important source of Islamic law after the Qur'an.
- The three major crime categories are *hudud*, the most serious; *ta'zir*, the least serious; and *qisas*, those for which the victim has a right to seek retribution and retaliation.
- The four major principles of Islamic law are the principle of individual responsibility, presumption of innocence, nullification of penalty by doubt, and guarantees for an accused.
- Under Islamic criminal law, the definition of crimes, the means of establishing proof, and appropriate punishments are intimately related. The types of punishment under consideration determine which legal rules govern a criminal trial.
- Islamic law has three degrees of murder (*qatl*): intentional murder, nonintentional murder, and accidental murder.
- The Islamic rules of proof in criminal trials are complicated by the intersection between Islamic sentencing and trial law. The boundaries of each category of permissible evidence will vary according to the punishment being contemplated in court.
- The most practical and effective method of proof allowed under Islamic law is confessional evidence.
- A confession that resulted from torture, beating, threats, deception, or any inhumane treatment will not be accepted.
- An accused person can withdraw a confession, even a voluntary one.
- The classic method for proof of criminal charges under Islamic law is the oral testimony of two pious Muslim males.
- The use of evidence other than eyewitness testimony and confession is controversial in Islamic law.
- If *shari'ah* judges are faced with doubts in the evidence, weak evidence can be supplemented by a procedure called *qasama* (oath).
- The Saudi Nizam Al-Assasy (Basic Law of Government), Article I, declares that Saudi Arabia is an Arab Islamic state with the Qur'an,

the holiest text of Islam, and the Sunnah (the sayings and practice of the prophet) as its constitution. The traditional subjects of law, including criminal law, are exclusively defined by the *shari'ah*. All legal matters are regulated by royal decrees.

- Traditional Islamic law provides for a very simple criminal procedure. There is no jury system. There is no prosecutor. Judges conduct the investigation and the examination and issue the verdict.
- The 1979 Islamic Revolution in Iran changed Iranian law fundamentally, especially Iranian criminal law. The 1979 Constitution provides that all legislation must be consistent with Islamic criteria.

Questions in Review

1. What are the principal differences between Islamic law and common law?
2. What role does religion play in Islamic law?
3. What role does a judge play in Islamic law? A prosecutor?
4. Explain how crimes are classified under Islamic law.
5. Explain the differences in classification of murders between Islamic law and common law.

Policing and Corrections under the Islamic Legal Model

7

Chapter Objectives

After studying this chapter, you should understand or be able to explain the following issues and concepts:

- The concept of blood money payments
- The role of the police in enforcing religion
- Saudi Arabia's record on human rights
- The law regarding arrests and searches under Islamic legal models
- Corrections under the Islamic legal models

Key Terms

Diyya: Blood money; money paid to victims of the crime by the offender.

Hudud: Crimes that are offenses against God, whose punishment is specified in the Qur'an and Sunnah.

Mubahith: A secret police unit in Saudi Arabia.

Mutawa: Religious police unit in Saudi Arabia.

Qisas: Crimes of physical assault and murder punishable by retaliation.

Ta'zir: Offenses whose punishment is not fixed by the Qur'an or Sunnah.

SAVAMA (Sazman-e Ettela'at va Amniat-e Melli-e): Iranian secret police and intelligence service in Iran.

Introduction

The police in those countries that are using the Islamic legal model for criminal justice are for the most part centralized and under the direct control of the central government. As noted in Photo 7.1, with the use of cameras in the patrol vehicles, many police cars are directly controlled from

Photo 7.1 Patrol car in Dubai. Note the camera fixed in the rear of the vehicle. This camera is controlled from police headquarters and not from the vehicle. It also transmits to police headquarters. An officer at headquarters may observe the actions of both the officer and the surroundings by viewing the camera. (Photo by Cliff Roberson.)

central headquarters. Those countries also have police units that specialize in enforcing religion, culture, and the Islamic style of life. When we discuss policing in civil or common law countries, there is a distinct separation of duties between policing, courts, and corrections. In Islamic law countries often those duties are interwoven. A similar situation exists when considering corrections under Islamic.

The Naif Arab University for Security Sciences (NAUSS), located in Riyadh, Saudi Arabia, is an intergovernmental organization operating under the aegis of the Council of Arab Ministers of Interior. It carries out various interdisciplinary and cross-sectoral activities to serve the needs of Arab states. The main institutions comprising NAUSS are the College of Graduate Studies, the Training College, the College of Forensic Sciences, the College of Language Studies, and the Research Centre/Computer and Information Centre. All Arab countries are members of NAUSS.

NAUSS prepares an annual work program. It comprises a digest list of all academic activities that NAUSS implements throughout the year, paying special attention to the various dimensions and objectives associated with the crime prevention program. It also considers the future needs of the Arab security personnel.

Saudi Policing

Saudi Arabia is a monarchy ruled by the al-Sa'ud family. As noted in Chapter 6, on Islamic law, the *shari'ah*, is the primary source of legislation, but the actual promulgation of legislation and implementation of policy is often mitigated by more mundane factors, such as political expediency, the inner politics of the ruling family, and the influence of intertribal politics, which remain strong in the modern kingdom.

Saudi Arabia has a centralized national police force that reports to the Ministry of the Interior, which also supervises the country's intelligence and counterintelligence bodies. Police interaction with civilians, particularly with foreigners, has often been described as heavy handed, but reports of human rights abuses are far less numerous and severe than those reported in other countries of the region. There is also a religious police force attached to the Committee for the Promotion of Virtue and the Prevention of Vice. Known as the *Mutawa* (plural, *Mutawwa'in*), this force operates in plain clothes and enforces such Islamic precepts as ensuring that women are properly veiled, that shops close during prayer, and that the fast is kept during Ramadan. Imposing impromptu corporal punishment for infractions is an accepted part of their duty. It is estimated that this police force has about 50,000 members. It is reported that members of the *Mutawa* get about $300 for every Saudi they arrest (Dammer and Fairchild, 2006).

The main police force in Saudi Arabia is called the Department of Public Safety (DPS). Figure 7.1 describes the organization of the Saudi police. The DPS handles most of the daily law enforcement functions in the country and is divided into the regular police and the *mubahith*. The *mubahith* is the secret police and is officially listed as the special investigative police of the General Directorate of Investigation. The *mubahith* handles matters involving domestic security and counterintelligence. It also conducts criminal investigations (Dammer and Fairchild, 2006).

Figure 7.1 Organization of the Saudi police.

Each of the country's 14 provinces has a general manager who controls police activities within that province. The province general manager reports to the provincial governor for police matters, and the governor is under the supervision of the director of public safety. The director of public safety is the head of the police and is an official in the Interior Ministry. In the past, the director has been a relative of the king. Most police officers are appointed to the local police forces by the director's office.

The King Fahd Security College is the police academy in Saudi Arabia. It is based in Al Riyadh. The college was founded in 1935. In 2007, it had more than 1300 students.

The Saudi police are generally divided between commissioned officers, who are graduates of the King Fahd Security College and hold ranks from lieutenant to general, and rank-and-file officers. The latter must be able to read and write and receive about 3 months of training before becoming police officers. Generally, the rank-and-file officers are not eligible for commissioned status.

The police generally must demonstrate reasonable cause and obtain permission from the provincial governor before searching a private home; however, warrants are not required by law.

Saudi Arabia's Record on Human Rights

According to the U.S. Department of State, the Saudi government's human rights record is poor. Citizens have neither the right nor the legal means to change their government. Security forces continue to abuse detainees and prisoners, arbitrarily arrest and detain persons, and hold them incommunicado in detention. In addition, there are allegations that security forces have committed torture. On October 1, 2002, the Council of Ministers approved a new law regarding punitive measures that would forbid harming detainees and allow those accused of crimes to hire a lawyer or legal agent. The law became effective in November 2002; however, at year's end, there were no reports of its implementation. Prolonged detention without charge is a problem. Security forces committed such abuses, in contradiction to the law, but with the acquiescence of the government. The *Mutawwa'in* continued to intimidate, abuse, and detain citizens and foreigners. Most trials are closed, and defendants usually appear before judges without legal counsel. The government infringes on citizens' privacy rights. The government prohibits or restricts freedom of speech, the press, assembly, association, religion, and movement. However, during 2002, the government continued to tolerate a wider range of debate and criticism in the press concerning domestic issues. Other continuing problems included discrimination and violence against women, discrimination against ethnic and religious minorities, and strict limitations on workers' rights.

Torture and Other Cruel, Inhuman, or Degrading Treatment or Punishment

Shar'iah (Islamic law) prohibits any judge from accepting a confession obtained under duress; however, there have been credible reports that Saudi authorities abused detainees, both citizens and foreigners. Ministry of Interior officials are responsible for most incidents of abuse of prisoners, including beatings, whippings, sleep deprivation, and at least three cases of drugging of foreign prisoners. In addition, there were allegations of torture, including beating with sticks, suspension from bars by handcuffs, and threats against family members. Torture and abuse are used to obtain required confessions from prisoners. There were reports that in detention centers some boys and young men were flogged, forced constantly to lie on hard floors, deprived of sleep, and threatened with whipping and other abuse.

The government has refused to recognize the mandate of the UN Committee against Torture to investigate alleged abuses, although it has invited the committee to visit the country. However, the government has pledged to cooperate with UN human rights mechanisms and announced in 2000 the establishment of a committee to investigate allegations of torture pursuant to its obligations under the Convention against Torture and Other Cruel, Inhuman, or Degrading Treatment or Punishment.

Arbitrary Arrest, Detention, or Exile

The law prohibits arbitrary arrest; however, the authorities at times make arrests and detain persons without following explicit legal guidelines. The *Mutawwa'in* generally are free to intimidate and bring to police stations persons whom they accuse of committing "crimes of vice," based on their own religious interpretations. There are few procedures to safeguard against abuse, although the government claims that it punishes individual officers who violate regulations. There have been few publicized cases of citizens successfully obtaining judicial redress for abuse of the government's power of arrest and detention; none were reported during 2002.

According to regulation, authorities may not detain suspects for longer than 3 days before charging them. However, serious exceptions have been reported. In practice, persons are held weeks or months and sometimes longer. The regulations also provide for bail for less serious crimes, although authorities at times release detainees on the recognizance of a patron or sponsoring employer without the payment of bail. If they are not released, authorities typically detain accused persons for an average of 2 months before sending the case to trial or, in the case of some foreigners, summarily deporting them. There is no established procedure providing detainees the right to inform their family of their arrest.

The *Mutawwa'in* have the authority to detain persons for no more than 24 hours for violations of the strict standards of proper dress and behavior. In the past, they sometimes exceeded this limit before delivering detainees to the police. During 2002, *Mutawwa'in* reportedly handed over detainees to police within the 24-hour period; however, in some cases prisoners were held by police for longer periods, depending on the offense. Current procedures require a police officer to accompany the *Mutawwa'in* at the time of an arrest. *Mutawwa'in* generally complied with this requirement. During the year, in the more conservative Riyadh district, reports continued of *Mutawwa'in* accosting, abusing, arresting, and detaining persons alleged to have violated dress and behavior standards.

The *Mutawwa'in* reportedly detained young men for offenses that included eating in restaurants with young women, making lewd remarks to women in shopping malls, or walking in groups through family-only sections of shopping centers. Women of many nationalities were detained for actions such as riding in a taxi with a man who was not their relative, appearing with their heads uncovered in shopping malls, and eating in restaurants with males who were not their relatives. Many such prisoners were held for days, sometimes weeks, without officials notifying their families or, in the case of foreigners, their embassies.

Policing in Pakistan

In 1947, when Pakistan became a nation, it inherited its police system from the British. During the colonial period, the emphasis of the police appeared to be on the intimidation of citizens as a means of deterring crime. To the early police, the concepts of service to and cooperation with the community were not paramount. The constraints that have slowed reform of the police system are an outdated legal and institutional framework, arbitrary and impulsive management of the police by the executive authority at every level, poor incentive systems, widespread corruption, and severe lack of resources for the enforcement of the law and maintenance of order (Suddle, 2003).

The present police forces in Pakistan were created in 2002 by the Police Order, which repealed the 1861 Police Act under which the police had been organized. The stated purpose of the Police Order was to ensure the neutrality of the police and their functional autonomy. Policing is now a function of each province or region. The present regional police units are the Punjab Police, Sindh Police, NWFP Police (North West Frontier Province Police), Balochistan Police, Islamabad Capital Territorial Police, Azad Jammu and Kashmir Police, and Northern Area Police.

The present specialized police forces in Pakistan include the Pakistan Railway Police, who monitor the railway system; the National Highways and

Motorway Police, who monitor the motorways and national highways; the Federal Investigative Agency, which investigates white collar crime, organized crime, and immigration; the Intelligence Bureau, which collects and analyzes information; and the Anti-Narcotics Force, which investigates drug trafficking and provides preventive programs (Das and Palmiotto, 2006, vol. 2).

The senior officer ranks in the police service are the inspector general, who heads a provincial police force, and a deputy inspector general, who directs the work of a division or "range," which coordinates police work within various parts of a province. There are also assistant inspectors general in each province. The principal focus of police activity is at the district level, which is headed by a superintendent, and the subdistrict level, usually under the direction of an assistant or deputy superintendent. The latter is not necessarily drawn from the Police Service of Pakistan. At each level, police officials report to the political or civil service heads of the respective administrative level; the inspectors general, however, have direct links to the federal Ministry of Interior. Larger municipalities have their own police forces, but these are responsible to the provincial structure of police authority (Suddle, 2003).

The great majority of police personnel are assigned to subdistricts and police stations and are not at the officer level. Their ranks are inspector, sergeant, subinspector, assistant subinspector, head constable, and constable. As one descends the rank hierarchy, education levels, skills, and motivation decrease precipitously—even dramatically at the lower levels. Although constables are supposed to have a modest amount of education, they are paid only the wages of an unskilled laborer, and a head constable—the height of aspiration for many policemen—is paid only at the level of a semiskilled worker (Suddle, 2003).

Policing in Iran

Until 1979, Iran was a constitutional monarchy. After the Islamic Revolution, the country was transformed into an Islamic Republic with a cadre of Iranian clerics leading the government. Iran's present police force was created in the 1930s and has been reformed several times since then.

Prior to the Islamic Revolution in 1978–1979, SAVAK (Organization of National Security and Information), the Iranian secret police and intelligence service, protected the regime of the shah by arresting, torturing, and executing many dissidents. After the shah's government fell, the organization was closed down. Following the departure of the shah in January 1979, SAVAK's 3000 central staff were targeted for reprisals; many of the senior officials were executed. SAVAK has been replaced by SAVAMA (Sazman-e Ettela'at va Amniat-e Melli-e Iran), later renamed the Ministry of Intelligence.

According to many sources, the new organization is structurally identical to the old one and retains many of the same people. However, since Iran does not have a free press, there is little reliable evidence that the new organization currently practices detention and torture on the same massive scale as SAVAK (Rezaei, 2002).

Iran has two primary police units. The national police operates with approximately 200,000 personnel, a figure that has not fluctuated much since 1979, and is under the Ministry of Interior. Its responsibilities include all cities with more than 5000 in population, a total of 20% of the nation's population. In addition, the national police is responsible for passport and immigration procedures, issuance and control of citizens' identification cards, driver and vehicle licensing and registration, and railroad and airport policing. Some of these duties were absorbed into the Ministry of the Pasdaran during the early years of the Revolution, and cooperation between these two branches seemed extensive.

The second unit is the Gendarmerie, which operates with approximately 74,000 personnel. It is subordinate to the Ministry of Interior. Its law enforcement responsibilities extend to all rural areas and to small towns and villages of fewer than 5000 inhabitants.

Iran also has approximately 40,000 police personnel who operate under the Ministry of Interior and Justice in specialized units. There is a riot police unit that specializes in rapid-response activities in urban areas and dispersing gatherings deemed dangerous to public order. There is also a marine police unit equipped with inshore patrol and harbor boats. In 2003, some 400 women became the first female members of the police force since the Iranian Revolution (Souryal, 2004; Tabar, 2003).

Corrections

And if anyone is slain wrongfully, we have given his heir authority to demand *Qisas* or to forgive.

Qur'an 17:33

Never should a believer kill a believer, except by mistake, and whoever kills a believer by mistake it is ordained that he should... pay blood money to the deceased's family, unless they remit it freely.

Qur'an 4:92

Help ye one another to righteousness and piety, but help ye not one another in sin and rancour.

Qur'an 5:2. Thus, participation in crime is subject to a *ta'zir* punishment.

According to Souryal et al. (2005, p. 405), the calculus of Islamic justice can be summarized in the following three principles:

1. The larger interest of society takes precedence over the interest of the individual.
2. While relieving hardship and promoting benefit are both among the primary objectives of *shari'ah*, the former takes precedence over the latter.
3. A bigger loss cannot be inflicted to relieve a smaller loss or a bigger benefit cannot be sacrificed for a smaller one. A smaller harm may be inflicted to avoid a bigger harm and a smaller benefit may be sacrificed for a larger benefit.

As explained in detail in Chapter 6, criminal punishment under Islamic law is divided into three categories: *hudud*, which are offenses against God, whose punishment is specified in the Qur'an and Sunnah; *qisas*, which are crimes of physical assault and murder punishable by retaliation; and *ta'zir*, which are penalties for offenses whose punishment is not fixed by the Qur'an or Sunnah. The two methods generally used in executions are beheading and stoning. It appears that beheading is the most popular method used.

Sentencing practices under Islamic law are based to a large extent on the Qur'an and therefore are very dogmatic. As noted by Dammer and Fairchild (2006), a nation's way of administering its sentencing reflects its deep-seated cultural and religious values. This explains, in part, why some Islamic punishments are considered cruel and unusual by Western standards.

In Islam, the life and dignity of individuals, the family and property of each individual, and certain freedoms are protected. However, the individual and the state are not separated. Rather, they are combined in the concept of the *umma* (the Islamic community). Thus, the individual, when being sentenced under Islamic law, does not stand in an adversary position vis-à-vis the state but is an integral part thereof.

Under *shari'ah*, punishment for sexual crimes varies according to the marital status of the parties. Male and female fornicators are lashed 100 times. Adulterers are stoned to death. Although stoning is not specified in the Qur'an, it was ordered by the Prophet Muhammad and enforced by him against Muslims and Jews. It has been followed ever since. In addition to stoning of the adulterer, the Prophet Muhammad is reported to have ordered banishment of the male fornicator. The application and interpretation of banishment vary according to each school of Islamic jurisprudence. Since sexual crimes are *hudud* crimes, once proven, their punishment cannot be reduced or changed and no mitigating factors can be considered (Nesheiwat, 2004).

Capital punishment is available for a number of crimes under Islam, both as a fixed punishment (e.g., for adultery) and occasionally as a discretionary *ta'zir* punishment. Under Islamic law, a punishment for murder arises from the principle of *qisas*, from the Arabic word *qassa* "to follow." *Qisas* is based on the principle that the method of punishment chosen should ensure that the offender is punished in the same way, and by the same means, as the victim of the crime that she or he committed. *Qisas* is a refinement of the biblical and pre-Islamic Arab notion of punishment for personal crimes. In pre-Islamic Arab culture, revenge for murder often involved escalating tribal warfare where, typically, several lives were taken in response to a single killing.

If the crime is murder, then the punishment is the death penalty, *qisasal-nafs* (*qisas* for life). For lesser personal injuries, *qisas ma doon al-nafs* (*qisas* for less than life) is available. However, carrying out the lesser punishment is sometimes difficult because of the strict requirement that the retaliatory wound be exactly the same as the original injury.

The right of *diyya* is held exclusively by the heirs of the victim. In capital cases, this means that *shari'ah* judges' involvement in *qisas* capital punishment is limited to reaching a verdict that the death penalty is available. Even the Saudi king has no power to commute a death penalty in these circumstances. The procedural requirement that all such matters be referred to the king does not connote the need for approval of the sentence, only confirmation of the guilty verdict pronounced by the courts.

In theory, the victim's heirs even have the right to exact the death penalty personally. However, a layperson's lack of expertise in beheading means that in practice the sentence will be carried out by an appointed executioner. Where the victim is Muslim, the heirs are defined by the judge.

The general rule is that the victim's heirs have three options under *qisas*. First, they can ask for the death penalty. Second, they can seek monetary compensation (*diyya*). Third, they can ask for forgiveness. Leniency is preferred as a matter of principle under Islamic law, which teaches Muslims respect for all life. Where there is more than one heir and they disagree, the most lenient position is applied.

If the victim's heirs waive the right to the death penalty, a *shari'ah* court may sentence a murderer to a discretionary, noncapital punishment if it feels that the killers are wicked, of bad character, or lack a sense of honor. The purpose of this rule is to provide for heirless victims, to compensate for what might be regarded as an overly forgiving heir, or, perhaps, to provide a more flexible punishment option than those permitted under *qisas* (Esmaeili and Gans, 2000).

Amputation

The use of corporal punishment is linked to provisions of Islamic justice. For example, Islamic law provides for amputation in cases of recidivism, especially with crimes such as theft or robbery. Reichel (2005) reports that the amputation procedure in Iran is accomplished by an electric guillotine that severs a hand in a tenth of a second. Reichel notes that the amputation device has been justified as an example of attempts to have better coordination of punishment between medical and political authorities (Reichel, 2005, p. 209).

Blood Money

In most Islamic nations, if a defendant is convicted of murder under conditions that fail to satisfy the requirements for capital punishment (e.g., the murder may not have been intentional or not committed with a deadly weapon, or it may have been proved by eyewitnesses who nonetheless could not give sufficiently detailed accounts), the victim's heirs' rights under *qisas* are limited to two options: to forgive the defendant completely, or to receive a fixed amount of monetary compensation, termed *diyya* (blood money). *Diyya* has a dual role in Islamic law: as a punishment in some criminal matters, and as a compensation device in civil matters. Under the Hanbali School of Jurisprudence, *diyya* is payable from the defendant's estate if the defendant dies before punishment.

The value of *diyya* was historically 100 camels. Under the Hanbali School, this can be paid in gold or silver, rather than camels. In 1987, the Saudi government, by royal decree, set the value of 100 camels in Saudi currency as 140,000 Saudi riyals (approximately $35,000). The *diyya* is halved for women victims and may be further halved if the victim was not a Muslim (Esmaeili and Gans, 2000).

Caning in Saudi Arabia

In 2003, Robert Thomas, an Australian, was sentenced to 16 months in prison and 300 lashes to be administered 50 strokes at a time. Thomas was jailed for a crime allegedly committed by his wife. He was deemed responsible for the actions of his wife after she was convicted of stealing hospital equipment, an offense she denied.

Thomas, 55, had lived in Saudi Arabia for 10 years and was running the sterilization department of the Prince Abdullah Bin Abdulaziz Hospital in Riyadh when he was arrested. Under Saudi Arabia's *shari'ah* law, he was found guilty of association when his Filipino wife, Lorna, was convicted and jailed for 16 months. Mr. Thomas's family in Melbourne was told that in Saudi culture, it was "inconceivable" that a woman could commit a crime without her husband's knowledge, the AFP news agency reported.

The beatings were restricted to a wrist and forearm action because Thomas was a Westerner. Under *shari'ah* court order, the Islamic holy book was held under the official's arm while he lashed Thomas.

"(The lashing) is to humiliate and control and I draw a large crowd as I am one of those Western ungodly people, but they shall never hear me yell," Mr. Thomas wrote on January 20 to his friend, Hilary Ash, in Melbourne.

Dunn (2003, p. 1)

Section 5:41: hand amputation for theft.

Section 5:32: death penalty for armed robbery

Section 24:2: 100 lashes for fornication

Section 24:4: 80 lashes for slander

Figure 7.2 Some punishments under the Qur'an.

An Indian worker in Roudhat Sudair, 150 km north of Riyadh, was sentenced to 70 lashes in public and deportation by a *shari'ah* court there for urinating on the walls of a mosque. The man, a non-Muslim tailor, was proved guilty of repeating the sacrilegious act several times with malicious intention. He was flogged at the courtyard of the Sabeen Mosque in Roudhat Sudair (Al-Fehaid, 2003).

Aid to Prisoners' Families

In most Islamic countries, there are programs that provide aid to prisoners' families. It is difficult to find information regarding the programs. One recent report was noted in the Saudi daily *Al-Watan*. The paper reported in 2007, citing an anonymous security source, that the Saudi Interior Ministry has spent over 115 million riyals over the last 3 years in financial aid for eligible prisoners and their families. The source stated that the aid given to the prisoners goes toward payment of debts, assisting family members in housing and health care, financing prisoners' weddings, and purchasing cars after they complete the program and are released. He added that prisoners' families that are needy receive monthly payments of 2000–3000 riyals (http://www.julescrittenden.com/2007/04/29/saudid-straight/, accessed September 25, 2007). Figure 7.2 shows a list of some common punishments under the Quran.

Corrections in Iran

According to Iran's Islamic Punishment Act 1991, Article 105, "the Islamic judge can decide in *Hudud* based on his knowledge in criminal cases related to both crimes against God and people. However, the judge is required to mention the basis of his knowledge in the judgment" (see Ashrafi, 1997).

In Iran, the Islamic Punishment Act 1993, Article 205, provides the following.

In intentional cases where there is no complaint or the family of the victim has waived the demand for *Qisas*, if the act of the killer has endangered the public order of society or promotes the killer or others to commit further crimes, then the killer should be sentenced to a discretionary jail sentence from 3 to 10 years.

Corrections in Pakistan

Pakistani courts can and do impose the death sentence as well as imprisonment, forfeiture of property, and fines. Imprisonment is either "rigorous"—the equivalent of hard labor for up to 14 years—or "simple," confinement without hard labor. Another form is "banishment," which involves serving in a maximum security prison for a period ranging from 7 years to life. In February 1979, Prime Minister Zia ul-Haq issued new laws (*hudud*) that punished rape, adultery, and the "carnal knowledge of a virgin" by stoning, first-time theft by amputation of the right hand, and consumption of alcohol by 80 lashes. Stoning and amputation, it should be noted, had not been carried out as of early 1994—at least not outside the tribal area, where tribal custom, rather than the Pakistani penal code, is the law of the land.

While many consider the punishment practices under the Islamic legal systems dogmatic, the confinement rates of the Islamic countries are very similar to those in other countries around the world. Their rates of confinement are not as high as the United States. Figure 7.3 provides a comparison of the confinement rates of selected countries in the world.

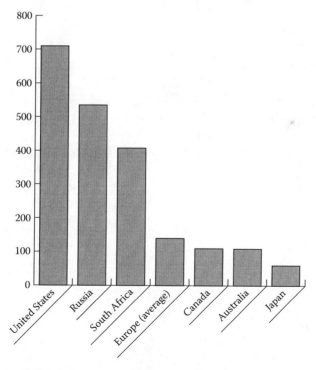

Figure 7.3 Confinement rates near this point. (From http://www.kcl.ac.uk/depsta/rel/icps/world-prison-population-list-2005.pdf, accessed September 20, 2007.)

Summary

- Policing in Islamic law countries is generally centralized and under the direct control of the government.
- Religion and law are interwoven in Islamic law countries.
- Saudi Arabia is a monarchy, and the monarch controls both the police and the courts.
- Saudi National Police report directly to the Ministry of the Interior. The main police force in Saudi Arabia is in the Department of Safety. Saudi police are divided in rank between commissioned officers and rank-and-file officers.
- Policing in Pakistan is a function of each province or region.
- The inspector general is the senior police officer in Pakistan.
- Iran is a constitutional monarchy.
- The SAVAMA is a highly controversial police unit in Iran.
- Islamic corrections are based on the Qur'an or Sunnah.
- Capital punishment is used in Islamic law nations.
- Blood money is often paid by an offender to the victim's family in the settlement of a dispute.
- Caning is used as a punishment in most Islamic countries.

Questions in Review

1. Is caning an effective punishment? Justify your response.
2. What are some of the issues involved when the justice system is based on a religious concept?
3. How does Islamic punishment differ from punishment in the United States?
4. How does Islamic policing differ from policing in non-Islamic countries?

The Socialist Law Model
The Courts

8

Chapter Objectives

After studying this chapter, you should understand or be able to explain the following issues and concepts:

- The judicial systems under the socialist models
- How confessions are handled under the socialist models
- Public trials under the socialist models
- The legislative bases of law under the socialist models
- How cases are prosecuted under the socialist models

Key Terms

Cuotas: Cuban units of a fine that have variable values. For example, one person may be subject to a fine of 100 cuotas at one peso each, while another may be subject to the same fine but at a rate of two pesos per cuota.

People's mediation of disputes: An informal justice system in China.

Primary people's courts: County criminal courts in China.

Procurate: Prosecutor.

Provincial courts: Felony courts in Cuba.

Supreme People's Court: The highest court in China.

Supreme People's Procurate: The highest legal supervisor in China.

Telephone law: A term that was used in the Soviet Union to refer to political trials in which the judges were instructed by party officials by telephone.

Introduction

With the breakup of the Soviet Union, the tradition of socialist law has gone into a state of suspended animation. After the fall, the Soviet republics and the satellite states of Central and Eastern Europe soon rejected Soviet law.

Currently, it survives only in partial form in the communist-governed juris-dictions of Cuba, North Korea, Vietnam, and China (Glenn, 2000).

Prior to the fall, the court system acted to ensure party control of judicial decisions at all levels. Trial courts consisted of a judge, who was selected by party officials and who almost always was a party member, and two carefully chosen laypersons, who were under pressure to agree with the judge. The system was designed to give the outward appearance of popular par-ticipation without actually involving it. Control over judicial decisions was also exercised by allowing easy appeals through higher judicial levels to the supreme courts of the Soviet republics and the Supreme Court of the Soviet Union. Cases of political importance were subject to the so-called telephone law—legal decisions dictated by telephone calls from party officials to judges.

Cliff Roberson first visited the Soviet Union in 1974 with a group of judges. They were picked up at their hotel and went to observe a criminal trial in Moscow. On the way to the court, the translator and guide told this joke:

> A student at the University of Moscow was asked by a professor: "What is God?"
> The student replied: "God is a mistaken idea of the capitalistic society, there is no God."
> The professor then stated: "Very good. You pass." The student replied: "Thank God."

That there is no God is one of the basic tenets of socialist law. Second, since there is no God, there can be no God-given set of laws or commandments that citizens are required to obey. Under socialist law, law is considered a system of rules that corresponds to the interests of the dominant class.

Legal System of Russia

While the socialist legal model originated in historical Russia, the present nation known as Russia became the Russian Federation following the disso-lution of the Soviet Union in December 1991. After the breakup of the Soviet Union, the newly independent Russian Federation emerged. The present legal system of Russia is truly a mixed system, but because of its historical significance to the socialist legal model, it is discussed in this section.

In 1722, Tsar Peter I created a procuracy office, which was responsible for prosecution of criminals and for supervising the entire criminal justice sys-tem, including the police and the courts. In 1864, the system was reformed and the prosecutorial power was restricted to the prosecution of cases. The reform also established an independent judiciary and trial by jury, but both were eliminated after the Russian Revolution of 1917.

Photo 8.1 A mobile police substation providing information on the identity of a thief in Prague. (Photo by Cliff Roberson.)

The procuracy was revived during the Soviet period, when prosecutors became the central administrators of the entire justice system. Trials were heard by a panel consisting of one career judge and two "people's assessors," all of whom were appointed by local Communist Party officials. The Soviet constitution invested the procurator general with the responsibility of supervising the observance of the law by all government ministries and institutions subordinate to them, as well as by individual officials and citizens. The procurator was not the president of a court or a tribunal but rather purportedly was a watchdog of legality, charged with ensuring the strict observance of the constitution and laws by all government officials and citizens.

The Soviet countries have adopted many of the modern practices of other countries. For example, Photo 8.1 shows a mobile police station in Prague, which is similar to many mobile stations used in Western countries.

Judicial System of Russia

- Supreme Court of the Russian Federation (consists of 170 members organized into the Judicial Panel for Civil Affairs, the Judicial Panel for Criminal Affairs, and the Military Panel. Highest court in the system.
- Constitutional Court (consists of 19 members); note—in February 2014, Russia's Superior Court of Arbitration was abolished and its former authorities transferred to the Supreme Court, which in addition to being the country's highest judicial authority for appeals, civil, criminal, administrative cases, and military cases,

and the disciplinary judicial board, now has jurisdiction over
economic disputes.
- Judge selection and term of office: All members of Russia's three
highest courts are nominated by the president and appointed
by the Federation Council (the upper house of the legislature);
members of all three courts are appointed for life.
- Subordinate courts: Higher Arbitration Court; regional (*kray*) and
provincial (*oblast*) courts; Moscow and St. Petersburg city courts;
autonomous province and district courts; note—the 14 Russian
Republics have court systems specified by their own constitutions.

Source: CIA World Fact Book, available at: https://www.cia.gov/
library/publications/resources/the-world-factbook, accessed
May 14, 2015.

With the collapse of the Soviet Union in 1991, juries have been reintroduced,
but the pretrial phase has not been reformed. Presently, the criminal procedure is very similar to Continental or civil law. Also after the fall of the Soviet
Union, laws were passed to ensure the independence of judges from local politics, and prosecutorial supervision of the courts was eliminated. Prosecutors
still, however, maintained fairly broad power in Russia (Pakes, 2004).

The Supreme Court is Russia's highest judicial body. It supervises the
activities of all other judicial bodies and serves as the final court of appeal.
The Supreme Court was supplemented in 1991 by a Constitutional Court,
which reviews Russian laws and treaties. The Constitutional Court is presided over by 19 judges, who are nominated by the president and approved
by the Federation Council. Appointed to life terms, judges for both the
Supreme Court and the Constitutional Court must hold a law degree. The
Constitutional Court has the power of judicial review, which enables it to
rule on the constitutionality of laws. The Russian legal system was reformed
in an attempt to overcome the repression practiced during the Soviet era by
requiring public trials and guaranteeing a defense for the accused.

The Russian system for training lawyers and judges is very rigid compared to many Western countries. Photo 8.2 is a picture of the University of
Moscow where many Soviet lawyers and judges are educated.

Judicial System of the Czech Republic

- Highest court(s): Supreme Court (organized into Civil Law and
Commercial Division, and Criminal Division each with a court
chief justice, vice justice, and several judges); Constitutional
Court (consists of 15 justices); Supreme Administrative Court
(consists of 28 judges).

Photo 8.2 The University of Moscow is one of the leading institutions in Russia dealing with the education of lawyers. (Photo by Cliff Roberson.)

- Judge selection and term of office: Supreme Court judges are proposed by the Chamber of Deputies and appointed by the president; judges are appointed for life; Constitutional Court judges are appointed by the president and confirmed by the Senate; judges are appointed for 10-year renewable terms; Supreme Administrative Court judges are selected by the president of the Court.
- Subordinate courts: High Court; superior, regional, and district courts.

Source: CIA World Fact Book, available at: https://www.cia.gov/
library/publications/resources/the-world-factbook, accessed
May 14, 2015.

People's Republic of China

The Chinese legal system is a work in progress.

Pittman B. Potter (2004)

In the last 20 years, legal reforms and the establishment of rule of law have once again taken center stage as part of the new law and development movement. ...Of course, many will question whether a socialist rule of law is truly rule of law, especially given the many imperfections in the Chinese legal system and China's well-documented human rights abuses.

Peerenboom (2006, p. 823)

China is a unitary, multiethnic socialist country with 31 provinces, autonomous regions, and municipalities directly under the authority of the central government. Some cities and autonomous prefectures also operate directly under provincial and autonomous regional governments (Guo, 2002).

China's criminal justice system consists of police, procurates (prosecutors), courts, and correctional institutions. The police and corrections are administered at the national level by the Ministry of Public Security and the Ministry of Justice. The Supreme People's Court is the highest judicial court. The Supreme People's Procurate is the highest authority for legal supervision. Its main function is the prosecution of cases. There are justice bureaus, procurates, and courts at various levels of the government to fulfill their respective duties in their own jurisdictions.

Judicial System of China

- Highest court(s): Supreme People's Court (consists of over 340 judges including the chief justice, 13 grand justices organized into a civil committee and tribunals for civil, economic, administrative, complaint and appeal, and communication and transportation cases).
- Judge selection and term of office: Chief Justice is appointed by the People's National Congress; the term is limited to two consecutive 5-year terms; other justices and judges are nominated by the chief justice and appointed by the Standing Committee of the People's National Congress.
- Subordinate courts: Higher People's Courts; Intermediate People's Courts; District and County People's Courts; Autonomous Region People's Courts; Special People's Courts for military, maritime, transportation, and forestry issues.

Note: In late 2014, China unveiled planned judicial reforms.

Source: CIA World Fact Book, available at: https://www.cia.gov/library/publications/resources/the-world-factbook, accessed May 14, 2015.

The legal system of the People's Republic of China is best described as Marxist. The first article of the penal code declares that the thoughts of Marx, Lenin, and Mao Zedong are the guiding principles of the law. The Chinese socialists view criminal law as a tool of the ruling class (synonymous with the state) to be used as a coercive force to repress the ruled. The criminal law represents the interests of the ruling class, which defines certain acts as crimes.

In judicial activities, public security branches, people's procurates, and people's courts there are divisions of labor, with assigned responsibilities and checks and balances to ensure the accurate and effective enforcement of the law. The division of labor includes the following:

- Public security branches, which are responsible for the investigation, detention, and preparatory examination of criminal cases.
- People's procurates, responsible for approving arrests, conducting procuratorial work (including investigation), and initiating public prosecution. People's courts, responsible for adjudication.
- Prisons or other places of reform through labor, responsible for sentence execution.

No other branch, organization, or individual has the right to exercise the powers assigned to those branches or courts.

The People's Mediation of Disputes is an informal justice system that has a significant role in criminal justice. The Mediation of Disputes is available, however, only in criminal cases of private prosecution.

Prior to the People's Republic of China, each Chinese dynasty had its own criminal laws. A common characteristic of these was that the criminal justice systems were operated by administrative officials. With the establishment of the People's Republic of China in 1949, the Communist Party came into power for the first time in China. One of the party's first priorities was to establish a socialist legal system.

A new constitution was adopted in 1954 at the National People's Congress, the highest legislative body of the country. New codes of criminal law, civil law, criminal procedure law, and civil procedure law were prepared.

In 1966, the Cultural Revolution stopped the legal reform process. In 1978, the Third Plenary Session of the 11th Central Committee of the Chinese Communist Party ended the Cultural Revolution campaign and reemphasized the institutionalization and legislation of the socialist democracy and the stability, continuity, and authority of law.

The draft of the criminal law was revised more than 30 times before it was formally adopted at the second session of the 5th National People's Congress in July 1979. The Criminal Procedure Law of the People's Republic of China was also adopted at the same session in 1979. For the period from 1949 to 1979, there were no formal legal standards or codes to guide judges in the trying of criminal cases. Since then, the criminal code has been revised several times, with major revisions in 1982 and 1990.

Public Trials in China

In 1954, public trials were guaranteed in the first Constitution established by the People's Republic of China. They were abolished following the Anti-rightist Campaign and the Great Leap Forward in the late 1950s, when courts public trials were denounced for bourgeois Western liberalism. Public trials were reestablished after 1978 as a means of representing the regularization and systematization of justice administration after nearly two decades of closed trials and kangaroo courts.

Supreme People's Court vice president Zhu Minshan explains the need for public trials:

> The content of all propaganda must be directly related to trial work... First and foremost, we must employ concrete trials to the full, and bring into full play, the use of the courtroom as a stage for propaganda. It is well documented that if trials are conducted properly, their educational effects will be great. On the other hand, if trials are not conducted well, it may result in a loss of confidence in court work and in the legal system in general, on the part of those who attend trials.
>
> **Trevaskes (2004, p. 6)**

According to Trevaskes (2004), the reopening of the trial to the general public in the post-1978 period became a symbol of Deng Xiaoping's vision of a renewed socialist rule of law. Trevaskes states that this examination of trials and sentencing rallies shows that despite the two-decade long push to effect a new modernist legal culture based on professionalism, regularity, and bureaucratic rationality, criminal justice practices in China have continued to rely on the crude theatrics of expressive punishment that have been employed since the days of revolution.

Procedure in a Typical Chinese Criminal Trial

- Prosecutor reads the bill of prosecution to the court.
- Defendant answers to the bill.
- Victim is offered an opportunity to make a statement.
- Prosecutor may question the defendant about the bill.
- Judge may question the defendant.
- Prosecutor presents his or her evidence.
- Defendant may present evidence.
- Statements of witnesses who did not appear in court are read.
- Prosecutor and defense present arguments.
- The court closes and the panel of judges deliberate.
- Findings are announced in open court.
- If a finding of guilt, defendant is advised of the time limit for an appeal.

Crimes

Crimes in China are divided into eight classes:

1. Crimes of counterrevolution: crimes that endanger the People's Republic, for example, treason, espionage, and rebellion

2. Crimes that endanger public security: crimes that endanger the life and wealth of many people as well as the security of public and private property, for example, arson, breaching dikes, causing explosions, spreading poison, causing traffic accidents, illegal manufacturing, trading in or transporting guns or ammunition, and causing major manufacturing accidents
3. Crimes that undermine the socialist economic order, for example, smuggling, speculation, falsely passing off trademarks, and illegal cutting of trees
4. Crimes that infringe upon the right of the person and/or the democratic rights of citizens, for example, homicide, bodily injury, rape, promoting prostitution, trafficking in people, unlawful detention of another person, unlawful intrusion into another person's residence, falsely accusing and framing, defamation, insult and humiliation, giving false evidence or testimony, and using torture to coerce a statement
5. Crimes involving property rights, for example, robbery, stealing, swindling, corruption, and extortion by blackmail
6. Crimes involving disrupting of the social order, for example, disrupting public affairs, official documents, certificates or seals, harboring criminals, concealing stolen goods, hooligan activities, and gambling
7. Crimes involving the family, for example, bigamy, abuse of a family member, abandonment, and abducting a child
8. Crimes that constitute a dereliction of duty, for example, bribery and subjecting imprisoned persons to corporal punishment and abuse

Chinese procedure law categorizes crimes into crimes of public prosecution and crimes of private prosecution.

In China, as in many common and civil law systems, the age of criminal responsibility is 16 years. A juvenile between the ages of 14 and 16 years who commits homicide, infliction of serious bodily injury, robbery, arson, habitual theft, or any other crime that seriously undermines the social order is, however, punished as an adult.

Court System

China has four levels of criminal courts: the Supreme People's Court, the Higher People's Courts, the Intermediate People's Courts, and the Primary People's Courts. The highest court is the Supreme People's Court. It handles major criminal cases that have national importance, and appeals or protests brought against the judgments and orders of the Higher People's Court and the People's Military Court. The court also hears cases of protest brought by

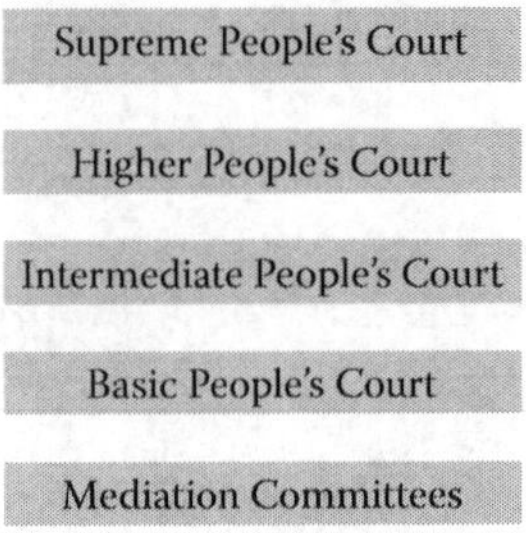

Supreme People's Court

Higher People's Court

Intermediate People's Court

Basic People's Court

Mediation Committees

Figure 8.1 Chinese court structure.

the Supreme People's Procurate. In addition, the court supervises the administration of justice by lower courts at different levels, such as the Higher People's Courts. Figure 8.1 shows the Chinese court structure.

The Higher People's Courts are courts in the different provinces, autonomous regions, and municipalities. There are 31 of these courts, which handle cases of first instance, cases that are transferred from people's courts at lower levels, cases of appeals, protests brought against judgments and orders of the Intermediate People's Courts, and cases of protests brought by people's procurates. They also supervise the administration of justice by lower courts.

The Intermediate People's Courts are established in the prefectures, cities, and autonomous prefectures within the jurisdiction of provinces and municipalities. China has approximately 400 of these courts, which handle cases of first instance, cases that are transferred from the Primary People's Courts, appeals and protests brought against judgments and orders of the Primary People's Courts, and cases of protests lodged by the people's procurates. They also supervise the administration of justice in the Primary People's Courts.

The Primary People's Courts are established in counties, autonomous counties, cities (at country level), and municipal districts. There are more than 3000 Primary People's Courts, which handle all criminal cases except those that fall within the jurisdiction of the higher courts. A Primary People's Court may also set up a number of people's tribunals in the area under its jurisdiction, depending on the local conditions, population size, and crime rate. People's tribunals are components of the Primary People's Courts. A tribunal's sentences and orders carry the same impact and meaning as those of the Primary People's Courts.

The president of the Supreme People's Court is elected by the National People's Congress. The vice presidents, presidents, vice presidents of the chambers, and judges of the Supreme People's Court are appointed or removed by the Standing Committee of the National People's Congress. The presidents of local people's courts are elected by the local people's congresses at different levels. China maintains the National University of Judges and training centers for the education of judges. In addition, the Supreme People's Court established the Chinese Training Center for senior judges.

Confessions

Under Chinese criminal procedure law, the police cannot use torture to coerce confessions or gather evidence through threats, enticement, deceit, or other unlawful methods. Any interrogation of a suspect must be conducted by the investigating personnel of the people's procuratorates or the public security branches. There must be at least two investigating personnel present during interrogation. The interrogator is required to first ask the defendant whether he or she engaged in a criminal act and then let the defendant state the circumstances of guilt or innocence. The defendant must answer the investigation personnel's questions relevant to the crime, but may refuse to answer questions that are not relevant.

Law of Search and Seizure

The police may conduct searches of the persons, articles, residences, and other relevant places of defendants for the purpose of gathering evidence and apprehending criminals. They may also search people who they believe are hiding criminals or evidence. The officers generally need a search warrant and must show a search warrant to the person to be searched.

  As in U.S. criminal procedure, the police may search without a search warrant if an emergency arises during the arrest or detention process. The suspect, family members, neighbors, or other eyewitnesses are usually present during the search. If articles or documents are discovered that can be used as evidence, they are usually examined by eyewitnesses and/or the person being searched. As in many U.S. jurisdictions, after the search, an inventory of the seized items is made in duplicate, with one copy given to the person who was searched.

Rights of an Accused

In addition to the right to defend themselves, defendants may also request assistance from an attorney, citizens approved by a people's organization or authorized by the people's court; or close relatives of the defendant. The accused has the right to be informed of the nature of the accusation; the right to participate in proceedings in his or her native spoken and written language; to apply for new expert evaluation or inspection during the courtroom hearing; to request the chief judge to ask certain questions to witnesses or else ask them directly; to make a final statement after the chief judge has announced the closing of the debate; to raise a counterclaim against the private prosecutor in a case of private prosecution; and to request that members of the judicial panel, the court clerk, the public prosecutor, expert witness, or interpreters withdraw from the case. An accused is entitled to the assistance of a defense lawyer of his or her own choice. In cases where the public prosecutor brings a public prosecution and defendant has not authorized anyone to be his or her defender, the people's court may designate a defender. The appellate rights of an accused include the right to appeal and the right to petition judgments or orders, which have become legally effective, to the people's courts or the people's procurates.

Court Procedures

After a suspect is arrested, his or her family is supposed to be notified within 24 hours of the reasons for the arrest and the place of custody. Notification is not required, however, when it would hinder the investigation.

After the police have investigated an offense, they will make a recommendation as to whether the suspect should be prosecuted. Then the police will transfer the case file to the procurate's office. The procurate then reviews the case and makes a decision on whether to prosecute the suspect.

If the decision is to prosecute, then the procurate initiates a public prosecution in a court. The court reviews the case prosecuted by the procurate. If the evidence is sufficient, the court can decide to open the court session for adjudication, in which the suspect is formally brought to trial. The procurate may grant exemption from prosecution for certain minor crimes.

The severity of crime and the dangerousness of the suspect are the primary considerations when deciding whether a suspect should be incarcerated before or while awaiting trial. If a suspect is considered a threat to the community or the crime carries a prison sentence, the suspect is usually put in jail to await trial.

Except in cases under private prosecution, most cases are tried by a collegial panel, which consists of one judge and two people's representatives, who decide the guilt of the defendant and the sentence to be imposed if the defendant is found guilty. Criminal trials in the high people's courts or the Supreme People's Court are conducted by a collegial panel composed of one to three judges and two to four people's assessors. In carrying out their duties in the people's courts, people's assessors have equal rights with judges. The adjudication of appealed and protested cases in the people's courts is conducted by a collegial panel composed of three to five judges.

Legal System of Cuba

Cuba is described by the U.S. State Department as a democratic-centralist state organized according to a Marxist–Leninist model. The Communist Party of Cuba is the only official political party. The national government is divided into executive, legislative, and judicial branches. The executive branch consists of a Council of State and a Council of Ministers. The president of the Council of State serves as the president of Cuba. The national legislative branch consists of an elected, unicameral body known as the National Assembly of People's Power. The Supreme Court of Cuba serves as the nation's highest judicial branch of government. It is also the court of last resort for all appeals from convictions in provincial courts (Michalowski, 2002).

Excerpts from the Constitution of Cuba as Amended in 2002

Article 56: The home is inviolable. Nobody can enter the home of another against his will, except in those cases foreseen by law.

Article 58: Freedom and inviolability of persons is assured to all those who live in the country.

Nobody can be arrested, except in the manner, with the guarantees and in the cases indicated by law.

The persons who has been arrested or the prisoner is inviolable in his personal integrity.

Article 59: Nobody can be tried or sentenced except by the competent court by virtue of laws which existed prior to the crime and with the formalities and guarantees that the laws establish.

Every accused person has the right to a defense.

No violence or pressure of any kind can be used against people to force them to testify. All statements obtained in violation of the above precept are null and void and those responsible for the violation will be punished as outlined by law.

Article 60: Confiscation of property is only applied as a punishment by the authorities in the cases and by the methods determined by law.

Article 61: Penal laws are retroactive when they benefit the accused or person who has been sentenced. Other laws are not retroactive unless the contrary is decided for reasons of social interest or because it is useful for public purposes.

Article 62: None of the freedoms which are recognized for citizens can be exercised contrary to what is established in the Constitution and by law, or contrary to the existence and objectives of the socialist state, or contrary to the decision of the Cuban people to build socialism and communism. Violations of this principle can be punished by law.

Article 63: Every citizen has the right to file complaints with and send petitions to the authorities and to be given the pertinent response or attention within a reasonable length of time, in keeping with the law.

Article 64: Every citizen has the duty of caring for public and social property, observing work discipline, respecting the rights of others, observing standards of socialist living and fulfilling civic and social duties.

Article 65: Defense of the socialist homeland is the greatest honor and the supreme duty of every Cuban citizen.

The law regulates the military service which Cubans must do.

Treason against one's country is the most serious of crimes; those who commit it are subject to the most severe penalties.

Judicial System of Cuba

- Highest court(s): People's Supreme Court (consists of court president, vice president, 41 professional justices, and NA lay judges; organized into the "Whole," State Council, and criminal, civil, administrative, labor, crimes against the state, and military courts).
- Judge selection and term of office: Professional judges are elected by the National Assembly to serve 2.5-year terms; lay judges are nominated by workplace collectives and neighborhood associations and elected by municipal or provincial assemblies; lay judges are appointed for 5-year terms and serve up to 30 days per year.
- Subordinate courts: People's Provincial Courts; People's Regional Courts; People's Courts.

Source: CIA World Fact Book, available at: https://www.cia.gov/library/publications/resources/the-world-factbook, accessed May 14, 2015.

The Cuban legal system is a composite of the three major stages of Cuban history. Photo 8.3 shows a typical Cuban court. Reflecting its past as a Spanish colony, Cuba is a civil law state that emphasizes written codes rather than precedent as the source of law, and the utilization of an inquisitorial system of criminal procedure similar to that of Spain and France. Intermingled with this are elements of common law, such as habeas corpus, and a greater separation of courts and prosecutors than is normally characteristic of Marxist–Leninist states (Michalowski, 2002). Similar to the courts in many countries, the Cuban courts have limited space to adequately file their records as noted in Photo 8.4.

It is also guided by Marxist legal theory and shaped by close ties to the former Soviet Union that have added a clearly socialist character to the Cuban legal system. Key elements of Cuba's "socialist legality" are an emphasis on substantive rather than juridical measures of justice; the use of law as a proactive tool for socialist development; direct citizen involvement in the judicial and crime control procedures; and a system of state-organized law collectives to provide low-cost legal services nationwide (Michalowski, 2002).

In Cuba, an act is a crime when it is prohibited by the law and is socially dangerous or harmful (*socialmente peligrosa*). Violations of law that are not considered socially dangerous or harmful are regarded as infractions (*contravenciones*)

Photo 8.3 A justice court on the outskirts of Havana, Cuba. (Photo by Cliff Roberson.)

Photo 8.4 Storage of court records in a justice court in Havana, Cuba. (Photo by Cliff Roberson.)

and are noncriminal citation offenses. Crimes are divided into felony and misdemeanor offenses very similar to the breakdown in the United States. Felony crimes are those that may be punished by a sentence exceeding 1 year of imprisonment or a fine of more than 300 *cuotas* (see Key Terms).

Felonies are prosecuted in provincial courts. Misdemeanor offenses are adjudicated in municipal courts and carry maximum penalties below the 1-year/300-*cuota* level. Felony crimes in Cuba encompass an array of offenses against persons or property, including murder, rape, assault, death or injury by vehicle, robbery, burglary, larceny, vehicle theft, arson, and drug trafficking. Except for the crimes of murder, rape, and robbery, each of the felonies also has a less serious misdemeanor equivalent.

As in other socialist law countries, the Cuban penal code enumerates various offenses against socialist organization. These offenses constitute a regular part of the criminal caseload in Cuba. Primarily among them are misuse of employment in a state-run enterprise for illegal personal gain (*malversación*), illegally obtaining money or property channeled from a state economic venture (*receptación*), trading involving foreign currency (*trafico de divisas*), slaughter and distribution of livestock not authorized by the socialist distribution system (*sacrificio ilegal*), and leaving or attempting to leave the country without complying with emigration requirements (*salida ilegal*).

Unlike civil and common law nations, Cuba places few formal limits on police discretion to stop and/or interrogate citizens. A central juridical assumption of the Cuban system is that no criminal case exists until an initial investigation (*fase preparatoria*) has established that a crime has been committed and that a suspect is the probable offender. Because there is no formal criminal case, the judicial philosophy is that citizens have little need for procedural protection during the initial stage of the investigative process. Only recently was Cuban criminal procedure modified to allow defense attorneys to enter cases as soon as a suspect is arrested or is the target of an investigation. Since arrests are considered as part of the precase, investigative stage, the use of a warrant procedure, which is characteristic of most legal systems, is not available in the Cuban penal process.

The Cuban constitution does require that warrants be obtained from a judge before the police may conduct a search of a home. The warrants, as under common law, must specify the place to be searched and the nature of the material being sought. A warrant is not necessary, however, if the home was the scene of the crime. Where the crime scene is in a home, the procedural law permits investigators to search the premises and to remove any items that may be considered evidence.

Court Structure

The Cuban court system consists of the Supreme Court, provincial courts, municipal courts, and military courts. The Supreme Court is divided by areas of jurisdictional or responsibility (*salas*), with divisions for penal, civil and administrative, labor, state security, and military cases. Provincial courts have similar areas of responsibility, with the exclusion of the military. Municipal courts have no formal division, but some of the larger municipal courts are subdivided into sections with specific responsibilities.

Trial Procedure

Cuban law requires that in all criminal cases, guilt is to be established in court. While criminal suspects can confess guilt, they cannot be convicted solely on the basis of a confession or a plea. An accused person has the right to a trial not by a jury, but by a judicial panel. In felony cases in provincial courts, these panels consist of five judges, three of whom are trained jurists with law degrees and two of whom are lay judges. Lay judges are citizens chosen to serve. In less serious cases, the defendant is usually tried by a municipal court consisting of one jurist and two lay judges. Defendants have the right to a defense counsel. Cuba has a system of law collectives (*bufetes colectivos*) designed to provide public access to legal counsel.

During the pretrial preparation phase (*fase preparatoria*), police investigators and/or prosecutors assemble the evidence and witnesses. If this evidence is considered by the prosecutor as sufficient, the prosecutor issues the equivalent of a bill of indictment (*conclusiones provisionales*). The bill is sent to the court of first instance and to the accused's defense attorney, if he or she has one that time.

In felony cases, the prosecution normally will be a prosecutor (*fiscal*) from the provincial office of the attorney general during trial. In less serious cases, the prosecution is generally represented by a police investigator.

Under Cuban law, police cannot detain a suspect longer than 24 hours without submitting the case to an investigator. In felony cases, the investigator must submit the case to a prosecutor within three working days. The prosecutor's office then has a maximum of three working days within which either to release the suspect or to submit the case for a judicial review if the accused is to be kept in custody until trial. This review is made by the court that will adjudicate the case. The court is required to either approve detention or order release, and its decision is final.

Pretrial confinement (*prision provisional*) is required to be limited to those who have committed crimes that caused public fear (murder, rape, robbery), who are suspected of multiple offenses, or who may flee prosecution. Pretrial incarceration is not considered appropriate in misdemeanor cases unless the suspect has given false identification or given indications of flight from prosecution.

Extradition from Cuba

Cuban citizens cannot be extradited for crimes committed in other countries. Non-Cubans can be extradited, except as noted, for crimes committed in other countries in accordance with bilateral extradition treaties. Cuba does not allow the extradition of any person for offenses related to "fighting imperialism, colonialism, neocolonialism, fascism, racism or for defending the democratic principles or rights of working people."

Summary

- Since the fall of the Soviet Union, socialist law has gone into a state of suspended animation in most countries.
- Under the Soviet Union, the court system acted to ensure party control of judicial decisions.
- That there is no God was a basic tenet of socialist law. Since there is no God, there can be no God-given laws.
- Law is a system of rules that corresponds to the interests of the dominant class.
- The present legal system of Russia is a mixed system.
- Under the tsar and the Soviet Union, the procuracy office was responsible for supervising the criminal justice system.
- The People's Republic of China has a socialist legal model.
- China's system is best described as a Marxist system.
- Chinese socialists view criminal law as a tool of the ruling class.
- The Cultural Revolution of 1966 stopped China's legal reform process, but the reform started again in the late 1970s.
- In China, public trials were in the 1950s denounced as bourgeois Western liberalism, but were reestablished in 1978.
- The most serious crime in China is classified as a crime of the counterrevolution.
- China has four levels of criminal courts.
- In Cuba, the civil law system has been reformed to meet the socialists' goals of the government.
- Cuba places few limits on the power of the police.

Questions in Review

1. What was the primary function of the courts under the Soviet Union?
2. How does the socialist law model differ from the civil law model?
3. Why did the Soviets dislike the concept of public trials?
4. How is the Cuban legal system different from the Chinese system?
5. What are the key differences between a criminal trial under the socialist legal model and one under the common law model?

Policing and Corrections under the Socialist Law Model

9

Chapter Objectives

After studying this chapter, you should understand or be able to explain the following issues and concepts:

- The status of public trust in the police for the socialist legal models
- The functions of the police in socialist legal model countries
- Correction principles under the socialist legal model
- The use of force by the police in socialist legal model countries
- Sentencing rallies in China

Key Terms

Chinese Ministry of Public Security: The highest police agency in the People's Republic of China.

Chinese People's Armed Police: A police agency in the People's Republic of China that is a part of the armed forces.

Guanzhi: Chinese punishment imposed for minor offenses. Offenders continue to work at their place of employment and to receive wages, but are under the supervision of a public security agent.

Juyi: Common Chinese punishment minor offenses. Offenders are deprived of freedom and confined in a detention house, rather than a prison institution. Generally, offenders may go home several days each month and can earn money for work.

Kanshou house: A Chinese detention house that holds offenders awaiting trial.

Procuratorate: Chinese prosecution agency or prosecutor.

Russian Militia: The Russian police agencies that are tasked with protecting life, physical health, rights and freedoms of citizens, property, and the interests of the state and society from criminal and other unlawful infringements.

Sentencing rally: A public rally in China after a criminal trial to publicly announce the criminals' sentences to an audience, usually organized to be attended by local work units and local party committees.

Watching units: Small units of the Russian Militia.

Introduction

In this chapter, we will examine policing and corrections in those nations that embrace the socialist legal model. For the most part, both policing and corrections in those countries do not meet the standards advocated in most Western countries. A primary reason for this is that policing and corrections in Western countries are used to protect the public, whereas in the socialist nations they are used to advance the purposes of the state. In the next section, we will examine an attempt to impose a Western policing concept, community policing, on certain socialist countries whose citizens have had a traditional distrust of the police.

Public Trust and Community Policing

Public trust in the police in many Eastern European countries is extremely low. In those countries that were formerly part of the Soviet Union, the negative image of police that developed during the Soviet era still exists. The reputation of the police units continues to be one in which the police routinely violates human rights, are involved in corruption, and act primarily in the pursuit of their own interests (Beck, 2004).

During the 1990s, the police forces of the former Soviet Union suffered from a crisis in funding, which left them understaffed, poorly trained and equipped, and demoralized. The police are also unprepared to combat the growing crime rates and new patterns of criminality. As a result, high levels of public distrust are also accompanied by strong perceptions of the police as incompetent, unprofessional, and ineffective in coping with crime (Beck, 2004).

Beck (2004) notes that most international policing assistance provided to those former Soviet countries has focused on promoting Westernized approaches, in particular the development of community policing model. The U.S. concept of community policing can be considered a philosophy and an organizational strategy that promotes a new partnership between the people and their police. It is based on the premise that the police and the community must work together as equal partners to identify, prioritize, and solve contemporary problems such as crime, drugs, fear of crime, social and physical disorder, and overall neighborhood decay, with the goal of improving the overall quality of life in the area (Beck, 2004).

Fundamental to a community policing approach is a nonconfrontational and broadly supportive relationship between the police and the community they are tasked to serve. While there are doubts about the efficacy of this approach in the United States and Western Europe, it has been the model of first choice for international donor agencies. According to Beck, the history of experimenting with community policing in postcommunist countries is rather short, with most programs starting in the late 1990s. Some examples include police training initiatives promoted in Russia and Ukraine by the UK's Foreign and Commonwealth Office and by the Department for International Development of the U.S. State Department.

Many analysts think community policing is unlikely to develop in postcommunist societies because of cultural, organizational, sociostructural, political, and other factors. For example, in Hungary, the possibilities for adoption of community-based models of policing are severely limited by the continued weakness of local communities in relation to the state. In Poland, it may be unreasonable to consider community policing in a country that is still in the process of struggling with its own identity.

Brogden (1999) has argued that in the former Soviet countries, centralized organization, cultural perceptions of the role and practices of the state police, and legal limitations of the police mandate—apart from a range of factors in relation to resources and tradition—militate against community policing development.

Policing in Russia

The Russian Militia is a public agency and a part of the executive branch of government. The Militia is tasked with protecting life, physical health, rights, and freedoms of citizens; protecting property and the interests of the state and society from criminal and other unlawful infringements. The Militia is divided into the Criminal Militia and the Public Security Militia. While both organizations are under the Ministry of Internal Affairs, the Public Security Militia is also subordinated to local authorities. The Criminal Militia's missions include the prevention, suppression, and exposure of criminal offenses that require a preliminary investigation, the organization of searches for persons who have escaped from bodies of inquiry, investigations under judicial bodies involving persons who avoid the execution of criminal punishment, and investigations of missing persons and of other persons as the law prescribes.

The missions of the Public Security Militia and the local militia include the task of ensuring the personal security of citizens; ensuring the public security; protection of public order; prevention and suppression of criminal offenses and minor delinquencies; the disclosure of criminal offenses that do not require a preliminary investigation; investigation of criminal offenses in the form of inquiry; and the rendering of assistance to citizens, officials, businesses, establishments, organizations, and public associations (Nikiforov, 2002).

The Department of Taxation Police is an independent police organization. The Taxation Police are charged with the prevention, suppression, and exposure of taxation crimes and infringements; safeguarding taxation inspection; and protection of the department's officers.

Cities with population in excess of 300,000 generally have their own special detachment of the Militia. Cities of between 50,000 and 300,000 population have *watching units* of 8–12 officers. There are also watching units for railways and water departments. The Militia is authorized to use firearms, rubber batons, tear gas, and fire hoses.

The police forces, like in many other countries, spend a portion of their assets on traffic control. Photo 9.1 shows a Russian police officer directing traffic.

To qualify for the Militia, an individual must pass professional training in specialized higher or secondary educational establishments of the Ministry of Internal Affairs or other state departments. To qualify for the professional training, the individual must be 18–35 years old and have a secondary education and no previous convictions. An officer serves a probation period lasting from 3 months to 1 year.

An individual unhappy with treatment received by a member of the Militia may file a complaint against the actions to higher officers or Militia unit, to a prosecutor, or to a court (Nikiforov, 2002).

Photo 9.1 Moscow has traffic problems similar to all major cities in the world. Traffic control requires a substantial portion of the Moscow police agencies' budgets. (Photo by Cliff Roberson.)

Policing in the People's Republic of China

In the People's Republic of China, the police agencies include the Ministry of Public Security at the central level, the local public security bureaus at various levels, and public security forces for railways, highways, navigation, air transport, forests, and other fields. The organizational structure of the police from top to bottom is as follows: Ministry of Public Security; Provincial Public Security departments/bureaus; Prefectural Public Security departments/ bureaus; County Public Security bureaus; local police stations.

The Public Security Offices of the Ministry of Railways and Public Security Offices of the Ministry of Communications also fall under the authority of the Ministry of Public Security. The Ministry of Public Security, which operates under the State Council, is the highest police agency in the country. Local public security agencies are responsible for public security in their respective localities under the dual leadership of local government and higher public agencies. The public security forces for railways, highways, navigation, air transport, forests, and other special fields are under the administrative leadership of their respective ministries or departments and the professional leadership of higher public security agencies. They cooperate closely with the local public security agencies.

The Chinese People's Armed Police Force is a part of the nation's armed forces, a component of the public security force, and a branch of the People's Police under the leadership of the Central Military Commission and the Ministry of Public Security. The local armed police are under the leadership of the local public security agencies and higher organizations of the armed police. Their principal duties include inner guard, frontier control and inspection, and exit and entry control, as well as firefighting (Guo, 2002).

Complaints against police misbehavior are handled by the supervisory bureau or sections within the Ministry of Public Security or lower public security branches. Any citizen may prosecute the illegal behavior of police officers and bring the case to a people's procurate or a people's court, and can initiate petition to the higher public security branch. The criminal law stipulates:

> ...the use of torture to coerce a statement is strictly prohibited. State personnel who inflict torture on an offender to coerce a statement are to be sentenced to not more than 3 years of fixed-term imprisonment or criminal detention. Whoever causes a person's injury or disability through corporal punishment is to be handled under the crime of injury and given a heavier punishment.

Article 136

Most police officers graduate from the police universities of the country or the police academies of provinces. Under special circumstances, police

Photo 9.2 A Hong Kong police station. (Photo by Cliff Roberson.)

agencies can also recruit as new staff individuals who do not have a diploma from a police university or school. It is required, however, that an applicant be a graduate of a senior high school or university, be under the age of 25, and be of strong physique.

The colleges or academies that are run by the Ministry of Public Security train the directors of public security (or bureaus) of provinces, autonomous regions, and municipalities. The colleges and schools at the levels of province, autonomous region, and municipality train the directors of county public security bureaus, the leaders of the public security branch bureaus in the municipalities, and the leader's subordinates, such as section chiefs and squad heads. Schools attached to the prefectures and municipalities under the provincial government train section chiefs, station leaders, squad heads, and other police officers. Training periods last an average of 6 months and vary for different trainees. A typical police station in China is similar to the one shown in Photo 9.2, which is one such station in Hong Kong.

Use of Force by Police in China

The rules for the use of force by the police are very similar to those in most Western countries. The Chinese police carry pistols, batons, and handcuffs when performing their duties. They are permitted to use guns to stop a crime or defend themselves. Specifically, they can use deadly force as a last resort to stop situations where the offender tries to resist or escape apprehension, steals weapons carried by police, or attacks police officers while being arrested or detained; the offender is in the process of committing a violent crime and putting citizens' lives in danger; the offender is attacking an object under guard by the police; a group of offenders raid a prison and/or prisoners are escaping, rioting, murdering, or stealing guns from security officers; or the offender physically threatens the life of a police officer.

Before using their pistols, the police must issue an oral warning or fire a warning shot. Only when these warnings do not affect the criminal behavior can police fire.

Police Detention

The Chinese police may detain an individual under the following circumstances:

- An individual who is a major suspect in a violent or serious crime
- A person who is preparing to commit a crime, is committing a crime, or is discovered immediately after committing a crime
- A person who is identified as having committed a serious crime by a victim or eyewitness
- A person discovered to have criminal evidence on his or her person or at his or her residence
- An individual who attempts to commit suicide, to escape, or to become a fugitive after committing the crime
- An individual who has the opportunity to destroy or falsify evidence or collude with others to devise a false account of events
- Where a person's true identity is unknown and he or she is suspected of committing crimes in several geographic areas
- A person who is beating, smashing, and looting and undermining work production or the social order (Guo, 2002)
- The police can arrest any suspect for whom a warrant for arrest has been issued by a chief prosecutor.

Public Crime Statistics

It was not until 1986 that crime statistics were made public by the People's Republic of China. In 1987, the Ministry of Public Security presented the first group of crime statistics data in the *China Law Yearbook of 1987*. The data included statistics from 1981 to 1986 and were compiled by the China Law Society, which has thereafter published updates of criminal justice data every year. The data presented by the ministry included the number of crimes recorded by the police, the rates of recorded crime, and the number of arrests made by the police.

Policing in Cuba

Policing in Cuba is under the Ministry of the Interior, which is responsible to the Council of State. The Ministry has three directorates: Security, Technical Operations, and Internal Order and Crime Prevention. The Internal Order and Crime Prevention section contains the three subdirectorates: corrections, fire protection, and policing.

As in most countries, traffic regulation is a large part of the police's responsivities. Photo 9.3 shows a Cuban officer directing traffic.

The subdirectorate for policing is responsible for the National Revolutionary Police (PNR). The PNR is tasked with uniform policing, criminal investigation, crime prevention, control of juvenile delinquency, and traffic control. It is divided into municipal divisions, each with its own police chief. The local PNR agencies are responsible to the national directorate of the PNR through a hierarchical structure that incorporates provincial levels of oversight (Michalowski, 2002).

The Security division is responsible for policing crimes against the state security, such as espionage and sabotage. The Ministry of the Interior and the National Revolutionary Police are closely integrated with the Revolutionary Armed Forces (FAR). The FAR was established after the revolutionary victory of 1959.

Photo 9.3 A police officer directing traffic in Havana, Cuba. Note that most of the cars were in Cuba before the U.S. embargo in 1960. (Photo by Cliff Roberson.)

In addition to the PNR, the Cuban system of control utilizes the Committees for the Defense of the Revolution (CDR) as auxiliary eyes and ears of the police. The CDR maintains nightly neighborhood watches known as *la guardia* to prevent crime. They deal with juvenile deviance and assist crime victims. The CDR is also responsible for promoting compliance with a variety of noncriminal requirements, such as water and electricity conservation, pet inoculation, and public health requirements. Active CDR members (*cederistas*) may also provide the police or ministry with information about activities they consider suspicious or deviant. There is no formal *watchdog* or citizen-review body devoted specifically to overseeing police in Cuba (Michalowski, 2002).

Corrections in Russia

Under the Russian Criminal Procedure Code, the judge, unless the accused demands to be sentenced by the entire court, decides on the punishment in cases where the permissible punishment may not exceed 5 years of confinement. In cases where the punishment may exceed 5 years of confinement, the punishment is decided by the judge and two peoples' assessors, who act as regular judges and have the same rights to participate in the determination of the sentence.

The decisions are made by a majority vote. If the case was conducted by three professional judges, then the three judges determine the punishment (Nikiforov, 2002).

The range of criminal punishments in Russia includes capital punishment, imprisonment, fines, reforming works without imprisonment, publicity, dismissal from office, deprivation of the right to hold certain positions or perform certain activities, restitution of financial damage, and additional punishments, such as confiscation of property and deprivation of special military or other ranks. Under the constitution of 1993, a capital sentence may be imposed only for serious violent offenses against human life. Executions are performed by firing squads.

Imprisonment in Russia

The Russian penitentiary system has approximately 780 reforming labor institutions (*ispravitelno-trudovich colonii*) and 13 prisons. There are about 60 educational-labor institutions for juvenile criminals. Men and women are confined in separate institutions, as are adult and juvenile criminals. The penitentiary system is controlled by the Main Department for Reformation Affairs, part of the Ministry of Internal Affairs.

Prisoners, based on good behavior and labor, are encouraged by premiums and given permission to spend additional money for food and everyday goods, permission for additional short visits up to 4 hours and long visits up to 3 days, and permission to receive additional mail and parcels.

Based on excellent behavior and honest labor, prisoners may be released early or may be placed in less restrictive punishment.

Prisoners are required to work, and wages are paid for their labor according to the quality and quantity of their work and in compliance with the national economy's standards and rates. The 1993 constitution prohibits forced work, but it is not clear whether these provisions are enforced.

Corrections in China

A collegial panel imposes the sentence in a criminal case based on the facts of the crime, the nature and circumstances of the crime, and the degree of harm done to society, in accordance with the relevant stipulations of the criminal law. Any property illegally obtained by a convicted defendant may be forfeited. In addition, he or she may be ordered to make restitution or pay compensation to the victims. As in most Western countries, any contraband or tools used in committing the crime may also be forfeited.

If there is a disagreement among the collegial panel as to the appropriate sentence, the minority defers to the majority, although the opinion of the minority is entered into the trial transcript. In cases involving serious crimes, the president of the court may submit the matter to an adjudication committee for discussion and decision. When a case has been submitted to an adjudication committee, the collegial panel carries out the decisions of the adjudication committee.

Sentencing Rallies in China

Although mass trials and mass rallies were employed as far back as the revolutionary era of the 1930s, and into the early 1950s, the sentencing rally, first appearing in the early 1950s, is officially the property of the courts.

According to Trevaskes (2004), very little on this topic has been published either in China or in the West. Trevaskes describes the sentencing rally in China as a legal ritual, a ceremony conducted in a public venue such as a stadium, the site of the crime, or the criminal's workplace. The public rally is organized after a criminal trial to publicly announce the criminals' sentences to an audience that usually has been organized to attend by local work units and local party committees. A typical rally begins with a group of convicted criminals brought out on stage, handcuffed and under the guard of a line of court police. The criminals may have placards around their necks and tied to their backs, which detail the criminal's name, the nature of the offense, and the sentence given. They usually stand at the front of the stage under guard, in front of a group of legal and political officials including senior heads of the police, procuratorate, and courts, and local government and party dignitaries. Following a period of speech making by politicians and judges, a judge will announce sentencing.

The death penalty may not be imposed on a person under the age of 18 years. If a criminal is under 16 years old, instead of punishment, the head of the family or guardian is ordered to subject the person to discipline. When necessary, the person may also be given shelter and rehabilitation by the government.

China uses five types of principal penalties and three kinds of accessory penalties. The principal penalties include *guanzhi* (control), *juyi* (criminal detention), fixed-term imprisonment, life imprisonment, and the death penalty.

Guanzhi is imposed for minor offenses. The offender continues to work at his or her place of employment and continues to receive wages, but is under the supervision of a public security agent. In addition, the offender must make periodic reports of his or her circumstances. The *guanzhi* penalty period can last from 3 months to 2 years.

Juyi is also a common punishment for minor offenses. The offender is deprived of freedom and confined in a detention house, rather than a prison institution. Generally, the offender may go home on several days each month and can earn money for work. The *juyi* penalty period can last from 15 days to 6 months. Fixed-term imprisonment sentences may be between 6 months and 15 years. The fixed-term imprisonment sentence may increase to 20 years if combined with other penalties.

Accessory penalties may include fines, deprivation of political rights, and confiscation of property. The supplementary punishments can also be applied independently.

In China, the death penalty may be imposed for crimes such as murder, rape, and serious property crimes. It may not be imposed on juveniles under the age of 18 years or on women who are pregnant at the time of adjudication. Persons between the ages of 16 and 18 years may be sentenced to death if the crime is particularly heinous. However, they are given a 2-year suspension of execution period.

If a criminal is sentenced to death, but immediate execution is not considered essential, a two-year suspension of execution may be announced at the same time the sentence is imposed, followed by the carrying out of reform-through-labor activities. If the offender repents and demonstrates meritorious service upon the expiration of the 2-year period, his or her sentence may be reduced to fixed imprisonment between 15 and 20 years. If there is evidence that the offender has resisted reform, the death penalty is to be executed upon the order of the Supreme People's Court. The method of execution in China is by shooting.

Chinese Prisons

The penal institutions in China are officially known as reform-through-labor organs or labor reform institutions. China has five basic types of institutions for imprisonment:

1. Prisons
2. Reform-through-labor institutions, where offenders serve a minimum of 1 year of fixed-term imprisonment
3. Reform houses for juvenile delinquents
4. Juyi houses (criminal detention houses), which house offenders sentenced to criminal detention
5. Kanshou houses (detention houses), which house offenders awaiting trial

Most offenders (about 61%) are imprisoned for property crimes, and the second largest group (34%) is that of offenders convicted of violent crimes.

Corrections in China are administered under the Reform-Through-Labor Administration. That administration is under the direct authority of the Ministry of Justice. Most Chinese correctional officers are graduates of correctional academies or are former military men. There are two levels of training institutions. The Central Administrative Cadres of College for Reform-Through-Labor and Reeducation Through Labor, located in Baoding, Hebei Province, exists at the central level as an advanced training institute for senior officers such as wardens. Correctional schools at the provincial level train the other correctional officers.

Early Release of Prisoners

Chinese prisoners can have sentences reduced for good behavior or be released on parole. Parole is granted to prisoners who have served more than half of their sentences and who show improvement in their behavior and/or attitude.

Prison Conditions

Prisoners who are able to work must do so, but those who cannot because of illness, age, or other reasons may be excused. Chinese prisons provide both educational and vocational programs. Vocational education is a major part of the education program. The government provides material needs such as food, clothing, and housing. Prisoners have the right to vote, unless they have been stripped of their political rights. Prisoners may exchange letters with relatives and friends. Prisoners are permitted visits from family members, no more than twice a month.

Corrections in Cuba

In Cuba, criminal sentences are adjudged by the judicial panel that determined the offender's guilt. Similar to many U.S. court systems, in municipal courts, sentences are generally announced at the time of the trial. In felony cases, there is usually a delay of several weeks between a guilty finding and the announcement of the sentence.

Cuban judicial procedure allows the sentencing authority to consider all evidence entered into the case, including that entered prior to a finding of guilty. Trial and pretrial documents as well as in-court testimony normally incorporate information concerning the social character, work history, personal associations, and prior criminal record of the defendant, and may be considered by judges in their sentencing decisions. There are no special sentencing hearings and no formal procedures for gathering presentencing information beyond what is revealed at trial (Michalowski, 2002).

Range of Punishments

The Cuban Penal Code enacted in 1988 allows for the following sentences: capital punishment, incarceration, correctional labor with confinement to a work site, correctional labor without confinement, probation, fines, and public chastisement (*la amonestación*).

Typical prison sentences for first-degree murder range from 15 to 20 years. Those for crimes like trafficking in foreign currency or burglary of an uninhabited dwelling generally range from 2 to 5 years. Possession of illegal drugs can carry a confinement period of 6 months to 2 years.

The death penalty may be used only for "heinous" crimes such as multiple murders, murder of a child, murder associated with torture, or treason. The mode of execution is by firing squad. Defendants under the age of 20 years or pregnant at the time of the offense or at the time of sentencing are not subject to the death penalty (Michalowski, 2002).

Confinement in Cuba

There are prisons and *granjas* in the Cuban penal system. Their prisons are fenced and sometimes walled facilities, especially in the case of older prisons. *Granjas* are open farms without gates or fences. *Granjas* are used to house offenders convicted of relatively minor offenses, while prisons are for felony-equivalent violators. The prisons are administered nationwide through the Penal Directorate of the Ministry of Justice.

Cuban prisoners are expected to complete the equivalent of a high school degree if they do not have one. If they do not have a trade, they are expected to learn one. Prisoners not taking an educational program are expected to work. Prisoners are paid the same wage for their work in prison that they would receive on the outside. One-third of their income is taken to pay for upkeep in prison; the remainder may be used to support any dependents or purchases. Both male and female prisoners are allowed conjugal visits from formal or common law spouses approximately every 60 days, depending upon their conduct.

Summary

- The establishment of community policing in those Eastern European countries that were formerly part of the Soviet Union has for the most part been a failure.
- The Russia Militia is a public agency and part of the executive branch of the national government.
- The Criminal Militia functions as a nationwide law enforcement agency in Russia.
- The Russian Department of Taxation Police is separate from the militia and enforces the tax laws in Russia.
- The police in the People's Republic of China are under the Ministry of Public Safety.
- Provincial public security forces are also under the direction of the provincial governors in China.
- In China, local public security forces are responsible for public security in their localities under the dual direction of local and higher governments.
- Chinese police have authority to use force similar to that in common law countries.
- Policing in Cuba is under the Ministry of the Interior.
- The Cuban Security division is responsible for policing crimes against the state.
- In Russia, a capital sentence may be imposed only for serious violent offenses against human life. Executions are performed by firing squads.
- Russian prisoners are required to work and are paid wages for their labor. In China, the death penalty may not be imposed upon a person under the age of 18 years.
- The death penalty in China may be suspended for a period of up to 2 years.

Questions in Review

1. Why are there problems in establishing community policing in those Eastern European countries that were formerly part of the Soviet Union?
2. How does the public perceive *the police* in most socialist nations compared to the common law nations? Why the difference?
3. Explain the present police organizational structure in Russia.
4. Should other countries adopt *sentencing rallies*? Justify your opinion.

Mixed-Law Models

10

Chapter Objectives

After studying this chapter, you should understand or be able to explain the following issues and concepts:

- How crimes are prosecuted in the mixed model countries
- How the different countries' judicial systems work
- Policing in the mixed-legal model countries
- Corrections in the different countries under the mixed-legal model

Key Terms

Cognizable crimes: Serious crimes in Indian law.

Dharma: An ancient Indian code that set the "right rules of conduct."

Grave crimes: Serious crimes in Sri Lanka criminal law.

Pataka: Ancient Indian concept of sin.

Primary courts: Lower-level courts in Sri Lanka.

Subjails: Jails used for holding individuals sentenced to less than 1-month confinement or awaiting trial.

Supreme Court of Cassation: The highest court of appeals in Bulgaria.

Introduction

In this chapter, the mixed model of law is examined for three countries. The first country discussed is Bulgaria. At one time, Bulgaria was one of the communist countries in Eastern Europe. Its present legal system is based on a civil law system, with Soviet law influence. In addition, Bulgaria has accepted the jurisdiction of the International Court of Justice. The second country explored is India, whose legal system is based on a combination of civil law and common law. The final country is Sri Lanka, which has a highly complex mixture of English common law, Roman-Dutch law, Muslim law, and customary laws. For the most part, the basis of Sri Lanka's criminal law and procedure is the common law model. Countries that have mixed-legal models include not only those discussed but also American Samoa, Bangladesh, Bahrain, Botswana, Burma, Cameroon, Chad, Republic of Congo, Cyprus, Hong Kong, Iraq, Kenya, Kuwait, Malaysia, Malta, Philippines, South Africa, Tunisia, and United Arab Emirates.

Bulgarian System of Law

Bulgaria is divided into nine provinces. Presently, it is a unitary multiparty republic with one legislative body. Bulgaria became part of the European Union in 2007. Its population is about 8 million, and its land area is about 43,000 square miles. The population is fairly homogeneous, with ethnic Bulgarians making up about 85% of the total.

Founded in the seventh century AD, Bulgaria is one of the oldest nations on the European Continent. At one time its territory was part of the Ottoman Empire, from which it gained independence in 1908. In 1944, the Soviet Union declared war on Bulgaria, and in that same year a communist-dominated coalition, called the Fatherland Front, seized power from the coalition government formed to arrange an armistice with the Allies. In 1947, the communist leaders adopted the Dimitrov Constitution, which was modeled after that of the Soviet Union. In 1990, the Bulgarian National Assembly formally removed the clauses guaranteeing the existence of the Communist Party from its constitution and in 1991 adopted a new constitution (Bojadjieva, 2002).

The 1991 constitution established a parliamentary government and guaranteed direct presidential elections, separation of powers, and freedom of speech, press, conscience, and religion. In addition, the constitution required the return of properties that had been confiscated by the previous communist governments.

The judiciary is an independent branch of the government. It consists of the courts, prosecutor's offices, and investigative agencies, which are all independent institutions within the judiciary. They are structured on the basis of territorial and functional principles.

Bulgarian Court System

The Bulgarian judicial system became an independent branch of the government under the 1991 constitution. In 1994, the National Assembly passed the Judicial Powers Act to further delineate the role of the judiciary. In 2003, Bulgaria adopted amendments to the constitution that aimed to improve the effectiveness of the judicial system by providing for the removal of judges for misconduct and removing their immunity against criminal prosecution.

The Bulgarian court system consists of the Supreme Court of Cassation, Supreme Administrative Court, Constitutional Court, local courts, courts of appeal, and military courts. The 1991 constitution provides that specialized courts may also be established. Extraordinary courts are not allowed by the constitution. The Supreme Court of Administration and Supreme Court of Cassation are the highest courts of appeal and determine the application of all laws. The court that interprets the constitution and constitutionality of laws and treaties is the Constitutional Court. Its 12 justices serve 9-year terms and are selected by the president, the National Assembly, and the Supreme Courts.

Bulgaria has a High Judicial Council, with about 25 members, which appoints judges, prosecutors, and investigators. The members of the council are appointed by the National Assembly and judicial authorities.

Trial courts are generally composed of one judge and two lay persons. If the maximum punishment for a crime exceeds 15 years in prison or is capital punishment, the trial court is composed of three judges and four lay persons. Generally, appellate courts are composed of three judges. Judges must have a law degree. They enjoy immunity and are elected by the Supreme Judicial Council. They cannot be replaced, except for cause, after they have completed their third year in office. The presidents of the Supreme Court of Cassation and the Supreme Administrative Court and the general prosecutor are appointed by the president of the Republic on a motion of the Supreme Judicial Council.

Bulgarian Prosecutors

The structure of the prosecutor's offices corresponds to the structure of the courts. There is a General Prosecutor's Office, appellate office, and district and regional prosecutor's office. The general prosecutor guides and supervises all the prosecutors. The prosecutors enforce the law by bringing charges against criminal suspects and supporting the charges in criminal trials, by overseeing the execution of punishments, and by taking part in civil and administrative suits when required to do so by the law.

Crime Classification

The Bulgarian Penal Code classifies crime into three categories:

1. Severe crimes, punishable by more than 5 years of imprisonment or by capital punishment
2. Particularly severe crimes, those in which the criminal act or the perpetrator has demonstrated a particularly high degree of social danger
3. Petty crime, one with insignificant harmful consequences

Trial Procedure

There are two stages in the criminal prosecution of a defendant under the Bulgarian criminal justice system: pretrial investigation and court hearing. The prosecutor initiates the pretrial investigation. A police investigator may also initiate an investigation, but must immediately inform the prosecutor. If the case is under the jurisdiction of the lowest court, then normally a pretrial investigation is initiated if the person was detected while committing the crime or has been caught immediately after the crime has been committed; if there are obvious traces of the crime on the body or clothes of the perpetrator; or if the suspect goes personally to the police or the prosecutor and admits committing the crime.

Generally, investigative agencies, such as the National Investigation Agency and regional investigation agencies, perform the pretrial investigation in criminal cases, while the prosecutor guides and supervises the activities. Investigators are required to follow the written instructions of the prosecutor. Investigation reports are delivered to the prosecutor, who determines whether the act is definable as a crime and has the features of the specific crime charged; if there are grounds to dismiss, suspend, or divide the case; if the circumstances concerning the case have been clarified; if the accusation is supported by the collected evidence; whether there are substantial violations of the procedural rules; if the causes of the particular crime have been investigated; and if it is necessary to change the measures employed to prevent evasion of prosecution.

After examining the results of the pretrial investigation, the prosecutor will formulate an indictment and bring the case to court, return the case for additional investigation, dismiss the case on grounds provided for by the Code of Criminal Procedure, or suspend the case on grounds provided for by the Code of Criminal Procedure—the last usually when the crime perpetrator is not known.

If the investigation determines that there are grounds to initiate a court trial, a prosecutor will issue an indictment, or if the crime is a private crime, the victim will issue a complaint. The prosecutor may take part in a private criminal prosecution if he or she determines that it is in the public interest. The parties to a trial may include the prosecutor, the defendant and defense counsel, and the private complainant or the private accuser and their counsel.

Like criminal trials in the United States, cases may be tried only in the jurisdiction of the court in the region where the crime has been committed unless agreed otherwise by the defendant. Criminal cases are generally public trials, except when the law requires closed trials. Trials involving minor defendants are not open to the public.

The court determines the sentence on the grounds of evidence collected by the court. The sentence may be appealed by the defendant or prosecutor.

Lower appellate courts examine the entire proceedings, checking whether there were errors in fact-finding and in application of the law. Except for written documents, appellate courts cannot collect additional evidence or impose a harsher sentence unless the prosecutor appealed it. Sentence may be further appealed to the Supreme Court under conditions explicitly formulated by the Code of Criminal Procedure.

Judicial System of Bulgaria

- Highest court(s): Supreme Court of Cassation (consists of a chairman and approximately 72 judges organized into penal, civil, and commercial colleges); Supreme Administrative Court (organized into two colleges with various panels of 5 judges each); Constitutional Court (consists of 12 justices); note— Constitutional Court resides outside the Judiciary.
- Judge selection and term of office: Supreme Court of Cassation and Supreme Administrative judges are elected by the Supreme Judicial Council or SJC (consists of 25 members with extensive legal experience) and appointed by the president; judge tenure NA; Constitutional Court justices are elected by the National Assembly and appointed by the president and the SJC; justices are appointed for 9-year terms with the renewal of 4 justices every 3 years.
- Subordinate courts: Appeals courts; regional and district courts; administrative courts; courts martial.

Source: CIA World Fact Book available at website: https://www.cia.gov/ library/publications/resources/the-world-factbook, accessed May 14, 2015.

Bulgarian Police System

The Bulgarian National Police is a specialized department within the Ministry of Interior. Its mission includes the prevention, detection, and investigation of crimes and the securing of the public order. The National Police's activities are regulated by constitutional limitations, the National Police Act, the Decree of the Council of Ministers for the application of the National Police Act, and by other statutes and regulations.

The National Police is comprised of officers and sergeants. It has a militaristic organizational structure. It is structured according to the administrative divisions of the country and is composed of the Directorate of the National Police, 27 police departments in the Sofia Directorate of Interior and the Regional Directorates of Interior, municipal police departments, and

230 An Introduction to Comparative Legal Models of Criminal Justice

neighborhood police stations. There are also subdivisions in various territories, which correspond to the specific tasks of the National Police, such as the Criminal Police, Economic Police, Police Unit for Securing the Public Order, and Traffic Police.

Corrections in Bulgaria

Criminal sentences include imprisonment, correctional work without imprisonment, confiscation, fines, exile without imprisonment, deprivation of the right to hold a certain office, deprivation of the right to practice in certain professions, deprivation of the right to live in a certain place, deprivation of the right to bear decorations already received or to enjoy titles of honor, deprivation of a military rank, and public reprimand.

Under the Code of Criminal Procedure, capital punishment was permissible only in the most severe crimes. It was not imposed on persons who were younger than 20 years old or on women who were pregnant when the crime was committed or when trial was held. The method of execution was by firing squad. In 1990, a moratorium on executions was introduced.

The decision formally to abolish the death penalty in Bulgaria was made on the day, December 11, 1998, on which the world celebrated the 50th anniversary of the Universal Declaration of Human Rights. Following the National Assembly's vote to remove the death penalty from the Penal Code, Bulgaria joins the growing number of countries that have irrevocably renounced the use of this cruel and inhuman punishment. According to Amnesty International, more than 100 countries around the world have abolished it either in law or in practice.

The last execution in Bulgaria occurred on November 4, 1989, a year in which 14 people were executed there. Throughout the 1980s, Bulgaria had one of the highest execution rates in Europe, with 27 people executed in 1986, 20 in 1987, and 26 in 1988. While a moratorium on executions was introduced in 1990, the courts continued to pass death sentences on those convicted of aggravated murder. According to an unofficial report published in 1998, 22 men were under sentence of death (Amnesty International, 2007).

Confinement in Bulgaria

Bulgaria confinement facilities are one of three types. Centers for correction and work of the open type are used for offenders who for the first time have been given a maximum sentence of 3 years of imprisonment for deliberate crimes or a maximum of 5 years of imprisonment for crimes of negligence. Centers for correction and work of the semiopen type are used for offenders who for the first time have been given a maximum sentence of 3–5 years of imprisonment for deliberate crimes or for offenders who are sentenced for crimes of negligence but do not serve their punishment in open-type facilities. Centers for correction and work of the closed type and prisons are used for all other persons sentenced to imprisonment.

Each facility has its own regime. Regimes are classified as lenient, general, strict, and highly strict. The sentence generally defines the regime the offender will be placed under. Sentenced offenders are housed separately from convicted offenders who are awaiting sentence and from arrested defendants. Prisoners may earn money by working. Educational and vocational training programs are available at no cost to the prisoners. The type of regime operating at the prison defines prisoners' rights and restrictions.

The correctional facilities are under the supervision by the Ministry of Justice. There are no private prisons. Prison activities are managed by the General Department of Prisons, which also has a Scientific and Methodological Council for Prison Studies.

Sentencing of Children in South Africa

In South Africa, children for purposes of criminal sentencing are persons under the age of 18 years. The South African Child Justice Act of 2008 established a separate criminal justice system for children. The philosophy of the system is that sentencing should be what is best in the interest of the child and that children should not be incarcerated unless incarceration is unavoidable. Children under the age of 10 years cannot be prosecuted. Children between the ages of 10 and 14 years are presumed to lack criminal capacity unless it is proven that they have it. Children over the age of 14 years are presumed to have criminal capacity.

The Child Justice Act has two basic aims:

- Whenever possible, child offenders should be diverted from the criminal justice system.
- When diversion is not advisable, child offenders should be dealt with in child justice courts.

When children are diverted, they do not enter formal criminal proceedings but are referred to alternative processes without a formal trial, conviction, or sentencing. The alternative processes may require the child to perform services and tasks or to undergo training. Frequently, however, these requirements are perceived by the children to be punitive.

Source: William F.M. Luyt. (2015). Sentencing and incarceration in a Democratic South Africa. In: Mathieu Deflem (Ed.), *Punishment and Incarceration: A Global Perspective*. Bigley, UK: Emerald Books, pp. 203–227.

Indian System of Law

India attained its independence from the British in 1947 and became a democracy in 1950. India's constitution provides for a quasi-federal system of government. The president is the head of state. There is a Council of Ministers, headed by the prime minister, to aid and advise the president. The Indian legal system is a mix of adversarial and accusatorial. In civil law, they have made an attempt to respect and preserve the tenets of both Hindu and Muslim jurisprudence. An informal justice system operates in the rural areas in civil and family matters.

Indian Legal History

Ancient India's jurisprudence was Hindu ruled and was based on the concept of *dharma*, the rules of right conduct. Under this concept, the king had no independent authority but derived his powers from *dharma*, which he was expected to uphold. There was a clear distinction between a civil wrong and a criminal offense. Civil wrongs were related mainly to disputes over wealth and property rights. Criminal acts were based on the concept of *pataka*, or sin.

The Mauryan Dynasty, which controlled most of India during the fourth century BC, had a strict system of punishments that included mutilation and the death penalty for trivial offenses. During the second century AD, the Dharmasastra code was drawn up by the Hindu jurist Manu. This code established the crimes of assault and other bodily injuries and property offenses such as theft and robbery. The judicial hierarchy was formed during the fourth to sixth centuries under the rule of the Gupta Dynasty. The early judiciary consisted of the guild, the folk assembly or the council, and the king. Judicial decisions were conformed to legal texts.

India was subjected to a series of invasions by Muslims beginning in the eighth century and ending in the fifteenth century, when a mixed invading group of Persians, Turks, and Mongols set up the Moghul Empire. They occupied most of the northern region and enforced Islamic criminal law that classified all offenses on the basis of the penalty each merited. These included retaliation (blood for blood), specific penalties (as for theft and robbery), and discretionary penalties (see Chapter 6).

The British arrived in India in the early seventeenth century as traders, notably those of the East India Company. The Company acquired Indian territory for commercial reasons at first, but later assumed powers of governance. The Company considered the Muslim criminal law irrational and draconian and brought about reforms with a series of regulations that modified or expanded the definitions of some offenses, introduced new offenses, and modified penalties to make them more logical and reasonable.

In 1857, the authority enjoyed by the East India Company was transferred to the British government by an act of Parliament. Prior to that date, India was a loose collection of kingdoms.

In 1860, the first Indian Penal Code (IPC) was adopted. The IPC, based on English common law, defined crimes and established punishments for violations of the crimes. In 1861, a Code of Criminal Procedure was enacted that established the rules to be followed in all stages of investigation, trial, and sentencing. A new Code of Criminal Procedure was adopted in 1974. The IPC and the 1974 Code of Criminal Procedure form the major part of Indian criminal law system. A number of special and local laws, such as the Arms Act, Prohibition Act, and Immoral Traffic (Prevention) Act, supplement the two codes.

Crime Classifications in India

The IPC establishes nearly 300 offenses into two classes, cognizable and noncognizable crimes. Cognizable crimes include murder, rioting, rape, kidnapping and abduction, robbery, organized robbery, housebreaking (burglary), and theft. Noncognizable crimes are less serious than cognizable crimes. Crimes are also classified as "bailable" or "nonbailable," depending on their severity.

Indian Court System

The Supreme Court of India is the highest court and is located in New Delhi. Other judicial bodies at the Union level take the form of tribunals whose members may be from the judiciary or from the civil service. The Supreme Court of India is a court of records and hears appeals from any judgments of a High Court. The Supreme Court has the power to issue prerogative writs in the nature of habeas corpus, mandamus, prohibition, quo warranto, and certiorari in the enforcement of fundamental rights.

Each state or group of states has a High Court. The High Court is also a court of record and hears appeals from the district courts. The High Court has the power to grant writs. Below the High Court is a Court of Sessions, of which the judge, in his or her capacity as district judge, also handles civil cases. Some courts of sessions have additional or assistant judges who also exercise the powers of a Sessions Judge.

At the district level, the lower criminal courts (subdivisional courts) are headed by magistrates (submagistrates and subdivisional magistrates) with jurisdiction over certain lesser offenses. One of the magistrates in a district is appointed as the chief judicial magistrate. Magistrates also commit for trial to the Court of Sessions certain offenses, such as murder, that must be tried by Sessions Judges.

Magistrates try and dispose of lesser offenses and oversee and assist the police in the maintenance of public peace, particularly in matters such as dispersal of an unlawful assembly posing threat to public tranquility, and the handling of disputes over immovable property. The Criminal Procedure Code provides that the government may appoint executive magistrates, civil servants who look after magisterial functions in addition to their own administrative duties. The district magistrate also appoints the senior civil servants in a district.

Special courts may be appointed to handling a variety of problems, including terrorist violence, family disputes, juvenile delinquency, theft of forest wealth, corruption among public officials, and various socioeconomic offenses (such as adulteration, hoarding, and black-marketing of essential food articles).

Judges of the Supreme Court and the High Courts are appointed by the president of India acting on the advice of the executive and after a process of consultation with the existing judges. Judges who have sat on a High Court for at least 5 years, or have practiced as advocates in a High Court for 10 years, or who, in the opinion of the president, are distinguished jurists are all eligible for the Supreme Court. A judge appointed to a High Court must have held a judicial office for at least 10 years or must have been an advocate in the High Court for 10 years. Sessions judges are appointed by the state governor in consultation with the High Court. Other judicial appointments are made by the governor after consultation with the State Public Service Commission and the High Court.

Judicial System of India

- Highest court(s): Supreme Court (the chief justice and 25 associate justices); note—Parliament approved an additional 5 judges in 2008.
- Judge selection and term of office: Justices are appointed by the president to serve until the age of 65.
- Subordinate courts: High Courts; District Courts; and Labour Court.

Note: In mid-2011, India's Cabinet approved the "National Mission for Justice Delivery and Legal Reform" to eliminate judicial corruption and reduce the backlog of cases.

Source: CIA World Fact Book available at website: https://www.cia.gov/library/publications/resources/the-world-factbook, accessed May 14, 2015.

Policing in India

The Indian Police are a civil authority under the prime minister of the Union (as the national government is known) and in the states under the chief ministers and their respective councils of ministers. Major union police forces are the Central Bureau of Investigation (CBI), Border Security Force, Central Reserve Police Force, Central Industrial Security Force, and the Indo-Tibetan Border Police. Each of these forces is headed by a director or director general with the status of a three-star general in the army. The CBI is controlled by the Department of Personnel of the Union government, headed by a minister of state who reports to the prime minister. The other forces are controlled by the Union Ministry of Home Affairs, headed by a cabinet minister.

Most of the police agencies in India are the agencies of the states. Each state has its own police force under the supervision of a director general of police (DGP), who is equivalent in rank to his counterpart in the Union government forces. A number of additional directors general or inspectors general of police (IGPs) who look after various portfolios, such as personnel, law and order, intelligence, crime, armed police, training, and technical services, are located at the state police headquarters and report directly to the DGP. Major cities in a state are headed by a commissioner of police who reports to the DGP. Areas outside the cities are divided into districts of varying sizes. Each district is headed by a superintendent of police (SP) and supervised by a deputy inspector general (DIG), whose jurisdiction is composed of a group of three or four districts.

In each district and city, the basic police unit is a police station (PS). A few police stations have an outpost (OP), which is a ministation for serving remote or trouble-prone localities. The number of police stations depends on the size of the state and the district. The state of Madhya Pradesh, the largest state in land area, has 1101 police stations and 554 outposts. While the larger districts have an average of 22 police stations, the smaller ones have 15.

Each police station is headed by a subinspector or inspector, referred to as the station house officer (SHO). A designated number of constables, the lowest rank in the police force, and head constables are assigned to each police station. In some states, there are additional ranks, such as assistant subinspector or assistant police inspector. While urban police stations often have certain functional divisions, such as law and order and crime and traffic, no such divisions exist in rural or village police stations.

An armed reserve at the district headquarters, under the command of the superintendent of police, handles public disturbance problems, such as religious or caste riots and clashes between political rivals. There are a few battalions of the Special Armed Police (SAP) used for more serious situations. The SAP is deployed by the DGP when the situation warrants it.

There is a criminal investigation department in every state police department. Headed by an additional director of general police or IGP, it is a specialized agency for conducting sensitive inquiries into allegations against public figures or police personnel. More importantly, it is entrusted with the investigation of important criminal cases that cannot be solved by the district police.

The minimum educational qualification for a constable and a subinspector or inspector is a high school diploma; an undergraduate college degree is required for entry into the ASP and DSP level. Physical requirements include a minimum height of 5 feet 5 inches, good eyesight, and minimum attainments in a physical efficiency test consisting of running, jumping, climbing, and throwing. Psychological tests are not yet used in a majority of forces. Superintendents of police (SPs) are recruited by the Union government on the basis of a national competitive exam and are appointed into what is known as the Indian Police Service (IPS). The IPS officers are assigned to the states and the Union territories. Positions in the central forces are filled generally by IPS officers selected from the state agencies.

Criminal Process in India

After the police complete an investigation and obtain a legal opinion from the prosecuting personnel, the police investigator either establishes a charge sheet, accompanied by statements of witnesses, before a competent magistrate, or, in the event of insufficient evidence, files a final report indicating that no further action will be taken. If a suspect is charged, during the trial it is the responsibility of the investigating officer to assist the prosecutor, including the production of witnesses.

Police may arrest, without a warrant and without an order from a magistrate, any person who has committed or is suspected to have committed a cognizable offense. Police may also arrest persons without a warrant for the purpose of preventing a crime. From a practical standpoint, only a few arrests are made on the basis of a warrant.

The Indian Evidence Act provides that confessions made to police officers are not admissible as evidence. If the confession leads to evidence, the evidence may be used against the defendant. Any confession made to a magistrate during an investigation after the person has been warned can be used in evidence.

An accused may be represented in court by a pleader, and the accused is not required to be physically present in court. The accused is entitled to receive without delay a copy of the police report, the first information report, and all statements and confessions on which the prosecution proposes to rely for proving its case.

Any evidence admitted for trial must be recorded in the presence of the accused or his pleader. If the accused pleads guilty, the judge shall record the plea and may, using his or her discretion, convict the accused thereon. The right to a jury trial no longer exists in India. A person accused of a criminal offense has a right to be defended by a pleader of his or her choice. If the accused is indigent, the court will assign a pleader at state expense.

Normally, a police investigation and the filing of a charge sheet with a magistrate precede a criminal trial. If the magistrate finds on the basis of the record that there is sufficient ground for prosecution, a summons or warrant is issued. Warrants are used for offenses punishable with death, life imprisonment, or prison terms exceeding 2 years.

At a hearing, the magistrate determines whether the charges against the accused are correctly framed. This is accomplished after the accused has been provided with a copy of the police report and other documents in the trial folder. The magistrate may alter or add any charge and explain the charge to the accused. If the magistrate finds that a cited offense is triable exclusively by a higher court, he or she commits the case to the higher court after notifying the prosecutor. After the magistrate has approved the charge or charges, the trial commences, with a public prosecutor presenting his or her witnesses. Indian criminal law does not provide for plea bargaining.

Prosecutors

Cases are generally presented in magistrate's court by an assistant public prosecutor, who is a full-time government counsel. A public prosecutor (PP) is also available at every district headquarters to conduct cases before the sessions court. A state prosecutor generally represents the prosecution before the High Court. In addition, any person, including a police officer of a rank at or above inspector, who has not investigated the case may conduct a prosecution in a magistrate's court after receiving permission of the court or the public prosecutor.

The trial judge determines the sentence at the end of the trial without a special sentencing hearing. Defendant is required to be present when the sentence is announced unless his or her absence has been approved by the court or the sentence involves only a fine.

Corrections in India

The range of penalties that may be given in a criminal case includes capital punishment, life imprisonment, imprisonment, forfeiture of property, and fines. Defendants under the age of 21 years who are convicted of an offense punishable with a fine or with imprisonment for not more than 7 years may be released on probation. Community-based treatment is also available. Probation with and without supervision is the primary community-based treatment. The probation department functions under the Home Department in most states and under the Welfare Department in the other states. Generally, punishment takes the form of a term of imprisonment or fine or some combination of both.

Capital punishment can be imposed for murder and certain specified offenses against the Union, including waging war against the government of India, attempting or abetting war, or mutiny. Special circumstances are needed in murder cases before imposing the death penalty. The death penalty can be imposed when an individual serving a life sentence attempts to murder, even if a nonfatal injury results from the attempt. Hanging is used as the method of execution.

Confinement in India

There are five types of prisons in the states: central prisons for individuals serving confinement in excess of 1 month; special prisons for women serving more than 1 month; subjails, which are used for individuals serving less than 1 month or awaiting trial; corrective schools for adolescent convicts from 16 to 23 years old; and open-air prisons, which hold nonviolent individuals serving less than 1 year.

The administration of prisons in India is the responsibility of the various states or the territorial administration. The central government is largely concerned with policy formulation and planning services. In each state, the head of prison administration is an inspector general, who is usually a police officer. He or she has deputy inspectors general to look after the jails in each of the various geographical ranges into which the state is divided.

Sri Lankan System of Law

Sri Lanka is governed by the parliament and the president, who is directly elected by the citizens. The country is divided into 8 provinces and 25 administrative districts. Its justice system is the responsibility of the central government, although the provincial councils maintain regional police departments. Each province and district is headed by a provincial council and a district council, respectively. The members of the councils are popularly elected. The governor is appointed by the president (Karunaratne, 2002).

The judicial branch includes the Supreme Court, a Court of Appeal, the High Court, district courts, and magistrate courts. The highest court is the Supreme Court. Judges are appointed. The chief justice and the other justices of the Supreme Court are appointed for life by the president.

Criminal Justice System

The Sri Lankan justice system consists of a highly complex mixture of common law, civil law, Islamic law, and customary laws. The criminal justice system is mostly English common law and is an adversarial system of justice, with the attorney general (AG) as the principal law officer of the state. The district attorney and state counsels in AG's department handle prosecutions in serious cases. The bulk of prosecutions in minor cases are tried in magistrates' courts by a police officer.

Sri Lanka's penal code was first adopted in 1883 and was based on Indian law. In 1898, the Criminal Procedure Code was adopted; it was replaced in 1973 by the Administration of Justice Act. This act was later replaced by the Code of Criminal Procedure Act of 1979 and the Judicature Act of 1978 as amended by the Judicature Act of 1979.

Crime Classification

The Penal Code divides crime into two categories: grave crimes, which are indictable, and minor offenses, which are nonindictable. The grave crimes include abduction, arson and mischief, burglary, cattle and goat theft, grievous hurt, hurt by knife, homicide, attempted homicide, rape, riot, robbery, "unnatural offenses," extortion, cheating, misappropriation, criminal breach of trust over rupees 1000 theft of bicycles, theft of property over rupees 100, theft of praedial (farm) produce, counterfeiting currency, offenses against the state, offenses under the Offensive Weapons Act, and exchange control offenses.

Sri Lanka's Court System

The hierarchy of the judicial system is as follows: the Supreme Court of the Republic of Sri Lanka, the Court of Appeal of the Republic of Sri Lanka, the High Court of the Republic of Sri Lanka, district courts, magistrates' courts, and primary courts. The criminal trial courts are the primary courts, magistrates' courts, district courts, and High Court. Cases may be appealed to the Court of Appeal and further review may be sought in the Supreme Court. The High Court is the court of first instance for all prosecutions initiated with an indictment. The Supreme Court exercises final appellate jurisdiction as well as special jurisdiction for alleged violations of fundamental rights and freedoms guaranteed by the constitution.

The justices to the Supreme Court and the judges of the Appeal and High courts are appointed by the president. The judges of the lower courts are appointed by the Judicial Service Commission, an administrative body composed of three Supreme Court justices headed by the chief justice.

Policing in Sri Lanka

The police force of Sri Lanka is modeled after the British police and is largely centralized. The police department is under the minister of defense/internal security, a position usually held by the president. The police department is organized in a military-style hierarchical structure and is led by the IGP. Assistant superintendents of police oversee police stations within their districts and report to the deputy inspectors general.

Police duties include patrol, detection, investigation, executing warrants, running local jails, traffic control, testifying in court, record keeping, maintaining order, service to the community, and providing security to VIPs and to large community gatherings. There is a Central Investigation Department patterned after Scotland Yard. It conducts difficult and politically sensitive investigations. There is also a Special Task Force of police commandos who are specially trained to fight terrorists.

Most police officer training is undertaken at the Sri Lanka Police College. The probation period of a recruit is considered to be a continuation of the process of training. The Police Higher Training Institute conducts management and promotion training courses for officers from the rank of subinspector up to that of superintendent of police. There is also training available from other institutions locally and from institutions abroad.

A police officer may, without a warrant, arrest any person in cases of directly witnessed or grave offenses. The majority of arrests are made without warrants. A person arrested has to be produced before a magistrate without unnecessary delay, within 24 hours in case of arrest without a warrant, or be released on bail. An arrested person may be detained in custody by order of a magistrate, pending investigation, for 15 days. Confessions given to a police officer are not admissible into evidence in a court of law, but voluntary judicial confessions are admissible.

Trial Procedures

An accused is considered "innocent until proven guilty." The accused has the right to notification of the charges, the right to answer to the charges, the right to present witnesses, the right to confront and cross-examine opposing witnesses, and the right to legal representation. The accused has the right to a trial by jury in cases involving grave offenses.

Minor offenses may be resolved between the persons concerned. The consent of a magistrate is required if court proceedings have already begun in a court of law. An attorney is provided for indigent defendants.

Generally, a case starts with a police investigation and an arrest. Indictments are required for grave offenses, which may be tried only by a High Court. Indictments are presented by the district attorney in the name of the AG. Prosecution is conducted by a district attorney in cases involving grace offenses.

Most cases involve nongrave offenses and are tried in magistrates' court by the officer in charge of a police station. Sometimes, the police are assisted by a state counsel. For the most part, prosecution is required if sufficient evidence is available to substantiate the charge. The police officer who prosecutes a case in magistrates' court has only limited discretion. The AG or a district attorney has discretion not to prosecute for substantial reasons, but such discretion is rarely exercised.

Alternatives to trial in Sri Lanka include negotiated settlements between the concerned parties, dispute resolution, plea bargaining, and medical or some other kind of supervised treatment.

In cases that are decided by dispute resolution, generally a judge of the Primary Court summons the accused and aggrieved persons to appear before him or her to ascertain if there are acceptable bases for settling the underlying dispute amicably. A resolution has the same effect of an acquittal.

Sentencing Process

The trial judge imposes the sentence and may impose any sentence or other penalty prescribed by statute. Generally, prior to sentencing, a special sentencing hearing is held. Sri Lanka uses the following penalties: fines, imprisonment, probation, capital punishment, suspended sentence, community service, and institutional treatment.

Disenfranchisement may be used for offenses committed while holding public office. Corporal punishment, public punishment, banishment, and exile are not used or available under the law. The death penalty was reintroduced in 1960 after the assassination of the prime minister of Sri Lanka; it is carried out by hanging. The death penalty has rarely been used. As of November 2007, Sri Lanka had not executed a person since the 1970s.

Judicial System of Sri Lanka

- Highest court(s): Supreme Court of the Republic (consists of the chief justice and 10 justices); note—the court has exclusive jurisdiction to review legislation.
- Judge selection and term of office: The chief justice is appointed by the president; the other justices are appointed by the president with the advice of the chief justice; all justices hold office until the age of 65.
- Subordinate courts: Court of Appeals; High Courts; Magistrate's Courts; municipal and primary courts.

Source: CIA World Fact Book available at website: https://www.cia.gov/library/publications/resources/the-world-factbook, accessed May 14, 2015.

Confinement in Sri Lanka

Sri Lanka's prisons are under the jurisdiction of the central government and are administered by the Department of Prisons. The commissioner of prisons, who is appointed by the minister of justice, is the chief administrator.

Remission of sentences is available through executive clemency, parole, and good time credit earned for good behavior. Inmates may learn trades, and there are some educational and vocational programs available.

Summary

- Bulgaria has a High Judicial Council that appoints the judges, prosecutors, and investigators. The members of the council are appointed by the National Assembly.
- Bulgarian trial courts are generally composed of one judge and two lay judges.
- The structure of the Bulgarian prosecutors' offices corresponds to the structure of the courts.
- There are two stages in the Bulgarian criminal trial: the pretrial and the hearing.
- The Bulgarian National Police is a specialized department in the Ministry of Interior and has a militaristic organizational structure.
- Bulgaria has formally abolished the death penalty.
- India's legal system is a mixture of adversarial and accusatorial systems. An informal legal system operates in India's rural areas in civil and family law matters.
- Each state or group of states in India has a High Court.
- Magistrates in lower criminal cases have jurisdiction over lesser crimes. The Indian police are under the jurisdiction of the prime minister of the union.
- Most Indian police agencies are agencies in the various states.
- The Indian Evidence Act prevents the use of confessions made to police officers.
- Capital punishment may be imposed in India for murder and other specified offenses.
- Sri Lanka is governed by a parliament and a president who is directly elected. Its justice system consists of a highly complex mixture of common law, civil law, Islamic law, and customary laws.
- Sri Lanka's police are modeled after the British system.
- Sri Lanka's prisons are under the jurisdiction of the central government and administered by the Department of Prisons.

Questions in Review

1. Explain the difference between the Bulgarian criminal procedure and India's.
2. What forms of corrections are used in Bulgaria?
3. Who selects the judges in Bulgaria? In India? In Sri Lanka?
4. Which of the three mixed systems provides more protection for defendants? Why?

International Courts **11**

Chapter Objectives

After studying this chapter, you should understand or be able to explain the following issues and concepts:

- The various international courts
- The judicial framework of the international courts
- How nations accept jurisdiction under international courts
- The status of the United States and international courts

Key Terms

Community law: The judgments of the Court of Justice of the European Communities together with its treaties, regulations, directives, and decisions.

Contentious cases: Cases before the International Court of Justice that involve an active dispute between two or more member nations and that have been submitted to the court by the nations involved.

Genocide: The systematic killing of a religious, racial, national, or ethnic group of people.

Judge-rapporteur: A judge who is appointed as the official reporter who monitors and supervises a case before the European Community Court of Justice.

Trial chamber: Panel of judges in the International Criminal Court that holds a hearing and makes decisions in a particular case.

Introduction

While there are at least 30 international courts and tribunes, only 3 will be examined in this chapter. See Table 11.1 for a list of the most important international courts. The three international courts that will be examined in this chapter are the International Criminal Court (ICC), the International Court

Table 11.1   Historical List of Major International Courts

International Court of Justice	Worldwide	1945 to Present	General Disputes	Primary Judicial Branch of UN
International Criminal Court	Worldwide	2002 to present	Criminal prosecutions	Rome Statute
Permanent Court of International Justice	Worldwide	1922–1946	General disputes	League of Nations Court
Appellate Body	Worldwide	1995–present	Trade Disputes within the WTO	Part of the World Trade Organization
International Tribunal for the law of the sea	Worldwide	1994–present	Martine disputes	UN Convention on the law of the sea in 1982
African Court of Justice	Africa	2006–present	Interpretations of A. treaties	African Union judicial branch in 2003
Inter-American Court of Human Rights	American Continent	1979–present	Human rights	Judicial branch of Organization of American States
European Court of Justice	Europe	1952–present	Interpretation of EU law	Highest court in the European Union on EU law
International Military Tribunal	Europe	1945–1946	Criminal Prosecutions	Nuremberg trials by Allied forces in WW II
European Union Civil Service Tribunal	Europe	2005–present	Civil disputes	Specialized Court of the European Union
African Court on Human Rights and Peoples Rights	Africa	2006–present	Human Rights	Est. by Protocol to the African Charter on Human and Peoples' Rights

of Justice (ICJ), and the Court of Justice of the European Communities. The ICJ, also known as the World Court, is the Supreme Court of the United Nations (UN). Photo 11.1 is a picture of the UN Headquarters. The ICC was established in 2002 as a court of last resort to prosecute the most heinous offenses in cases where national courts fail to act. Unlike the ICJ, which hears disputes between states, the ICC handles prosecutions of individuals. The Court of Justice of the European Communities is the judiciary for the European Union (EU). While the court now handles mostly civil matters, many leaders have advocated that it take a larger part in criminal justice problems in the EU, especially in dealing with transnational crimes and illegal drugs.

Photo 11.1 UN Headquarters, UN Plaza, New York City, New York. (Photograph courtesy of the Library of Congress Prints and Photographs Division.)

ICC

The ICC is intended to complement existing national judicial systems, and therefore, it only exercise its jurisdiction when certain conditions are met, such as when national courts are unwilling or unable to prosecute criminals or when the UN Security Council or individual states refer investigations to the court. The ICC was established by the Rome Statute of the ICC, so called because it was adopted in Rome, Italy, on July 17, 1998, by the United Nations Diplomatic Conference of Plenipotentiaries on the Establishment of an International Criminal Court. The Rome Statute is an international treaty, binding only on those nations that formally express their consent to be bound by its provisions. The ICC's jurisdiction includes the crime of genocide, and the statute adopts the same definition of the offense as found in the UN Convention on Genocide (see box). Although the Rome Statute was widely praised and signed by 140 countries, few countries in the Middle East or Asia joined. By 2002, China, Russia, and the United States had declined to participate, and the United States had threatened to withdraw its troops from UN peacekeeping forces unless its citizens (both military and civilian) were exempted from prosecution by the ICC. As of 2007, more than 100 countries had ratified the treaty.

The ICC has four principal divisions: the Presidency, the Judicial Divisions, the Office of the Prosecutor, and the Registry. The president is the senior judge chosen by his or her peers in the Judicial Division. It is the Judicial Division that hears cases before the court. The Office of the Prosecutor is led by the chief prosecutor who investigates crimes and initiates proceedings before the Judicial Division. The Registry is headed by the registrar and is charged with managing all the administrative functions of the ICC, including the headquarters, detention union, and public defense office.

As of 2015, 36 individuals have been indicted in the ICC. Those indicted include Ugandan rebel leader Joseph Kony, Sudanese president Omar al-Bashir, Kenyan president Uhuru Kenyatta, Libyan leader Muammar Gaddafi, and Ivorian president Laurent Gbagbo. The ICC has been accused of selected enforcement because all of the official investigations as of 2015 have been in Africa.

Genocide

Raphael Lemkin is credited with developing the word "genocide" in 1944. He combined the Greek word *genos* ("race") with the Latin root *cide* ("killing"). Genocide is defined by the UN to mean any of the following acts committed with intent to destroy, in whole or in part, a national, ethnic, racial, or religious group, including (a) killing members of the group, (b) causing serious bodily or mental harm to the members of the group, (c) deliberately inflicting on the group conditions of life calculated to bring about its physical destruction in whole or in part, (d) imposing measures intended to prevent births within the group, or (e) forcibly transferring children of the group to another group.

Excerpts from the UN Convention on Genocide

Article III
The following acts shall be punished: (a) Genocide; (b) conspiracy to commit genocide; (c) direct and public incitement to commit genocide; (d) attempt to commit genocide; (e) complicity in genocide.

Article IV
Persons committing genocide or any of the other acts enumerated in Article III shall be punished, whether they are constitutional responsible rulers, public officials, or private individuals.

Source: Convention on the Prevention and Punishment of the Crime of Genocide. Adopted by the UN General Assembly on December 9, 1948.

The United States and the ICC

President Bill Clinton signed the ICC Statute on December 31, 2000. In May 2002, President George W. Bush and his administration declared that they would no longer consider the United States legally bound by that signature.

This acts as a nullification of it. In addition, the U.S. Congress enacted two pieces of legislation that were designed to hinder the operations of the ICC. The United States' stated opposition to the ICC is based on preserving sovereignty over its citizens and a fear that the court may become a vehicle for other countries to criminalize and punish actions by U.S. citizens (Yacoubian, 2003).

Establishment of the Court

After the adoption of the Rome Statute, the UN convened the Preparatory Commission for the International Criminal Court. As with the Rome Conference, all nation-states were invited to participate in the Preparatory Commission. Among its achievements, the Preparatory Commission reached consensus on the Rules of Procedure and Evidence and the Elements of Crimes. These two texts were subsequently adopted by the Assembly of States Parties. Together with the Rome Statute and the Regulations of the Court adopted by the judges, they comprise the court's basic legal texts, setting out its structure, jurisdiction, and functions.

By July 2002, the requisite number of countries (60) had ratified the agreement and the court began sitting. As of 2007, 105 nation-states had become parties to the statute. The states parties meet as the Assembly of States Parties and exercise management oversight and legislative control of the court. The court is not part of the UN, but it maintains a cooperative relationship with the UN. The ICC is based in The Hague, the Netherlands, although it may also sit elsewhere (ICC website: http://www.icc-cpi.int/about/ataglance/establishment.html, accessed November 2, 2007).

The ICC is now a permanent judicial body with the mission to prosecute and adjudicate individuals accused of genocide, war crimes, and other crimes against humanity. It is an independent institution composed of four organs: the Presidency, the judicial divisions, the Office of the Prosecutor, and the Registry. Recently, there has been a strong movement to include within its jurisdiction international drug trafficking and trafficking in humans.

The ICC's first hearing was held in 2006 to decide whether charges should be brought against Thomas Lubanga, who was accused of recruiting child soldiers in Congo (Kinshasa). In the following year, the court's prosecutor announced charges stemming from atrocities committed in the Darfur region of Sudan.

President of the ICC

The Presidency is responsible for the overall administration of the court, with the exception of the Office of the Prosecutor, and for specific functions assigned to the Presidency in accordance with the statute. The Presidency is composed of three judges of the court, elected to the Presidency by their fellow judges for a term of 3 years.

Judicial Divisions

The Judicial Divisions consists of 18 judges organized into the Pretrial Division, the Trial Division, and the Appeals Division. The judges of each division sit in chambers, which are responsible for conducting the proceedings of the court at different stages. Assignment of judges to divisions is made on the basis of the nature of the functions each division performs and the qualifications and experience of the judge.

Prosecutor

The Office of the Prosecutor is responsible for receiving referrals and any substantiated information on crimes within the jurisdiction of the court, for examining them, and for conducting investigations and prosecutions before the court. The office is headed by the prosecutor, who is elected by the state parties for a term of 9 years. The prosecutor is assisted by two deputy prosecutors, one with responsibility for investigations and one with responsibility for prosecutions.

Registry

The Registry is responsible for the nonjudicial aspects of the administration and servicing of the court. The Registry is headed by the registrar, who is the principal administrative officer of the court. The registrar exercises his or her functions under the authority of the president of the court. The registrar is elected by the judges for a term of 5 years.

Other Offices

The ICC also includes a number of semiautonomous offices, such as the Office of Public Counsel for Victims and the Office of Public Counsel for Defence. These offices fall under the Registry for administrative purposes but otherwise function as wholly independent offices. The Assembly of States Parties has also established a trust fund for the benefit of victims of crimes within the jurisdiction of the court and the families of these victims.

Jurisdiction and Admissibility

The ICC exercises jurisdiction over genocide, crimes against humanity, and war crimes. These crimes are defined in detail in the Rome Statute. In addition, a supplementary text of the "Elements of Crimes" provides a breakdown of the elements of each crime. The court has jurisdiction over individuals accused of these crimes. This includes those directly responsible for committing the crimes as well as others who may be liable for the crimes, for example, by aiding, abetting, or otherwise assisting in the commission of a crime. The latter group also includes military commanders or other superiors whose responsibility is defined in the statute.

The ICC does not have universal jurisdiction. The court may exercise jurisdiction only if the accused is a national of a state party or a state otherwise accepting the jurisdiction of the court, the crime took place on the territory of a state party or a state otherwise accepting the jurisdiction of the court, or the UN Security Council has referred the situation to the prosecutor, without regard to the nationality of the accused or the location of the crime.

The court's jurisdiction is also limited to events taking place since July 2002. In addition, if a state joins the court after July 2002, the court has jurisdiction only after the statute entered into force for that state. Such a state may nonetheless accept the jurisdiction of the court for the period before the statute's entry into force. However, in no case can the court exercise jurisdiction over events before July 2002.

Even if the ICC has jurisdiction, it does not necessarily act. The principle of "complementarity" provides that some cases will be inadmissible even though the court has jurisdiction. In general, a case will be inadmissible if it has been or is being investigated or prosecuted by a state with jurisdiction. However, a case may be admissible if the investigating or prosecuting state is unwilling or unable genuinely to carry out the investigation or prosecution. For example, a case would be admissible if national proceedings were undertaken for the purpose of shielding the accused person from criminal responsibility. In addition, a case will be inadmissible if it is not of sufficient gravity to justify further action by the court.

Procedure

The Assembly of States, Parties, or the UN Security Council may refer situations of crimes within the jurisdiction of the ICC to the prosecutor. The prosecutor evaluates the available information and commences an investigation unless he determines there is no reasonable basis to proceed. The prosecutor may also begin an investigation on his own initiative. In doing so, he receives and analyzes information submitted by a variety of reliable sources. If the prosecutor concludes that there is a reasonable basis to proceed with an investigation, he requests a pretrial chamber to authorize an investigation.

A prosecutor's investigations cover all facts and evidence relevant to an assessment of criminal responsibility. The prosecutor investigates incriminating and exonerating circumstance equally and is expected to respect the rights of the accused. During the investigation, each situation is assigned to a pretrial chamber.

The pretrial chamber is responsible for the judicial aspects of proceedings. Among its functions, the pretrial chamber, on the application of the prosecutor, may issue a warrant of arrest or a summons to appear if there are reasonable grounds to believe a person has committed a crime within the jurisdiction of the court. Once a wanted person has been surrendered to or voluntarily appears before the court, the pretrial chamber holds a hearing to confirm the charges that will be the basis of the trial.

Following the confirmation of charges, the case is assigned to a trial chamber of three judges. The trial chamber is responsible for conducting fair and expeditious proceedings with full respect for the rights of the accused. The accused is presumed innocent until proven guilty by the prosecutor beyond reasonable doubt. The accused has the right to conduct the defense in person or through counsel of his or her choosing. Victims may also participate in proceedings directly or through their legal representatives.

Upon conclusion of the proceedings, the trial chamber issues its decision, acquitting or convicting the accused. If the accused is convicted, the trial chamber issues a sentence for a specified term of up to 30 years or, when justified by the extreme gravity of the crime and the individual circumstances of the convicted person, life imprisonment. The trial chamber may also order reparations to victims.

Duties of States That Are Parties

The ICC relies on international cooperation, in particular from states. State parties are expected to cooperate with the court in its investigations and prosecutions. State parties may cooperate in arresting persons wanted by the court, providing evidence for use in proceedings, relocating witnesses, and enforcing the sentences of convicted persons. The court may also receive cooperation from non–state parties and may enter into arrangements or agreements to provide cooperation. International organizations also provide important support to the court. Foremost among these is the UN. In 2004, the president of the ICC and the secretary-general of the UN concluded the Negotiated Relationship Agreement between the ICC and the UN. This agreement provides for institutional relations, cooperation, and judicial assistance between the court and the UN while reaffirming the independence of the court.

Selected Court Cases

By 2007, four situations had been referred to the prosecutor. Three state parties (Uganda, the Democratic Republic of the Congo, and the Central African Republic) referred situations occurring on their territories to the court, and the Security Council, acting under Chapter VII of the UN Charter, referred a situation on the territory of a non–state party (Sudan).

After analyzing the referrals for jurisdiction and admissibility, the prosecutor commenced investigations in three situations—Uganda, the Democratic Republic of the Congo, and Darfur in Sudan. In July 2005, the court issued the first arrest warrants with regard to the situation in Uganda. At the end of 2007, the prosecutor was monitoring situations in other countries, including Côte d'Ivoire, a non–state party, which declared its acceptance of jurisdiction over crimes on its territory.

Frequent Questions Asked of Court Personnel and Their Answers

Why Is an ICC Necessary?

This past century has seen some of the worst atrocities in the history of humanity. In too many cases, these crimes have been committed with impunity, which has only encouraged others to flout the laws of humanity. States representative of the international community met in order to negotiate and agree upon the establishment of a treaty-based ICC to help end impunity and the gross violations of international humanitarian law.

What Are the Key Features of the ICC?

Based in The Hague, the Netherlands, the ICC is the first ever permanent international institution with jurisdiction to prosecute individuals responsible for the most serious crimes of international concern: genocide, crimes against humanity, and war crimes.

The court shall exercise jurisdiction over the crime of aggression once a provision is adopted defining the crime and setting out the conditions under which the court shall exercise jurisdiction with respect to it.

The jurisdiction of the ICC will be complementary to national courts, which means that the court will only act when countries themselves are unable or unwilling to investigate or prosecute.

The jurisdiction and functioning of the court is governed by the provisions of the Rome Statute. The ICC also has strong protections for due process, procedural safeguards to protect it from abuse, and furthers victims' rights and gender justice under international law.

When Did the Rome Statute of the ICC Enter into Force?

The ICC Statute entered into force on July 1, 2002, 60 days after the sixtieth ratification needed to create the court was received on April 11 at a special event at the UN, when 10 countries simultaneously deposited their instruments of ratification.

Does "Complementarity" Mean that the ICC Can Never Prosecute If a Country Holds Its Own Trial?

The ICC will complement national courts so that they retain jurisdiction to try genocide, crimes against humanity, and war crimes. If a case is being considered by a country with jurisdiction over it, then the ICC cannot act unless the country is unwilling or unable genuinely to investigate or prosecute. A country may be determined to be "unwilling" if it is clearly shielding someone from responsibility for ICC crimes. A country may be "unable" when its legal system has collapsed.

Who Can Initiate Proceedings?

Proceedings before the ICC may be initiated by a State Party, the prosecutor, or the UN Security Council. The jurisdiction of the ICC is based on "complementarity," which allows national courts the first opportunity to investigate or prosecute.

Can the ICC Be Used to Try Crimes Committed before the Rome Treaty Entered into Force?

The ICC will not have retroactive jurisdiction and therefore will not apply to crimes committed before July 1, 2002, when the statute entered into force.

Why Is the Court Not Exercising Its Jurisdiction over the Crime of Aggression?

The Rome Statute included the crime of aggression within the jurisdiction of the court. However, the States Parties must adopt an agreement setting up a definition of aggression and the conditions under which the court could exercise its jurisdiction. A review conference will be held in 2009, 7 years from the date that the Rome Statute entered into force, during which the matter will be discussed.

Can the ICC Deal with Terrorist Acts within Its Existing Jurisdiction?

The ICC will have jurisdiction over genocide, crimes against humanity, and war crimes. The ICC may be able to prosecute terrorist acts only if they fall within these categories.

How Is the ICC Different from the Ad Hoc Tribunals for Rwanda and the Former Yugoslavia?

The ICC is the product of a multilateral treaty, whereas the tribunals for the former Yugoslavia and Rwanda were created by the UN Security Council. These tribunals were created in response to specific situations and will be in existence for a limited time period. The ICC is a permanent international criminal tribunal and will avoid the delays and costs of creating ad hoc tribunals.

How Is the ICC Different from the International Court of Justice?

The ICJ does not have criminal jurisdiction to prosecute individuals. It is a civil tribunal that deals primarily with disputes between states. The ICJ is the principal judicial organ of the UN, whereas the ICC is independent of the UN.

Where Is the ICC Located?

The ICC has established its headquarters in The Hague, the Netherlands. The court is currently located at Maanweg 174, 2516 AB, The Hague, the Netherlands, with postal address P.O. Box 19519, 2500 CM, Den Haag, the Netherlands.

Chronology of the Development of the ICC

1945: Nuremberg Tribunal, the establishment of an international military tribunal by the "London Agreement" to try Nazi war criminals.

1946: Tokyo Tribunal, established by the Allied Powers of World War II, a military tribunal for the Far East known to prosecute Japanese war criminals.

1947: UN Convention on the Prevention and Punishment of the Crime of Genocide adopted. Article I of the Convention states that genocide is "a crime under international law," and article VI indicated that persons charged with the offense of genocide "shall be tried by a competent tribunal of the State in the territory of which the act was committed or by such international penal tribunal as may have jurisdiction."

1949–1954: The International Law Commission (ILC) (established by the UN) prepared several draft statutes for an ICC, but differences of opinions forestalled further developments.

1989: UN General Assembly requested the ILC to resume work on an ICC with jurisdiction to include drug trafficking.

1993: The UN Security Council established the ad hoc International Criminal Tribunal for the former Yugoslavia to hold individuals accountable for the atrocities committed as a part of what was known "ethnic cleansing."

1994: The ILC completed its work on the draft statute for an ICC and submitted the draft statute to the UN General Assembly.

1995: The Ad Hoc Committee on the Establishment of an International Criminal Court met twice. After the General Assembly had considered the committee's report, it created the Preparatory Committee on the Establishment of an International Criminal Court to prepare a widely acceptable consolidated draft text for submission to a diplomatic conference.

1996–1998: The Preparatory Committee met and held its final session in March and April of 1998, when it completed the drafting of the text.

1998: Adoption of the Statute of the International Criminal Court at the UN Conference of Plenipotentiaries in Rome with the participation of representatives of 160 states, 33 intergovernmental organizations, and a coalition of 236 nongovernmental organizations. There were 120 countries that voted in favor, 7 against, and 21 abstained. The ICC was established not as an organ of the UN but as an independent organization with an independent budget.

January 16, 2002: There was as agreement between the UN and the government of Sierra Leone for the establishment of the Special Court for Sierra Leone to try individuals responsible for "those who bear greatest responsibility for crimes committed in Sierra Leone during the country's violent conflict after 30th November 1996."

April 11, 2002: Sixty ratifications of the statute of the ICC were required before the statute could be enforced. The sixtieth instrument of ratification was deposited with the UN secretary-general when 10 countries simultaneously deposited their instruments of ratification as provided by Article 126 of the Rome Statute.

July 1, 2002: The Rome Statute entered into force on July 1, 2002. Anyone who commits any of the crimes under the statute after this date is liable for prosecution by the court. Court commences its basic operations when it formally begins its work.

(Information for chronology obtained from ICC website, http://www.icc-cpi. int/about/ataglance/establishment.html, accessed November 2, 2007.)

Trial Procedure of the ICC

Basically, the court proceeds under a modified adversarial proceeding. The prosecutor presents the case and the accused is represented by a defense counsel. The registrar is responsible for retaining and preserving the evidence and other materials offered during the hearing, subject to any order of the trial chamber (panel of judges).

If the presiding judge does not give directions, the prosecutor and the defense shall agree on the order and manner in which the evidence shall be submitted to the trial chamber. If no agreement can be reached, the presiding judge makes the decisions. The prosecution and the defense have the right to question witnesses about relevant matters related to the witness testimony and its reliability, the credibility of the witness, and other relevant matters. The trial chamber has the right to question a witness before or after the witness is questioned by a participant. The defense has the right to be the last to examine a witness.

Unless otherwise ordered by the trial chamber, a witness other than an expert, or an investigator if he or she has not yet testified, shall not be present when the testimony of another witness is given. However, a witness who has heard the testimony of another witness shall not for that reason alone be disqualified from testifying. The presiding judge shall declare when the submission of evidence is closed. The prosecutor and the defense are allow to make their closing statements. The defense has the opportunity to speak last. After the closing statements, the trial chamber retires to deliberate, in private. The trial chamber shall inform all those who participated in the proceedings of the date on which the trial chamber will announce its decision.

International Court of Justice

The ICJ is housed in the Peace Palace in The Hague, the Netherlands. It is one of the six principal organs of the UN and the only one not located in New York. The ICJ's mission is to settle legal disputes submitted to it by member nations and to give advisory opinions on legal questions referred to it by authorized UN organs and specialized agencies. The ICJ has 15 judges, who are elected for terms of office of 9 years by the UN General Assembly and the Security Council. It is assisted by a Registry, its administrative organ. Its official languages are English and French.

The court is the result of a long search for methods for the peaceful settlement of international disputes, the origins of which can be traced back to Classical times. The modern history of international arbitration is generally considered to date from the Jay Treaty of 1794 between the United States of America and Great Britain. This treaty provided for the creation of mixed commissions, composed of American and British nationals in equal numbers, whose task would be to settle a number of outstanding questions between the two countries. During the nineteenth century, the United States and the United Kingdom used the commissions, as did other states in Europe and the Americas, to settle disputes between nations.

Another phase of international commissions began in 1870s. One of the more famous such commissions was the Alabama Claims arbitration in 1872 between the United Kingdom and the United States. Under the Treaty of Washington of 1871, the United States and the United Kingdom agreed to submit to arbitration claims by the United States for alleged breaches of neutrality by the English during the American Civil War. The two countries agreed to certain rules governing the duties of neutral governments that were to be applied by the tribunal, which they agreed should consist of five members, to be appointed respectively by the heads of state of the United States, the United Kingdom, Brazil, Italy, and Switzerland, the last three states not being parties to the case. The arbitral tribunal's award ordered the United Kingdom to pay compensation and it duly complied.

The Hague Peace Conference of 1899, convened at the initiative of the Russian Tsar Nicholas II, is considered the beginning of the modern history of international arbitration. The chief object of the conference was to discuss peace and disarmament. It ended by adopting the Convention on the Pacific Settlement of International Disputes, which dealt not only with arbitration but also with other methods of peaceful settlement, such as good offices and mediation.

The 1899 Convention made provision for the creation of permanent machinery that would enable arbitral tribunals to be set up as desired and would facilitate their work. This institution, known as the Permanent Court of Arbitration, consisted in essence of a panel of jurists selected from a panel designated by each country acceding to the convention. The convention also created a permanent bureau, located at The Hague, with functions corresponding to those of a court registrar or a secretariat, and it laid down a set of rules of procedure to govern the conduct of arbitrations. The name "Permanent Court of Arbitration" was not an accurate description of the machinery set up by the convention, which represented only a method or device for facilitating the creation of arbitral tribunals as and when necessary. The Permanent Court of Arbitration was established in 1900 and began operating in 1902.

In 1907, a second Hague Peace Conference, to which the states of Central and South America were also invited, revised the convention and improved the rules governing arbitral proceedings. Some participants would have preferred the conference not to confine itself to improving the machinery created in 1899. The United States, the United Kingdom, and Germany submitted a joint proposal for a permanent court, but the Conference was unable to reach agreement upon it. The Conference confined itself to recommending that states should adopt a draft convention for the creation of a court of arbitral justice as soon as agreement was reached "respecting the selection of the judges and the constitution of the court." In 1913, the Permanent Court of Arbitration took up residence in the Peace Palace, which had been built for it through a gift from Andrew Carnegie.

The work of the two Hague Peace Conferences and the ideas they inspired in statesmen and jurists had some influence on the creation of the Central American Court of Justice, which operated from 1908 to 1918, as well as on the various plans and proposals submitted between 1911 and 1919 both by national and international bodies and by governments for the establishment of an international judicial tribunal, which culminated in the creation of the Permanent Court of International Justice (PCIJ) within the framework of the League of Nations after the end of World War I.

Permanent Court of International Justice

Article 14 of the Covenant of the League of Nations gave the Council of the League responsibility for formulating plans for the establishment of a PCIJ, such a court to be competent not only to hear and determine any dispute of an international character submitted to it by the parties to the dispute, but also to give an advisory opinion upon any dispute or question referred to it by the League Council or by the Assembly. It remained for the League Council to take the necessary action to give effect to Article 14.

At its second session, early in 1920, the Council appointed an Advisory Committee of Jurists to submit a report on the establishment of the PCIJ. In August 1920, a report containing a draft scheme was submitted to the Council, which, after examining it and making certain amendments, laid it before the first Assembly of the League of Nations, which opened at Geneva in November of that year. The Assembly instructed its Third Committee to examine the question of the court's constitution. In December 1920, after an exhaustive study by a subcommittee, the committee submitted a revised draft to the Assembly, which unanimously adopted it. This was the Statute of the PCIJ.

By the time of the next meeting of the Assembly, in September 1921, a majority of the members of the League had signed and ratified the protocol. The statute thus entered into force. It was to be revised only once, in 1929, the revised version coming into force in 1936. The PCIJ was a working reality.

Unlike earlier tribunals, the PCIJ was a permanently constituted body governed by its own statute and rules of procedure, fixed beforehand and binding on parties having recourse to the court. It had a permanent Registry, which served as a channel of communication with governments and international bodies. Its proceedings were largely public and provision was made for the publication in due course of the pleadings, of verbatim records of the sittings, and of all documentary evidence submitted to it.

In principle, the PCIJ was accessible to all nations for the judicial settlement of their international disputes, and they were able to declare beforehand that for certain classes of legal disputes they recognized the court's jurisdiction as compulsory in relation to other nations accepting the same obligation. The PCIJ was empowered to give advisory opinions upon any dispute or question referred to it by the League of Nations Council or Assembly.

Although the PCIJ was brought into being by the League of Nations, it was not a part of the League. Between 1922 and 1940, the PCIJ dealt with 29 cases between nations and delivered 27 advisory opinions. The PCIJ had its last public sitting on December 4, 1939. In 1940, the PCIJ was removed to Geneva, with a single judge remaining at The Hague, together with a few Registry officials of Dutch nationality.

Establishment of the International Court of Justice

In 1942, the U.S. Secretary of State and the foreign secretary of the United Kingdom declared themselves in favor of the establishment or reestablishment of an international court after the war, and the Inter-American Juridical Committee recommended the extension of the PCIJ's jurisdiction. Early in 1943, the UK government took the initiative of inviting a number of experts to London to constitute an informal Inter-Allied Committee to examine the matter. This committee held 19 meetings, which were attended by jurists from 11 countries. In its report, which was published on February 10, 1944, it recommended the establishment of the PCIJ.

In October 1943, following a conference between China, the USSR, the United Kingdom, and the United States, a joint declaration was issued recognizing the necessity of establishing at the earliest practicable date a general international organization, based on the principle of the sovereign equality of all peace-loving states, and open to membership by all such states, large and small, for the maintenance of international peace and security. This declaration led to exchanges between the Four Powers at Dumbarton Oaks, resulting in the publication in October 1944 of proposals for the establishment of a general international organization, to include an international court of justice.

The ICJ was established in 1945 by the San Francisco Conference, which also created the UN. The PCIJ met for the last time in October 1945, when it was decided to take all appropriate measures to ensure the transfer of its archives and effects to the new ICJ, which was to have its seat in the Peace Palace. The judges of the PCIJ all resigned in January 1946, and the election of the first members of the ICJ took place in February 1946, at the first session of the UN General Assembly and Security Council. In April 1946, the PCIJ was formally dissolved, and the ICJ met for the first time. The first case was submitted in May 1947. It concerned incidents in the Corfu Channel and was brought by the United Kingdom against Albania. From May 22, 1947, to November 4, 2007, 136 cases were entered in the General List.

Resolution of Cases

Cases before the ICJ are resolved in one of three ways. First, they can be settled by the parties at any time during the proceedings. Second, a state can discontinue the proceedings and withdraw at any point. Third, the court can deliver a verdict.

The ICJ decides disputes in accordance with international law as reflected in international conventions, international custom, general principles of law recognized by civilized nations, judicial decisions, and writings of the most highly qualified experts on international law. Although the judges deliberate in secret, their verdicts—rendered in both English and French—are delivered in open court. Any judge who does not agree in whole or in part with the court's decision may file a separate opinion, and few decisions represent the unanimous opinion of the judges. The court's judgment is final and without appeal.

Practice Directions

The ICJ has adopted "practice directions" for use by nations appearing before it. They are the result of the court's ongoing review of its working methods. The highlights of those directions are summarized as follows:

- The ICJ discourages the practice of simultaneous deposit of pleadings in cases brought by special agreement.
- It expects future special agreements to contain provisions as to the number and order of pleadings, in accordance with the Rules of Court. Such provisions shall be without prejudice to any issue in the case, including the issue of burden of proof.
- If the special agreement contains no provisions on the number and order of pleadings, the court will expect the parties to reach agreement to that effect, in accordance with the Rules of Court.
- Each of the parties should, in drawing up its written pleadings, bear in mind the fact that these pleadings are intended not only to reply to the submissions and arguments of the other party but also, and above all, to present clearly the submissions and arguments of the party that is filing the proceedings. In the light of this, at the conclusion of the written pleadings of each party, a short summary of its reasoning should appear.
- The court has noticed an excessive tendency toward the proliferation and protraction of annexes to written pleadings. It strongly urges parties to append to their pleadings only strictly selected documents.
- Where one of the parties has a full or partial translation of its own pleadings or of those of the other party in the other official language of the court, these translations should as a matter of course be passed to the Registry of the court. The same applies to the annexes. These translations will be examined by the Registry and communicated to the other party. The latter will also be informed of the manner in which they were prepared.
- With the aim of accelerating proceedings on preliminary objections made by one party under the Rules of Court, the time limit for the presentation by the other party of a written statement of its observations and submissions shall generally not exceed 4 months from the date of the filing of the preliminary objections.

- The oral statements made on behalf of each party shall be as succinct as possible within the limits of what is requisite for the adequate presentation of that party's contentions at the hearing. Accordingly, they shall be directed to the issues that still divide the parties and shall not go over the whole ground covered by the pleadings or merely repeat the facts and arguments these contain.
- The court requires full compliance with these provisions and observation of the requisite degree of brevity. Where objections of lack of jurisdiction or of inadmissibility are being considered, oral proceedings are to be limited to statements on the objections. (ICJ website: http://www.icjcij.org/homepage/index.php?lang=en, accessed November 4, 2007.)

Jurisdiction of the ICJ

Article 93 of the UN Charter provides that all 193 UN members are automatically parties to the court's statute. The ICJ acts as a world court. It has a dual jurisdiction: it decides, in accordance with international law, disputes of a legal nature that are submitted to it by states (jurisdiction in contentious cases), and it gives advisory opinions on legal questions at the request of the organs of the UN or specialized agencies authorized to make such requests (advisory jurisdiction).

Contentious Cases

Only nations (member states of the UN and other states that have become parties to the Statute of the Court or have accepted its jurisdiction under certain conditions) may be parties to contentious cases. The court is competent to entertain a dispute only if the states concerned have accepted its jurisdiction in one or more of the following ways:

- By entering into a special agreement to submit the dispute to the court.
- By virtue of a jurisdictional clause: typically when they are parties to a treaty containing a provision whereby, in the event of a dispute of a given type or disagreement over the interpretation or application of the treaty, one of them may refer the dispute to the court.
- Through the reciprocal effect of declarations made by them under the statute whereby each has accepted the jurisdiction of the court as compulsory in the event of a dispute with another state having made a similar declaration. A number of these declarations, which must be deposited with the UN secretary-general, contain reservations excluding certain categories of dispute.

Advisory Proceedings

Advisory proceedings before the ICJ are open only to organizations and agencies of the UN. The UN General Assembly and Security Council may request advisory opinions on "any legal question." Other UN organs and specialized agencies that have been authorized to seek advisory opinions can do so only with respect to legal questions arising within the scope of their activities.

When the ICJ receives a request for an advisory opinion, it is empowered to hold written and oral proceedings. After the request is filed, the ICJ draws up a list of those states and international organizations that will be able to furnish information on the question before the court. Those states are not in the same position as parties to contentious proceedings: their representatives before the court are not known as agents and their participation, if any, in the advisory proceedings does not render the court's opinion binding upon them. In general, the states listed are the member states of the organization requesting the opinion. Any state not consulted by the court may ask to be.

It is rare, however, for the ICJ to allow international organizations other than the one having requested the opinion to participate in advisory proceedings. With respect to nongovernmental international organizations, the court has rejected all such requests by private parties to participate in the proceedings.

Participants may file written statements, which sometimes form the object of written comments by other participants. The written statements and comments are regarded as confidential, but are generally made available to the public at the beginning of the oral proceedings. States are then usually invited to present oral statements at public sittings. Advisory proceedings are concluded by the delivery of the advisory opinion at a public sitting.

Court of Justice of European Communities

The European Court of Justice (ECJ) is the highest court in the EU in matters of EU law. The Court of Justice of the European Communities, together with the national courts of the 27 member nations, constitutes the EU's judiciary. The court's main task is to interpret EU law uniformly and to rule on its validity.

It answers questions referred to it by the national courts, which play a vital role, as they apply community law at the local level. The EU enacts its own legislation, known as regulations, directives, and decisions. While it is not possible to appeal the decisions of national courts to the ECJ, the national courts frequently refer questions of EU law to the ECJ. It is ultimately for the national courts to apply the resulting interpretations to the facts in any given case. The Court of Justice of the European Communities is composed of three courts: the Court of Justice (created in 1952), the Court of First Instance (created in 1988), and the Civil Service Tribunal (created in 2004) (CJEC, 2007).

The Court of Justice is composed of 27 judges and 8 advocates general. The judges and advocates general are appointed by a common accord by the governments of the EU's member states for a renewable term of 6 years. They are chosen from among lawyers whose independence is beyond doubt and who possess the qualifications required for appointment, in their respective countries, to the highest judicial offices, or who are of recognized competence.

The judges of the court elect one of themselves as president of the court for a renewable term of 3 years. The president directs the work and staff of the court and presides at hearings and deliberations of the full court or the grand chamber.

The advocates general assist the court. They are responsible for presenting, with complete impartiality and independence, an "opinion" in the cases assigned to them. The registrar is the institution's secretary-general and manages its departments under the authority of the president of the court.

The court may sit as a full court, in a "grand chamber" of 13 judges, or in chambers of three or five judges. It sits as a full court in the particular cases prescribed by the statute of the court (e.g., in proceedings to dismiss the European ombudsman or a member of the European Commission who has failed to fulfill his or her obligations) and where the court considers that a case is of exceptional importance. It sits in a grand chamber when a member state or an institution that is a party to the proceedings so requests, and in particularly complex or important cases. Other cases are heard by chambers of three or five judges. The presidents of the chambers of five judges are elected for 3 years and those of the chambers of three judges for 1 year.

Judicial System of European Union

- Note: The European Court of Justice (ECJ) ensures that EU law is interpreted and applied uniformly throughout the EU, resolves disputed issues among the EU institutions and with member states, issues opinions on questions of EU law, referred by member state courts.
- Highest court(s): European Court of Justice (consists of 28 judges—1 from each member state); the court may sit as a full court, in a "Grand Chamber" of 13 judges in special cases, but usually in chambers of 3–5 judges.
- Judge selection and term of office: judges appointed by the common consent of the member states to serve 6-year renewable terms.
- Subordinate courts: General Court; Civil Service Tribunal.

Source: CIA World Fact Book available at website: https://www.cia.gov/library/publications/resources/the-world-factbook, accessed May 14, 2015.

Excerpts from the Establishing Treaty

A. Treaty on European Union Court of Justice of the European Communities
Article 35

1. The Court of Justice of the European Communities shall have jurisdiction, subject to the conditions laid down in this Article, to give
   preliminary rulings on the validity and interpretation of framework
   decisions and decisions, on the interpretation of conventions established under this Title(1) and on the validity and interpretation of
   the measures implementing them.
2. By a declaration(2) made at the time of signature of the Treaty of
   Amsterdam or at any time thereafter, any Member State shall be able
   to accept the jurisdiction of the Court of Justice to give preliminary
   rulings as specified in paragraph 1.
3. A Member State making a declaration pursuant to paragraph 2 shall
   specify that either:
   (a) any court or tribunal of that State against whose decisions there
       is no judicial remedy under national law may request the Court
       of Justice to give a preliminary ruling on a question raised in a
       case pending before it and concerning the validity or interpreta-
       tion of an act referred to in paragraph 1 if that court or tribunal
       considers that a decision on the question is necessary to enable it
       to give judgment, or
   (b) any court or tribunal of that State may request the Court of
       Justice to give a preliminary ruling on a question raised in a case
       pending before it and concerning the validity or interpretation of
       an act referred to in paragraph 1 if that court or tribunal consid-
       ers that a decision on the question is necessary to enable it to give
       judgment.
4. Any Member State, whether or not it has made a declaration pursuant to paragraph 2, shall be entitled to submit statements of case or
   written observations to the Court in cases which arise under paragraph 1.
5. The Court of Justice shall have no jurisdiction to review the validity
   or proportionality of operations carried out by the police or other
   law enforcement services of a Member State or the exercise of the
   responsibilities incumbent upon Member States with regard to the
   maintenance of law and order and the safeguarding of internal
   security.
6. The Court of Justice shall have jurisdiction to review the legality of framework decisions and decisions in actions brought by a
   Member State or the Commission on grounds of lack of competence,

infringement of an essential procedural requirement, infringement of this Treaty or of any rule of law relating to its application, or misuse of powers. The proceedings provided for in this paragraph shall be instituted within 2 months of the publication of the measure.

7. The Court of Justice shall have jurisdiction to rule on any dispute between Member States regarding the interpretation or the application of acts adopted under Article 34(2) whenever such dispute cannot be settled by the Council within 6 months of its being referred to the Council by one of its members. The Court shall also have jurisdiction to rule on any dispute between Member States and the Commission regarding the interpretation or the application of conventions established under Article 34(2)(d).

The Court of Justice cooperates with all the courts of the member states, which are the ordinary courts in matters of EU law. To ensure the effective and uniform application of EU legislation and to prevent divergent interpretations, the national courts may, and sometimes must, refer to the Court of Justice and ask it to clarify a point concerning the interpretation of EU law, so that they may ascertain, for example, whether their national legislation complies with that law. A reference for a preliminary ruling may also seek the review of the validity of an act of EU law.

The Court of Justice's reply is not merely an opinion, but takes the form of a judgment or reasoned order. The national court to which it is addressed is, in deciding the dispute before it, bound by the interpretation given. The Court of Justice's judgment likewise binds other national courts before which the same problem is raised.

It is thus through references for preliminary rulings that any European citizen can seek clarification of the EU rules that affect him. Although such a reference can be made only by a national court, all the parties to the proceedings before that court, the member states and the European institutions may take part in the proceedings before the Court of Justice. In that way, several important principles of EU law have been established by preliminary rulings, sometimes in reply to questions referred by national courts of first instance.

Proceedings before the Court

The Court of Justice determines whether a member state has fulfilled its obligations under EU law. Before bringing the case before the Court of Justice, the Commission conducts a preliminary procedure in which the member state is given the opportunity to reply to the complaints against it. If that procedure does not result in the member state's terminating the failure, an action for infringement of EC law may be brought before the Court of Justice.

The action may be brought by the Commission as, in practice, is usually the case, or by a member state. If the court finds that an obligation has not been fulfilled, the state must bring the failure to an end without delay. If, after a further action is brought by the Commission, the Court of Justice finds that the member state concerned has not complied with its judgment, it may impose on it a fixed or periodic financial penalty.

By an action for annulment, the applicant seeks the annulment of a measure (regulation, directive, or decision) adopted by an institution. The Court of Justice has exclusive jurisdiction over actions brought by a member state against the European Parliament and/or against the Council (apart from Council measures in respect of state aid, dumping, and implementing powers) or brought by one EU institution against another. The Court of First Instance has jurisdiction, at first instance, in all other actions of this type and particularly in actions brought by individuals.

These actions enable the lawfulness of EC institutions' failures to act to be reviewed. However, such an action may be brought only after the institution concerned has been called on to act. Where the failure to act is held to be unlawful, it is for the institution concerned to put an end to the failure by appropriate measures. Jurisdiction to hear actions for failure to act is shared between the Court of Justice and the Court of First Instance according to the same criteria as for actions for annulment.

Appeals on points of law only may be brought before the Court of Justice against judgments and orders of the Court of First Instance. If the appeal is admissible and well founded, the Court of Justice sets aside the judgment of the Court of First Instance. Where the state of the proceedings so permits, the court may itself decide the case. Otherwise, the court must refer the case back to the Court of First Instance, which is bound by the decision given on the appeal.

Decisions of the Court of First Instance on appeals against decisions of the European Union Civil Service Tribunal may, in exceptional circumstances, be reviewed by the Court of Justice.

Whatever the type of case, there is always a written stage and usually an oral stage, which takes place in open court. However, a distinction must be drawn between references for preliminary rulings, and other actions, known as direct actions.

A national court may submit questions to the Court of Justice about the interpretation or validity of a provision of EC law, generally in the form of a judicial decision in accordance with national procedural rules. When that request has been translated into all the Community languages by the court's translation service, the Registry notifies the parties to the national proceedings of it and also all the member states and the institutions. A notice is published in the Official Journal of the European Union stating, inter alia, the names of the parties to the proceedings and the content of the questions.

The parties, the member states, and the institutions of the EU have 2 months within which to submit written observations to the Court of Justice.

Direct actions before the court must be brought by application addressed to the Registry. The registrar publishes a notice of the action in the Official Journal, setting out the applicant's claims and arguments. At the same time, the application is served on the party sued, who has 1 month within which to lodge a defense. The applicant may lodge a reply and the defendant a rejoinder, the time allowed being 1 month in each case. The time limits for lodging these documents must be complied with unless an extension is granted by the president.

In either an action by a member state or a direct action, a judge-rapporteur and an advocate general, responsible for monitoring the progress of the case, are appointed by the president and the first advocate general, respectively.

In all proceedings, once the written procedure is closed, the parties are asked to state, within 1 month, whether and why they wish a hearing to be held. The court decides, after reading the report of the judge-rapporteur and hearing the views of the advocate general, whether any preparatory inquiries are needed, what type of formation the case should be assigned to, and whether a hearing should be held for oral argument, for which the president will fix the date. The judge-rapporteur summarizes, in a report for the hearing, the facts alleged and the arguments of the parties and any interveners. The report is made public in the language of the case at the hearing.

The case is argued at a public hearing, before the bench and the advocate general. The judges and the advocate general may put to the parties any questions they consider appropriate. Some weeks later, the advocate general delivers his opinion before the Court of Justice, again in open court, analyzing in detail the legal aspects of the case and suggesting completely independently to the Court of Justice the response that he or she considers should be given to the problem raised. This marks the end of the oral procedure. If it is decided that the case raises no new question of law, the court may decide, after hearing the advocate general, to give judgment without an opinion.

The judges deliberate on the basis of a draft judgment drawn up by the judge-rapporteur. Each judge of the formation concerned may propose changes. Decisions of the Court of Justice are taken by majority and no record is made public of any dissenting opinions. Judgments are signed by all the judges who took part in the deliberation, and their operative part is pronounced in open court. Judgments and the opinions of the advocates general are available on the court's Internet site on the day they are pronounced or delivered. They are, in most cases, subsequently published in the *European Court Reports*.

Where a question referred for a preliminary ruling is identical to a question on which the court has already been called to rule, or where the answer to the question admits of no reasonable doubt or may be deduced from existing case law, the Court of Justice may, after hearing the advocate general, give its decision by reasoned order, citing in particular a previous judgment relating to that question or the relevant case law.

The expedited procedure enables the court to give its rulings quickly in very urgent cases by reducing the time limits and omitting certain steps in the procedure. On application by one of the parties, the president of the court may decide, after hearing the other parties, whether the particular urgency of the case requires the use of the expedited procedure. Such a procedure can also be used for references for preliminary rulings. In that case, the application is made by the national court seeking the preliminary ruling.

Applications for interim measures seek suspension of the operation of measures that an institution has adopted and that form the subject matter of an action, or any other interim order necessary to prevent serious and irreparable damage to a party.

There are no court fees for proceedings before the Court of Justice; however, the court does not meet the fees and expenses of the lawyer entitled to practice before a court of a member state by whom the parties must be represented. However, a party unable to meet all or part of the costs of the proceedings may, without having to instruct a lawyer, apply for legal aid. The application must be accompanied by all necessary evidence establishing the need.

In all direct actions, the language used in the application (which may be one of the 23 official languages of the EU) will be the "language of the case," that is, the language in which the proceedings will be conducted. With references for preliminary rulings, the language of the case is that of the national court that made the reference to the Court of Justice. Oral proceedings at hearings are interpreted simultaneously, as required, into various official languages of the EU. The judges deliberate, without interpreters, in a common language, which, traditionally, is French.

Court of First Instance

The Court of First Instance is made up of at least one judge from each member state. The judges are appointed by the agreement of the member state governments for a renewable mandate of 6 years. They appoint their president, for a period of 3 years, from among themselves. They appoint a registrar for a mandate of 6 years.

The judges carry out their tasks in a totally impartial and independent manner. Unlike the Court of Justice, the Court of First Instance does not have permanent advocates general. However, that task may, in exceptional circumstances, be carried out by a judge.

The Court of First Instance sits in chambers of five or three judges or, in some cases, as a single judge. It may also sit as a grand chamber (13 judges) or as a full court when the legal complexity or importance of the case justifies it. Approximately three-quarters of the cases brought before the Court of First Instance are heard by a chamber of three judges. The presidents of the chambers of five judges are elected from among the judges for a period of 3 years. The Court of First Instance has its own Registry, but uses the services of the Court of Justice for its other administrative and linguistic requirements.

The Court of First Instance has jurisdiction to hear the following types of actions:

- Direct actions brought by natural or legal persons against acts of EU institutions (addressed to them or directly concerning them as individuals) or against a failure to act on the part of those institutions, for example, a case brought by a company against a commission decision imposing a fine on that company
- Actions brought by the member states against the commission
- Actions brought by the member states against the council relating to acts adopted in the field of state aid, dumping, and acts by which it exercises implementing powers
- Actions seeking compensation for damage caused by EU institutions or their staff
- Actions based on contracts made by the EU that expressly give jurisdiction to the Court of First Instance

Actions Relating to EU Trademarks

The rulings made by the Court of First Instance may, within 2 months, be subject to an appeal, limited to questions of law, to the Court of Justice. Disputes between the EU and its staff members are heard by the Civil Service Tribunal. However, there is a right of appeal, limited to questions of law, to the Court of First Instance.

The Court of First Instance has its own rules of procedure. In general, the proceedings include a written phase and an oral phase. An application, drawn up by a lawyer or agent and sent to the Registry, opens the proceedings. The main points of the action are published in a notice, in all official languages, in the Official Journal of the European Union. The registrar sends the application to the other party to the case, which then has a period within which to file a defense. The applicant may file a reply, within a certain time limit, to which the defendant may respond with a rejoinder.

Any person who can prove an interest in the outcome of a case before the Court of First Instance, as well as the member states and the EU institutions, may intervene in the proceedings. The intervener files a statement in intervention, supporting or opposing the claims of one of the parties, to which the parties may then respond. In some cases, the intervener may also submit its observations at the oral phase.

During the oral phase a public hearing is held. When the lawyers are heard, the judges can put questions to the parties' representatives. The judge-rapporteur summarizes, in a report for the hearing, the facts relied on and the arguments of each party and, if applicable, of the interveners. This document is available to the public in the language of the case.

The judges then deliberate on the basis of a draft judgment prepared by the judge-rapporteur and the judgment is delivered at a public hearing. The procedure before the Court of First Instance is free of court fees. However, the costs of the lawyer entitled to appear before a court in a member state, by whom the parties must be represented, are not paid by the Court of First Instance. Even so, an individual who is not able to meet the costs of the case may apply for legal aid.

An action brought before the Court of First Instance does not suspend the operation of the contested act. The court may, however, order its suspension or other interim measures. The president of the Court of First Instance or, if necessary, another judge rules on the application for interim measures in a reasoned order. Interim measures are granted only if three conditions are met: (1) the substance of the main proceedings must appear, at first sight, to be well founded; (2) the applicant must show that the measures are urgent and that it would suffer serious and irreparable harm without them; and (3) the interim measures must take account of the balance of the parties' interests and of public interest.

The order is provisional in nature and in no way prejudges the decision of the Court of First Instance in the main proceedings. In addition, an appeal against it may be brought before the president of the Court of Justice.

Expedited procedure allows the court to rule quickly on the substance of the dispute in cases considered to be particularly urgent. Expedited procedure may be requested by the applicant or by the defendant.

The language used for the application, which may be 1 of the 23 official languages of the EU, will be the language of the case. The proceedings in the oral phase of the procedure are simultaneously interpreted, as necessary, into different official languages of the EU. The judges deliberate, without interpreters, in a common language, traditionally French.

From the beginning of its operation until the end of 2006, the court ruled on more than 5200 cases. Its case law has developed in particular in the fields of intellectual property, competition, and state aid.

Examples of Cases Brought before the Court of First Instance

Community trademarks: The company Henkel applied to the Office for Harmonization in the Internal Market (Trade Marks and Designs) (OHIM), which is responsible for promoting and managing EU trademarks, for registration of a trademark for a washing powder or dishwasher tablet. The 3D trademark applied for was in the form of a round tablet with two layers colored white and red. The application was rejected by OHIM, and the applicant brought an action before the Court of First Instance for annulment of the decision. According to an EU regulation, it is not possible to register a trademark that is not distinctive. In this case, the contested trademark was made up of the form and arrangement of the colors of the product—that is, by the appearance of the product itself. The court took the view that trademark would not allow consumers, when choosing which product to buy, to distinguish between the goods covered by the trademark and those made by another manufacturer. Consequently, it dismissed the company's action, since OHIM had been right to conclude that the 3D trademark was not distinctive.

Mergers: Airtours, a British company selling package tours from the United Kingdom, wished to acquire a competitor, First Choice. The Commission was informed by Airtours of this proposed merger. The Commission declared the merger incompatible with the common market on the ground that it would have led to Airtours having a collective dominant position. Airtours brought an action before the Court of First Instance for annulment of the Commission's decision. The court stated that a merger may be prohibited if it will lead directly and immediately to the creation or reinforcement of a collective dominant position, significantly distorting effective competition in the market over a long period. The court concluded that, because the Commission had made a number of errors of assessment, it had not shown sufficient evidence of the negative effects of the merger on competition, and the court therefore annulled the contested decision.

Cartels: EU law prohibits all agreements between companies, all decisions by associations of companies, and all concerted practices that are likely to affect trade between member states and that have the intention or effect of preventing, restricting, or distorting competition within the common market. Following a complaint, the Commission made certain checks and, in 1998, adopted a decision finding that a number of companies participated in a set of prohibited agreements and practices in the European district heating market. The Commission imposed fines amounting to a total of around 92 million euros on the companies participating in that cartel. The Court of First Instance dismissed almost entirely the actions for annulment brought against the Commission's decision, after finding that there was proof of, first, the existence of the various elements constituting the overall agreement and, second, the individual involvement of the companies in the anticompetitive conduct for which they had been held liable, except with regard to the length of time one of the companies participated in the agreement and the geographical range of the agreement as regards another company.

The fines imposed by the Commission were, moreover, on the whole confirmed by the court in the total sum of 83,410,000 euros. However, the fines imposed on two companies were reduced.

State aid: By a law of 1991, a banking organization owned outright by the Land of North Rhineland-Westphalia and having the task of granting financial assistance for the building of housing was transferred to a banking organization governed by public law. The Land received as payment a sum much lower than the market price. The Commission decided that the transaction was unlawful state aid, incompatible with the common market. According to the Commission, the difference between the market value and the amount paid was the sum of around 808 million euros, and this constituted unlawful state aid. The Land and the two banking organizations then sought annulment of the Commission's decision before the Court of First Instance. The court ruled that the Commission, which is subject to a duty to give reasons, had failed to give sufficient reasons for its estimate of the market value. The court therefore annulled the Commission's decision.

Access to documents: Ms. Hautala, a member of the European Parliament, had asked the Council of the European Union to send her a report on arms exports. Relying on its power to refuse access to such a document in order to protect the public interest in the field of international relations, the Council refused to release the report because it contained sensitive information, the disclosure of which might harm the relations of the EU with nonmember states. In this situation, Ms. Hautala brought an action before the Court of First Instance seeking annulment of the Council's decision refusing to send her the report. In its judgment, the court restated the principle that the public must have the widest possible access to documents, exceptions to that rule having to be interpreted and applied strictly. It said that the Council should have considered the possibility of editing certain pages likely to harm international relations and therefore looked into whether partial access to the document could be authorized. Since the Council had not taken that step, the court annulled its decision.

Civil Service Tribune

The Civil Service Tribune has jurisdiction to hear and determine at first instance disputes between the EU and its employees, which represents some 150 cases a year for approximately 35,000 members of EU institutions' staffs. These disputes concern not only questions to do with working relations in the strict sense (pay, career progress, recruitment, disciplinary measures, etc.), but also the social security system (sickness, old age, invalidity, accidents at work, family allowances, etc.).

It also has jurisdiction in cases concerning certain specific employees, in particular those of Eurojust, Europol, the European Central Bank, and the Office for Harmonization in the Internal Market. It may not hear and determine cases between national administrations and their employees. The decisions given by the tribunal may, within 2 months, be subject to an appeal, limited to questions of law, to the Court of First Instance (http://curia.europa. eu/en/coopju/apercu, accessed November 8, 2007).

Summary

- The ICJ is the Supreme Court of the UN.
- The ICC, unlike the ICJ, handles the prosecution of individuals.
- The ICC was established by the Rome Statute in 1998.
- The ICC's jurisdiction includes crimes of genocide.
- The ICC is now a permanent judicial body with the mission to pros- ecute and adjudicate individuals accused of genocide, war crimes, and crimes against humanity.
- Both the ICC and the ICJ are located in The Hague.
- The ICJ is the result of a long search for methods for the peaceful settlement of disputes between nations.
- The ICJ was established in 1945 by the San Francisco Conference and replaced the PCIJ.
- The Court of Justice of the European Communities, together with the national courts of the members, constitutes the European Community's judiciary. The court's main task is to interpret com- munity law uniformly and to rule on its validity. It also answers questions referred to it by the national courts.

Questions in Review

1. Explain the differences between the ICC and ICJ and why two are needed.
2. Why is the United States not a member nation of the ICC?
3. What is the jurisdiction of the ICC? The ICJ?
4. What three methods are used to resolve cases before the ICJ?
5. Why does the ICC not exercise jurisdiction over crimes of aggression?

International Criminal Justice Agencies and Associations 12

Chapter Objectives

After studying this chapter, you should understand or be able to explain the following issues and concepts:

- The important international criminal justice agencies
- How Interpol works
- How Interpol works to reduce human trafficking
- The role of the International Association of Chiefs of Police
- The role of the United Nations (UN) in combating crime

Key Terms

Human trafficking: The exploitation of migrants often for purposes of forced labor and prostitution.

IACP: International Association of Chiefs of Police.

Interpol: The International Criminal Police Organization.

Private international law: The legal framework composed of conventions, protocols, model laws, legal guides, uniform documents, as well as other documents and instruments, which regulates relationships between individuals in an international context.

Transnational criminal organizations: Criminal organizations that operate in more than one nation.

Introduction

In this chapter, we will explore some of the more prominent international criminal justice agencies. Many of those organizations are affiliated with or are a part of the UN. The first international organization examined is the

International Criminal Police Organization, more commonly known as Interpol. This chapter in no way, however, attempts to present all the international organizations or agencies involved in criminal justice.

Interpol

Interpol, the formal name of which is the International Criminal Police Organization, is the world's largest such agency. It has 190 member countries and was created in 1923. It facilitates cross-border police cooperation and supports and assists all organizations, authorities, and services whose mission is to prevent or combat international crime. Interpol attempts to facilitate international police cooperation even where diplomatic relations do not exist between particular countries.

Interpol works within the limits of existing laws in different countries and subject to the Universal Declaration of Human Rights. Its constitution prohibits any intervention or activities of a political, military, religious, or racial character. The president of Interpol and the secretary-general work closely together in providing strong leadership and direction to the organization (http://www.interpol.int, accessed November 5, 2007).

Structure

Interpol's structure consists of five general sections:

1. *General Assembly*: Interpol's supreme governing body, it meets annually and comprises delegates appointed by each member country. The assembly takes all important decisions related to policy, resources, working methods, finances, activities, and programs.
2. *Executive Committee*: A 13-member committee elected by the General Assembly, it comprises the president, three vice presidents, and nine delegates covering the four regions. The General Assembly and the Executive Committee form the organization's governance.
3. *General Secretariat*: Located in Lyon, France, the General Secretariat operates 24 hours a day, 365 days a year, and is run by the secretary-general. Officials from more than 80 countries work side by side in any of the organization's four official languages: Arabic, English, French, and Spanish. The secretariat has six regional offices—in Argentina, Côte d'Ivoire, El Salvador, Kenya, Thailand, and Zimbabwe—and a liaison office at the UN in New York.

4. *National Central Bureau* (*NCB*): Each Interpol member country maintains a National Central Bureau staffed by national law enforcement officers. The NCB is the designated contact point for the General Secretariat, regional offices, and other member countries requiring assistance with overseas investigations and the location and apprehension of fugitives.

5. *Advisers*: These are experts in a purely advisory capacity, who may be appointed by the Executive Committee and confirmed by the General Assembly.

The organizational chart for Interpol is set forth in Figure 12.1.

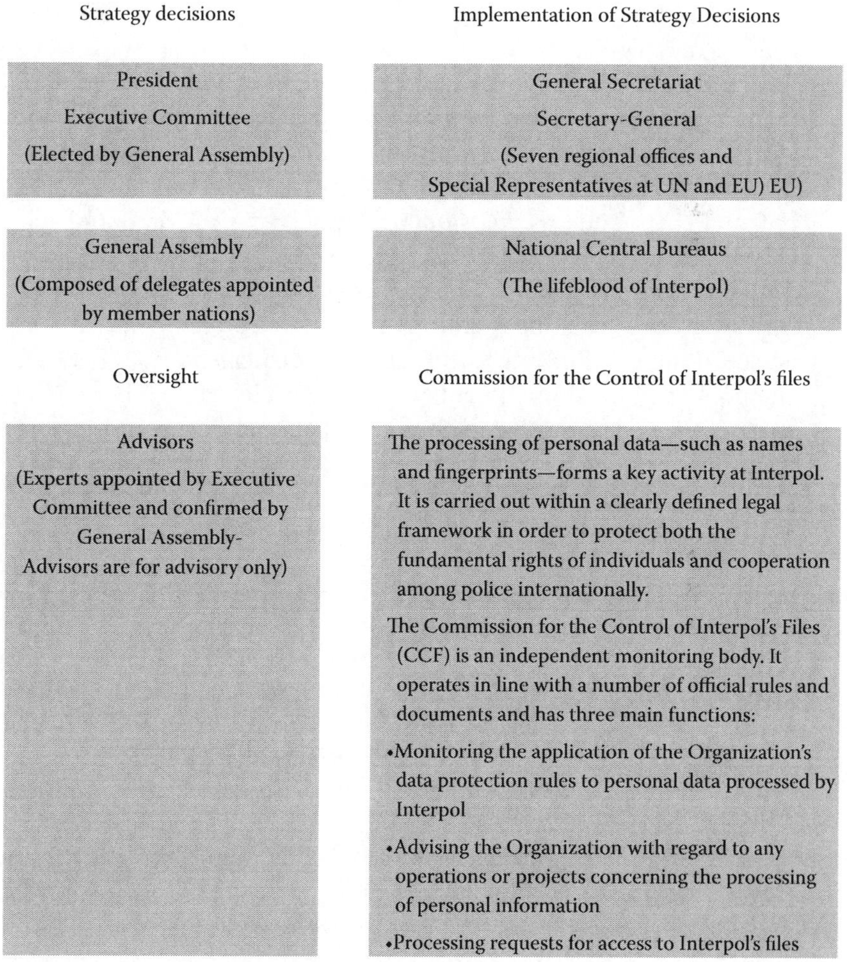

Strategy decisions	Implementation of Strategy Decisions
President Executive Committee (Elected by General Assembly)	General Secretariat Secretary-General (Seven regional offices and Special Representatives at UN and EU) EU)
General Assembly (Composed of delegates appointed by member nations)	National Central Bureaus (The lifeblood of Interpol)
Oversight	Commission for the Control of Interpol's files
Advisors (Experts appointed by Executive Committee and confirmed by General Assembly- Advisors are for advisory only)	The processing of personal data—such as names and fingerprints—forms a key activity at Interpol. It is carried out within a clearly defined legal framework in order to protect both the fundamental rights of individuals and cooperation among police internationally. The Commission for the Control of Interpol's Files (CCF) is an independent monitoring body. It operates in line with a number of official rules and documents and has three main functions: •Monitoring the application of the Organization's data protection rules to personal data processed by Interpol •Advising the Organization with regard to any operations or projects concerning the processing of personal information •Processing requests for access to Interpol's files

Figure 12.1 Organizational chart for Interpol.

Core Functions

Interpol's activities are based on the following four core functions:

1. *Secure global police communication services*: Interpol runs a global police communications system called I-24/7, which provides police around the world with a common platform through which they can share crucial information about criminals and criminality.
2. *Operational data services and databases for police*: Interpol's databases and services ensure that police worldwide have access to the information and services they need to prevent and investigate crimes. Databases include data on criminals, such as names, fingerprints, and DNA profiles, and on stolen property, such as passports, vehicles, and works of art.
3. *Operational police support services*: Interpol supports law enforcement officials in the field with emergency support and operational activities, especially in its priority crime areas of fugitives, public safety and terrorism, drugs and organized crime, trafficking in human beings, and financial and high-tech crime. A Command and Coordination Centre operates 24 hours a day, 7 days a week.
4. *Training and development*: Interpol provides focused police training initiatives for national police forces and also offers on-demand advice, guidance, and support in building dedicated crime-fighting components. The aim is to enhance the capacity of member countries to effectively combat serious transnational crime and terrorism. This includes sharing knowledge, skills, and best practices in policing through Interpol channels and the establishment of global standards on how to combat specific forms of crimes.

Trafficking in Human Beings

One of Interpol's goals is to end the abuse and exploitation of human beings for financial gain. Women from developing countries and young children all over the world are especially vulnerable to trafficking, smuggling, or sexual exploitation. Trafficking in women for sexual exploitation is a multibillion-dollar business that involves citizens of most countries and helps sustain organized crime. As a violation of human rights, it destroys the lives of its victims. Human trafficking is distinct from people smuggling in that it involves the exploitation of the migrant, often for purposes of forced labor and prostitution. People smuggling denotes the procurement, for financial or material gain, of illegal entry into a state of which the smuggled person is neither a citizen nor a permanent resident. Criminal networks that smuggle and traffic in human beings for financial gain increasingly control the flow of migrants across borders.

Definition of Human Trafficking

Trafficking in persons is the action of recruitment, transportation, transfer, harboring, or receipt of persons by means of the threat or use of force, coercion, abduction, fraud, deception, abuse of power or vulnerability, or giving payments or benefits to a person in control of the victim, for the purposes of exploitation, which includes exploiting the prostitution of others, sexual exploitation, forced labor, slavery or similar practices, and the removal of organs.

Corruption *Things being done internationally*

Interpol has identified corruption as a priority crime area that warrants its full resources and efforts to fight it. The organization has embarked on a campaign to raise 15 million euros to create the world's first academic institute dedicated to the study and prevention of corruption. Interpol has been actively involved in supporting initiatives to curb corruption since it hosted the First International Conference on Corruption-Related Crimes in 1998 at its General Secretariat in Lyon, France. As the world's largest international police organization, Interpol is particularly concerned about the role corruption plays in terrorism and other international crimes. The globalization of crime in general makes it also necessary for law enforcement in different countries to work together to develop various means for fighting corruption.

Interpol established the Interpol Group of Experts on Corruption (IGEC) in 1998 and is currently in the process of developing the Interpol Anti-Corruption Office (IACO) and Interpol Anti-Corruption Academy (IACA). These components support anticorruption activities by establishing policies and standards, as well as conducting or assisting with education, research, training, investigations, and asset recovery operations.

These initiatives are consistent with the UN Convention against Corruption, which entered into force on December 15, 2005, as well as with the efforts of the UN Office on Drugs and Crime (UNODC) to strengthen the implementation of the convention.

Child Sexual Exploitation

Child sexual exploitation on the Internet ranges from posed photos to visual recordings of brutal sexual crimes. One of Interpol's main tools for helping police fight this type of crime is the Interpol Child Abuse Image Database (ICAID). Created in 2001, it contains hundreds of thousands of images of child sexual abuse submitted by member countries, thereby facilitating the sharing of images and information to assist law enforcement agencies with the identification of new victims.

The Interpol Specialist Group on Crimes against Children meets annually and brings together law enforcement investigators to facilitate and enhance the investigation of sexual crimes against children, including computer-facilitated crimes. Through research, education, and shared intelligence, the group promotes strategies that lead to the effective prosecution and treatment of individuals who have abused, or are at risk to abuse, children.

Project Childhood brings together Interpol, the UN Office on Drugs and Crime, and World Vision to combat child sexual exploitation and trafficking in southeast Asia. Interpol works with law enforcement agencies in the affected countries to strengthen their abilities to identify, arrest, and prosecute traveling sex offenders through enhanced intelligence sharing. The project is funded through the government of Australia's AusAID program.

Interpol Databases as of December 2006*

The Interpol wanted persons database currently contains about 190,000 circulations issued for the purpose of locating persons and 463,000 arrest requests, including 446,000 expulsion orders/deportations of foreigners.

The property database includes approximately 10.3 million items that are the subject of searches because of possible links to crimes. This total number includes, among others, the following items: 186,000 passenger cars; 36,000 trucks, including trailers; 107,000 mopeds, motorized bicycles, and motorcycles; 823,000 bicycles; 4,241,000 identity documents and drivers' licenses; and 220,000 firearms.

Public Safety and Terrorism   *Global Response to terrorism*

The growing possibility of terrorists launching attacks with biological or chemical weapons is a particularly urgent concern. A dedicated bioterrorism unit at the General Secretariat works to implement various projects with the close cooperation of Interpol National Central Bureaus and regional offices.

Interpol has made available various resources to support member countries in their efforts to protect their citizens from terrorism, including bioterrorism, firearms and explosives, attacks against civil aviation, maritime piracy, and weapons of mass destruction. Interpol collects stores, analyzes, and exchanges information about suspected individuals and groups and their activities. The organization also coordinates the circulation of alerts and warnings on terrorists, dangerous criminals, and weapons threats to police in member countries. A chief initiative in this area is the Fusion Task Force, which was created in the aftermath of the September 11, 2001, attacks in the United States.

---

* From Bundeskriminalamt (German Police), available at: www.bka.de, accessed November 7, 2007.

In order to help member countries report terrorist activity, Interpol has issued practical guidelines on the type of information required. Member countries are also encouraged to report on other crimes that may be linked to terrorism, such as suspicious financial transactions, weapons trafficking, money laundering, falsified travel and identity documents, and seizures of nuclear, chemical, and biological materials.

Drugs

Drug abuse and the problems associated with it continue to grow in most parts of the world. The global abuse of drugs and the drug trafficking situation is becoming more complex, in part because of political and economic changes around the world that have led to increasingly open borders between many countries. Drug trafficking is frequently linked to other serious crimes, such as people smuggling, organized prostitution, and travel-document counterfeiting. It is often cited as a means to finance the more violent and destructive activities of criminal and terrorist organizations, because of the major cash benefits derived from relatively minimal time and investment.

Interpol's primary drug control role is to identify new drug trafficking trends and criminal organizations operating at the international level and to assist all national and international law enforcement bodies concerned with countering the illicit production, trafficking, and abuse of cannabis, cocaine, heroin, and synthetic drugs. The agency's efforts include collecting and analyzing data obtained from member countries for strategic and tactical intelligence reports and disseminating these reports to the concerned countries; responding to and supporting international drug investigations; helping coordinate drug investigations involving at least two member countries; organizing operational working meetings between two or more member countries where Interpol has identified common links in cases being investigated in these countries; and organizing regional or global conferences on specific drug topics, the aims of which are to assess the extent of the particular drug problem, exchange information on the latest investigative techniques, and strengthen cooperation within law enforcement communities.

Interpol maintains close liaison with national law enforcement agencies and with nongovernmental organizations (NGOs) that have a counterdrug mandate. Information gathered and assessed by these NGOs is valuable in creating a more comprehensive assessment of drug trafficking and abuse issues. The UN Office on Drugs and Crime has not only information on drug trafficking and abuse studies but also reports on other criminal matters that have a global impact. The World Customs Organization has information regarding the harmonization of customs controls and practices, and it provides information on smuggling. Back issues of its magazine can be accessed through the website in PDF format, www.wcoomd.org.

Criminal Organizations

Definitions of what constitutes organized crime vary widely from country to country. Organized groups are typically involved in many different types of criminal activity spanning several countries. These activities may include trafficking in humans, weapons and drugs, armed robbery, counterfeiting, and money laundering. Interpol currently has projects targeting organized crime in two areas of high activity: Eurasia (Project Millennium) and Asia (Project AOC—Asian Organized Crime).

Financial and High-Tech Crimes

Interpol's chief initiatives in the area of financial and high-tech crime focus on payment (credit and debit) cards, money laundering, intellectual property crime, currency counterfeiting, and new technologies.

Currency counterfeiting and money laundering have the potential to destabilize national economies and threaten global security, as these activities are sometimes used by terrorists and other dangerous criminals to finance their activities or conceal their profits. Intellectual property crime is a serious financial concern for car manufacturers, luxury goods makers, media firms, and drug companies. Most alarmingly, counterfeiting endangers public health, especially in developing countries, where the World Health Organization estimates that more than 60% of pharmaceuticals are fake.

New technologies open up many possibilities for criminals to carry out traditional financial crimes in new ways. One notable example is "phishing," whereby a criminal attempts to acquire through e-mail or instant messaging sensitive information such as passwords or credit card details by pretending to be a legitimate business representative. With this information, the criminal can commit fraud and even money laundering. Interpol has stepped up its efforts in this area, working with stakeholders such as pharmaceutical makers, Internet service providers, software companies, central banks, and other relevant bodies to devise solutions to thwart criminals and protect consumers.

Fugitive Investigative Services

Fugitives pose a serious threat to public safety worldwide. They are mobile and opportunistic; they frequently finance their continued flight from the law through further criminal activities, which may result in criminal charges in more than one country. Fugitives also undermine the world's criminal justice systems. They may have been charged with a violation of the law but have not been arrested. They may have been released on bail and then fled to avoid prosecution, or perhaps they have escaped from prison. When fugitives flee, cases are not adjudicated, convicted criminals fail to meet their obligations, and crime victims are denied justice.

Interpol's activities in relation to international fugitives have been part of its core business since the organization's creation. Interpol circulates internationally, at the request of member countries, electronic diffusions and notices containing identification details and judicial information about wanted criminals. The Interpol Red Notice has been recognized in a number of countries as having the legal value to serve as a basis for provisional arrest. The persons concerned are wanted by national jurisdictions or international criminal tribunals, where appropriate, and the Red Notice is intended to help police identify or locate these individuals with a view to their arrest and extradition. Interpol created the Fugitive Investigative Service to offer more proactive and systematic assistance to member countries by providing investigative support to member countries in ongoing international fugitive investigations with a view to locating and arresting wanted persons; coordinating and enhancing international cooperation in the field of fugitive investigations; collecting and disseminating best practice and expert knowledge; and conducting and coordinating relevant research and serve as a global point of reference for fugitive-related information.

Interpol's Other Areas of Crime

While not considered priority crime areas within the organization's current operational framework, other issues of concern for law enforcement in which Interpol remains active include genocide, war crimes and crimes against humanity, environmental crime, and law enforcement corruption. Interpol supports member countries and ad hoc international criminal tribunals in the location and apprehension of persons wanted for such crimes primarily through the organization of working group meetings and conferences, publication of Red Notices, and provision of other investigative assistance.

Environmental crime is a serious and growing international problem, with criminals violating national and international laws put in place to protect the environment. In the pursuit of financial gain, criminals are polluting the world's natural resources and pushing commercially valuable wildlife species closer to extinction, thereby significantly harming the biological integrity of the planet.

With the goal of improving the quality of police forces and the services they provide, Interpol works with law enforcement around the world to help ensure that police officials, as civic leaders and role models, remain faithful to the tenets of their profession. The organization has undertaken the task of developing and implementing an anticorruption strategy, with the objective not only of raising awareness of the major issues but also of enhancing law enforcement's ability and effectiveness to fight corruption within its ranks.

National Central Reference Points Network

In cybercrime investigations, it is vital that police can swiftly seize digital data evidence while the majority of it is still intact, as well as cooperate across borders when a cyberattack involves multiple jurisdictions. Interpol has established a designated network of investigators working in national computer crime units, called National Central Reference Points (NCRPs), to facilitate operational contact among member countries as quickly as possible. These contacts are available 24 hours a day, 7 days a week, and are able to receive or provide information and/or requests for assistance. The NCRPs are essential prerequisites for the establishment of an early warning system. As of August 2007, 111 Interpol National Central Bureaus had designated NCRPs.

International Cybercrime Conference

Interpol organizes an International Conference on Cybercrime every 2 years to provide a forum for the exchange of knowledge and expertise in cybercrime investigation. The conference, hosted by member countries' police services, brings together experts from law enforcement, private industry, and academia to present and discuss the latest technologies in the fight against cybercrime.

Interpol's Red Notice

The Interpol is known for issuing "red notices." A red notice is an alert requested by a member state indicating that it seeks an individual's arrest. Once the notice is disseminated, other member states can choose to act or not act on the notice. Most states, however, will arrest and extradite anyone with a red notice. In the calendar year 2010, over 6000 red notices were issued.

A red notice can have other consequences. Frequently, the subjects' bank accounts are frozen or closed or they may find it impossible to open a new account, to obtain or keep employment, or to apply for loans and other lines of credit because of the existence of the red notice. There are six other types of notices as noted in the following, but red notices are far more frequently used.

1. **Yellow notice:** A request for help in locating missing persons or identifying persons who are unable to identify themselves.
2. **Blue notice:** A request for additional information such as movement about a person in relation to a crime.
3. **Black notice:** A notice that seeks information on unidentified bodies.
4. **Green notice:** A notice that provides warnings or criminal intelligence about persons who have committed criminal offenses and are likely to repeat those crimes in other countries.

5. **Orange notice:** A notice that warns police and international organizations about potential threats from disguised weapons, parcel bombs, or other dangerous materials.
6. **Purple notice:** A notice designed to provide information on modi *operandi*, procedures, objects, devices, and hiding places used by criminals.

Europol

The European Police Office (Europol) in The Hague was established for the purpose of improving cooperation between the European Union (EU) member states with regard to the prevention and suppression of crime. Europol is the European Union's law enforcement organization that handles criminal intelligence. Another mission is to assist the law enforcement authorities of member states in their fight against serious forms of organized crime. Europol does not have any independent investigative or executive powers. All 25 EU member states are represented in Europol. The information exchange between the individual member states is carried out through the National Liaison Office in The Hague.

The establishment of Europol was agreed on in the Maastricht Treaty on European Union in February 1992. Based in The Hague, Netherlands, Europol started limited operations in January 1994 in the form of the Europol Drugs Unit (EDU), fighting against drugs. Progressively, other important areas of criminality were added. As of January 1, 2002, the mandate of Europol was extended to deal with all serious forms of international crime as listed in the annex to the Europol Convention. The Europol Convention was ratified by all member states and came into force on October 1, 1998. Following a number of legal acts related to the convention, Europol commenced its full activities on July 1, 1999.

Europol supports the law enforcement activities of the member states, mainly against illicit drug trafficking, illicit immigration networks, terrorism, forgery of money (counterfeiting of the euro) and other means of payment, trafficking in human beings (including child pornography), illicit vehicle trafficking, and money laundering. Other main priorities for Europol include crimes against persons, financial crime, and cybercrime. This applies where an organized criminal structure is involved and two or more member states are affected.

Europol supports the EU in the following ways:

- Facilitating the exchange of information, in accordance with national law between Europol liaison officers (ELOs); ELOs are seconded to Europol by the member states as representatives of their national law enforcement agencies

- Providing operational analysis in support of operations
- Generating strategic reports (e.g., threat assessments) and crime analysis on the basis of information and intelligence supplied by member states and third parties
- Providing expertise and technical support for investigations and operations carried out within the EU, under the supervision and the legal responsibility of the member states concerned
- Being also active in promoting crime analysis and harmonization of investigative techniques within the member states

The Europol Computer System

The Europol Convention states that Europol shall establish and maintain a computerized system to allow the input, access, and analysis of data. The convention lays down a strict framework for human rights and data protection, control, supervision, and security. The Europol Computer System has three principal components: an information system, an analysis system, and an index system (http://www.europol.europa.eu, accessed November 7, 2007).

International Association of Chiefs of Police

The International Association of Chiefs of Police is the world's oldest and largest nonprofit membership organization of police executives, with more than 20,000 members in more than 89 different countries. The IACP's leadership consists of the operating chief executives of international, federal, state, and local agencies of all sizes. The organization characterizes itself as follows:

Founded in 1893, the association's goals are to advance the science and art of police services; to develop and disseminate improved administrative, technical, and operational practices and promote their use in police work; to foster police cooperation and the exchange of information and experience among police administrators throughout the world; to bring about recruitment and training in the police profession of qualified persons; and to encourage adherence of all police officers to high professional standards of performance and conduct.

Since 1893, the International Association of Chiefs of Police has been serving the needs of the law enforcement community. Throughout those past 100-plus years, we have been launching historically acclaimed programs, conducting groundbreaking research and providing exemplary programs and services to our membership across the globe.

Professionally recognized programs such as the FBI Identification Division and the Uniform Crime Records system can trace their origins back to the IACP. In fact, the IACP has been instrumental in forwarding breakthrough technologies and philosophies from the early years of our establishment to now, as we approach the twenty-first century. From spearheading national use of fingerprint identification to partnering in a consortium on community policing to gathering top experts in criminal justice, the government, and education for summits on violence, homicide, and youth violence, IACP has realized our responsibility to positively affect the goals of law enforcement (IACP, 2007).

International Police Association

The International Police Association is an independent body made up of members of the police service, whether on active duty or retired, and without distinction as to rank, sex, race, language, or religion. Its purpose is to create bonds of friendship and to promote international cooperation. The association was formed in 1950 because a police sergeant from Lincolnshire, England, Arthur Troop, wanted to create a channel for friendship and international cooperation among police officers. It is the largest police organization in the world with more than 300,000 members. National sections exist in 60 countries throughout the world.

It is committed to the principles set out in the Universal Declaration of Human Rights as adopted by the UN in 1948. Its aims include the development of cultural relations among its members, a broadening of their general knowledge, and an exchange of professional experience; in addition, it seeks to foster mutual help in the social sphere and to contribute, within the limits of its possibilities, to peaceful coexistence between peoples and to the preservation of world peace.

Membership of the International Police Association is open to serving and retired policemen and women of all ages. Each member country (IPA section) is permitted to apply its own criteria as to who can or cannot be regarded as a police officer for the purpose of membership. Each section also determines its own membership fees (www.ipa-iac.org, accessed November 5, 2007).

United Nations Crime Prevention and Criminal Justice Network

The UN Crime Prevention and Criminal Justice Program Network of Institutes consist of the UN Crime Prevention and Criminal Justice Division and a number of interregional and regional institutes around the world as well as specialized centers. It was developed to assist the international community in strengthening international cooperation in the crucial areas of

288 An Introduction to Comparative Legal Models of Criminal Justice

crime prevention and criminal justice. The division serves as the substantive secretariat of the Commission on Crime Prevention and Criminal Justice, Economic and Social Council (ECOSOC), and the General Assembly and the Congresses on the Prevention of Crime and Treatment of Offenders. It is responsible for the overall coordination of the Network of Institutes' activities.

UN Commission on Crime Prevention and Criminal Justice

The 40-member UN Commission on Crime Prevention and Criminal Justice formulates international policies and recommends activities in the field of crime control. It offers nations a forum for exchanging information and settling on ways to fight crime on a global level. The commission is a subsidiary body of the Economic and Social Council and formulates draft resolutions for action by the council. These resolutions eventually direct the work of UNODC's Crime Programme.

The commission, which arose from a ministerial meeting held in Versailles in 1991, was preceded by a more technically focused Committee on Crime Prevention and Control, formed in 1971 to replace an earlier expert advisory committee and tackle a broadened scope of the UN interest in criminal justice policy.

In 1997, UNODC was also tasked with the responsibility for crime prevention, criminal justice, and criminal law reform. The office works with member states to strengthen the rule of law, promote stable and viable criminal justice systems, and combat the growing threat of transnational organized crime through its Global Programme against Corruption, Global Programme against Organized Crime, Global Programme against Trafficking in Human Beings, and its Terrorism Prevention Branch (TPB).

Priority areas mandated by the council when it established the commission in 1992 are international action to combat national and transnational crime, including organized crime, economic crime, and money laundering; promoting the role of criminal law in protecting the environment; crime prevention in urban areas, including juvenile crime and violence; and improving the efficiency and fairness of criminal justice administration systems.

Aspects of these principal themes are selected for discussion at each annual session of the Vienna-based commission. The commission formulates draft resolutions for action by the Economic and Social Council. These resolutions eventually direct the work of the Centre for International Crime Prevention.

International Center for Criminal Law Reform and Criminal Justice Policy

Founded in 1991, the Vancouver-Based International Centre is a joint initiative of the University of British Columbia, Simon Fraser University, and the International Society for the Reform of Criminal Law, with contributions from the government of Canada and the province of British Columbia. The center is a component of the UN Crime Prevention and Criminal Justice Programme. Through its activities, the center contributes to the priorities of Canada and the UN in the field of criminal law and criminal justice. The international center's mission is to improve the quality of justice through reform of criminal law, policy, and practice. The center promotes democratic principles, the rule of law, and respect for human rights in criminal law and the administration of criminal justice, domestically, regionally, and globally. The primary role of the center is to provide advice, information, research, and proposals for policy development and legislation. Since information and knowledge are primary, the center is actively involved in education and training. Where appropriate, the center also provides technical assistance to governments and other agencies.

The international center is a not-for-profit organization. It relies upon financial support from foundations, academic institutions, governments, and individual donations. The program, as it now exists, was created in 1991 by UN General Resolution 46/152. The new political will that found an expression in that resolution is being translated into action by creating the essential mechanisms for practical collaboration against common problems, providing a framework for interstate cooperation and coordination to respond to the serious new forms and transnational aspects and dimensions of crime, establishing information exchanges concerning the implementation and effectiveness of the UN norms and standards in crime prevention and criminal justice, and providing means of assistance, particularly to developing countries, for more effective crime prevention and more humane justice.

The center issues two valuable publications for law enforcement agencies. The *Criminal Justice Assessment Toolkit* from the UN Office on Drugs and Crime is a practical guide intended for use by those charged with the assessment of criminal justice systems and the implementation of criminal justice reform. The *Handbook on Restorative Justice Programmes* is one of a series of practical tools developed by the UN Office on Drugs and Crime to support countries in the implementation of the rule of law and the development of criminal justice reform. It introduces the reader to restorative justice programs and processes (http://www.icclr.law.ubc.ca, accessed November 5, 2007).

Criminal Justice Reform Unit

The Criminal Justice Reform Unit (CJRU) is part of the UNODC Rule of Law Section in the Division for Operations' Human Security Branch. The CJRU contributes toward the mandate of UNODC by assisting developing countries, countries emerging from conflict, and countries with economies in transition in building the capacity of their justice systems to operate more effectively within the framework of the rule of law and with particular attention to vulnerable groups, such as women and children (General Assembly Resolution, 59/159 of February 3, 2005). The CJRU oversees project development and provides substantive support for project implementation in the general area of justice reform, including juvenile justice, penal reform, restorative justice, alternatives to imprisonment, victim support, and monitoring and civilian oversight of criminal justice performance.

Criminal justice reform is at the heart of the mandate of the UN. Successive UN crime congresses, the first UN Congress on the Prevention of Crime, and the Treatment of Offenders, having been held in Geneva in 1955, have explored ways in which criminal justice systems can operate both more effectively and more humanely. The most recent crime congresses, held in Vienna in 2000 and in Bangkok in 2005, have continued to strengthen the role of the UN in the area of criminal justice reform. The Vienna Declaration and its Plans of Action, in particular, highlighted the importance of criminal justice reform. The Commission on Crime Prevention and Criminal Justice has in successive sessions continued to underscore the importance of effective global responses in the area of criminal justice reform. The mandate to assist states in building fair and effective criminal justice systems is also contained in resolutions by the main policy-making organs of the UN: the General Assembly and the Economic and Social Council.

The CJRU works on the implementation and operationalization of the UN Standards and Norms in Crime Prevention and Criminal Justice. These include the *Code of Conduct for Law Enforcement Officials* (GA Resolution 34/169), the *United Nations Rules for the Protection of Juveniles Deprived of Their Liberty* (GA resolution 45/113), the *Basic Principles on the Independence of the Judiciary* (ECOSOC Resolution 1989/60), the *United Nations Standard Minimum Rules for the Administration of Juvenile Justice* (GA resolution 40/33), the *United Nations Standard Minimum Rules for the Treatment of Prisoners* (ECOSOC resolution 1984/47), the *United Nations Standard Minimum Rules for Non-Custodial Measures* (GA resolution 45/110), the *Basic Principles of Justice for Victims of Crime and Abuse of Power* (ECOSOC 1989/57), and the Guidelines on Justice in Matters Involving Child Victims and Witnesses of Crime (http://www.unodc.org/unodc/en/criminal_ justice. html, accessed November 6, 2007).

Office for Drug Control and Crime Prevention

The UN International Drug Control Programme (UNDCP) was established in 1991. In October 2002, UNDCP was renamed the UN Office on Drugs and Crime (UNODC), which also administers the Fund of UNDCP. UNODC works to educate the world about the dangers of drug abuse and to strengthen international action against drug production, trafficking, and drug-related crime through alternative development projects, illicit crop monitoring, and anti-money-laundering programs. UNODC also provides accurate statistics through the Global Assessment Programme (GAP) and helps to draft legislation and train judicial officials as part of its Legal Advisory Programme.

Globalization has created an environment where illicit drugs, crime, and terrorism can flow easily across borders. The welfare gains to be had from open trade and flow of public goods are, however, offset by the globalization of threats to human security. UNODC interventions are therefore designed to assist member states in their struggle against illicit drugs, crime, and terrorism. In the Millennium Declaration, member states also resolved to intensify efforts to fight transnational crime in all its dimensions, to redouble efforts to implement the commitment to counter the world drug problem, and to take concerted action against international terrorism.

The three key parts of the UNODC work program are as follows:

1. Research and analytical work to increase knowledge and understanding of drugs and crime issues and expand the evidence base for policy and operational decisions
2. Normative work to assist states in the ratification and implementation of the international treaties; the development of domestic legislation on drugs, crime, and terrorism; and the provision of secretariat and substantive services to the treaty-based and governing bodies
3. Field-based technical cooperation projects to enhance the capacity of member states to counteract illicit drugs, crime, and terrorism (http://www.odccp.org/crime_cicp_sitemap.html, accessed November 5, 2007)

Institutes of the UN Crime Prevention and Criminal Justice Program Network

The UN Crime Prevention and Criminal Justice Program Network consists of the UN Office on Drugs and Crime and a number of interregional and regional institutes around the world as well as specialized centers. The network has been developed to assist the international community in strengthening cooperation in the crucial area of crime prevention and criminal justice. Its components provide a variety of services, including exchange of information, research, training, and public education. The network includes the following agencies:

PNI: United Nations Crime Prevention and Criminal Justice Programme Network Institutes

UNICRI: United Nations Interregional Crime and Justice Research Institutes, Turin, Italy

UNAFEI: United Nations Asia and Far East Institute for the Prevention of Crime and the Treatment of Offenders, Tokyo, Japan

ILANUD: United Nations Latin American Institute for the Prevention of Crime and the Treatment of Offenders, San José, Costa Rica

HEUNI: European Institute for Crime Prevention and Control, affiliated with the United Nations, Helsinki, Finland

UNAFRI: United Nations African Institute for the Prevention of Crime and the Treatment of Offenders, Kampala, Uganda

NAUSS: Naif Arab University for Security Sciences, Riyadh, Saudi Arabia

AIC: Australian Institute of Criminology, Canberra, Australia

ICCLR and CJP: International Centre for Criminal Law Reform and Criminal Justice Policy, Vancouver, Canada

ISISC: International Institute of Higher Studies in Criminal Sciences, Siracusa, Italy

NIJ: National Institute of Justice, Washington, D.C., United States

RWI: Raoul Wallenberg Institute of Human Rights and Humanitarian Law, Lund, Sweden

ISPAC: International Scientific and Professional Advisory Council of the United Nations Crime Prevention and Criminal Justice Programme, Milan, Italy

ICPC: International Centre for the Prevention of Crime, Montreal, Canada

KICJP: Korean Institute of Criminal Justice Policy, Seoul, Korea

ISS: Institute for Security Studies, Pretoria, South Africa

Commission on Narcotic Drugs

The Commission on Narcotic Drugs was established in 1946 by the Economic and Social Council of the UN. It is the central policy-making body within the UN system for dealing with all drug-related matters. The commission analyzes the world drug abuse situation and develops proposals to strengthen international drug control.

UN Terrorism Prevention Branch

While the TPB is part of the UNODC, it operates as an independent agency. In 2002, the General Assembly approved an expanded program of activities for the TPB. The expanded program focuses on the provision of assistance to states, upon request, in the legal and related aspects of counterterrorism, especially for ratifying and implementing the universal legal instruments against terrorism and for strengthening the capacity of the national criminal justice systems to apply the provisions of these instruments in compliance with the principles of rule of law. In addition, the TPB's program of work entails the provision of substantive input on related counterterrorism issues to intergovernmental bodies, especially the Crime Commission, the Economic and Social Council, the General Assembly, and the UN Congress on Crime Prevention and Criminal Justice. The TPB also provides specialized input on relevant counterterrorism issues for the UN Secretariat in wide initiatives and coordinates its activities with other entities and organizations. Appendix C of this book contains excerpts of the UN General Assembly's Resolution on Counter Terrorism.

International Narcotics Control Board

The International Narcotics Control Board (INCB) is the independent and quasi-judicial control body for the implementation of the UN drug conventions. It was established in 1968 by the Single Convention on Narcotic Drugs of 1961. INCB is independent of governments as well as of the UN; its 13 members serve in their personal capacity.

Transnational Organized Crime

On November 15, 2000, the General Assembly adopted the first UN treaty against transnational organized crimes (Resolution 55/25). It is the main international instrument in the fight against transnational organized crime. It opened for signature by member states at a high-level political conference convened for that purpose in Palermo, Italy, on December 12–15, 2000, and entered into force on September 29, 2003. The convention is further supplemented by three protocols, which target specific areas and manifestations of organized crime: the Protocol to Prevent, Suppress and Punish Trafficking in Persons, Especially Women and Children; the Protocol against the Smuggling of Migrants by Land, Sea, and Air; and the Protocol against the Illicit Manufacturing of and Trafficking in Firearms, their Parts and Components and Ammunition. Countries must become parties to the convention itself before they can become parties to any of the protocols.

The convention represented a major step forward in the fight against transnational organized crimes and signifies recognition by member states of the seriousness of the problems posed by it, as well as the need to foster and enhance close international cooperation in order to tackle those problems. States that ratify this instrument commit themselves to taking a series of measures against transnational organized crime, including the creation of domestic criminal offenses (participation in an organized criminal group, money laundering, corruption, and obstruction of justice); the adoption of new and sweeping frameworks for extradition, mutual legal assistance, and law enforcement cooperation; and the promotion of training and technical assistance for building or upgrading the necessary capacity of national authorities (http://www.odccp.org/palermo, accessed November 6, 2007).

Trafficking in Humans

The Protocol to Prevent, Suppress and Punish Trafficking in Persons, especially Women and Children, was adopted as part of General Assembly Resolution 55/25. It entered into force on December 25, 2003. A summary of this protocol follows this section. It is the first global legally binding instrument with an agreed definition on trafficking in persons. The intention behind this definition is to facilitate convergence in national approaches with regard to the establishment of domestic criminal offenses that would support efficient international cooperation in investigating and prosecuting cases of trafficking in persons. An additional objective of the protocol is to protect and assist the victims of trafficking with full respect for their human rights.

The Protocol against the Smuggling of Migrants by Land, Sea and Air, adopted as part of General Assembly Resolution 55/25, entered into force on January 28, 2004. It deals with the growing problem of organized criminal groups who smuggle migrants, often at high risk to the migrants and at great profit for the offenders. A major achievement of the protocol is that for the first time in a global international instrument, a definition of smuggling of migrants was developed and agreed upon. The protocol aims at preventing and combating the smuggling of migrants, as well as promoting cooperation among state parties, while protecting the rights of smuggled migrants and preventing the worst forms of their exploitation, which often characterize the smuggling process.

United Nations and Juvenile Justice

According to the United Nation's Fact Sheet on Juvenile Justice, Youth are disproportionately represented in statistics on crime and violence, both as victims and as perpetrators, and in many developed countries violent crimes are being committed at younger ages than in the past. Moreover, there is growing concern that, in some countries, the proportion of violent crimes committed by youth has been increasing.

Between two-thirds and three-quarters of all offenses committed by young people are committed by members of gangs or groups, which can vary from highly structured criminal organizations to less structured street gangs. Even those young people who commit offenses alone are likely to be associated with groups.

Though poverty and unemployment are not, by themselves, causes of violence, they become important factors when coupled with other triggers such as lack of opportunity, inequality, exclusion, the availability of drugs and firearms, and a breakdown in access to various forms of capital, justice, and education.

The UN motivated by the information contained in its fact sheet has strengthened its programs on juvenile justice through the adoption of the World Program of Action for Youth. The UN defines juveniles as young people between the ages of 15 and 24 years. According to the UN present strategies to tackle juvenile delinquency are often too narrowly focused on tough penalties and law enforcement. To address these issues, the UN contends that meaningful alternatives for socialization and achievement of young people can be achieved by

- Providing rural areas with socioeconomic opportunities and services to promote rural development as well as discourage young people from migrating to urban areas
- Providing recreational, sport, and leisure activities
- Improving school quality, incorporating into school programs seminars and lessons to raise awareness about issues related to violence, and expanding access to/retention in schools for high-risk individuals and communities, with meaningful after-school group activities
- Providing tailored apprenticeship programs that enable youth to enter the labor market through an alternative, effective channel
- Preventing violence by involving families and entire communities, raising awareness of the importance of domestic support in the prevention of juvenile crime, and setting up information campaigns and training and educational programs for family members or guardians

The UN stresses that preventive measures should address the root causes of criminality, rehabilitation programs, and services. To help accomplish this, the UN has developed the "Manual for the measurement of juvenile justice indicators." The UN has also published the 1985 *United Nations Standard Minimum Rules for the Administration of Juvenile Justice* ("The Beijing Rules") (United Nations, 1985) and the 1990 Guidelines for the Prevention of Juvenile Delinquency (also referred to as "The Riyadh Guidelines") (United Nations, 1990). These documents established basic actions to prevent children and young people from engaging in criminal activities as well as to protect the human rights of youth already found to have broken the law. The UN's focus on safeguarding the human rights of children and young people was strengthened by the Convention on the Rights of the Child (CRC) (United Nations, 1989), which entered into force in 1990.

In 1995, the UN adopted the World Programme of Action for Youth (WPAY) (UN, 1995). This program provides a policy framework and practical guidelines for national action and international support to improve the situation of young people.

Differences between Trafficking and Smuggling

There are three important differences:

1. *Consent*: The smuggling of migrants, while often undertaken in dangerous or degrading conditions, involves migrants who have consented to the smuggling. Trafficking victims, on the other hand, have either never consented or, if they initially consented, that consent has been rendered meaningless by the coercive, deceptive, or abusive actions of the traffickers.
2. *Exploitation*: Smuggling ends with the migrants' arrival at their destination, whereas trafficking involves the ongoing exploitation of the victim. From a practical standpoint, victims of trafficking also tend to be affected more severely and to be in greater need of protection from revictimization and other forms of further abuse than are smuggled migrants.
3. *Transnationality*: Smuggling is always transnational, whereas trafficking may not be. Trafficking can occur regardless of whether victims are taken to another state or only moved from one place to another within the same state.

United Nations Protocol to Prevent, Suppress, and Punish Trafficking in Persons, Especially Women and Children

Articles 1, 2, and 4 of this protocol set out the relationship between the protocol and its parent instrument, the UN Convention against Transnational Organized Crime, the basic purpose of the protocol, and its scope of application. The protocol is not a stand-alone instrument. It must be read and applied together with the parent convention, and each country is required to become a party to the convention in order to become party to the protocol. Protocol offenses are deemed to be convention offenses for the purposes of extradition and other forms of cooperation, and most of the provisions must be read together.

The convention has general powers for dealing with transnational organized crime, while each protocol has additional provisions that supplement those of the convention and that focus on the specific subject matter of the protocol. This is an important asset for national legislators, prosecutors, and law enforcement agencies because of the complexity of major criminal organizations and the diverse range of crimes in which they engage: the combination of the convention and one or more protocols makes it possible for countries to attack trafficking in the broader context of organized criminal groups and not just as one distinct area of criminal activity.

The application of the protocol is governed by the same rules as is the application of the convention: between state parties, both instruments apply in any case involving the investigation or prosecution of an offense that is suspected of being "transnational in nature" and involving an "organized criminal group," as defined in the convention. These conditions govern international cooperation between parties but not the domestic law adopted pursuant to the convention and its protocols. Domestic law should apply regardless of whether trafficking or other illicit activities involve transnational organized crime, so that prosecutors do not need to prove these elements in domestic courts: trafficking in human beings is a crime whether it crosses national borders or not and regardless of whether it can be linked to organized crime.

The basic purpose of the protocol is to prevent and combat trafficking, to protect and assist victims, and to promote international cooperation. Victims and witnesses are also dealt within the parent convention, but the protection of, and assistance to, victims is specified as a core purpose of the protocol in recognition of the acute needs of trafficking victims and the importance of victim assistance, both as an end in itself and as a means to support the investigation and prosecution of trafficking crimes.

"Trafficking in persons" is defined in Article 2 of the protocol, the first time that the international community has developed and agreed to a definition. Essentially, trafficking consists of actions in which offenders gain control of victims by coercive or deceptive means or by exploiting relationships, like those between parents and children, in which one party has relatively little power or influence and is therefore vulnerable to trafficking.

Once initial control is gained, victims are moved to a place where there is a market for their services and where they often lack language skills and other basic knowledge that would enable them to seek help. Destinations are commonly in foreign countries, but that is not always the case; international borders do not have to be crossed. Upon arrival at their destination, victims are forced to work in difficult, dangerous, and usually unpleasant occupations, such as prostitution, the production of child pornography, or general labor, in order to earn profits for the traffickers. Like other smuggled or trafficked commodities, victims are sometimes simply sold by one criminal group to another, but unlike other commodities, they can be made to work for long periods after arrival at their final destination, generating far greater profits for traffickers at all stages of the process.

Article 3, paragraph (a) of the protocol, defines trafficking as follows:

> "Trafficking in persons" shall mean the recruitment, transportation, transfer, harbouring or receipt of persons, by means of the threat or use of force or other forms of coercion, of abduction, of fraud, of deception, of the abuse of power or of a position of vulnerability or of the giving or receiving of payments or benefits to achieve the consent of a person having control over another person, for the purpose of exploitation. Exploitation shall include, at a minimum, the exploitation of the prostitution of others or other forms of sexual exploitation, forced labour or services, slavery or practices similar to slavery, servitude or the removal of organs.

Several significant issues were resolved in developing this definition and other protocol provisions. The broad range of forms taken by modern trafficking was difficult to cover in a single provision, particularly with the degree of clarity needed to form the basis of criminal laws adopted by national legislatures. The definition, criminalization requirements, and other elements of both the convention and its protocols, therefore, set only minimum standards, which countries can exceed or supplement in accordance with their needs. The definition uses language such as "at a minimum" to express this principle, and Article 34, paragraph (3) of the convention, expressly authorizes measures that are "more strict or severe" than those required by the instruments.

The role of victim consent was also a difficult issue. On one hand, negotiators were aware that victims often consent to their initial recruitment based on deception or misinformation about where they will be taken and what will happen when they arrive. The reality is that any initial consent is usually rendered meaningless, if not by the initial deception, then by the use of force or other coercive or abusive conduct on the part of traffickers.

On the other hand, requiring countries to make the consent of victims completely irrelevant could exclude valid defenses and raise constitutional or other problems in many countries. The solution was to specify that, while consent may initially be raised by accused traffickers, consent to initial recruitment is not the same as consent to the entire course of trafficking, and any alleged consent to exploitation must be deemed irrelevant if any of the means of trafficking listed in the definition have occurred (i.e., the threat or use of force, coercion, abduction, fraud, deception, the abuse of power or a position of vulnerability, or of the giving or receiving of payments or benefits to achieve the consent of a person such as a parent).

A third issue was whether the protocol should focus on women and children, who are the most common victims of trafficking, or it should extend to all persons. Negotiators referred this question back to the General Assembly, which expanded the original mandate to include trafficking in all "persons" regardless of age or gender (GA/RES/54/126), and the protocol was finalized on that basis.

In addition to taking action against traffickers, the protocol in Part II requires states that ratify it to take some steps to protect and assist victims of trafficking. These supplement the more general provisions of the parent convention for the protection of victims and witnesses, recognizing that victims of trafficking are often in greater danger and in greater need of assistance and support, particularly if repatriated to their countries of origin. Under the protocol, trafficking victims would be entitled to some degree of confidentiality, information about legal proceedings involving traffickers, and assistance in making representations in such proceedings at an appropriate stage. Under both instruments, countries must also endeavor to provide for the basic safety and security of victims, and the protocol requires that victims be afforded "the possibility of obtaining compensation for damage suffered."

The protocol also calls for further social assistance to victims in areas such as counseling, housing, education, and health-care needs, although these are not obligatory. The obligations of states regarding victims fall upon whichever state the victim is in at a given time.

The legal status of trafficked persons and whether they would eventually be returned to their countries of origin was also the subject of extensive negotiations. Generally, the developed countries to which persons are often trafficked take the position that there should not be a legal right to remain in their countries as this would provide an incentive for both trafficking and illegal migration. Countries whose nationals were more likely to be trafficked sought as much protection and legal status for trafficked persons as possible.

The agreed-upon provision (Art. 8) requires countries to "facilitate and accept" the return of victims who are their nationals or who had legal residency rights when they were trafficked into the destination country, and then incorporates a series of safeguards to protect victims. Repatriation should be voluntary, if possible, and must take into consideration the safety of the victim and the status of any ongoing legal proceedings. This also helps to ensure the viability of prosecutions by reducing the likelihood that witnesses will be repatriated before they can testify. A further safeguard provision (Art. 14) protects other fundamental interests, including those of trafficking victims who are also asylum seekers, and the principle of nondiscrimination.

Under Part III (Prevention, cooperation, and other measures; Arts. 9–13), law enforcement agencies of countries that ratify the protocol are required to cooperate in such things as the identification of offenders and trafficked persons, sharing information about the methods of offenders, and the training of investigators, law enforcement, and victim support personnel (Art. 10). Countries are also required to implement security and border controls to detect and prevent trafficking (Arts. 11–13). These measures include strengthening their own border controls, imposing requirements on commercial carriers to check passports and visas, setting standards for the technical quality of passports and other travel documents, protecting the production and issuance of travel documents from fraud and corruption, and ensuring the expeditious cooperation of security personnel in establishing the validity of their own documents on request.

These precautions are equally important for the prevention of trafficking in persons and the smuggling of migrants, and identical requirements have been included in both protocols, a fact that may also make joint implementation easier for countries that wish to do so. Joint implementation may also have advantages for law enforcement and prosecution agencies, which would be able to deal with cases initially as migrant smuggling until the added elements of improper recruitment and exploitation necessary to build a trafficking case can be established.

Social methods of prevention, such as research, advertising, and social or economic support, are also provided for. The specific provisions of the protocol (Art. 9) should be read in conjunction with the parallel provisions of the convention (Art. 31), which contains additional language dealing with the alleviation of social conditions and the need for public information campaigns. These are particularly important with respect to trafficking, where the willingness—and in some cases desperation—of potential victims to relocate and their ignorance of trafficking and the true conditions in the destinations to which they are trafficked have been identified as major contributing factors. In addition to general social prevention measures, the protocol also calls for measures to prevent revictimization, where victims who are returned to their countries of origin are simply trafficked out again.

Trafficking in Firearms

The Protocol against the Illicit Manufacturing of and Trafficking in Firearms, their Parts and Components and Ammunition was adopted by General Assembly Resolution 55/255 on May 31, 2001. It entered into force on July 3, 2005. The objective of the protocol, which is the first legally binding instrument on small arms that has been adopted at the global level, is to promote, facilitate, and strengthen cooperation among state parties in order to prevent, combat, and eradicate the illicit manufacturing of and trafficking in firearms, their parts and components, and ammunition. By ratifying the protocol, states make a commitment to adopt a series of crime control measures and implement in their domestic legal order three sets of normative provisions. The first one relates to the establishment of criminal offenses related to illegal manufacturing of, and trafficking in, firearms on the basis of the protocol requirements and definitions; the second to a system of government authorizations or licensing intending to ensure legitimate manufacturing of, and trafficking in, firearms; and the third to the marking and tracing of firearms.

Excerpts of the United States' Act: Victims of
Trafficking and Violence Protection Act of 2000

22 U.S. CODE § 7101

An Act to combat trafficking in persons, especially into the sex trade, slavery, and involuntary servitude, to reauthorize certain Federal programs to prevent violence against women, and for other purposes.

SEC. 102. PURPOSES AND FINDINGS

(a) PURPOSES.—The purposes of this division are to combat trafficking in persons, a contemporary manifestation of slavery whose victims are predominantly women and children, to ensure just and effective punishment of traffickers, and to protect their victims.

(b) FINDINGS.—Congress finds that:

(1) As the twenty-first century begins, the degrading institution of slavery continues throughout the world. Trafficking in persons is a modern form of slavery, and it is the largest manifestation of slavery today. At least 700,000 persons annually, primarily women and children, are trafficked within or across international borders. Approximately 50,000 women and children are trafficked into the United States each year.

(2) Many of these persons are trafficked into the international sex trade, often by force, fraud, or coercion. The sex industry has rapidly expanded over the past several decades. It involves sexual exploitation of persons, predominantly women and girls, involving activities related to prostitution, pornography, sex tourism, and other commercial sexual services. The low status of women in many parts of the world has contributed to a burgeoning of the trafficking industry.

(3) Trafficking in persons is not limited to the sex industry. This growing transnational crime also includes forced labor and involves significant violations of labor, public health, and human rights standards worldwide.

(4) Traffickers primarily target women and girls, who are disproportionately affected by poverty, the lack of access to education, chronic unemployment, discrimination, and the lack of economic opportunities in countries of origin. Traffickers lure women and girls into their networks through false promises of decent working conditions at relatively good pay as nannies, maids, dancers, factory workers, restaurant workers, sales clerks, or models. Traffickers also buy children from

302 An Introduction to Comparative Legal Models of Criminal Justice

poor families and sell them into prostitution or into various types of forced or bonded labor.

(5) Traffickers often transport victims from their home communities to unfamiliar destinations, including foreign countries away from family and friends, religious institutions, and other sources of protection and support, leaving the victims defenseless and vulnerable.

(6) Victims are often forced through physical violence to engage in sex acts or perform slavery-like labor. Such force includes rape and other forms of sexual abuse, torture, starvation, imprisonment, threats, psychological abuse, and coercion.

(7) Traffickers often make representations to their victims that physical harm may occur to them or others should the victim escape or attempt to escape. Such representations can have the same coercive effects on victims as direct threats to inflict such harm.

(8) Trafficking in persons is increasingly perpetrated by organized, sophisticated criminal enterprises. Such trafficking is the fastest growing source of profits for organized criminal enterprises worldwide. Profits from the trafficking industry contribute to the expansion of organized crime in the United States and worldwide. Trafficking in persons is often aided by official corruption in countries of origin, transit, and destination, thereby threatening the rule of law.

(9) Trafficking includes all the elements of the crime of forcible rape when it involves the involuntary participation of another person in sex acts by means of fraud, force, or coercion.

(10) Trafficking also involves violations of other laws, including labor and immigration codes and laws against kidnapping, slavery, false imprisonment, assault, battery, pandering, fraud, and extortion.

(11) Trafficking exposes victims to serious health risks. Women and children trafficked in the sex industry are exposed to deadly diseases, including HIV and AIDS. Trafficking victims are sometimes worked or physically brutalized to death.

(12) Trafficking in persons substantially affects interstate and foreign commerce. Trafficking for such purposes as involuntary servitude, peonage, and other forms of forced labor has an impact on the nationwide employment network and labor market. Within the context of slavery, servitude, and labor or services which are obtained or maintained through coercive conduct that amounts to a condition of servitude, victims are subjected to a range of violations.

(13) Involuntary servitude statutes are intended to reach cases in which persons are held in a condition of servitude through nonviolent coercion. In *United States v. Kozminski*, 487 U.S. 931 (1988), the Supreme Court found that section 1584 of title 18, United States Code, should be narrowly interpreted, absent a definition of involuntary servitude by Congress. As a result, that section was interpreted to criminalize only servitude that is brought about through use or threatened use of physical or legal coercion and to exclude other conduct that can have the same purpose and effect.

(14) Existing legislation and law enforcement in the United States and other countries are inadequate to deter trafficking and bring traffickers to justice, failing to reflect the gravity of the offenses involved. No comprehensive law exists in the United States that penalizes the range of offenses involved in the trafficking scheme. Instead, even the most brutal instances of trafficking in the sex industry are often punished under laws that also apply to lesser offenses, so that traffickers typically escape deserved punishment.

(15) In the United States, the seriousness of this crime and its components is not reflected in current sentencing guidelines, resulting in weak penalties for convicted traffickers.

(16) In some countries, enforcement against traffickers is also hindered by official indifference, by corruption, and sometimes even by official participation in trafficking.

(17) Existing laws often fail to protect victims of trafficking, and because victims are often illegal immigrants in the destination country, they are repeatedly punished more harshly than the traffickers themselves.

(18) Additionally, adequate services and facilities do not exist to meet victims' needs regarding health care, housing, education, and legal assistance, which safely reintegrate trafficking victims into their home countries.

(19) Victims of severe forms of trafficking should not be inappropriately incarcerated, fined, or otherwise penalized solely for unlawful acts committed as a direct result of being trafficked, such as using false documents, entering the country without documentation, or working without documentation.

(20) Because victims of trafficking are frequently unfamiliar with the laws, cultures, and languages of the countries into which they have been trafficked, because they are often subjected to coercion and intimidation including physical detention and debt bondage, and because they often fear retribution and

forcible removal to countries in which they will face retribution or other hardship, these victims often find it difficult or
impossible to report the crimes committed against them or to
assist in the investigation and prosecution of such crimes.

(21) Trafficking of persons is an evil requiring concerted and vig-
orous action by countries of origin, transit or destination,
and by international organizations.

(22) One of the founding documents of the United States, the
Declaration of Independence, recognizes the inherent dignity and worth of all people. It states that all men are created equal and that they are endowed by their Creator with
certain unalienable rights. The right to be free from slavery
and involuntary servitude is among those unalienable rights.
Acknowledging this fact, the United States outlawed slavery
and involuntary servitude in 1865, recognizing them as evil
institutions that must be abolished. Current practices of sexual slavery and trafficking of women and children are similarly abhorrent to the principles upon which the United States
was founded.

(23) The United States and the international community agree
that trafficking in persons involves grave violations of human
rights and is a matter of pressing international concern. The
international community has repeatedly condemned slavery and involuntary servitude, violence against women, and
other elements of trafficking, through declarations, treaties, and United Nations resolutions and reports, including the Universal Declaration of Human Rights; the 1956
Supplementary Convention on the Abolition of Slavery, the
Slave Trade, and Institutions and Practices Similar to Slavery;
the 1948 American Declaration on the Rights and Duties of
Man; the 1957 Abolition of Forced Labor Convention; the
International Covenant on Civil and Political Rights; the
Convention Against Torture and Other Cruel, Inhuman or
Degrading Treatment or Punishment; United Nations General
Assembly Resolutions 50/167, 51/66, and 52/98; the Final
Report of the World Congress against Sexual Exploitation of
Children (Stockholm, 1996); the Fourth World Conference
on Women (Beijing, 1995); and the 1991 Moscow Document
of the Organization for Security and Cooperation in Europe.

(24) Trafficking in persons is a transnational crime with national
implications. To deter international trafficking and bring its
perpetrators to justice, nations including the United States
must recognize that trafficking is a serious offense. This is

done by prescribing appropriate punishment, giving priority to the prosecution of trafficking offenses, and protecting rather than punishing the victims of such offenses. The United States must work bilaterally and multilaterally to abolish the trafficking industry by taking steps to promote cooperation among countries linked together by international trafficking routes. The United States must also urge the international community to take strong action in multilateral fora to engage recalcitrant countries in serious and sustained efforts to eliminate trafficking and protect trafficking victims.

International Police Executive Symposium

The International Police Executive Symposium (IPES) brings police researchers and practitioners together to facilitate cross-cultural, international, and interdisciplinary exchanges for the enrichment of the policing profession. It encourages discussions and writing on challenging topics of contemporary importance through an array of initiatives including conferences and publications. Founded in 1994 by Dilip K. Das, the IPES is funded by the benefaction of institutional supporters and sponsors that host IPES events around the world.

The International Police Executive Symposium's major annual initiative is a 4-day meeting on specific issues relevant to the policing profession. Past meeting themes have covered a broad range of topics from police education to corruption. Meetings are organized by the IPES in conjunction with sponsoring organizations in a host country. To date, meetings have been held in North America, Europe, and Asia.

The IPES's annual meetings bring together ministers of interior and justice, police commissioners and chiefs, scholars representing world-renowned institutions, and many more of the criminal justice elite from more than 60 countries throughout the world. The meetings facilitate interaction and the exchange of ideas and opinions on all aspects of policing. The agenda is structured to encourage dialog in both formal and informal settings. Meeting participants are requested to present papers discussing the meeting's theme from the perspective of each presenter's country. Compilations of selected papers from each meeting have been published or are in preparation for publication. Photo 12.1 is a picture of an IPES workshop on human trafficking.

IPES advocates, promotes, and propagates the idea that policing is one of the most basic and essential avenues for improving the quality of life in all nations, rich and poor, modern and traditional, large and small, peaceful and strife ridden. IPES actively works to drive home to all its office bearers,

Photo 12.1 IPES workshop on trafficking in humans, held in Canada. (Photo by Cliff Roberson.)

supporters, and admirers that, in order to reach its full potential as an instrument of service to humanity, policing must be fully and enthusiastically open to collaboration between research and practice, global exchanges among the police of all nations in the world, UNIVERSAL dissemination and sharing of best practices, and generating thinking police leaders and followers, reflecting and writing on the issues challenging to the profession (http://www.ipes, accessed November 7, 2007).

International Policy Institute for Counter-Terrorism

Founded in 1996, the International Policy Institute for Counter-Terrorism (ICT) is an academic institute facilitating international cooperation in the global struggle against terrorism. ICT is an independent think tank providing expertise in terrorism, counterterrorism, homeland security, threat vulnerability and risk assessment, intelligence analysis, and national security and defense policy.

ICT also serves as a joint forum for international policy makers and scholars to share information and expertise through research papers, situation reports, and academic publications for worldwide distribution. A number of international seminars, workshops, and conferences are organized monthly by ICT to discuss and educate on global and regional issues of security, defense, and public policy making in order to facilitate the exchange of perspectives, information, and proposals for policy action. ICT administers the largest public domain research database on the Internet encompassing global terrorist attacks, terrorist organizations, and activists, in addition to statistical reports.

ICT draws upon a comprehensive and international network of individuals and organizations with unique expertise on terrorism and counterterrorism research, public policy analysis, and education dispersed all over the world, including the United States, the European Union, and Israel, among others. An acclaimed management and research staff at ICT spearheads the Institute's efforts to coordinate the struggle against global terrorism and leads a worldwide team of affiliates and academic partners working to encourage cooperation among experts and disseminate innovative ideas for policy makers in the fight against terrorism.

ICT is a nonprofit organization located at the Interdisciplinary Center (IDC), Herzliya, Israel, which relies exclusively on private donations and revenue from events, projects, and programs. One of ICT's first initiatives was to develop an objective definition for "terrorism" as "the deliberate use of violence aimed against civilians in order to achieve political ends." According to ICT, terrorism is becoming an increasingly international and multidisciplinary activity, carried out by networks rather than classic organizations. In order to counter such terrorism, security agencies must adapt themselves to operate at least as efficiently as the terrorists themselves.

Just as the terrorists have formed networks, so must counterterrorists learn to network between like-minded organizations and individuals. The ICT was designed to meet this challenge. While its activities are academic in nature, the participating institutes are all involved in recommending policy for their respective countries while serving as a model for cooperation with international agencies. This is primarily done with the organization and promotion of conferences and information exchange. Noteworthy examples include the conference on "International Terrorist Threats to the Olympic Games," in addition to the publication of an ICTAC newsletter for members' updates (http://www.ict.org, accessed November 8, 2007).

Organization of American States

The Organization of American States, located in Washington, D.C., is the world's oldest regional organization, dating back to the First International Conference of American States, held in Washington, D.C. in 1889–1890. At the meeting, the International Union of American Republics was established. The OAS came into being in 1948 with the signing in Bogotá, Colombia, of the Charter of the OAS, which entered into force in December 1951. It was subsequently amended by the Protocol of Buenos Aires, signed in 1967, which entered into force in February 1970; by the Protocol of Cartagena de Indias, signed in 1985, which entered into force in November 1988; by the Protocol of Managua, signed in 1993, which entered into force in January 1996; and by the Protocol of Washington, signed in 1992, which entered into force in September 1997.

The organization was established in order to achieve among its member states—as stipulated in Article 1 of the Charter—"an order of peace and justice, to promote their solidarity, to strengthen their collaboration, and to defend their sovereignty, their territorial integrity, and their independence."

Presently, the OAS brings together all 35 independent states of the Americas and constitutes the main political, juridical, and social governmental forum in the Hemisphere. In addition, it has granted permanent observer status to 69 states as well as to the European Union (EU). The organization uses a four-pronged approach to effectively implement its essential purposes, based on its main pillars: democracy, human rights, security, and development.

The Organization of American States (OAS), though not solely a law enforcement agency, brings together the nations of the Western Hemisphere to strengthen cooperation on democratic values, defend common interests, and debate the major issues facing the region and the world. The OAS is the region's principal multilateral forum for strengthening democracy, promoting human rights, and confronting shared problems such as poverty, terrorism, illegal drugs, and corruption. It plays a leading role in carrying out mandates established by the hemisphere's leaders through the Summits of the Americas.

With four official languages—English, Spanish, Portuguese, and French—the OAS reflects the diversity of the hemisphere's peoples and cultures. It is made up of 35 member states: the independent nations of North, Central, and South America, and the Caribbean. The government of Cuba, a member state, has been suspended from participation since 1962; thus only 34 countries participate actively. Nations from other parts of the world participate as permanent observers, which allows them to follow closely the issues that are critical to the Americas. The member countries set major policies and goals through the General Assembly, which gathers the hemisphere's ministers of foreign affairs once a year in regular session. Ongoing actions are guided by the Permanent Council, made up of ambassadors appointed by the member states.

The OAS, through its Department of International Legal Affairs, plays a central role in the harmonization and codification of private international law in the Western Hemisphere. The principal component of this work is the Inter-American Specialized Conferences on Private International Law, which the OAS hosts approximately every 4–6 years. Known by their acronym in Spanish as CIDIP, these conferences have produced 26 widely enacted international instruments (including conventions, protocols, uniform documents, and model laws), which shape the inter-American private law framework (http://www.oas.org/ key_issues/eng/KeyIssue_Detail. asp?kis_sec=20, accessed November 8, 2007).

Article 3 of the Charter of the OAS

The American States reaffirm the following principles:

a. International law is the standard of conduct of States in their recipro-cal relations;

b. International order consists essentially of respect for the personality, sovereignty, and independence of States, and the faithful fulfillment of obligations derived from treaties and other sources of interna-tional law;

c. Good faith shall govern the relations between States;

d. The solidarity of the American States and the high aims which are sought through it require the political organization of those States on the basis of the effective exercise of representative democracy;

e. Every State has the right to choose, without external interference, its political, economic, and social system and to organize itself in the way best suited to it, and has the duty to abstain from intervening in the affairs of another State. Subject to the foregoing, the American States shall cooperate fully among themselves, independently of the nature of their political, economic, and social systems.

f. The elimination of extreme poverty is an essential part of the promo-tion and consolidation of representative democracy and is the com-mon and shared responsibility of the American States;

g. The American States condemn war of aggression: victory does not give rights;

h. An act of aggression against one American State is an act of aggres-sion against all the other American States;

i. Controversies of an international character arising between two or more American States shall be settled by peaceful procedures;

j. Social justice and social security are bases of lasting peace;

k. Economic cooperation is essential to the common welfare and pros-perity of the peoples of the Continent;

l. The American States proclaim the fundamental rights of the individual without distinction as to race, nationality, creed, or sex.

m. The spiritual unity of the Continent is based on respect for the cultural values of the American countries and requires their close cooperation for the high purposes of civilization;

n. The education of peoples should be directed toward justice, freedom, and peace.

Child Wise

Child Wise is an Australian charity dedicated to protecting children everywhere. Child Wise is unique. It is the only Australian-based organization working exclusively to prevent the sexual abuse and exploitation of children in Australia, Asia, and the Pacific. Child Wise combines direct support, advocacy, community education, research, program implementation, and training to provide an innovative, highly specialized, and enduring service to communities in Australia and overseas.

Child Wise works to end the sexual exploitation of children by providing direct assistance and support to individuals and community and through programs that seek to raise awareness about child abuse, provide professional and community training, and build the capacity of individuals, organizations, and communities to combat child abuse (http://childwise.net/our-work.php, accessed November 8, 2007).

Summary

- There are many international associations involved in criminal justice. Interpol attempts to facilitate international police cooperation.
- Interpol is not involved itself in political, military, religious, or racial character issues in nations.
- Interpol's core functions are secure global communication services, operational data services and databases for police, operational police support services, and training and development.
- The International Association of Chiefs of Police is the world's oldest and largest membership organization of police executives.
- The IACP was founded in 1893.
- The International Police Association was founded in 1950 to create bonds of friendship and to promote international cooperation.
- The UN has a wide assortment of programs and agencies involved in international criminal justice issues.

Questions in Review

1. Why are international law enforcement agencies important?
2. What is the purpose of Interpol?
3. Should the UN take a more active role in criminal justice? Justify.
4. Why is there an increased emphasis on trafficking in humans?
5. What are the primary functions of the International Association of Chiefs of Police?

Appendix: Excerpts from the World Justice Project—Rule of Law Index 2014*

Four Universal Principles of the Rule of Law

The World Justice Project (WJP) uses a working definition of the rule of law based on four universal principles, deprived from internationally accepted standards. The rule of law is a system where the following four universal principles are upheld:

1. The government and its officials and agents as well as individuals and private entities are accountable under the law.
2. The laws are clear, publicized, stable, and just; are applied evenly; and protect fundamental rights, including the security of persons and property.
3. The process by which the laws are enacted, administered, and enforced is accessible, fair, and efficient.
4. Justice is delivered timely by competent, ethical, and independent representatives and neutrals who are of sufficient number, have adequate resources, and reflect the makeup of the communities they serve.

Rule of Law Index Factors

The WJP used nine aggregate indicators (or factors), which are further disaggregated into 47 specific indicators or subfactors. The factors are

- Factor 1: constraints on government powers
- Factor 2: absence of corruption
- Factor 3: open government
- Factor 4: fundamental rights
- Factor 5: order and security
- Factor 6: regulatory enforcement
- Factor 7: civil justice
- Factor 8: criminal justice
- Factor 9: informal justice

* Reprinted by permission of the World Justice Project, Washington, DC, 2005.

311

Comments and Rankings on Selected Factors

Factor 2: Absence of Corruption

The absence of corruption—conventionally defined as the use of public power for private gain—is one of the hallmarks of a society governed by the rule of law, as corruption is a manifestation of the extent to which government officials abuse their power for their own interest. WJP used three forms of corruption: bribery, improper influence by public or private interests, and misappropriation of public funds or other resources (embezzlement).

Selected Comparative Ranking of Factor 2

Rank	Country	Score
1	Denmark	0.96
2	Norway	0.94
7	Netherlands	0.88
11	Japan	0.84
12	Germany	0.83
14	Canada	0.81
15	United Kingdom	0.80
20	France	0.78
21	United States	0.75
25	Spain	0.69
46	South Africa	0.49
78	Mexico	0.37

Factor 4: Fundamental Rights

In 1948, the United Nations General Assembly adopted the Universal Declaration of Human Rights. Its Preamble explicitly recognizes the centrality of fundamental rights to the rule of law, stating that "it is essential, if man is not to be compelled to have recourse, as a last resort to rebellion against tyranny and oppression, that human rights should be protected by the rule of law…." The WJP in this factor considered how effectively countries uphold and protect a menu of rights and freedoms that are firmly established under international law. These rights include the right to equal treatment and the absence of discrimination, the right to life and security of the person, due process of law and rights of the accused, freedom of belief and religion, the absence of arbitrary interference with privacy, freedom of assembly and association, and the protection of fundamental rights.

Selected Comparative Ranking of Factor 4

Rank	Country	Score
1	Sweden	0.91
2	Denmark	0.90
6	Netherlands	0.85
8	Germany	0.84
14	Spain	0.78
15	United Kingdom	0.78
16	Canada	0.77
18	France	0.76
20	Japan	0.75
27	United States	0.71
41	South Africa	0.62
60	Mexico	0.55

Factor 8: Criminal Justice

An effective criminal justice system is a key aspect of the rule of law, as it constitutes the conventional mechanism to redress serious grievances and bring action against individuals for offenses against society. Effective criminal justice systems are capable of investigating, prosecuting, adjudicating, and punishing criminal offenses successfully, reliably, and in a timely manner through a system that is impartial and nondiscriminatory, as well as free of corruption and improper government influence, all while ensuring that the rights of both the victims and the accused are effectively protected.

Selected Comparative Ranking of Factor 8

Rank	Country	Score
1	Finland	0.85
3	Denmark	0.84
4	Norway	0.83
9	Netherlands	0.75
14	United Kingdom	0.72
15	Canada	0.72
16	Germany	0.71
18	Japan	0.69
22	United States	0.65
25	Spain	0.61
47	South Africa	0.45
97	Mexico	0.25

References

Al-Fehaid, A. (2003, January 20). Indian flogged for sacrilege. *Arab News* (Riyadh/ Jeddah), p. 1.

Amnesty International (2007). Amnesty's country dossiers. Retrieved March 28, 2015, from http://web.amnesty. org.

Aronowitz, A. A. (2002). Germany. In *World Factbook of Criminal Justice Systems.* Washington, DC: U.S. Department of Justice, Office of Justice Programs Bureau of Justice Statistics.

Ashrafi, G. H. (1997). *Majmu'a kamil qawanin wa muqarrat jazae'i* [The complete collection of criminal laws and regulations]. In R. Poters (Ed.), *Crime and Punishment in Islamic Law.* Cambridge, UK: Cambridge University Press.

Banton, M. P. (2007). Centralization versus decentralization. Retrieved March 30, 2015, from *Encyclopaedia Britannica.* Available at http://www.britannica. com/ eb/article-36610.

Bahgat, A. (1993). *The Prophets of God.* Cairo, Egypt: Dar-al-Shoruk.

Barrionuevo, A. (2007, October 14). A violent police unit, on film and in Rio's street. *New York Times*, p. A-3.

Bayley, D. H. (1992). Comparative organization of the police in English-speaking countries. In M. Tonry and N. Morris (Eds.), *Crime and Justice: A Review of Research* (Vol. 21, pp. 509–545). Chicago, IL: University of Chicago Press.

Beck, A. (2004, December). Understanding the criticality of context in developing community policing: A post Soviet case study (NCJRS Publication No. 207976). Washington, DC: U.S. Department of Justice.

Begley, S. (2007, April 30). The anatomy of violence. *Newsweek*, pp. 40–47.

Beharry v. Reno, 183 F. Supp. 2d 584 (E.D.N.Y. 2002).

Berman, H. J. (2005). The foundations of law: The historical foundations of law. *Emory Law Journal, 54,* 13, 13–24.

Bingham, T. (2010) *The Rule of Law.* New York: Penguin.

Birzer, M. and Roberson, C. (2006). *Policing Today and Tomorrow.* Upper Saddle River, NJ: Prentice-Hall.

Board of Canal & Lock Comm'rs v. Willamette Transp. & Locks Co., 6 Ore. 219 (Oregon, 1877 [1877]).

Bojadjieva, J. (2002). Bulgaria. In *World Factbook of Criminal Justice Systems.* Washington, DC: U.S. Department of Justice, Office of Justice Programs Bureau of Justice Statistics.

Borricand, J. (2002). France. In *World Factbook of Criminal Justice Systems.* Washington, DC: U.S. Department of Justice, Office of Justice Programs Bureau of Justice Statistics.

Bowen, C. D. (1956). *The Lion and the Throne: The Life and Times of Sir Edward Coke.* New York: Little, Brown.

Brazil (2007). *Encyclopaedia Britannica Online*. Retrieved March 16, 2016, from http://www.britannica.com/eb/article-222825.

Brogden, M. (1999). Community policing as cherry pie. In R. Mawby (Ed.), *Policing across the World: Issues for the Twenty First Century* (pp. 167–186). London, UK: UCL Press.

Bureau of Justice Statistics (2006, May). Law enforcement management and administrative statistics: Local police departments, 2003, NCJ 210118. Rockville, MD: NCJ. Retrieved April 2, 2015, from http://www.ojp.usdoj.gov/bjs/pubalp2.htm#lpd.

Bundeskriminalamt (German Police). www.bka.de, accessed April 1, 2015.

Calgary Police (2007). Core values. Retrieved March 21, 2015, from http://www.gov.calgary.ab.ca/police/about/core_values.html.

Calvi, J. V. and Colemen, S. (2000). *American Law and Legal Systems* (4th edn.). Upper Saddle River, NJ: Prentice-Hall.

Canivet, G. (2003). The interrelationship between common law and civil law. *Louisiana Law Review*, *63*, 937.

Coker v. Georgia, 433 U.S. 584 (1977).

Dalrymple, T. (2005, October 24). The meaning of beheading. *National Review*, pp. 30–32.

Dammer, H. R. and Fairchild, E. (2006). *Comparative Criminal Justice Systems* (3rd edn.). Belmont, CA: Wadsworth.

Das, D. and Palmiotto, M. (Eds.). (2006). *World Police Encyclopedia*. New York: Routledge.

Dawson, R. O. (1969). *Sentencing: The Decision as to Type, Length, and Conditions of Sentence*. Boston, MA: Little, Brown.

Deflem, M. and Swygart, A. J. (2001). Comparative criminal justice. In M. A. Dupont-Morales, M. Hooper, and J. Schmidt (Eds.), *Handbook of Criminal Justice Administration* (pp. 51–68). New York: Marcel Dekker.

Dicey, Albert Venn (A. V.) (1889). *An Introduction to the Study of the Law of the Constitution*. London, UK: MacMillan.

Dixon v. United States, 126 S.Ct. 2437 (2006).

Du, X. and Zhang, L. (1990). *China's Legal System*. Beijing, China: New World Press.

Dunn, M. (2003, March 6). Aussie prisoner vows not to scream. *Courier-Mail* (Brisbane, Australia), p. 1.

Encyclopaedia Britannica. (2007). Beheading. Retrieved March 25, 2015, from *Encyclopaedia Britannica*. http://www.britannica.com/eb/article-9014134.

Enmund v. Florida 458 U.S. 782 (1982).

Esmaeili, H. and Gans, J. (2000, March 22). Islamic law across cultural borders: The involvement of Western nationals in Saudi murder trials. *Denver Journal of International Law and Policy*, *28*(2), 145–148.

Frase, R. S. (1990). Comparative criminal justice as a guide to American law reform: How do the French do it, how can we find out, and why should we care? *California Law Review*, *78*, 542.

Furman v. Georgia, 408 U.S. 238 (1972).

Garland, D. (2001). *The Culture of Control: Crime and Order in Contemporary Society*. Chicago, IL: University of Chicago Press.

Garner, B. (Ed.). (1961). *Black's Law Dictionary* (6th edn.). St. Paul, MN: West.

Garza, A. (2015, March 29). Mexicans expect and deserve better from their country. *Houston Chronicle*, C-1.

Glendon, M., Gordon, M., and Carozza, P. (1999). *Comparative Legal Traditions*. St. Paul, MN: West.

Glenn, H. P. (2000). *Legal Traditions of the World*. New York: Oxford University Press.

Godfrey v. Georgia, 446 U.S. 420 (1980).

Gregg v. Georgia, 428 U.S. 153 (1976).

Guo, J. (2002). China. In *World Factbook of Criminal Justice Systems*. Washington, DC: U.S. Department of Justice, Office of Justice Programs Bureau of Justice Statistics.

Hallaq, W. B. (2005). *The Origins and Evolution of Islamic Law*. New York: Cambridge University Press.

Harasani, H. (2014). Islamic law as a comparable model in comparative legal research devising a method. *Global Journal of Comparative Law* 3, 186–202.

Haykal, M. H. (1976). *The Life of Muhammed*. New York: North American Trust Publications.

Holmes, O. W. (1881). *The Common Law*. New York: Little, Brown.

Horton, C. (1995). *Policing Policy in France*. London, UK: Policy Studies Institute. International Association of Chiefs of Police (IACP). http://www.theiacp.org, accessed April 4, 2015.

International Centre for Prison Studies (2007). A human rights approach to prison management. Retrieved April 11, 2015, from http://www.kcl.ac.uk/depsta/rel/icps.

Iran (2007). *Encyclopaedia Britannica Online*. Retrieved April 1, 2015, from http://www.britannica.com/eb/article-230059.

Kalmthout, A. and Tak, P. (1988). *Sanctions Systems in the Member States of the Council of Europe, Part I*. Norwell, MA: Kluwer Law & Taxation.

Kamali, M. H. (1999). *Maqasid al-Shariah: The Objectives of Islāmic Law*. Islāmic Research Institute, Pakistan.

Karunaratne, N. H. A. (2002). Sri Lanka. In *World Factbook of Criminal Justice Systems*. Washington, DC: U.S. Department of Justice, Office of Justice Programs Bureau of Justice Statistics.

Kolbert, C. F. (Trans.) (1979). *Digest of Roman Law*. London, UK: Penguin Classics.

Kurian, G. T. (1989). *World Encyclopedia of Police Forces and Penal Systems*. New York: Facts on File.

Labardini, R. (2005). Life imprisonment and extradition: Historical development, international context, and the current situation in Mexico and the United States. *Southwestern Journal of Law and Trade in the Americas, 11*, 1–140.

Langer, M. (2004). From legal transplants to legal translations: The globalization of plea bargaining and the Americanization thesis in criminal procedure. *Harvard International Law Journal, 45*, 1–69.

Lepsius, O. (2006). Human dignity and the downing of an aircraft: The German Federal Constitutional Court strikes down a prominent anti-terrorism provision in the new Air-Transport Security Act. *German Law Journal, 7*, 9. Retrieved from http://www.germanlawjournal.com/article.php?id=756.

London Metropolitan Police (2015). Retrieved March 21, 2015, from http://www.met. police.uk/index.shtml.

Lux v. Haggin, 69 Cal. 255, 10 P. 674 (1886).

Maartinez-Aguero v. Gonzales, 2005 U.S. Dist. LEXIS 2412 (W.D. Tex. 2005).

McKenzie, I. K. (1994). Regulating custodial interviews in a comparative study. *International Journal of Sociology of Law, 22*, 239–259.

Meier, B.-D. (2004). Alternatives to imprisonment in the criminal justice system. *Federal Sentencing Reporter, 16*, 222–249.

Merryman, J. H. (1985). *The Civil Law Tradition: An Introduction to the Legal Systems of Western Europe and Latin America* (2nd edn.). Stanford, CA: Stanford University Press.

Michalowski, R. (2002). Cuba. In *World Factbook of Criminal Justice Systems*. Washington, DC: U.S. Department of Justice, Office of Justice Programs Bureau of Justice Statistics.

Morris, N. and Rothman, D. (Eds.). (1995). *Oxford History of Prisons*. New York: Oxford University Press.

Nader, M. M. J. (1990). *Aspects of Saudi Arabian Law*. Riyadh, Saudi Arabia: Nader.

Nesheiwat, F. K. (2004). Honor crimes in Jordan: Their treatment under Islamic and Jordanian criminal laws. *Penn State International Law Review, 23*, 251–291.

Nestler, C. (2003). Model penal code: Sentencing in Germany. *Buffalo Criminal Law Review, 7*, 109–135.

Nikiforov, I. V. (2002). Russia. In *World Factbook of Criminal Justice Systems*. Washington, DC: U.S. Department of Justice, Office of Justice Programs Bureau of Justice Statistics.

Opolot, J. (1980). *An Analysis of World Legal Traditions*. Jonesboro, TN: Pilgrimage.

O'Sullivan, E. and O'Donnell, I. (2007). Coercive confinement in the Republic of Ireland: The waning of a culture of control. *Punishment & Society: The International Journal of Penology, 9*, 27–48.

Pakes, F. (2004). *Comparative Criminal Justice*. Devon, UK: Willan.

Peerenboom, R. (2006). Mixed reception: Culture, international norms, and legal change in East Asia: Article: What have we learned about law and development? Describing, predicting, and assessing legal reforms in China. *Michigan Journal of International Law, 27*, 823–849.

People v. Defore, 242 N.Y. 13 (1926).

Pizzi, W. T. (1993). Understanding prosecutorial discretion in the United States: The limits of comparative criminal procedure as an instrument of reform. *Ohio State Law Journal, 54*, 1325–1369.

Potter, P. B. (2004). *Legal Reform in China: Institutions, Culture, and Selective Adaptation*. Washington, DC: American Bar Foundation.

Rahmdel, M. (2006). The role of the courts in the reform of Iranian criminal law policy. *Criminal Law Forum, 17*, 59–70.

Reckless, W. (1961). *The Crime Problem* (3rd edn.). New York: Appleton-Century-Crofts.

Reichel, P. (2005). *Comparative Criminal Justice Systems* (4th edn.). Upper Saddle River, NJ: Prentice-Hall.

Rezaei, H. (2002). The Iranian criminal justice under the Islamization project. *European Journal of Crime, Criminal Law and Criminal Justice, 10*, 54–69.

Roberson, C. (2003). *Criminal Procedure Today* (2nd edn.). Upper Saddle River, NJ: Prentice-Hall.

Roberson, C., Wallace, H., and Stuckey, G. (2015). *Judicial Procedures* (10th edn.). Columbus, OH: Pearson.

Royal Canadian Mounted Police (2007). Retrieved March 23, 2015, from http://www.rcmp-grc.gc.ca/ccaps/contract_e.htm.

Sanad, N. (1991). *The Theory of Crime and Criminal Responsibility in Islamic Law: Shari 'a.* Chicago, IL: University of Illinois at Chicago.

Schacht, J. (1964). *An Introduction to Islamic Law.* Oxford, UK: Clarendon Press.

Shirk, D. A. (2010) Change & challenges in the judicial sector. *Justice Reform in Mexico* (pp. 3–6). San Diego, CA: Trans-Border Institute.

Souryal, S. (2004). *Islam, Islamic Law, and the Turn to Violence.* Huntsville, TX: Criminal Justice Center, Sam Houston State University.

Souryal, S., Alobied, A. I., and Potts, D. W. (2005). The penalty of hand amputation for theft in Islamic justice. In C. Fields and R. Moore, Jr. (Eds.), *Comparative and International Criminal Justice* (2nd edn.). Long Grove, IL: Waveland.

State ex rel. Walsh v. Hine, 59 Conn. 50, 21 A. 1024, 1890 Conn. LEXIS 4, 10 L.R.A.83 (1890).

State v. Rocker, 52 Haw. 336, 475 P.2d, 684, 1970 LEXIS 135 (Haw. 1970).

Stein, J. (1999). *Roman law in European History.* Cambridge, UK: Cambridge University Press.

Steiner, E. (2003). Early release for seriously ill and elderly prisoners: Should French practice be followed? *Probation Journal, 50,* 267–276.

Suddle, M. S. (2003). Reforming Pakistan police: An overview. In *United Nations Asia and Far East Institute for the Prevention of Crime and Treatment of Offenders Annual Report for 2001 and Resource Material Series* (pp. 94–106). Tokyo, Japan: UNAFEI.

Tabar, K. (2003). The rule of law and the politics of reform in post-revolutionary Iran. *International Sociology, 18,* 96–113.

Trevaskes, S. (2003). Public sentencing rallies in China: The symbolizing of punishment and justice in a socialist state. *Crime, Law and Social Change, 39,* 359–382.

Trevaskes, S. (2004). Propaganda work in Chinese courts: Public trials and sentencing rallies as sites of expressive punishment and public education in the People's Republic of China. *Punishment & Society, 6,* 5–21.

Turner, J. (2006). Judicial participation in plea negotiations: A comparative view. *American Journal of Comparative Law, 54,* 199–294.

Tyler, L. and King, I. (2000). Arming a traditionally disarmed police: An examination of police use of CS gas in the U.K. *Policing: International Journal of Police Strategies and Management, 23,* 390–400.

Ullmann, W. (1962). Bartolus and English jurisprudence. In *Bartolo da Sassoferrato: Studi e documenti per il VI centenario* (vol. 1). Rome, Italy: Giuffre Editore, pp. 47–73.

United States v. Wade, 388 U.S. 218 (1957).

United Nations (1985). United Nations Standard Minimum Rules for the Administration of Juvenile Justice ("The Beijing Rules"). 29 November. A/RES/40/33. Available from http://www2.ohchr.org/english/law/pdf/beijingrules.pdf, accessed May 13, 2015.

United Nations (1989). Convention on the Rights of the Child. 20 November. A/RES/44/25, accessed May 13, 2015.

United Nations (1990). United Nations Guidelines for the Prevention of Juvenile Delinquency ("The Riyadh Guidelines"). 14 December. A/RES/45/112. Available from http://www2.ohchr.org/english/law/juvenile.htm, accessed May 13, 2015.

United Nations (1995). World Programme of Action for Youth to the Year 2000 and Beyond. December 14, 1995. A/RES/50/81. Available from http://www.un.org/Docs/journal/asp/ws.asp?m=A/RES/50/81, accessed May 13, 2015.

Usmani, M. T. (2006). The Islamization of law in Pakistan: The case of *hudud* ordinances. *The Muslim World*, 96, 287–304.

Vago, S. (1997). *Law and Society* (5th edn.). Upper Saddle River, NJ: Prentice-Hall.

Van Caenegem, R. C. (1988). *The Birth of the English Common Law* (2nd edn.). Cambridge, UK: Cambridge University Press.

Van Houten v. State, 46 N.J.L. 16, 17 (1884).

Vidmar, N. (1996). Pretrial prejudice in Canada: A comparative perspective of the criminal jury. *Judicature*, 79, 249–255.

Wiechman, D. J., Kendall, J. D., and Azarian, M. K. (1996). Islamic law: Myths and realities. *CJ International*, 12, 1–17.

Wisneski v. State, 2007 Md. LEXIS 188 (Md. 2007).

Woodson v. North Carolina, 428 U.S. 280 (1976).

World Justice Project (2014). *Rule of Law Index: 2014*. Washington, DC: World Justice Project.

Wright, A. (2002). *Policing: An Introduction to Concepts and Practice*. Devon, UK: Willan.

Yacoubian, G. S., Jr. (2003). Should the subject matter jurisdiction of the International Criminal Court include drug trafficking? *International Journal of Comparative Criminology*, 3, 175–190.

Index

A

American ethnocentrism, 4
Appointed counsel, 33, 50, 82
Arraignment, 33, 45, 47, 51
Australian legal system, 66–67
Australia's AusAID program, 280

B

Bailiff, 33, 51–52
Basilica, 110, 133
BGS, *see Bundegrenzschutz*
BKA, *see Bundeskriminalamt*
Brazil
　criminal justice
　　authorization, 130
　　caught in the act, 130
　　defendants, 132
　　evidence, 131
　　felonies and misdemeanors, 129
　　informal process, 130
　　judicial system, 132
　　jurisdictions, 131
　　jurors, 132
　　legal rights, 131
　　legal scholarship, 129
　　legislature, 129
　　prosecutors, 132
　　trial process, 131
　law enforcement
　　BOPE, 142
　　civil and military state police,
　　　141–142
　　federal police, 141
　　federal, state and municipal
　　　levels, 141
　　political repression, 141
　　violence and corruption, 141
Brazilian state police special operations, 142
Bulgarian system of law
　confinement facilities, 230–231
　correctional work, 230
　court system, 226–227
　crime classification, 227
　establishment, 226
　judicial system, 226, 229
　police, 229–230
　prosecutors, 227
　sentencing of children, South Africa, 231
　trial procedure, 228–229
Bundegrenzschutz, 135, 139
Bundeskriminalamt, 135, 139

C

Canadian Narcotic Control Act 1970, 82
CDR, *see* Committees for the Defense of the
　　　Revolution
Child Justice Act, 231
Child sexual exploitation, 279–280
Child Wise, 310
China
　central government, 196
　Chinese legal system, 195
　confessions, 200
　court system, 199–200
　crimes, 198–199
　criminal justice system, 196
　criminal procedure law, 197
　criminal trial, 198
　Cultural Revolution, 197
　division, labor, 197
　judicial system, 196
　Ministry of Justice, 196
　Ministry of Public Security, 196
　People's Mediation of Disputes, 197
　People's Republic of China, 196–197
　public trials, 197–198
　Supreme People's Court, 196
Chinese People's Armed Police, 213
Civil law model, 1, 15–17, 26–27
　Belgian police system, 136
　canon law, 111
　commercial law, 111–112
　common law, 117
　Concordia discordantium canonum, 111
　corrections

confinement, 148–149
criminal justice systems, 142
death penalty, 151
expert witnesses, 143
fines, 151
legal reform, 143
parole, 150–151
plea bargaining (*see* Plea
    bargaining)
political and economic
    structures, 143
pretrial diversion (*see* Pretrial
    diversion)
probation, 149
psychological/psychiatric
    evaluation, 143
punishment, 142
Spanish prison, 143–144
development, national legal systems,
    112–113
enforcement agencies, multiple force
    law, 136
federal authority, 136
Federal Constitutional Court, 121
German court system, 120
German legal science, 114–115
judicial system
    Germany, 121
    Spain, 127
jurisdictions, 108, 120
jury system, 126
legal systems, 108
legislation, 109
Napoleonic Code, 113–114
national governments, 136
national police agencies, France, 136
police forces, 136
principals, 108
Rikspolis, 136
Roman law, 109–110
tribal and feudal laws, 108–109
Civil police model, 73, 104
Civil Service Tribune, 273–274
CJRU, *see* Criminal justice reform unit
Code of Criminal Procedure Act of
    1979, 239
Codification, 22, 33, 56, 66, 107, 114, 115,
    161, 301
Commercial law, 19–20, 31, 107–109,
    111–112, 133
Committee for the Promotion of Virtue and
    the Prevention of Vice, 179

Committees for the Defense of the
    Revolution, 217
Common law, 1, 14–15
    Canadian legal system, 62
    court structure, 62–63
    England consisted of legal remedies,
        34–35
    English Court System Today
        Court of Queen's/King's Bench,
            53–54
        Crown Court, 55
        England, Wales and Scotland, 53
        highest court, 52
        magistrates' court, 54–55
        Royal Courts of Justice, 55
        Supreme Court of Judicature, 54
    exclusionary rule, 57
    feudal land law, 35
    Henry II, 35–37
    judiciary, 64–65
    Justice Benjamin Cardozo, 57–59
    the Magna Carta, 38
    practice of law, 59–61
    provincial and territorial superior
        courts, 63–64
    right to fair trial *vs.* freedom of the
        press, 65
    Sir Edward Coke, 38–39
    Sir William Blackstone, 39–41
    in the United States, 41–42
    United States *vs.* United Kingdom,
        55–56
    U.S. Court Systems Today
        court of appeals, 42–43
        district courts, 43–44
        federal system, 42
        magistrates, 44
Common law countries
    corrections
        convicted felons, 91
        conviction of misdemeanor, 91
        presentence investigation, 91
        prison sentence range, 91–92
        sentencing in United Kingdom, 94
        United Kingdom and Wales, 93–94
        U.S. prison population, 92–93
    sentencing, 89–90
Community policing
    Canada, 87
    common law model, 81–82
    concepts, 76, 104
    establishment, 222

IACP, 287
principles, 71
and public trust, 210–211
program, 10
socialist legal model
   station, 76
Comparative criminal justice, 1
Comparative jurisprudence, 1
Comparative study, criminal justice, 3
Concordia discordantium canonum, 111
Conditional discharge, 135, 143–144
Confinement
Bulgaria, 230–231
California Penal Code, Section
   1170(a), 95
Cuba, 221–222
English purposes, 95–96
France, 148
India, 238
Ireland, 96–97
Pakistan, 189
period of, 91
pretrial, 207
prisoners, 71, 89
probation, 98, 99, 104
punishment, 28
rates of incarceration, 4, 94–95, 104
Russia, 217
Sri Lanka, 242
in the United States, 95
Constitution Act, 1867, 62
Constitutional Reform Act 2005, 68
Convention on the Rights of the
   Child, 295
Corporal punishment, 71, 98, 173, 179, 186,
   199, 241
Corpus Juris Civilis, 109–110, 112
Corruption
absence of, 13, 311, 312
crimes, 199
and fraud, 300
free of, 313
Germany, 147
Global Programme, 288
IACA, 279
IACO, 279
identification, Interpol, 279, 283
India, 234
IPES, 305
official, 302
Pakistan, 182
public officials, 234

public trust and community
   policing, 210
and violence, Brazil, 141
Court clerk, 33, 51, 201
Court of Justice of European
   Communities
actions, EU trademarks, 270–271
advocates general, 264
annulment, action of, 267
appeals, 267
Civil Service Tribunal, 273–274
Court of First Instance
   access to documents, 273
   cartels, 272–273
   community trademarks, 271–272
   judges, 269–270
   mergers, 272
   outcome cases, 270
   rules of procedure, 270
   state aid, 272–273
   type of actions, 270
direct actions, 267–268
ECJ, 263
EU judicial system, 264
expedited procedure, 269
fees, 269
interim measures, 269
judges, 264
judgments, 268
jurisdiction, 267
languages, 269
member states, 267
national court, 267–268
preliminary proceedings, 266
public hearing, 268
question of law, 268–269
rule, 268–269
treaty establishment, 265–266
written procedure, 267–268
Court system
Brazil, 132
British, 34
Bulgaria, 226–227
Canada, 62, 64
control, judicial decisions, 192
Cuba, 206–207
function, 10–11
German, 120
India, 233–234
People's Republic of China, 196,
   199–200
Russia, 193–194

Soviet Union, 208
Sri Lanka, 239
United Kingdom, 52–55
US, 33, 34, 42–44, 221
CPIA, *see* Criminal Procedure and
    Investigations Act 1996
CRC, *see* Convention on the Rights of
    the Child
Criminal case
    bailiff, 51–52
    Brazil, 129
    China, 197–198, 200, 218
    clerk of the court, 51
    court commissioners, 52
    court reporter, 52
    Cuba, 206–207
    defendant, 46
    defense counsel, 49–50
    India, 235, 237, 242
    Iran, 188
    Japan, 98
    large jurisdictions, 131, 145
    participants, 44–45
    privileged communication, 50–51
    prosecuting attorney, 46–48
    right to represent oneself, 50
    Saudi Arabia, 169–170
    Scotland, 65
    serious, 147
    state accuses, 10
    state attorney general, 48–49
    state courts, US, 42
    trial judge, 45–46
    trial procedure, Bulgaria, 228
Criminal Justice Act 2003, 94
Criminal Justice and Public Order Act of
    1994, 81
Criminal Justice Reform Unit,
    289–290
Criminal Law Reform Acts, 118, 119
Criminal organizations, 275, 282,
    294, 297
Criminal Procedure and Investigations Act
    1996, 57
Cuba
    civil and common law nations, 206
    constitution, 203–204
    corrections (*see* Policing and
        corrections)
    Council of State and Council of
        Ministers, 202
    court structure, 206–207

crime, 204, 206
Cuban penal code, 206
extradition, 207–208
Felony courts, 191
government, 308
judicial system, 204
justice court, Havana, 205
Marxist-Leninist model, 202
national legislative branch,
    202–203
policing (*see* Policing and corrections)
socialist legality, 204
state-organized law, 204
storage, court records in Havana, 205
Supreme Court of Cuba, 203
trial procedure, 207
Cybercrime
    Europol, 285
    International Conference, 284–285
    investigations, 284
    RCMP, 83
    and terrorism, 4

D

Death penalty, Germany
    accused rights, 123–124
    age, 123
    attorneys, 124
    conditions, 125
    criminal offenses classification, 122
    defendant, 124
    district court level, 125
    Federal Constitutional Court, 122
    German court structure, 122–123
    injured party, 125
    National Socialist regime, 121
    plea bargaining, 125
    principle of territoriality, 126
    Public Prosecutor's Office, 124
    regional courts, 125
    senates, 122
    tax authorities, 124
    undesirable populations, 122
Death penalty, the United States, 102–103
Decretum Gratiani (Gratian's Decree), 111
Department of Public Safety, 179
Deterrence, 28, 29, 71, 88–89, 118, 143
DPS, *see* Department of Public
    Safety
Drug abuse, 281, 292
Dual federalism, 33, 42, 69

E

Economic and Social Council, 288, 290, 292–293
"Elite Squad", 142
English Police and Criminal Evidence Act, 1984, 59
English Statement of Purposes, 95–96
Ethnocentrism, 1, 4, 31
Europol Computer System, 285–286
Exegetical system of teaching, 1, 19

F

Federal government
    Brazil, 141
    Canada, 62, 64
    criminal trial, 34
    death penalty statute, 102
    Germany, 119
    power, 121
    United States, 74
Federal investigative agency, 183
Federal Republic of Germany, 118, 119, 138
Feudal laws, 108–109
Financial and high-tech crimes, 282
France
    adoption, Napoleonic Code, 109
    civil law, 15, 20, 24, 112, 153
    criminal justice
        Chamber of Accusation, 128
        French legal system, 127
        investigation, 128
        judicial system, 129
        magistrates, 128
        police, correctional and assize courts, 127
        public minister, 128
    confinement, 148
    death penalty, 151
    fines, 151
    Interpol, 276, 279
    judge, 152
    judicial system, 129
    law enforcement
        administrative and judicial police, 137
        antiterrorist operations, 137
        divide and conquer strategy, 137
        National Police and the National Gendarmerie, 137

OJPs, 137
        police court, 138
        police forces, 137
        political, economic and social issues, 137
        prosecutor, 138
    legal culture, 146
    Napoleonic Code, 113–114, 136, 161
    National police agencies, 136
    parole, 150
    plea bargaining, 145
    police model, 73
    probation, 149
    punishment, 167
    violence, 29
France's Napoleonic Code, 161
FRG, see Federal Republic of Germany
Fugitive investigative services, 282–283

G

General Directorate of Investigation, 179
German civil law system
    court levels, 119–120
    criminal justice system, 119
    criminal law reform, 118–119
    Draft of a Penal Code, 118
    Federal Republic of Germany, 119
    GDR, 118
    Grand Criminal Law Commission, 118
    juvenile courts, 120
    Nazi era (1933–1944), 118
    Unification Treaty Act 1990, 119
German legal science, 114–115
Germany
    civil law, 15, 20, 24
    confinement, 148
    death penalty (see Death penalty, Germany)
    judicial system, 121
    law enforcement
        BGS, 139
        BKA, 139
        FRG, 138
        joint security program, 140
        jurisdictions, 138
        juvenile justice, Turkey, 140–141
        police components, 140
        police directorate, 140
        police structure, 139
        Potsdam Agreement, 139
        reunification, 139

parole, 150
plea bargaining, 145–147
pretrial diversion, 143–144
probation, 149
punishments, 28
state police model, 73
Guilty
adultery, 166
confessions, 164
Crime Laboratory of the Dubai Police
Department, 165–166
evidence, 165
eyewitnesses, testimony, 164–165
hadith, 165
intentional murder, 164
Islamic sentencing and trial law, 164

H

High-tech crimes, 282
House arrest, 98, 101–102
Human trafficking, 275
Interpol, 278–279
UN Crime Prevention and Criminal
Justice Program Network, 294

I

IACP, *see* International Association of
Chiefs of Police
ICAID, *see* Interpol child abuse image
database
ICC, *see* International Criminal Court
ICJ, *see* International Court of Justice
ICT, *see* International Policy Institute for
Counter-Terrorism
Incapacitation, 28, 29, 71, 89–90, 95
Incarceration, 88, 97–98, 100, 124, 150, 207
Independent nations/states, 2
Indian Evidence Act, 236, 242
Indian system of law
confinement, 238
constitution, 232
corrections, 237–238
court system
High Court, 233
judges, 234
magistrates, 233–234
special courts, 234
Supreme Court, 233
crime classifications, 233
criminal process, 236–237

legal history, 232–233
police, 235–236
prosecutors, 237
Indictment, 33, 48, 55, 58, 123, 124, 105,
207, 228, 240
Instrument of control, 9–10
Interfoto Picture Library Ltd. *vs.* Stiletto
Visual Programmes Ltd., 6
International Association of Chiefs of
Police, 275, 286–287, 310
International Center for Criminal Law
Reform and Criminal Justice
Policy, 288–289
International Court of Justice
arbitration, 258
commissions, 257–258
disputes settlement, 257, 260–261
establishment, 260
Hague Peace Conference, 258
location, 257
permanent court, 259
practice directions, 261–262
International Courts
European Communities (*see* Court
of Justice of European
Communities)
ICC (*see* International Criminal
Court)
ICJ (*see* International Court of
Justice)
lists, 245–246
UN Convention on genocide, 247
International Criminal Court
ad hoc tribunals, 254
admissibility, 250–251
advisory proceedings, 263
contentious cases, 262
crime of aggression, 254
developments, 255–256
divisions, 247–248
establishment, 249
features, 253
headquarters, 255
and ICJ, 255
judicial divisions, 250
jurisdiction, 247, 250–251, 262
laws of humanity, 253
national courts, 254
national judicial systems, 247
offices, 250
President, 249
procedure, 251–252

prosecutions of individuals, 246
prosecutor, 250
registry, 250
Rome Statute, 247, 253
Rome Treaty, 254
sovereignty, 249
State parties, 252
Statute, 248
trial procedure, 256–257
International criminal justice agencies
Child Wise, 310
Europol, 285–286
IACP, 286–287
ICT, 306–307
International Police Association, 287
Interpol (*see* Interpol)
IPES, 305–306
juvenile justice, UN (*see* United Nations and juvenile justice)
OAS (*see* Organization of American States)
organizations, 275–276
UN Crime Prevention and Criminal Justice Program Network, 287–294
International Criminal Police Organization, *see* Interpol
International Narcotics Control Board, 293
International Police Association, 287, 310
International Police Executive Symposium, 305–306
International Policy Institute for Counter-Terrorism, 306–307
Interpol
advisers, 277
child sexual exploitation, 279–280
core functions, 278
corruption, 279, 285
creation, 276
crimes against humanity, 283
criminal organizations, 282
databases, 280
development, police forces and services, 283
drug abuse, 281
environmental crime, 283
executive committee, 276
financial and high-tech crimes, 282
fugitives, 282–283
general assembly, 276
genocide, 283
human trafficking, 278–279
International Conference, cybercrime, 284–285
International Criminal Police Organization, 276
NCB, 277
NCRPs, 284
organizational chart, 277
public safety and terrorism, 280–281
war crimes, 283
Interpol Anti-Corruption Academy, 279
Interpol Anti-Corruption Office, 279
Interpol child abuse image database, 279
Interpol Group of Experts on Corruption, 279
Interpol's Red Notice, 284–285
IPES, *see* International Police Executive Symposium
Iran
adoption, Islamic law, 157, 161
amputation procedure, 186–187
corrections, 188
criminal law, 165
Gendarmerie, 184
Islamic law model, 172–173
Islamic Punishment Act 1993, 188
Islamic Revolution, 183
judicial system, 173
marine police unit, 184
Ministry of Intelligence, 183
Ministry of Interior and Justice, 184
national police, 184
Organization of National Security and Information, 183
SAVAK, 183–184
Iran's Islamic Punishment Act 1991, 188
Islamic jurisprudence, 11, 155, 160, 164, 165, 185, 232
Islamic law model, 2
al-Qushayri and al-Ghazali, 157
benefit, society, 157
characterization, 157
civil/common law model, 157
crime categories, 161
criminal justice, 157
English colonies, 156
France's Napoleonic Code, 161
French colonial influence, 156–157
geographical location, 156

Hanbali school of thought, 156
and Iran, 172–173
law legal tradition, 156
legal systems, 156
legislator, 160
mazalim courts, 161
Middle East and North Africa, 156
Muslim and non-Muslim
    countries, 157
national legal system, 156
origins and evolution, 159–160
and Pakistan, 170–172
penal law, 162–163
principles, 161–162
procedures, 161
Prophet Muhammad, 156
public and private behavior, 161
punishment, 167–168
qatl al-amd, 163
qisas, 163
Qur'an, 160
Saudi Arabia, 161
Shari'ah, 157, 160–161
sunnah and *hadith,* 160
universal Muslim community, 156
Islamic legal model, policing and
    corrections
amputation, 186–187
blood money, 187
caning, 187–188
capital punishment, 185–186
central government, 177
Council of Arab Ministers of
    Interior, 178
criminal punishment, 185
diyya, 186
family and property, 185
Islamic justice, 185
NAUSS, 178
patrol car, Dubai, 177–178
policing, civil/common law
    countries, 178
prisoners' families, 188
qisas, 186
sexual crimes, 185
1979 Islamic Revolution in Iran, 175

J

Judicature Act of 1873, 54
Judicature Act of 1978, 239
Judicature Act of 1979, 239

Jurisprudence, 2, 7–8, 11, 107, 115, 155, 165,
    185, 187, 232
Jus gentium, 2
Justice Project Index, 13

L

Law enforcement systems, policing, 27–28
London Metropolitan Police
    Authority
in Calgary, Canada, 84–85
mission, 76
PCSOs, 82
policing in Canada, 82–84
principles, 85–87

M

Martial law model, 73, 104
Mesopotamian system, 3
Mexico's reform movement, 24–25
Misdemeanor, 34, 40, 44, 48–49, 67, 91, 122,
    127, 129, 144, 206–207
Mixed-law models, 23, 24
    Bulgaria, 226–231
    India (*see* Indian system of law)
    legal system, 225
    Sri Lanka, 238–242
MPA, *see* London Metropolitan Police
    Authority

N

Naif Arab University for Security Sciences,
    178, 292
Napoleonic Code, 20, 109, 113–114, 161
Narcotic Control Act, 86
National Central Bureau, 277
National Central Reference
    Points, 284
National Criminal Intelligence
    Service, 78
Nation's criminal justice system, 3, 5, 7
Natural law, 2, 8, 9, 17, 115
NAUSS, *see* Naif Arab University for
    Security Sciences
NCB, *see* National Central Bureau
NCIS, *see* National Criminal Intelligence
    Service
NCRPs, *see* National Central Reference
    Points
NYPD officers, 78–79

O

OAS, *see* Organization of American
States
Offensive Weapons Act, 239
Office for Harmonization in the Internal
Market, 271–272
Organization of American
States, 246
Charter, Art. 3, 309
democracy, human rights, security and
development, 308
establishment, 307–308
functions, 308–309
member countries, 308
official languages, 308

P

Pakistan
Article 31, Pakistan's Constitution
(1973), 171–172
banishment, 189
community, 182
confinement rates, 189
corrections, 189
education, 183
Federal Investigative Agency, 183
imprisonment, 189
Islamic law model, 22
legal and institutional framework, 182
police activity and service, 183
police order, 182
political/civil service, 183
railway police, 182–183
regional police units, 182
stoning and amputation, 189
Parole, 92, 135, 150–151, 220, 242
PCSOs, *see* Police Community Support
Officers
Permanent Court of International Justice,
246, 258, 259
Plea bargaining
adjust/dismiss charges, 147
civil law systems, 145
common law systems, 147
court deliberates, 147
dominant penal philosophy, 146
economic and utilitarian model, 146
functional equivalent, 148
imprisonment, 146
judge and defense counsel, 145

judges and prosecutors, 147
legal reformers, 146
pretrial diversion, 148
proactive approach, 147
Sri Lanka, 241
win-win contract and rational
allocation, 146
Police and Criminal Evidence Act of
1984, 80–81
Police and Magistrates' Court Act
of 1994, 81
Police Community Support Officers, 77, 82
Police force
Bulgaria, 229–230
India, 235–236
Sri Lanka, 240
Police Service of Pakistan, 182–183
Policing and corrections
China
conditions, prisons, 220
early release of prisoners, 220
prisons, 220
sentencing, 218–219
in common law countries
civil police model, 73
community policing, 81–82
criminal justice system, 73
current policing in United States, 75
definition, 72
deviance/civil order control, 72–73
hiring requirements, 78–79
local police, England and Wales,
77–78.
martial law model, 73
New York City Police Department,
75–76
police powers and use of discretion,
80–81
quasi-military model, 73
salaries, English and U.S. Police
Officers, 79
state police model, 73
training of new officers, 80
U.S. and English police
Cuba
CDR, 217
confinement, 221–222
directorates, 216
range of punishments, 221
security division, 216
subdirectorates, 216
traffic regulation, 216

Islamic legal model (*see* Islamic legal
    model, policing and corrections)
People's Republic of China
    armed police force, 213
    colleges/academies, 213–214
    complaints, police misbehavior, 213
    crime statistics, 215
    detention, 215
    Hong Kong police station, 214
    organizational structure, 213
    police agencies, 213
    public security, 213
    use of force, 214–215
public trust and community, 210–211
Russia, 211–212
    Criminal Procedure Code, 217
    determination of sentence, 217
    imprisonment, 217–218
    judges, 217
    punishment, 217
    Western countries, 210
Positive law approach, 2, 8–9
Precedent, 2, 3, 14, 15, 34, 39, 65, 121, 204
Pretrial diversion, 131, 148
    conditional discharge, 143–144
    conditional waiver, 145
    criminal caseload, 145
    minor offenses, 144
    orders and instructions, 144
Probation, 135
    Brazil, 149, 150
    conditional release, 98
    Cuba, 221
    defendant's sentence, 98
    in England, 99
    Europe, 149
    France, 149
    Germany, 149
    India, 238
    period, 79, 80, 212
    "recognizance", 98
    Saudi Arabia, 172
    service, 93, 97
    Sri Lanka, 240
    standard rules, State of Texas, 100–101
    US, 99–100, 149
Prosecuting attorney, 34, 44, 46–49, 51
Prosecutions
    accusatorial *vs.* inquisitorial
        systems, 116
    bill of, 198
    Bulgaria, 227, 228

characteristics, inquisitorial system, 116
CIPA, 57–58
common law *vs.* civil law models, 117
compulsory, 147
coordination, 48
criminal, 74
cross-examination, witnesses, 51
and enforcement process, 82
function, policing, 138
India, 236, 237
inquisitorial, 117–118
Italian penality, 116–117
judges, 117
private, 199, 201–202
public interest, 125, 145, 197
responsibility, 192
Sri Lanka, 237, 239, 240
trial procedure, 207
Public safety and terrorism, 280–281
Punishments, 21, 28–29, 89, 116–118, 160,
       162–165, 172–173, 188, 217, 219,
       221, 227, 232, 237

Q

Quasi-military model, 73

R

RCMP, *see* Royal Canadian Mounted
       Police
Rehabilitation, 72
    approach, 90, 95
    China, 219
    crimes, confinement of
        individuals, 28, 89
    Germany, 143
    probation period, 100
    programs, UN, 295
    rationale of, 119
    treatment/correction, 29, 88
Religious law, 2, 3, 14
Retained counsel, 34
Retribution, 72
    approach, 90
    attempts, 89
    Chinese legal system, 195, 198
    corrections, 88
    crimes, confinement of individuals, 28
    European Union Court of Justice, 268
    framework, 290
    Germany, 143

Islamic law, 161
"just deserts", 89
meaning, 88
principles, 293
and punishment, 118
and revenge, 88
trafficking, 302
UN, 288–289
UNODC, 288–289
victims of trafficking, 303, 304
Roman law, 18–19
ancient sources, 18
Basilica, 110
Corpus Juris Civilis, 109–110
glossators and commentators, 110
revival of, 18–19
vulgarized/barbarized, 110
Royal Canadian Mounted Police, 27–28, 83,
87–88, 136
Rule of law, the United Nations, 11–13
Russia
Communist Party officials, 193
Constitutional Court, 193–194
criminal justice system, 192
Czech Republic, 194–195
education institution of lawyers, 195
The Hague Peace Conference of
1899, 258
ICC, 247
imprisonment, 217–218
judge selection and term of office, 194
mobile police station, Prague, 193
policing, 211–212
prisoners, 222
punishments, 28
Russian Federation, 192
Russian police agencies, 209
Russian Revolution of 1917, 192
socialist model of law, 23
Soviet Union in 1991, 194
subordinate courts, 194
Supreme Court of the Russian
Federation, 193
University of Moscow, 194–195
Russian Federation, 192

S

Saudi Arabia
Abdul Aziz Ibn Abdar-Rahman, 168
Arabian Peninsula, 169
arbitrary arrest, 181

citizens and foreigners, 181
Committee for the Promotion of Virtue
and the Prevention of Vice, 179
crimes of vice, 181
criminal procedure, 169
DPS, 179
General Directorate of Investigation, 179
human rights record, 180–181
Islamic legal model, 156–157, 169
King Fahd Security College, 180
legislation, 179
Medina, 168
Ministry of Interior, 179, 181
Mubahith, 177
Mutawa, 177
Mutawwa'in, 182
NAUSS, 177, 292
oil and natural gas products, 168
organization, Saudi police, 179
patron/sponsoring employer, 181
The Prophet Muhammad, 158
public safety, 180
Qur'an, 169
safeguards, 169
Saudi Ministry of Justice, 169
security and military matters, 169
shari'ah, 169
Supreme Judicial Council, 169
torture and abuse, 181
Turkish Ottoman Empire, 168
Scottish legal system, 65
Socialist law model, 2
court system, 192
law of search and seizure, 201
procedures, 202
rights of an accused, 201–202
Soviet Union, 191–192
Socialist law model
China (*see* China)
Cuba (*see* Cuba)
policing and corrections (*see* Policing
and corrections)
Russia (*see* Russia)
South African Child Justice Act
of 2008, 231
Sri Lankan system of law
confinement, 242
courts, 239
crime classification, 239
criminal justice, 239
governance, 238
penalties, 241

police force, 240
punishment, 241
sentencing process, 241
trial procedures, 240–241
State police model, 73
Substantive criminal law, 6, 34, 56

T

Terrorism and public safety, 280–281
Texas Code of Criminal Procedure, Article
    42.12, 100–101
TPB, *see* UN terrorism prevention
    branch
Trafficking and smuggling
   differences, 296
   firearms (*see* Trafficking in firearms)
   UN protocol
     action against traffickers, 299
     agreed-upon provision, Art. 8, 299
     application, 297
     Article 2, 297
     control, 297
     convention offenses, 296
     definition, Art. 3, 298
     issues, 298
     prevention, cooperation and
      measures, 299–300
     protection, 299
     purpose, 297
     relationship, 296
     repatriation, 299
     transnational organized crime, 296–297
     victim consent, 298
     women and children, 298
Trafficking in firearms
   excerpts of the United States' Act
     concerted and vigorous action, 304
     involuntary servitude statutes, 303
     organized criminal enterprises, 302
     penalties, 303
     physical detention and debt
      bondage, 303
     physical violence, 302
     protection, 303
     purposes, 301
     range of violations, 302
     sex industry, 301
     transnational crime with national
      implications, 304–305
     transport victims, 302
     victims to serious health risks, 302

violations of human rights, 304
violations of laws, 302
women and children, 301–302
   protocol, 300
Transnational crime, 2, 4, 246, 278–288,
    291, 301, 304
Tribal laws, 108–109

U

UN Crime Prevention and Criminal Justice
    Program Network
   areas, 288
   CJRU, 289–290
   crime control, 288
   division, 288
   drug control and crime prevention,
    290–291
   human trafficking, 294
   INCB, 293
   Institutes, 291–292
   International Center for Criminal Law
    Reform and Criminal Justice
    Policy, 288–289
   international cooperation, 287–288
   interregional and regional institutes, 287
   TPB, 288, 292–293
   transnational organized crimes, 293–294
   UNODC, 288
UNDCP, *see* UN International Drug
    Control Programme
Unification Treaty Act of August 31, 1990, 119
UN International Drug Control
    Programme, 290–291
United Nations and juvenile justice
   CRC, 295
   fact sheet, 294
   gangs/groups, 294
   motivation, 295
   penalties, 295
   poverty and unemployment, 295
   preventive measures, 295
   violent crimes, 294
   WPAY, 296
Universal Declaration of Human Rights,
    Article 5, 97
UN Office on Drugs and Crime, 279, 288,
    291–292
UN terrorism prevention branch,
    292–293
UN World Programme of Action for
    Youth, 296

V

Violence
  causes of, 295
  comparative, 29–30
  and corruption, Brazil, 141
  and discrimination, 180
  IACP, 286, 287
  ICT, 307
  and juvenile crime, 288, 294, 295
  prevention, 295
  prisoners, 151
  sexual, 147
  terrorist, 234
  Victims of Trafficking and Violence
      Protection Act of 2000, 301–305
  witness, 57

W

War crimes, 249, 250, 253–254, 283
Women in Mexico's prisons, 150–151
WPAY, *see* UN World Programme of
    Action for Youth